MATCH DAY

ULSTER LOYALISM AND THE BRITISH FAR-RIGHT

By Tony Simms

INTRODUCTION

*T*his story is dedicated to all the victims of the Birmingham pub bombings, both Catholic and Protestant, who lost their lives on the 21st of November 1974. May they rest in peace. We will never forgive – we will never forget.

Jane Davis aged 17
Desmond Reilly aged 20
Eugene Reilly aged 23
Maureen Roberts aged 20
Marilyn Nash aged 22
Pamela Palmer aged 19
Stephen Whalley aged 21
Lynn Bennett aged 18
Anne Hayes aged 19
Michael Beasley aged 30
Maxine Hambleton aged 18

John Jones aged 51
Charles Grey aged 44
John Rowlands aged 46
Stanley Bodman aged 51
Trevor Thrupp aged 33
James Caddick aged 40
Paul Davies aged 20
Neil Marsh aged 20
Thomas Chaytor aged 28
James Craig aged 34

CHAPTER 1

$\mathcal{I}$ was born in Birmingham in 1972, to my mother Brenda and my father Ron. My Mom and Dad were both English – 'old school Brummies' from Summer Lane. With my father being Church of England and my mother a Roman Catholic. We lived over the south side of the city in an area called Kings Norton, which was very supportive of Birmingham City Football Club. I shared a loving household with my two older sisters and as I can recall they spoilt me rotten. My mother was a very hands on mother – always hugging us and telling us how much she loved us. I suppose it was like most homes in Birmingham at the time, the man at work – and the women left at home to bring up the kids. My mother spent her school years in a real strict Roman Catholic school and she told me many horror stories about the place – even into her late 60's she would still talk about it. My father was always in full time employment working all the hours he could. He was not as open with his affection as my mother, nevertheless, we knew he was there for us even if he was not one to throw his arms around you. We were not a very rich family. I can recall as a kid my mother putting cardboard in all of our shoes during wintertime to stop the rain and snow from getting through the holes.

However, it is fair to say everyone liked them as they were two lovely decent people.

As I started junior school, my mother made friends with a Jamaican woman named Clara whose son David was in my class. They became very close friends for a number of years and additionally, my mother had a number of female Jamaican friends who she met through Clara. I can still remember when David first joined our school as he was the only Black lad in the class. All the kids used to stare at him because he was different. As my mother and his became close, so did David and I, and we would also remain friends for many years. David's football club of choice was Liverpool. I can still remember when I used to visit David's home that his mother used to make us Jamaican dumplings; they were delicious. I tried to get my own mother to make some but not being from the West Indies she did not know how to make them – and I reluctantly had to force them down myself.

David's family were a smashing bunch of people – church going Black Christians – and his father Patrick actually taught me how to swim. He was a lovely man. Patrick used to listen to the original Jamaican Ska music and his favourite artists were Laurel Aitken, Prince Buster, Jimmy Cliff and The Pioneers. When I first heard the music, even though I was very young, it thrilled me to the bone. I used to love the beat of the music and David and I would mess around dancing to it in his living room. When the 2-Tone scene hit the British charts we were already fans of the music. We were both big fans of The Specials, who were from Coventry. I was very jealous of David and his family because they had a car, whereas no one from my side of the family even had a driving licence. We used to play football with a rolled up sock in David's living room. To look back now it is still hard to believe what road I would eventually end up taking in my later life, as like I have already stated they were a brilliant family, and they invited me into their home with open arms.

My Dad was a Birmingham City fan and like most Dad's he tried to make me follow suit. He took me to Saint Andrews when I was eight years old but I can recall crying my eyes out as I did not like it there; I thought it was a dump. He took me a couple more times, however, I just would not get into it and I told my mother I did not want to go any more so that was the end of that. My Dad had a mate called Les Payne (R.I.P) who was a die-hard Aston Villa supporter, and during the season of 1980/81, offered to take me to Villa Park as he had a spare ticket. Aston Villa were formed in 1874, and were founder members of The Football League in 1888. There were loads of United's, lots of City's and Town's. A good number of Wanderer's and Rover's and even a few Albion's. All the same, there was only one Villa – the most unique name in British football.

William McGregor – Villa committee member – and founder of the Football league – once released a statement : "If there is a club in the country which deserves to be dubbed the greatest, few will deny the right of Aston Villa to share the highest niche of fame with even the most historic of other aspirants". Additionally, Aston Villa are a club that Birmingham City have spent so long envying due to us holding the fourth highest total of major honours in English football. Furthermore, as the years went by I would come to realise that Birmingham City had a 'deep rooted obsession' towards Aston Villa that went beyond the realms of reality. To envy a club more than you love your own is a very odd way to follow a football team.

My Dad told Les I did not like football, but that was not the case – I just did not like going to Saint Andrews. Now that may seem like a piss take statement from an Aston Villa supporter, although it was true. I cannot remember the game itself as I was very young. But the one thing I can recall was seeing the Holte End; a gigantic standing terrace that seemed to go on forever – it was huge. The noise coming out of the Holte End was amazing and when the Villa scored I was immediately hooked. It seemed like the ground was going to collapse there was that much noise coming from the huge terrace.

It is safe to say I spent more time looking at the chanting fans than the football itself. The Holte End back in those days held 28,000 people, and to a kid of ten I am sure you can understand the attraction of seeing such a mass of fans all going wild and singing so loud I thought the roof of the Holte End was coming off. I sat there completely open mouthed at what I had witnessed that afternoon. That was me now a Villa man now for life and I went down a number more times that season with Les. Little did I realise that we would become Champions. My first season down the football and my team wins the bloody title. How lucky was that?

Something else that caught my eye at the football during my first season was the crowd trouble that I would witness on the way home at full time. I was unaware at the time that this was a firm called the C-Crew; a multi-racial firm led by Paul Brittle and Danny Brown. What's more, as the years progressed I got to hear stories about the C-Crew as they were looked upon by most Villa lads as Villa's best ever hooligan mob. At this stage the C-Crew were a top firm and were a far superior outfit than Birmingham City before their pre-Zulu days. This season when Villa won the title I can remember going up town and it felt like the whole world had turned out to see my club Aston Villa show off that trophy. I was addicted by now and every second of the day I would be going on about Aston Villa. This used to drive my Dad nuts. Nonetheless, you do not pick your club your club picks you – and the following season after a mid-table league finish, Villa had reached the final of the European Cup against German giants Bayern Munich; the Germans were firm favourites.

I can still remember the night now. Camped in front the TV with my Mom – and my Dad sitting in the kitchen wishing it was Birmingham City; we can all have dreams. When Peter Withe put the ball in the net, like many households in Birmingham that night my mother and I went crazy! I don't think we would have screamed like that if we had won the pools. My Mom spent the last ten minutes of the game locked away in the toilet; her nerves were shot. I was just sitting there in my Villa hat and scarf glued to the TV. The rest is history, and as Dennis Mortimer went up to collect the trophy I was the proudest Villa fan in the world; I was ecstatic. In my first two seasons as a Villa supporter we had won the league and the European Cup (Followed in 1983, by winning the Super Cup). Who could ask for anything more? My Dad popped his head in from the kitchen and shouted in: "You were lucky". However, I was too busy jumping all round the living room to care about what he said. In spite of this, I was about to find out that this was not the beginning of Aston Villa dominating Europe as Liverpool had. We had reached our peak and dark days were ahead for the club I loved. At the same time, little did I know at this young age that my country was changing at a rapid pace, and furthermore that years from now I would become involved in British nationalist politics.

I started secondary school in the summer of 1983 – at Primrose Hill, Kings Norton. And even though I was far too young to be political, I could notice even back then that certain areas of Birmingham were changing for the worst – including Kings Norton. I sometimes heard Black lads saying that White parents turn their kids racist. Nevertheless, from my household my Mom and Dad were staunch Labour and always taught me to respect other races and cultures. My Dad never had a bad word to say about anybody, and my Mom having Jamaican friends obviously was not one to care about the colour of someone's skin. My early concerns about a changing Birmingham were not based on any sort of racial hatred. I hung around with a Black lad at senior school called Tony. Despite that, I could tell that something just was not right and that Birmingham was rapidly declining. I still kept in contact with David and his family, and their warmness towards me and my family never faded.

During 1985, race riots spread through the UK and closer to home in Handsworth, Birmingham. It started after an incident on the Lozells Road. Even though I was a young lad at the time my opinion was it was nothing but 'mob rule' tactics and a bloody excuse to riot. All excuses were made from heavy-handed police presence, to lack of jobs (which affected both White and Black communities). I saw it as a community breaking the law and rioting for 'rights' that we never had. The police oppressed White people as well, although you did not see the White community turning their areas into a war zone. My mates mother was a special constable and she told me that the riot had been on the cards for a while. It came as no surprise. That was my opinion and one I still stand by.

A lot of the blame for the unruly behaviour from the Black youths was that a large number were growing up with no father figure to guide them in the right direction. Now we all know that it is very unfair to label a whole community under one banner, but the riots signified to me the beginning of a failed multi-racial society in Birmingham. Even at my young age I could see problems arising all over Britain.

Little did I know at the time, that we had imported racial conflicts that would now be fought out on our streets – with our people and our police force caught in the crossfire. I remember thinking that our country cannot take in so many immigrants and consequently they will create there own settlements with their own values. Even with some of the opinions I was forming, I still had a number of Black friends who I had gone through school with. Like most lads at school, I was into my football and having a play up whichever way I could. I was not at all interested in girls; I was too much into my Villa addiction to bother with girls. Looking back on things now some of the things you say and do at school to other lads were terrible but it is just how you were at that age.

On the football front, Aston Villa who had once dominated Europe were relegated during the 1986/87 season, after being sent down by Sheffield Wednesday. After all the highs I had been through we were now in the old Division 2. I can still remember looking around at the fans and it was as if it was not real. How could this be happening when five years earlier we had been crowned kings of Europe? It was as if it was all a dream, yet not a good one a bloody horror. I was now going down with some friends and at full time I can recall seeing running battles by Witton Island. It was proper hands on fighting and the Sheffield Wednesday lads seemed proper up for it. The Sheffield lads were giving as good as they got. I stood there watching the fighting and it seemed to go on for ages and ages. I suppose some Villa fans were gutted about being relegated and wanted to take it out on someone, where as other Villa lads would have been looking for trouble regardless of the result. The firm at the time were called the Villa Youth – the old C-Crew had long disbanded. What's more, the Villa Youth looked to be doing a good enough job on Witton Island. I went home that day totally gutted from relegation, yet buzzing from seeing a running battle close up. And rightly or wrongly it did excite me.

The following week a right firm of Villa old-heads went to Man United away, and went in the seats in the Man United end. I had gone on the Travellers Club coaches from Villa Park, and being the last game of the season it was looked upon as a 'relegation party – we lost the match 3-1. I did not care too much about the result as it was such a play up with Villa taking about 3,000 fans to Old Trafford. Running battles took place at full time as the Villa fans left the ground. It was mental. The Villa old-heads more then held their own against top opposition and far superior numbers. Therefore, as we finally left the top tier we showed that when needed we could still turn out a good firm.

What happened to me and my friend Jamie a few weeks later had a lasting effect on me, and maybe to some extent played a part in me eventually getting involved in right-wing politics. Jamie and I had both been bought matching leather jackets by our parents and had gone up town to look around the sports shops and visit some arcades to play on the video games. We were standing in the arcade when a group of older Black lads surrounded us and said: "Yo White boys give us your jackets". We were about fifteen at the time and the Black lads were in their twenties. We were scared stiff as the one lad was making out to have a knife in his hand. Fortunately, the arcade manager came down the stairs after seeing something was going on. His fast response saved us from being mugged. Moreover, even as we were walking off the Black lads were shouting racist comments at us, enjoying the fact that they had the power over us. What could two wet behind the ears young White lads do in a situation like that? We jumped straight back on the bus and headed home – still intact with our leather jackets. We were both very shook up by everything that had happened.

This is when I concluded that there were two types of Black people. The ones like David and his family – my other mates from school – and the ones who had attempted to mug us up town. I am not saying for one second that White people do not commit crime. Having said that, many muggings were going on in Birmingham at the time, mostly carried out by young British born Black males – and a majority of the victims were White. This was not a statement put forward by a knuckle-dragging skin-head covered in tattoos. This was official police statistics, and like it or not it was a fact. In 1995, the Metropolitan Police Commissioner – Sir Paul Condon – was forced into admitting: "It is a fact that very many of the perpetrators of muggings are very young Black people". Now it goes without saying that no person or racial group should be singled out just because they are Black. On the other hand, should neither any person nor racial group be immune from criticism just because they are Black. If certain individuals or groups give you strong grounds to point them out for their actions, the fact that they may be Black should not exempt them from criticism. As long as the criticism is conducted in moderate language and it excludes and avoids any insults. This also includes pointing out crimes that are carried out by the White community, like anti-social behaviour, car theft, drunken disorderly, and burglary to feed their heroin addiction.

It was also around this time I noticed that in every newsagent you could buy Black pride newspapers, Asian pride newspapers and Irish community newspapers; the list went on. There were also radio-stations set up for the Black and Asian community, as well as endless TV programmes produced solely for non-Whites. I started to think: "How can this be in what's supposed to be England", and I began to feel we were being shoved aside whilst everybody else was being looked after.

I was a big record collector during this period and would pop into the Virgin megastore in town to browse through the music on offer. I mostly left with an addition to my 2-Tone record collection. It came to my attention that you could purchase some Rap music from Black power bands that was glorying killing police officers, drugs, rape and gang culture. As the years progressed I would come to describe this as 'Devil's Music'. Obviously, the young people who brought this music would be influenced by the lyrics. Why was the Virgin megastore authorising such music to be sold? I approached a member of staff to ask him the question; he did not want to know. Would the Virgin megastore have stocked music by White power skin-head bands? Not a chance. What is acceptable for Black people surely must be acceptable for White people, unless we live in an 'anti-White' society. But that cannot be the case in good old Blighty can it? The land of 'diversity', 'tolerance' and 'equality' – if only that was true.

I would not let this put me off my interest in music, therefore, I continued to visit the store on a regular basis. During another visit I stumbled across a CD that was called

'100 greatest Rebel songs'. This CD was openly glorifying the I.R.A. In addition, it was available to purchase as easy as picking up a CD from Abba, The Bee Gees or Queen. This made my opinion even stronger that something was very wrong in my country. My visits to the Virgin megastore had opened up my eyes that little bit more.

I was now in my last year at school and it is safe to say I was a bit more politically aware than most kids, even though I was still a million miles away from labelling myself with any political party. I would question to myself why did all the minority events in Birmingham have massive financial input and advertisement, yet come Saint George's day it passed by completely unnoticed. I would also question to myself why large numbers of British born non-Whites felt the need to continue their cultures here and to wave the flag of their homeland. In Britain, we have room for one flag – the British flag. We have room for one language – the English language. Moreover, we have room for one sole loyalty – and that is to British traditions and the British way of life. How can we make a society work with so many different people pulling in so many different directions? My opinion was the same then as it is now. That the government had not attempted to make the immigrants integrate. They had been encouraged to continue their ways and cultures in the UK, at what I believed to be at the expense of the White British people. Our culture was being smashed from within and it seemed to me like we were being targeted for extinction. If I wanted to be a foreigner I would have moved to another country. I did not expect to be a foreigner in my own land.

Some of the people arriving from Asia could not speak a word of English and were not attempting to integrate. They were going into their own communities and totally shutting themselves off from British society. There is nothing racist about believing that immigrants should learn English and that 'sealed ghettos' are unhealthy. The governments claim of racial and religious harmony was a lie; I could see divisions all over the place. In addition, it is fair to say I was carrying around a bit of anger due to the state of my country. I did not blame people for coming here from third world countries – let's face it we all want to better ourselves. Having said that, I did personally blame the immigrants for not attempting to fit in to our society. The problem to me was simple – our cultures were not compatible. I am not saying I thought everything about Britain was great, but we'd had a glorious past and I did not see any reason not to have bright future. Nevertheless, it was obvious to anybody with half a brain we were going way of track.

By now I had started to follow the Villa away on a regular basis with my mate Peter from Stockland Green. Like most lads my age, we started going to the local away games. I remember the one trip to Nottingham Forest. You could pay in on the day these days. There were thousands of Villa fans there. We were all playing up on the train and generally being noisy; I loved it. I will never forget the police escort from the train station. It seemed like we had taken the whole town over as we marched towards the ground. I can remember looking around and thinking: "We could take on the world with this mob", and I was like thousands of lads my age up and down the country now fully hooked on the buzz from the football.

During the old second division season 1987/88, that's when I started to follow the Villa all over the country and got to know who were some of our top boys. I started to put names to faces and got to know more people. The first people I linked up with were Mark and Jason (The Webb brothers) from Kings Norton. I met them on holiday and strangely enough we only lived five minutes up the road from each other. They knew everybody down the Villa. I also got to meet Phil and Rob Harrison, Carl and Russell Clinton, Kevin and Gary (The Jeens brothers) and C-Crew Clive. I also teamed up with Clive's brother Paul who was an old skin-head. Other mates at the time were Andy Kesterton, Andy O' Keefe, Tony Lynch, Ian Pritchard, Paul Walker and many more. These lads were around years before the Villa Hardcore came together. Moreover, not forgetting who is still one of my closest mates to this day – Gary Bardell – more commonly known as 'Barmy Bardell'. He is an absolute lunatic but god he makes you laugh. Some were tough lads and some were not but it did not matter as we were all Villa through and through. And we were to spend many seasons following the Villa everywhere. Even if it was for example Southampton away on a Tuesday night we would still go; we never missed a game.

As the years progressed we would all head the away games on the Friday night and make a weekend of it. Kev Jeens introduced me to lads like skin-head Neil, Luddy, Chris Jones, Fat Stan and Gary Reid (R.I.P) who were a part of Villa's top firm at the time. And fair play to them they took me in as one of their own and looked after me on match day; I loved being part of the 'inner circle'. Kev Jeens had been around with the C-Crew and he knew loads of the older lads – that way you got to know more people. We were drinking in the middle room of the Witton Arms pub at the time and had some right laughs in there. I was still though very wet behind the ears regarding the match day scene. However, I loved the atmosphere of the match day get together; there was a real 'buzz' in the air. Being so young I loved mixing with the big-boys. I suppose I was like hundreds if not thousands of lads my age – travelling with the hooligans but not directly one myself. It was advisable though not to get in a round with Chris Jones; god he could drink. I had heard of Villa's C- Crew, but did not know any of them because they were around in the early 80's when I still used to go down with Les as a kid. Anyhow, this season a number of them made a comeback to visit grounds we had not been to in years and I saw some right good action.

 I can recall Blackburn away. It was a top of the table clash and we lost. At full time as the Villa fans left the stadium there was an area just up from the ground full of trees and suddenly all Blackburn's lads started jumping down from the trees and into the Villa fans. The Villa regrouped and scattered them everywhere and it seemed like it carried on for about half hour – with the Villa not giving up without catching a few of the Blackburn lads and giving them a good kicking. They must have wished that they had stayed up in the trees instead of jumping down to get ran everywhere. Leeds away in the FA Cup was another one that I remember well. There were 6,000 Villa fans there and we took a right firm. Running battles occurred outside the away end before and after the game. Leeds were noted for being a top firm, however, the Villa more than matched them. I admit it was frightening, nevertheless, I loved the buzz of seeing mobs running at each other. To a young lad it was all so new, yet all so addictive. It gave you a focus and something to do, in what was sometimes a dull boring life. At Huddersfield away, we were ambushed as we left the ground. It was proper chaos as we were not expecting it. Large-scale violence broke out but it did not put me off – it just made me want to follow the

Villa even more. I was not getting involved in the trouble; I am not going to bullshit. I was still 'learning the ropes', but by now I was most certainly addicted to the whole match day experience.

The last game of the 1987/88 season, Villa went to Swindon looking for promotion and Swindon sent us a derisory 2,000 tickets. Before the game Villa were everywhere, thousands without tickets just hoping to be there when Villa got back into the top tier. As Peter and I got into our seats in the away end we could not believe the huge stand behind the goal that was totally empty. Thousands of Villa fans were locked out, yet a huge terrace was not being used on the day. A steward told us that they had not given Villa the tickets because of the fear of having thousands of Villa fans in the ground going mental if we were promoted. But all they had done was to have the problem outside the ground, with the police not knowing what to do with the thousands of Villa fans milling around outside.

There were also loads of forged tickets going around, so the tiny Villa end that was already packed started to fill up even more. I remember thinking how lucky I was to have a ticket in the seats. Even more so, when a few hundred Villa got in the away end by somehow forcing the gates open. There was also a good mob of Villa in the home end who were escorted around the pitch by the 'Old Bill'. As they walked past the Villa in the seats we all stood up to clap them. You could tell from a mile away it was our main lads and that season our firm was once again back on the map and full of confidence. The results that day went our way and a 0-0 draw was enough to send us up in second place behind Millwall.

The scenes afterwards were absolute joy as hundreds of Villa fans emptied on to the pitch and lifted Graham Taylor into the air like the hero he was. They carried him around for what seemed like forever and Chris Jones face was on every TV station and every local newspaper. Don't get me wrong, this was not like winning the league in 80/81 or the European cup in 81/82. That being said, to me it meant a lot more as I was now old enough to take it all in and truly appreciate it. I do not mind admitting to having tears in my eyes as we were now back in the big time at the first attempt. We had travelled this season in large numbers 'firm' and 'scarfers' alike to Leicester, West Brom, Huddersfield, Leeds twice, Stoke, Bradford, Barnsley, Man City, Blackburn, Bournemouth, Reading, Millwall, Palace and Swindon. Not forgetting the 10,000 Villa who made the short trip to Saint Andrews, where the Villa Youth more than made their presence known on that night game. Trouble kept going off in the Tilton Road, with the Villa Youth more than up for it and not budging an inch. There were also running battles after the game. I had also earlier in the season travelled to Middlesbrough away – it was on Valentines Sunday and hardly anyone bothered. Even so, what a moody place. They are nuts – truly evil, and without a doubt one of Britain's top firms. We got our coach bricked as we were heading away from the ground and spent the whole journey home without a single window in place. Some lads were shouting to stop the coach, even though I was relieved that we never as they were animals.

The only place I can recall us coming unstuck this season was Palace away, when a right good firm of Palace lads steamed us in the seats and got the result. They also brought a little, but tidy firm to Villa Park and kicked it off by Witton Station – so hats off to them for a double showing. Apart from that and some Zulus showing up in the Witton Lane seats at Villa Park, it had been an eventful season on and off the pitch. I had now left school and had to start to look for a job. I'd had a great year following the Villa but now the real work began.

CHAPTER 2

$\mathcal{I}$ had now left school in 1988, and was looking for a job in full time employment. I suppose like most youngsters I did not have a clue what type of career I wanted to get into. Just something so I could earn enough money to pay for my drink and my days out at the football. I went after dozens of jobs – office clerk, door-to-door sales representative, factory work, dentist assistant, plumbers mate – the list was endless. The boss at my Dad's factory offered me a job working on what was known as Slide-way Grinding. Although at the time I was going through a bit of a funny relationship with my Dad. Therefore, the idea of working with my Dad was not on the cards. Then one day I saw an advert in the local paper for a vacancy at an Engineering factory down in Digbeth. Digbeth was an area that I would come to find out had many pubs supporting the cause of Irish nationalism; The I.R.A. I phoned the place up, arranged for an interview and got the bus down there the next day. I got the job there and then.

It was only a little factory unit at the time. I was about to become very close friends with a guy there named Chris Butler (R.I.P) who really took me under his wing and was like a second father to me; what a top bloke. My Dad was delighted I had found a job. He had never been one to sit around at home all day claiming benefits, and he even came to the factory to see me. I can still remember the first day I finished work and as I got home he was waiting on the front gate for me – proud as punch that his son had got off his arse and found a job. He always instilled it into me to go out and find work – don't sit around on your arse wasting your life away. He was a great example and he passed his attitude down onto me from a young age.

The factory I started working at was only a tiny place consisting of 30 people. Apart from Chris, I would also become good friends with another bloke called Lenny. He was an old Jamaican guy who was a right character. He was the only Black person who worked there at the time but trust me we had some laughs. I have mentioned him for this reason. He was the very first Black man who I discussed politics with. I'd had Black friends before although we never talked about politics. He was a very proud Black man, proud of his race and his culture and very proud to be Jamaican – and rightly so. In addition, I opened up to him about some of my opinions. Even though we differed on many issues it was good to have political debates without the risk of getting a smack in the mouth for saying the wrong thing. We also used to wind each other up about race – but all in good fun. There was never any unpleasantness about it. That's how our relationship was. Moreover, it is fair to say we had a lot of time for each other.

He had moved here with his family from Jamaica, however, I admired how he was always very thankful for England giving him a home and a better life. Additionally, I respected him as a person. He said himself that the country was not as it used to be when he first moved here. Lenny was naturally a very funny bloke and I will never forget the time he sold me his old TV and gave me a lift home to my parents to drop it off. As we stood on the doorstep holding the TV, he looked at me and said: "I wonder what your parents will think with a Black man bringing a TV into the house. I suppose they will think I have pinched it". I totally cracked up laughing and so did Lenny. That's how we used to bounce off each other. He was always making jokes – mostly about himself. That was how we used to get through the long boring days and a good friendship had been built. I can still remember whilst he was having a chat with my Mom in the living room and I was in the kitchen making the coffees – and hearing him telling my Mom what a good kid I was and how well we got on. I was chuffed about that and it was nice of him to sing my praises so much. Likewise, I felt the same towards him. This is what annoys me when people throw words at me like 'extremist' and 'Nazi'. These people do not know me and do not know the amount of Black friends I have had over the years. Nevertheless, they love to stick this label around your neck if you happen to have anti-immigration views.

My job initially consisted of working on a circle cutter, chopping metal, press-work, making the drinks, fetching the sandwiches and general factory duties whilst I was being trained up. As I said, Chris really showed me the ropes and I cannot thank him enough for the time and effort he gave me throughout the years. Chris and his wife had never had kids and I got the feeling that was why we were so close. He was like a second father to me and I really mean that; I loved him like one of my own. He was so talented at his job and some of the brass lampshades he used to do were brilliant; he really knew his job inside out. To watch him work was amazing. His reputation was that good he was offered a managers job at a factory in Bournemouth. I was so upset when I heard he was leaving. He was all ready to move but then had to cancel it all due to the hospital finding his cancer. When he died it broke my heart. It was the first death of someone I really cared for and it hit me hard. To this day it still really upsets me to think how close he came to his dream only to have it snatched away so cruelly. If anybody deserved it he did. He was a proper good decent bloke who I still miss and think about to this day. A true gentleman who dedicated his time to training me up. I never really thanked him and that's what hurts.

After a brilliant promotion season with the Villa the next season 1988/89, was a bit of a disappointment to be honest. As quick as some of the C-Crew lads had made a comeback they were gone again. From taking a huge firm away, things hit a real low as far as an organised firm goes. The rave and drug scene was blamed for this and so I heard some of our 'top boys' were making money instead of bothering with football; I ain't knocking them. We still had loads of lads floating around who I rated but no leader. I can remember looking around at known faces like Gary Reid for example and thinking: "Why doesn't he run things?" However, no one seemed to want to be Villa's top lad.

Then in the quarter-final of the League Cup, we drew West Ham away. Everyone was going. It was a Wednesday night match and for some reason they never made the game all ticket. Thousands of Villa headed down south for the game. I travelled there with some lads from Perry Common in Erdington, and you could tell as soon as you got there that it was going to be one of those nights. The only thing that stopped you getting a kicking walking to the ground was a heavy police presence. Not that the 'Old Bill' would have cared mind – they made it quite clear they did not like

'Northerners'. Even queuing up outside the ground West Ham were trying to steam us, and you could tell even though we had the numbers that most Villa fans did not fancy their chances against this lot – myself included.

Then a disaster happened inside the ground just before kick off. With loads of Villa still outside, the turnstiles that were counting the amount of fans into the away end stopped working. You could still get in the ground, despite that no one knew how many fans were in the small end and it just kept filling up. We needed a far bigger end for the support we had brought. Instead of closing the away end they kept on letting in hundreds more. I suppose to be perfectly honest no one would have liked to be left outside on this particular night. The I.C.F would have turned you over as they were milling around outside looking for Brummies. You could tell that something was not right and fans were becoming scared due to the pressure of the crushing. The standing terrace next to us was full of West Hams lads – and I mean lads – so they could not move us along; that would have caused a riot.

The inevitable happened and the Villa had no option bar to go on the pitch. Even though I could try to claim this was as a bit of a showing from the Villa firm it was not like that at all. The sheer numbers of the travelling support simply forced us onto the pitch if you wanted to or not. How a Hillsborough or Heysel disaster did not happen I still do not know to this day – it was that bad. West Ham should have been severely fined or had their ground closed for a number of games for making such a catastrophic blunder by not shutting the away terrace. The local Birmingham paper the Evening Mail, was full of horror stories the next morning from Villa fans saying how they thought they were going to be crushed to death. The West Ham lads had no idea of the potential death trap in the away end and thought we were trying our luck.

West Ham then emptied out from the seats on the side. They were not at all happy with the Villa coming on the pitch and a proper firm of Hammers charged at the Villa. I think the Villa fans would have ran back in the away end given a chance, however, we had just abandoned that terrace. It was a no win situation. Fighting broke out on the side of the pitch but it was simply men against boys and like the C-Crew we never really stood a chance. The police formed a line to separate the two mobs as hundreds of Villa fans spent the whole game watching it from by the advertising hoardings. The Villa support that night was very vocal in what I can only describe as a 'menacing atmosphere'. West Ham won the game 1-0 – much to the relief of the Villa fans who were in short distance from the 'angry Hammers'. When the full time whistle blew the only thing that stopped a full-scale riot was hundreds upon hundreds of 'Old Bill' forming a human chain around the Villa end. Not that it stopped the West Ham lads trying to break through a number of times. These were a proper firm who let you know you were not welcome in East London. They were mental that night. It would be the same after the game with fans going back to the tube station and coaches.

The police kept us locked in for an hour but that only gave the I.C.F more time to re-group –which they did. I have never seen so many Villa fans terrified. When I finally got on the train coming home from Euston, I can remember sitting down smiling to myself that I was still alive; that is how bad it was. But not all fans were as lucky as me as some had been beaten up and left with the I.C.F 'calling card'. On the way home I got speaking to some older lads who were there for the FA Cup game in 1980, who said that tonight's experience was nothing compared to that occasion. I honestly cannot imagine how it must have been on that day. I had gone to West Ham when I suppose in many ways the I.C.F were on the decline, whereas the older lads had gone there during the height of the I.C.F. Let me just say, I was glad I was too young to make the earlier cup match in 1980, and West Ham was not a place I had any plans to rush back to in the near future. For obvious reasons, I would make my excuses next time we played West Ham away.

After a dull first season back in the top flight after flirting with relegation and the horrors of West Ham away in the League Cup, the next season was a complete turnaround. Graham Taylor really got us playing well and we were challenging Liverpool for the title. It really was a good time to be following the Villa again. There was a time we were even labelled favourites. We were taking thousands everywhere and filling every away end, yet still we had no firm this season. Don't get me wrong we had loads of known lads following the Villa (some who I really respected) but no one pulling the strings. Everyone just seemed to be doing their own thing.

I can remember us coming proper unstuck at Derby away at the old Baseball Ground. We had 6,000 fans there, however, we were just easy pickings for the D.L.F at full time. The problem was at Derby there was only one road in and one road out. I got a smack in the face myself at this game after leaving the ground. Derby had a good firm out and we got ran everywhere. For a second city club pushing for the title it was a bit embarrassing to have no firm for a club our size. It is simply how it was – totally no organisation. With the season drawing to a close our challenge faded away with three games to go. All the same, plans were already in motion for a huge turnout for Everton away last game of the season, followed by a trip to Blackpool afterwards. We had already sold our official 7,000 allocation for Godson Park, and with some fans thinking it may be a title decider a few thousand had obtained them for the home end as well. We took over all the pubs surrounding the ground. Villa fans were everywhere.

We were in the Blue House pub before the game and there was not an Everton fan in sight. The C-Crew had also took this pub over during the championship wining season. It was an Aston Villa invasion on Merseyside and a right party atmosphere was in the air. As I said, we were not organised this season, in spite of this, if Everton did have a firm out and saw our numbers they would not have fancied their chances due to the sheer mass of Villa fans that were there. It was such a sight – a sea of claret and blue – and all the old songs were coming out. In the ground the Villa support was the best I have ever heard it and the amount of Villa in the home end was amazing. You could have been fooled into believing we had won the title such was the atmosphere. I am not saying that Everton do not have any lads but at no stage did they try to move the Villa in the home end. Just the sheer amount of travelling fans meant we nearly took the ground over. It was mental and was one of my proudest moments as a Villa fan. Some Villa fans tried to make out it was a hooligan take over of Godson Park, but it was not like that at all; you will only get the truth from me. When I have read some hooligan books in the past they have made me cringe as you know they are full of bull-shit. Anyone who knows me will tell you I will not distort the facts just to make the Villa look good.

The game finished 3-3, but even if it would have been a title decider Liverpool won 9-0 and eventually won the league by a good few points. At full time we all refused to leave the ground until Graham Taylor came back out. We must have chanted: "We want Taylor", solidly for half an hour until our manager came out to salute us. He deserved our applauds as we had pushed the mighty Liverpool all season and played some lovely football. As well as getting us back up at the first attempt, Graham Taylor had now nearly taken us to the league title. What's more, he was regarded as the new 'messiah' of Villa Park. We all loved him. Ask anyone who was there that day and they will all tell you it was a very special occasion. Even the Everton fans clapped us as they left the ground. As always, we were about to take another backward step as shortly afterwards it was announced Graham Taylor was leaving for the England job. To say I was disappointed would be an understatement. Looking back now it is such a shame Graham Taylor came back for unsuccessful second stint as manager as it took the shine off all he had achieved the first time around.

On a more personal level, my life was about to change on two fronts. I would shortly become involved in politics as well as meeting the women who would become my future wife.

CHAPTER 3

I had now been left school about two years and was keeping down a steady job with a regular income. I had a been spending a lot of time over the Stockland Green/Erdington side of town, due to hanging around with a few mates from the Villa. Over my side of town all the pubs were Blue Nose pubs – The Cartland, The Bulls Head, The Navigation, The Fordrough, The Man on the Moon and many more I could mention. If I went in there I got shit. That's how the Blue noses are – rotten to the core. This explains why I did not really drink over my side of town. By now I knew most of the lads down the Villa. Nonetheless, I never claimed to be one of Villa's lads. I was just grateful they had took me in as one of their own and made me so welcome. Having said that, I was now in the 'loop' and very clued up as to what happened off the pitch as much as on it.

On the political front a certain day still stands out to me as what I would describe at the time as a 'wake up call'. For a lad who was already politically aware this was the tipping point. I had left work early and travelled through Digbeth to head back into town and what I saw sickened me. The day before had been St Patrick's Day where a massive march had passed through Digbeth, and there were posters everywhere with the slogan on 'FREE THE I.R.A PRISONERS' – hundreds of them. Now I am not saying that from an estimated 100,000 marchers that everyone had taken part in the postering campaign; that would be a crazy statement. Although no attempt had been made to remove them. Besides, whoever had put them up must not have faced any opposition in doing so. They were all along the stretch of road running back into the City Centre. What made me furious was after what had happened regarding the Birmingham bombings in 1974, they still had the nerve to do this. With a total lack of respect for the city and country they were all too happy to live in.

Now do not get me wrong, at this stage my knowledge of the troubles in Ulster were very limited. Despite that, I was aware of the terror the I.R.A had brought to our British streets and all the innocent, women, children, pensioners and British soldiers they had killed in the so-called war for 'IRELANDS FREEDOM'. I asked myself where was the freedom for the British soldier lying with his body blown into hundreds of pieces. I was only two years old at the time of the bombings, however, I can still remember as I got older my Dad telling me about the bombings and the panic in every household. The phoning around checking if loved ones were all right. Not to mention, the endless worry if you could not get hold of family members. That night Villa and Blues fans died together, Irish and English men and women died together, Catholic and Protestant; my Dad said it was absolute carnage. I understood the basics of the war in Ulster and that the I.R.A wanted the 'British Out' of Northern Ireland. Nonetheless, there was also a population of Protestant people in Ulster who were loyal to the Queen and the Crown, who wanted Ulster to remain under British rule. And were ready and willing to kill for their beliefs – just like the I.R.A. I found it very hypocritical how the republicans wanted the Unionist people out of Ulster, whilst they in far larger numbers were more than happy to live here in England. Moreover, having the freedom to promote their support for the I.R.A's terror campaign. From that day, I took a deeper interest and started to follow the situation in Ulster. This most certainly triggered my hatred towards the I.R.A and republicanism in general.

I headed back into town still pretty wound up. I then bumped into Tony who I had gone through school with. We were both heading home from work. He had by then took on a role as a Technical Designer; he worked on the outskirts of town. He was always a clever lad at school to be fair. Tony was not a Villa supporter like me, although he had been to the Villa with me on many occasions due to the fact we were close mates all through senior school and it was a way of keeping in touch. We started chatting and arranged to link up soon for a Villa game. As we agreed on a Saturday, he suddenly said to me: 'I have just remembered I have something on that night'. He was going to some nightclub with some mates who he had met after we had left school. I offered to miss the Villa game to link up with him as it would have been good to catch up. What he then said to me knocked me for six: 'Sorry you can't come, it's just for Black people and I couldn't take you with me; no way man'. I was stunned into silence to say the least. We had been mates for five years all through senior school and did everything together. Race was never an issue; we were hard to separate at school. We had some right play ups and never once had the Black and White thing been a problem. This was not the lad I had gone through school with. Something had changed and I did not like what I was seeing.

I had no problem with him finding his roots. I had also developed myself (which I would later come to describe) as British nationalist views. Although it had never made me act any different towards anyone – especially people I had grown up with and respected. I never judged people by the colour of their skin, but by the respect they showed me and their personality. I am not saying this is how every friendship ends up, nevertheless, since leaving school our racial differences had pulled us apart. We made an agreement to one-day meet up at the Villa but what he had said upset me. And as we parted I felt gutted because I knew we would never be the same again. No matter what my beliefs were I would never have said something like that to him – simply out of respect. I have never bumped into Tony from that day. During school days we did have a great friendship that I cannot deny. Moreover, he was a great lad for the five years I hung around with him.

As I carried on through town for the 65 bus to take me to Peter's house in Stockland Green, a paper seller from the Socialist Workers Party (a front group for the self-hating Anti-Nazi League) stopped me in the street. In the last few years they have changed their name to Unite Against Fascism/Hope not Hate. There was a little team of them spread out stopping people walking by. At this particular time I did not know who they were or what they stood for. A middle-aged shabbily dressed White guy started to tell me how immigrants were hard done by and how the immigration laws in this country were too strict. How he came to that conclusion I will never know. I was going to say to him: "I'm, sorry, what language are you speaking? As it sounds like bullshit". He kept rambling on about 'rights' for everyone else, but never once mentioning the 'rights' for the indigenous people who had lived here for tens of thousands of years.

I was beginning to get the gist of what this group were all about; they were as far-left as you could go. Communism is the most evil, murderous, ideology in the history of humanity – far worse than the Nazis. The problem with Communism's idea of free speech is that they are free to say what they like, but if anyone says anything back – they go into an outrage. After filling my head with 'loony-left' politics for five minutes, he offered me a newspaper to purchase which I instantly declined. Nonetheless, he forced one on to me free of charge. I thought I might as well take it and read it on the bus on the way over to Peter's. It had cost me nothing and it would help to pass the time on my journey. Hence, I sat down on the bus to read it. I can honestly say I could not believe some of the nonsense in there. I could not see how anybody could see things through their eyes. They were all for the ethnic minorities and it seemed to me that they could do no wrong and were beyond criticism. Yet at the same time they were all too quick to point out the evils of the White man and how we had a duty to the third world. If these people were all for fighting evil why weren't they down Digbeth ripping down the posters glorifying the I.R.A?

I quickly got the impression they found having pride in Britain outdated – even 'racist'. I learnt very quickly about groups like these and how they had selected memory when it came to what they opposed. I got the impression they were ashamed to be British and White, and were on some kind of a guilt trip. They were all White who were campaigning in the city centre; not one Black or Asian were in sight. These idiots were campaigning against their own people. I found it all very odd to be honest. It is something I have never seen happen from the non-White communities – people actively campaigning against their own. I still admire to this day how the Blacks and the Asians stick together within their own communities and help each other out. White people lost that a long time ago.

When I arrived at Peter's, I honestly wished I had taken another route home from work. Additionally, I remember thinking how we had lost control in our own country. Peter and I went the Brookvale pub on Slade Road, Stockland Green, and I told Peter about my day. Peter was like most English lads at the time. Not happy with how the country was heading but not bothered enough to say a lot about it. More importantly, worried about being labelled as being anti-immigration or worse still a 'racist'. A word that was by now was really starting to really take off. Pretty much the same as today like being known as a 'paedophile'. It carried a lot of power and a lot of fear – especially if you were suddenly labelled one. It put many people off from even having an opinion in case they were thrown into the 'racist' camp. Are you losing the debate ? Just shout 'RACIST' and you silence any opposition allowing you to claim victory. The word racist is actually a made up word that was invented by Leon Trotsky in 1927. Ever since, the word has been used to browbeat all dissenters of the Communist ideology. And it is still used in Britain to this day to shut down all resistance to immigration.

My patience was being tested by now. I could see freedom for one man but not for the next. St Patrick's Day was celebrated – you also had the Handsworth carnival in Birmingham, and the Notting Hill carnival in the London for example. The Notting Hill carnival is a yearly rampage of violence, drug dealing, rape and even murder. At the 2013 Notting Hill carnival, almost 300 people were arrested for a number of gruesome crimes. Despite that, the police and carnival organisers released a statement saying: "The carnival passed off as a largely peaceful affair, with no major incidents ruining the festivities". You could not make it up. But they would never ban it on politically correct grounds – unlike the NF/BNP marches that were banned on a regular basis. Likewise, every special event in the Asian calendar was promoted with specially released newspapers to highlight events like Diwali and Ramadan. Consequently, on St George's day not one cross of St George could be seen anywhere. I found it blatantly unfair.

Just as I thought the day could not get any worse, when I arrived home in Kings Norton I could tell when I walked in that something was not right. My sister Anne had been walking home from Bingo with her mate when they had been mugged by two Black youths off their heads on drugs. That was the last thing I wanted to hear after the day I'd had. I was fuming as I saw this as a racist attack, where they had singled out my sister because she was White, female and easy prey. It made me think back to the incident in the arcade up town years ago with Jamie when we came close to having our leather jackets taken off us. Like the fact or not, you did not hear much about Black on Black muggings. In spite of this, fair play to a local West Indian taxi driver who personally knew my sister. He had heard whispers about who may have carried out the mugging, and after a bit of personal detective work he had the names of the two lads who had done it. I really respected him for doing that for my family. Their names were given to the police, however, they had been found dead in their flat due to a drugs overdose the day before. To that end, that was the end of that and in my eyes it was two less scum bags on the streets.

Even after junkies had mugged my sister, it was around this time I started myself to dabble in low-level street drugs – something I still regret doing to this day. Like most lads I started smoking cannabis which then led onto speed, ecstasy and LSD. I am not blaming anyone bar myself for dabbling with drugs. The government had most certainly lost the war against drugs and they were freely available in every part of Birmingham. Over my side of town all the dealers were White lads.

This went against a lot of people's judgement of the Black drug dealer in his flash car. Obviously you had a number of Black lads in the drug trade, nevertheless, the majority of dealers over my way were White. Most of them worked full time and made an extra wage on the side by doing what they did. Taking drugs was like most things at the start. It all started good and you would feel on top of the world. But after a while the depression started to set in, as well as all the other side effects like anxiety, panic attacks and mood swings. That is something the drug dealers obviously do not tell you about. It was no one's decision to do this bar my own – so I am not blaming anybody for my embarrassing juvenile blunder. It was one of the biggest mistakes of my life as it has led to years of depression and being on anti-depression tablets. Jumping from one type of medication to another trying to find one that works; it has been hell.

I am not trying to justify my actions, however, at the time everybody was trying this and trying that. In addition, unfortunately I got caught up in the swing of things. I am also not trying to be a preacher. But I would strongly advise anybody thinking about dabbling with drugs to stay well clear. It is a fools game and the lows far exceed the highs. I would like to point out I am now drug free bar the medication from my doctor. Around this time a girl had caught my eye in the Greyhound pub in Erdington. I had been drinking in there with Peter from Stockland Green, and other lads I had met from the Villa like Ripper, Mogo, Etch, Carver, Jonny Moo and Stickman. They also used the Leopard pub in Erdington, which was a Villa stronghold. Erdington has always been a strong Villa area unlike Kings Norton. The girl in question was called Karen Cooke and she stood out to me straight away; I thought she was drop dead gorgeous. She was by far the best-looking bird in the pub and I suppose like many of the lads I had the feeling she was out of my league. Still, it did not stop me from wanting her.

Then the one day heading to Peter's, I saw Karen on the bus and sat next to her and we started talking. For some crazy reason she was single and this made me even more interested. Moreover, it is safe to say I was hooked by her good looks. I had fancied many girls before, however, Karen was a bit special. I thought she was beautiful. She lived with her mother and two sisters just off Slade Road, Stockland Green. I even used to time it right after work so that we caught the same bus together if I was going over to North Brum to see the lads from the Villa. Little did she know, but I would hold back at the bus stop until she appeared and then make out we had once again met by chance. But that was nothing of the sort. It was my way of bumping into her again and having another chance to see her and talk to her. Call it devious or whatever; it was my way of getting close to her and building up to asking her out for a date.

We would also meet in the Greyhound pub on Friday's – and I could tell after so long I was finally getting somewhere

– even if it was a slow process. We started going out drinking together all day Sunday up the Monte Carlo in Handsworth. This place had a terrible reputation but in all honesty we never had any hassle in there. These were the days when it was the only place doing all day Sunday drinking. Don't get me wrong there were some right dodgy characters in there. But if you went in there for a quiet drink and kept yourself to yourself you were as safe as houses. Due to it's location it was mostly used by the Black community – even though a number of Whites also used it on Sunday's – and it was a real good afternoon out. Not everyone's cup of tea I suppose, however, I never once sensed any racial tension in there and spoke to many decent Black people. It used to serve chicken and chips in a basket which was included in the entrance fee. I can remember the one Sunday when they had ran out of chicken and chips, and this Black lad shared his with me – fair play to him. We used the place for a couple of years and really used to look forward to a good Sunday drink. I also liked a majority of the music in there as I was brought up on Ska, Reggae, 2-Tone and Blue Beat. I suppose that for a British patriot like myself some would say that was going against the grain drinking in a Black club, nonetheless, it was just how it was. More importantly, I had finally landed the girl of my dreams and I was over the moon.

The football season of 1990-91, was a right let down after finishing runners up the season before to Liverpool. Graham Taylor had left for the England job and we had appointed Jozef Venglos as manager. Hardly anyone had heard of him and it is fair to say the fans never really took to him. We spent the whole season sitting just below mid-table, and after the season before going for the title it was another major disappointment at Villa Park. We had a couple of memorable games though like Inter Milan at home – god that was some night; one I will never forget. We beat the Italian giants 2-0 at the first leg at Villa Park and the atmosphere was truly fantastic. Some of the older lads said it reminded them of the atmosphere during the European Cup winning year. Villa Park was electric. For all that, at the second leg in Italy we lost 3-0 and we were out. Nevertheless, the atmosphere at the first game was one to savour forever.

Another good day out was Man United away just after Christmas, as thousands of Villa headed up north for a day out on the beer and a singsong. There were that many Villa there it was their biggest gate of the season. That was some achievement considering they had the visits of Liverpool, Arsenal and Man City. We still though had no organised firm at this stage. All the same, having a laugh and seeing the Villa win meant more to me than getting a result off the pitch. I just found it a bit strange how a club Villa's size with so many good lads had no firm. Every club goes through this I suppose and it is just how things were on the Villa Park terraces at the time.

At the end of the season it was agreed that Jozef Venglos was not the man to take Villa forward and he was relieved from his duties. The rumour mill was that Ron Atkinson was coming to take over the Villa Park hot-seat. Villa fans were buzzing at this prospect. After saying he was not leaving Sheffield Wednesday, suddenly he did a massive U-turn and resigned. The Board paraded him at the Villa Park press conference. We were all delighted as Big Ron had a great record of accomplishment as well as having a bubbly personality. Moreover, it was just the lift the club needed after a dull season under Jozef Venglos. Little did I know at the time but it captured the imagination of 'scarfers' and 'firm' alike, and the next season would see the emergence of a new organised firm who would later become to be known as the Villa Hardcore.

I was still very concerned about the political situation in our country. I recall thinking to myself that if the British people are destroyed by racial in breeding, then the British nation will cease to exist. Now let me state, I will defend myself all day long and stick with the fact that I am not a racist in the real true meaning of the word. Be as it may be, if people decide to label you one there is not a lot you can do about it. It is a sad unpleasant fact. It is a reality of life that you will get 'pigeon holed' for holding certain views – especially in politically correct Great Britain where you are not allowed to have your own opinion. I am not the first and I will certainly not be the last. Then one day whilst walking up by Kings Norton green, I saw two stickers on a lamppost and I stopped to see what they were. They were stickers from the National Front, with a phone number on them. The stickers said: "ARE YOU PROUD TO BE BRITISH AND WHITE" and: "KEEP ULSTER BRITISH-HANG THE I.R.A". I totally agreed with both of these slogans. Throughout the years I had seen many pro-Black, pro-Asian and pro-Irish republican advertisements in many, way, shapes and forms. And I found it a refreshing change to see something I could actually relate to myself.

I wrote the phone number down and phoned up for an information pack when I got home. My life was about to take me into my first journey into politics. I was about to become involved in what people refer to as the 'right-wing'. My country had fallen by the way side and I felt it my duty to try to do something about it.

CHAPTER 4
(*In memory of*
John Tyndall 1934 – 2005)

*T*here was a wave of elections coming up, yet like millions of others I had no hope for Britain whatever mainstream party got in. The mass media in Britain were speculating on the outcome. However, did it really matter? Would they really make any difference – Tory, Labour or Lib Dem. You can look back on years of Tory governments and Labour governments and they have done nothing to change the course of affairs. Since the end of the world wars (from which we have never recovered) there has been a threat in Britain; a national decline of the whole country – millions can now see it. A loss of the greatness that Britain had once held. A loss of power and a loss of will. And just rewinding a little – on the subject of the world wars – why do we have wars? We are ruled by an elite of very evil and greedy people who own the banks that control the governments and the media. They secretly fund both sides of the war for profit (as war makes money) and they manufacture the consent of the public through the propaganda of the media. War is when your government tells you who the enemy is – revolution is when you figure it out for yourself,

Not only that – I could see a dramatic fall in the quality of life in Great Britain – especially in my home town of Birmingham. For all that, no political party seemed to have the vision to try to stop it. People who emigrated to Australia, Canada or New Zealand who came back on family visits all say the same; how Britain has changed for the worse. The most shocking thing about Britain's decline is it has not happened from any outside military takeover. No external forces had imposed these situations on us, or the policies that were leading to our downfall as a nation. Everything had come from within. It was as if the leaders of Britain had imposed on us a kind of 'national death wish'. Within a lifetime of people still living today, an empire has been surrendered. An empire which had endless wealth and possibilities – just allowed to disintegrate. Moreover, without any defeat in a war – only the collapse of the will to rule.

Then in a blink of an eye, the nation that was once the workshop of the world suddenly gave up its place in the world as a major manufacturer. Today British people travel to work in foreign motor cars. When they reach work, they carry out their jobs with foreign made equipment. Then they use foreign machine tools and foreign computers. Then when they come home, they switch on foreign made televisions. When tens of thousands of British holidaymakers fly off on their summer breaks, they mostly fly out on foreign made planes. All this from a country that once showed itself to have industrial expertise – second to none. Britain was once responsible for more great inventions than any other nation. Because Britain today imports the things we used to make in our own factories, millions are growing up with little or no prospect of finding a job. Young men and women leaving university with skills and qualifications, find that those skills are of little use to them. What's more, this state of affairs is more or less accepted by a British nation that has gone to sleep. As the mainstream parties keep telling us; the future belongs to Asia, Japan, Korea, Singapore and China. Moreover, that the best we British can hope for (who once led the world in industry) is to be the 'yes' men for far eastern manufacturers. The assemblers for a few spare parts for Japanese or any other far eastern producers – if were lucky.

This is allowed to happen under the International free market. We are told if Britain wants a slice of the cake, that we have to compete in this free market. Goods are now flooding into our country made in factories in the Far East, where workers will slave away for next to nothing. How can we compete? It is impossible. Primary, the British worker has to worry about fighting for a job in the face of a tidal wave of cheap immigrant labour. When they are occupied in trying to get decent housing in competition with teeming millions of immigrants, they will not have time to think about how the International big businesses are robbing them blind with such a gigantic swindle as the European Union.

Whilst Britain is crying out for the investment it needs to modernise our factories – to research new techniques and to expand production – British capital is going abroad to finance our rivals. It is hardly surprising when with cheap labour freely available, British capitalists can make far bigger profits out of industries abroad than from industries at home. What industries are left in this country, when they need capital to expand, they have to seek it from abroad and be taken over whilst in the process. We have seen it with Jaguar, we have seen it with Rover, we have seen it with HP Sauce – and we have seen it with one great British industry after another. Bit by bit the assets of this country, the great efforts built up over centuries of hard work, sold on lock, stock and barrel to the highest bidder. As far as I was concerned we would get this economic future regardless if we had a Tory, Labour or Lib Dem government. Who ever were elected it would make no difference, as all the mainstream parties are dedicated to the same system.

It's the same in America. It does not matter who you vote for; Democrat or Republican – you get the same outcome; nothing changes. I risk sounding now like a 'conspiracy theorist' but it is no longer simply a 'theory' – what I'm about to say is a fact. The secret organisations of the world power elite are no longer a secret. They have plans (which are well advanced) to lead us into a one-world communist/ Marxist government. Nobody should doubt that we are now living under a form of dictatorship. And on the subject of America, anybody with half a brain who can see past the media's version of events will know that 9/11 was an inside job; it has Israeli fingerprints all over it. I do not have the time here to explain it in it's full entity, but it only takes a tiny bit of investigative work to uncover these horrific facts. It is clear for all to see that it was a controlled demolition – experts worldwide have confirmed this. Never forget that jet fuel burns at 1500 degrees (Maximum) where as steel melts at 2750 degrees. But the majority of people will not even dare to share their version of events for fear of being called 'crazy', a 'crank, or a 'conspiracy theorist' – which is a contemptuous term used primarily by the mainstream media to slander anyone who dares to question their monopoly on the truth and crimes committed by the government.

Even though certain individuals or groups have done their own research and have concluded that the official account of events is either lacking or inaccurate, they are still labelled 'conspiracy theorists' because they refuse to believe what the controlled media proclaim to be the truth. Society has become so fake that the truth actually bothers people. People get mad when you say 'inside job' because it places them in a position they do not want to live in. It never ceases to amaze me how so many people still believe the 'official' version of September 11th and gloss over the facts like the unexplainable collapse of Building 7. Likewise, the fact that not one CCTV camera at one of the most secure sites on US soil managed to pick up a plane hitting the Pentagon. In order to create global solutions, you have to create global problems. No matter how conspiracy minded you are, what the government is actually doing is worse than you ever could imagine.

The smartest thing for our rulers to do is to own both sides of every game so that they control the outcome. And if they do have to face any opposition they will eventually command that resistance as well. Moreover, who are these people with such amazing power and wealth? Dare I say, for the fear of being accused of being 'anti-Semitic'? Subversive Jewish writer, Moritz Steinschneider, invented the term 'anti-Semitic' in 1860. The term ever since has been used to silence those that dare to speak about or expose Jewish wrongdoing. To learn who rules over you, simply find out who you are not allowed to condemn. Archbishop Desmond Tutu said himself: "You know as well as I do, that the Israeli government is placed on a pedestal and to criticise it is to be immediately labelled 'anti-Semitic'. People are scared to say wrong is wrong, as the Jewish lobby is powerful. Very powerful". These people hold all the leading positions in all the mainstream television networks, the main newspaper chains and the Hollywood film studios. In addition, their role in British politics is equally marked. They hold a disproportionate level of political power in more or less every government – especially in America. Pointing this out is little more than a statistical observation. But this is not a new phenomenon; it has long been a major factor.

Toughened by centuries of persecution, they have risen to positions of prime importance in the business of the financial world. They weld unprecedented power in the world of finance and investment banking. Furthermore, they play an important role in the American governments policy towards the Middle East. Pro-Israeli Jews have taken control of American foreign policy and have succeeded in pushing the U.S.A and Britain into war in Iraq and other Muslim nations. No wonder so many British Muslims are becoming radicalised. They have seen the Middle East invaded and destabilised by illegal wars based on Tony Blair's lies. They have watched their countries invaded and their women and children killed by drones and air strikes. History repeats itself and one only has to look at past wars to note that interference from the West leads to displacement of populations on a grand scale. In their eyes they are repaying us back for every war-mongering Western leader.

If our people actually knew the grip they had on our government they would rise outraged, but our citizens do not have any idea what is going on. People do not want to hear the truth because they do not want to destroy their illusions. Silence is the common response from a fool. What's more, we will be dragged into further wars along with America against Israel's enemies. You can give a person knowledge but you cannot make them think for themselves. Some people want to remain fools only because the truth requires change.

I think it's only fair to elaborate in more detail regarding the 'Jewish Question', because as well as being a touch confusing to the everyday person in the street it is not all what it seems. It is widely known as Zionism, or as I prefer to call it...Rothschild Zionism. I have added the 'Rothschild' to highlight the true creators of Zionism and its controllers to this day. The Rothschild family is a family descending from Mayer Amschel Rothschild, a court Jew (Jewish banker) to the German Landgraves of Hesse-Kassel, in the Free City of Frankfurt who established his banking business in the 1760's. Unlike most previous court Jews, Rothschild managed to entrust his wealth and established an international banking family through his five sons. During the 19th century, the Rothschild family possessed the largest private fortune in the world as well as the largest private fortune in modern world history – referred to as the 'founding father of international finance'. They are estimated to be worth £500 Trillion dollars. Furthermore, they invisibly control and affect every aspect of the world we live in today. I will explain the connections later, but some background is required to put it in the framework that it needs to be seen.

Ask most people about Zionism and they will say: "That's the Jews". Whilst this is the impression the Rothschild network in politics and the media have sought very successfully to sell as common knowledge; actually what may astound you – it is not true. It represents only a minority of them and many others who are surprisingly not Jewish; anti-Zionism is not the same as anti-Semitism. Rothschild Zionism in its public expression is a political ideology based on a homeland for Jewish people in Palestine, and a belief that Jews are God's chosen race with a God-given right to the 'promised land' of Israel. In addition, they believe that the real borders of Israel must surround what is now Israel, which includes Gaza and the West Bank – still officially owned by the Palestinians. Nonetheless, at its inner core is a secret society created and controlled by the House of Rothschild. They have sought to promote the 'Zionism means all Jewish people' lie, so that they can rebuke anybody who dares to expose the truth about Rothschild Zionism and its agents in government, banking, business, media et (as I explained earlier). This is why most researchers will not even dare mention it even if they are aware enough to know it to be true.

The world's most extreme 'racists' and 'bigots' are after all, the Rothschild Zionists. You only have to look at the racist divisions within Jewish society itself, with the Black Jews from Ethiopia who are treated less than animals. Moving on from here, let us get past the calculated smokescreen that challenging Rothschild Zionism and the horrors of Israel means you are anti-Jewish, and instead look at the simple facts that they do not want you to acknowledge. Firstly, you do not have to be Jewish to be a Rothschild Zionist. Some of the most staunch Rothschild Zionists are Christian Zionists in the United States of America and beyond, including here at home in Great Britain. By contrast, a large number of Jewish people are not Zionists. Some even oppose it and support the Palestinians in their battle for survival against the overwhelming aggression from the Israel government and the military funded by America in terrorising indigenous inhabitants. I do not want people thinking I am 'Pro-Palestinian' – nor am I 'Pro-Israel – I am just pointing out a few facts. Jewish people organise protests and call for boycotts of Israel, in response to the Rothschild Zionist agenda for the Palestinians, nonetheless, how many people know about this who get all their 'information' from the mainstream media. Have your eyes been blinded by the lies?

No one who gets their news from the Rothschild controlled broadcasting services would be none the wiser to any of this, because they push only one line to throw you off the scent – Zionism means ALL Jewish people; end of story. The Rothschild's have a network of organisations that work within one another to target anybody or any organisation that gets close to exposing their horrific agenda. They will attack and undermine them in every way possible to stop the truth becoming known. Many Israelis connected to the Rothschild networks were sent to America after the state of Israel was established, to specifically produce children who would be American born citizens to infiltrate the US government in the following generations. Only 1.7% of the population of America are Jewish and a significant number of those will not be Rothschild Zionists. Doesn't that show the enormous power that these people hold? The American government scream about the 'war on terror' yet they are the biggest terrorists on the face of the planet.

After September 11th, the American government passed what was known as the 'Patriot Act' – which from the outside may all seem well and good. For all that, it is just a smoke screen to gain more control and power over the American people and take away more of their freedoms. You may be amazed to hear that the British Prime Minister, David Cameron, is a Rothschild Zionist 'puppet', and so is the leader of the Labour 'opposition' Ed Milliband, who got the job after a campaign in which his brother, David Milliband, was the other major candidate. This is in a country where the Jewish population is around 280,000, in a national population of 62 million and rising due to unlimited immigration. The key manipulating force in the previous UK government of Tony Blair and Gordon Brown was Peter Mandelson, who to this day flaunts his close connections to the Rothschild's with holidays at their mansion on the Greek island of Corfu. I could go on and on explaining about the Rothschild Zionists in greater detail, but I would need to write another story in itself. This is only a brief synopsis which barely skims the surface without going 'deeper down the rabbit hole'. If you stop and take your time, you will see the evidence is there hidden under a mountain of disinformation. Nevertheless, I hope this goes some way to explaining the 'Jewish Question'.

Now moving onto the European Union. Britain's membership of Europe has been a total disaster. Along with those from Asia, cheap imports from Europe have helped to cripple the UK job market to its knees. The EU is an Internationalist – Soviet style organisation – that seeks to eradicate national sovereignty, cultural identity and racial homogeneity. The United Kingdom can not control immigration and be in the EU. And let us never forget – it was the Tory Satanist and child killer Edward Heath who led the campaign for EU membership and signed us into the fascist/communist 'superstate' to appease the people pulling his strings. It makes me think are paedophiles deliberately chosen for positions of power so if they can't be bought they can be blackmailed? Let's not pull any punches here – our country is run by satanic – paedophile leaders – who control the masses using fear, false flags and the mainstream media. Now imagine the masses finally waking up to this 'sick agenda'. Many in the United Nations, notably Peter Sutherland, UN special representative on migration – are intent on destroying national identity in order to facilitate a one world government. Mass immigration is a vital tool in their armoury. The men and women like Peter Sutherland, are appalling examples of the leaders that we need to cast out at the earliest opportunity. The United Nations has for a long time been unfit for purpose; it's high time this incompetent Third World political gravy train was derailed.

Our fishermen face ruin due to the surrender of the controls of our sea borders, where Spanish anglers are allowed into our waters. In addition, our cattle farmers are in deep trouble. As all this has been happening our national sovereignty and our freedom to make our own decisions, and to control our own affairs as a nation has been steadily eroded. As power has been handed over without a fight, to what they decide to call the European Union. All this is a result of our politicians being weak and giving up on their own people. Believing us to be as weak as they are, when we should be standing up proud. We are strong enough to stand alone in the world. The strongest walls are not made of stone – they are made of brave men and women.

Despite all the evidence over the centuries that point this out, the government choose to ignore it. Repeatedly, over the centuries Britain has stood on its own. We had done so because in those days, those times in our former great history, our people believed in themselves. More importantly, we had leaders who believed in our destiny, our strength as a nation and our capabilities – and they were never proved wrong. Yet today this counts for nothing. Our politicians turn their back on British history. The record of Tory and Labour governments have been equally embarrassing.

Over the past 60 years we have seen a once stable, loyal, and law abiding country totally fall apart. We have seen crime hit record levels. We have seen the bedrock of family life almost collapse. We now have the highest divorce rate in Europe. Meanwhile, the church for where the British people once looked to for leadership, has given up on its responsibilities. Today our church leaders seem more concerned about political correctness and somebody being hungry in Africa, than about rape, murder and child molesters. When we look at the values that once held our society together we cannot avoid pointing a finger at the mass media. Night after night from the fancy screen in your living room, we get an endless barrage of sleaze, filth and planned brainwashing. Encouraging all the bad things that are tearing Britain apart. The mass media has corrupted journalism to the point where any unbiased dialogue on the subject of immigration is a non-starter. Look at the promotion of homosexuality. Yes, we all know it goes on, in spite of that it should not be promoted in the way that it is. I have met many good gay and lesbian people – all the same, my opinion is this. That it should be accepted – not promoted – especially not to schoolchildren. This comes as no surprise. It is the pattern of the road we have been travelling as a nation.

Something has to be done. Someone must stand up and say we cannot go this way any longer. We have to have a clean up in this country. We have to return to the ways which served our ancestors well over the centuries. We have to have decency, standards, order and respect. I realised this would not happen if we had either a Tory, or Labour government. Those who had allowed and encouraged the problem to grow for all these years were not going to suddenly provide the solutions. You cannot change people who do not see an issue in their actions. Their past records are not to be trusted, and as representatives of our nation they are too spineless. I used to pray from somebody to speak out and to stand up and defend our liberties. Then I realized...I am somebody.

One of the most terrible situations facing this country over the past 40 years has been the drop in the standards of education. This has happened due to a number of reasons. Inferior teaching, collapse of discipline at schools, decline in our sport and training – and the monster of it all – the creeping totalitarianism of political correctness. This has many features. The most insulting is criticism of national pride and the never-ending barrage and promotion of multi-culturalism. This results in the promotion of non-British cultures, whilst holding our own people back and destroying our culture. There is no attempt to install into our youth the basic principles of patriotism. Schools and universities have become the breeding grounds for all the ideas that are systematically rotting our nation from within. We have teachers telling our young children to believe what they were programmed to believe, and what they must teach if they wish to keep their jobs. And in doing so, we put our young kids – the brightest of our future – through a 'sausage machine' and turn them out the other end knowing nothing about British history. Our children are force fed a programme of left-wing indoctrination. The political left are an insecure crowd – so they compensate for their insecurities by coming up with immature political correct ideas. All 'leftists' care about is using victims to establish their Communist agenda. What they don't realise being very stupid, is that for example Muslim extremists will then turn on the 'leftists' and wipe them out to establish their Islamic state; they are digging their own graves.

Most people in this country regard political correctness as a terrible thing that has been imposed upon us. When in reality, it is only a small number of powerful people that are forcing it onto us. The same people I mentioned earlier. The shocking thing is these people have the power to impose their views and standards on everybody else – even if they do not agree with them. The British people have been bullied into not expressing perfectly legitimate and reasonable concerns over mass immigration. Better to be seen to be agreeing, than to be the one kicking up a stink over something springs to mind.

One feature of political correctness that stands out to me, is finding faults in the words in children's nursery rhymes. No longer being able to call a Blackboard a Blackboard and changing the words to 'Baa, Baa, Black Sheep'; it's madness. This however is just one example. But it does not stop there. Spy cameras that were put up in a Muslim area in Birmingham, were taken down once the political correct 'loonies' got involved. The cameras had been financed with funding from a counter-terrorism initiative to combat the movement of potential terrorist activity in the area. At the cost of many millions of pounds the spy cameras were taken down and the police were forced to apologise for upsetting the Muslim community. These cameras could have been in weeks, months or years to come, the saviour of a terrorist attack in Birmingham. Now they have been removed it puts all people at risk – regardless of race or religion. Political correctness is now more important than saving human life. This is what happens when crackpot political theorists are allowed to impose their warped ideology on the British people. The traitors who first decided to force multi-culturalism on the British people are long dead and buried and will not have to reap what they have sown. Unfortunately, the same can not be said for those of us still here living in this hell hole.

What was to surface in Rotherham in 2014, would shake British society to the core. The Labour Party knew about the abuse of 1,400 children by Islamic grooming gangs but decided to cover it up under political correctness. This has to be one of the biggest Paedophile scandals to have ever take place in the UK. The Labour Party was more concerned about the feelings of the Muslim community than justice for our children. Sarah Champion knew for over a year about the grooming gangs in Rotherham, yet she said nothing as she valued her job more than the child victims; these are the type of people we have representing us. We now live in a society where the authorities desire not to offend an ethnic-group, outweighs the desire to protect a child from a grooming gang. Then again, this was not only the case in Rotherham. You can also include to that list Dewsbury, Rochdale, Sheffield, Blackpool, Blackburn, Derby, Leeds, Oxford and my home city of Birmingham. The Labour Party has blood on their hands. We should also remember that 800 years ago in 1215, King John sealed the Manga Carta. Its values are the foundation of so many world democracies through the power of an idea – a principle that states that nobody, including the King, is above the law of the land.

Our masters though are not completely stupid. The way they manage to control our people is to take away a little bit of our freedom at a time. By doing so bit by bit, our people will not notice our rights being taken away up to the point when they then have complete control over our way of life. You will not even notice some of things they do against us as at the time they seem so insignificant. The political correct masters also occupy the commanding roles in education, media, arts, town and city councils. Yet nothing is done. What strange power does this lobby hold which makes it free from public criticism? Ninety-nine per cent of our politicians are totally in bed with this PC lobby. The only politician from the past twenty years I have any type of respect for is Norman Tebbit. He would now and again make some good strong views on immigration and political correctness, however, he stood alone. I waited thinking maybe with him speaking out it would give others in power some steel to debate these issues in parliament. I waited and waited, but it never happened. No matter who got into power the education system would get worse. All the leading politicians support all the loony ideas that have destroyed our schools. The teachers unions who force these ideas, are to large part Labours far-left activists. The Tories are no different. I have always found with the Tories they can talk a good fight – but they always fail to deliver with their promises. Their record in power is a disgrace. Like I have already told you, all the main three political parties work for the same hidden corporations? It's like having the option to vote for 'Tweedledum or Tweedledee'. The gap between talk and action is as wide as the Atlantic Ocean.

A short while ago I mention multi-culturalism, but only slightly touched on the subject. Now I will mention about the large-scale take over of most of our towns and cities; the relentless invasion of Britain. Yes, this is the great forbidden issue that you should not speak about. The one issue that made Enoch Powell a household name all those many years ago. Most politicians pander to the immigrants and say how they love their presence here – whilst themselves living in plush areas with private gates. Totally shut off from reality. This is the subject on which more than any other, all the mainstream parties have decided to ignore. Whilst at the same time to lie and to brainwash the British people into believing that immigration is a good thing.

What we have experienced in this country since the 1950's, is nothing short of an invasion. Moreover, it has been an invasion in which the complete make up of Britain has changed – maybe forever. It is a far more dangerous invasion than if an enemy army had invaded us during a time of war. This is an invasion which threatens the whole identity and character of Britain. And before anybody starts telling me about other invasions like the Saxons, Romans, Vikings and Normans, let us get this straight right at the beginning. These earlier invasions were by people from Northern Europe, whose character, whose cultures, whose standards and way of life were very little different from our own. There simply is no argument over invasions of old and the new invasion we have seen over the last 60 years. Especially from a section of the Asian/Muslim population who are worlds apart from us in almost every way you can imagine.

These immigrants have brought with them changes to the areas they have settled, which are so vast that the areas of old are now totally unrecognisable. In addition, the result is always the same. When the immigrants move in, the locals move out. Anyone who denies this fact is kidding himself or herself. The result is large parts of our towns and cities now look like outposts of the third world. The governments 'race replacement plan' is now in it's final stages. We have seen the results. I do not really need to spell it out to you because you will know what I already mean. If you have lived in or pass through these areas, you will know what I am talking about. You will know that the big experiment has not worked. I knew by now that this failed policy would not be tackled – no matter who got into power. All the mainstream politicians are totally committed to making Britain a multi-cultural society – if the British people want it or not.

One of the reasons that the MP's support this invasion, is that they are all chasing the immigrant vote. Therefore, they fall over each other to pander to them. This is one of the things that gives the ethnic minorities so much power. Look at how the Muslim community support any politician who speaks out against the occupation of Muslim nations. They are not voting for issues that are at the centre of Britain's interests – they are voting for issues that effect what they consider their 'homeland'. In a divided society as Britain is today, any ethnic group that can sway an election one way or the other are going to have enormous power.

We are approaching a situation where the ethnic minorities – still at the moment with smaller numbers than the native British – can actually have a big say in the running of this country by deciding which party should win the election. You do not need many millions to do this in a democracy; all you have to do is hold the balance of power. Moreover, this is what the ethnic minorities can do with the present system as it is. One of the features of the past 30-40 years has been the feeble response to the increase in violence and crime. Murder and riots in our inner cities – which is another result of multi-culturalism – has been dealt with kid gloves. Our once proud and decent police force, have been reduced to 'playing politics'. Fear of arresting and tackling criminals – paralysed by the thought of condemnation by 'harassing' ethnic minorities. This is a fact I know only to well for myself. Everywhere you can see what has happened to a country whose government has lost the will to govern.

When you bring different cultures into the same area and do so by bringing in very large numbers, you are creating a 'tinderbox' just waiting to explode. The problem is the different nationalities do not sense or feel any type of unity as their cultures develop separately. Our culture and way of life has been around for many centuries and to just drop it and let it fade away would be a huge mistake. Our culture has been brushed to the side. I wonder how other cultures around the world would react if the situation in Britain was reversed? How would other cultures react if millions of British people poured into Pakistan for example and opened up fish and chip shops, night-clubs and started building Christian churches? Would there be tolerance? Would there be acceptance of the British way of life? Whilst at the same time, they still have in their homelands their deeply-rooted traditions and culture – which bounds them to their land and their people. Britain is the place where our masters have decided to force their globalisation experiment, as they know the weakness of our people (which they have created) who will put up little if any resistance.

For all that, I want to focus on one subject that always stood out to myself and many others. What I am talking about is the cowardly response of government, one after the other, to the campaign of terror and murder by the I.R.A. I am not saying that the loyalist community were free of any wrong doing themselves, however, their loyalty to the British nation has never came into question. Over nearly four decades, the I.R.A and its criminal supporters have butchered not only British soldiers and police officers, but old folk, women, and little children. And in the face of that campaign what we have seen from our politicians has not been strength and solutions – but surrender. Concession after concession, retreat after retreat. Repeatedly, the British government have shown a total lack of will to put these terrorists down with the use of all the force available. And to defend the frontiers of our country – and Northern Ireland is our country. Let us make no bones about it. We must defend Northern Ireland against those who wish to destroy it.

In loyal Ulster we have the Unionist/Protestant community whose loyalty to the British nation is second to none. A loyalty demonstrated across the ages, from the battlefields of the Somme and beyond. Thousands of Volunteers left what they knew as 'the nine counties of Ulster'. They bravely went off to fight and die for King and country, but what happened when they returned home – the ones who did return? The counties that made Ulster up no longer numbered nine. Three counties had been sold away by those they fought to save. Yes, that was England's gratitude. The nine counties had been reduced to six, by a government who overlooked all they had fought for. That was the repayment for the endure made by the 36th Ulster Division. In spite of this, after all their loyalty towards Britain, governments have been willing to 'strike deals' over the future of our people. And let me make this perfectly clear yet again – the loyalists are our people. We have talked to the government of the Irish Republic, we have talked to the United States of America over the most loyal part of Great Britain – it should be our business, and no one else's business. In addition, by doing so, we have sent out a message to the I.R.A – terrorism works. If you murder enough people you will scare the British government into talking to you, doing deals with you; making special allowances. The list is endless. This horrid tale of weakness and betrayal in the face of the I.R.A's republican war machine is one of the most deplorable chapters in British history.

I knew whatever party got into power this would continue. In Tony 'Traitor' Blair's autobiography, he stated he wanted peace in Northern Ireland by having a United Ireland. It is there in print for the whole world to see for themselves. This was not a statement from an Irish Politician; it was from the British Prime Minister. After the Good Friday agreement was signed, Tony Blair announced he was becoming a Roman Catholic. Without throwing the sectarian tag at me doesn't this show behind the scenes whose side he was secretly on all along? A majority of the Labour party are also for a United Ireland. They are all in bed together. By now, I had seen a pattern emerging. Appeasement of Britain's enemies, betrayal of Britain's most loyal friends. It had become a habit. Both Tory and Labour were to blame. Moreover, as for the Liberals, if there is one thing this country does not need its more Liberalism.

The National Front wanted and offered something different. I wanted things to be as they used to be. With leaders not afraid to speak out for Britain and it's interests. If you live in a country where you can be arrested for fishing without a licence but not for entering that country illegally, it is safe to say something is very wrong. I wanted a future for our people which was worthy of it's past. The very first thing Britain needs to do again is to start truly acting like a nation. A nation that will stand on its own two feet – a nation that will look to its own people for salvation. A nation that will put its own people first – a nation that will fight for its own interests and defend its own borders. A nation with pride and honour – as we have in loyal Ulster. A nation we were once – when the world respected us.

We must immediately withdraw from Europe. And I'll say it again – OUT. Not renegotiate membership or accept the single currency – OUT. What this means in effect is a British stance of independence. The EU are trying to play god by changing Europe beyond all recognition. We would say to Europe: "Yes by all means let us be friends, let our nations co-operate when it is in our interests. And let us trade when it suits our interest to trade". However, we can do that without the European Union. If we did come out of Europe where would that leave us? It would leave us on a set of heavily populated islands on the edge of a continent – just like Japan. But the difference is we have far more farming land – we have coal and we have oil. Japan along with China have little of these modern resources, yet they have become the most successful nations of the modern world. They have done so by the nature of their own character and by the intelligence and the industry of their own people. Why can't we do the same? I am certain we could do the same, but we need one thing that China and Japan have – and that is a sense of our own worth. A sense of our own destiny, and above all a sense of patriotism. This would weld our people into a strong unit, which knows what it wants and where it is going. A nation with a will to fight for its own interests; a nation with a sense of identity and pride.

The United Kingdom once survived on our own for centuries and we can survive again. But are we on our own? Do we not have friends and kin-folk around the world? In Australia and New Zealand, there are over 15 million people of British stock occupying a huge continent vastly rich in mineral oil. If these people feel alienated from us today should we really be surprised? They came and fought with us in two world wars and what did we do? We abandoned them when we went into Europe. If we came out of Europe, could we win them back? Well nothing in life is certain but there is one very important factor working in our favour. Canada and Australia are big exporters of minerals and both these countries – plus New Zealand – are big exporters of food products. We could buy their minerals from them and we could buy their food from them at better prices than we could ever get in Europe. Self interest if nothing else to begin with, would make them foolish to turn us down. By doing this, we could achieve a larger market – which was what Europe was supposed to be all about in the first place. But with one big difference. We would be linking up with economies complementary to our own. Countries what sell what we need to buy and buy what we need to sell. Nevertheless, we cannot expect these countries to buy our products on sentiment alone.

To make such a system work we need a massive regeneration of the manufacturing industry here in Britain. When the Tories first came to power in 1979, they said this was their main objective. After four successive terms of government the simple fact is they had failed. They failed because their policies were wrong at the very first base. They put their faith in the International free market and we have seen the results. British industry gutted by cheap imports. The free market simply has not worked for Britain and it is time for a change in policy. The first thing we should do is to rebuild British manufacturing behind a 'PROTECTIVE WALL'.

We should gradually reduce imports of foreign goods, as our own industry grows to fill the gap. The final objective would be for all Britain's needs in manufactured products to be supplied by industries at home. This simple change of policy would create jobs for the millions of British people who are now unemployed. We need to start producing the goods that we now import from the Far East and Europe. As the imported cut price goods from around the world are gradually brought to a halt, the British wage would rise again. These products would be sold in a protected British home market. Shut off from the cut-price goods on offer from the sweatshops in Asia. Along with this, we would need a huge programme of investment. The mainstream parties look for investment from abroad. They are quite happy for foreign capital to buy up and control British industry. We need investment from British capital and to bring our industries back under British ownership. There is no other solution. We simply should not stand for British financial institutions investing money abroad for the benefit of our rivals. British finance should be regulated the same way as all other sensible nations regulate their finances. We should make finance work in favour of the British people and not for the interests of the International gamblers.

We must make our country once again, a decent place to live in. Towns and cities must return to being clean. On a recent trip to Germany, I was amazed how clean the country was – as well as the public transport. I felt a sense of shame when I compared the standards in Germany to Great Britain. Why can't we have the same degree of pride? We must reclaim the streets and parks and make them safe to walk around. A decent level of education must be a priority. We need to return to old traditional codes. Our politicians and the media are consistently going on about everyone's rights, but you never hear them talk about duties. What is a young person today ever taught about duties? If they are not taught about duties how can they have any idea what having duties are all about? When you consider that children are taught that having pride in Britain is out of date, even racist, it is not surprising the way today's youth are turning out. We must without hesitation educate our children to be proud of Britain and its history. It must become a priority in the classrooms. We must no longer be afraid to upset the left-wing 'fascist' bullyboys. The Japanese educate their children in patriotism from a young age, which is why their country is where it is today. I respect them for that. We must do the same. All tyranny needs to gain a foothold in a nation, is for people of good conscience to remain silent.

Now what about crime? I have always believed that crime stems from a collapse in values. My view is that this happens when people start to see no future in their life and give up hope. I have seen it for myself in Birmingham. Let's face it – there are no good examples from those above in positions of power. National Service should be brought back to re-install some standards in young people. Are you surprised with the political leaders that we have today how the young people are turning out. If the politicians do not live by rules themselves, how can they expect others to do so? Why should the youth of today give a damn about their country, when they have not been taught any different? Standards must be raised in Britain again to restore us as a great nation. A nation that people are once again proud to belong to – under leaders they can respect. We must restore the death penalty for child killers, Irish republican terrorists and their allies. We must have tougher jails and longer jail sentences.

The situation in Ulster needs putting to bed for good. We must send out a message that regardless of what happens by republican terrorists that they will never win. The new wave of attacks by Dissident republicans will have no impact over the future of Northern Ireland. That means a declaration that Northern Ireland will remain British for all time – and with no ifs or buts. No more talks about the future of Northern Ireland. Least of all with America, who should be told abruptly to keep their nose out of British politics; the same goes for the Irish Republic. Furthermore, we must eradicate I.R.A terror glorification marches on British streets. If the I.R.A want to march send them to the Republic; Ulster is not for sale.

We need some control at our borders to stop immigration. At the airports and seaports, the third world and Eastern Europeans are still pouring in as we speak; crippling the job market. It is madness to let this continue. Britain is a tiny island who simply cannot cope any longer. Do not believe the government lies about imposing controls – nothing is being done. The time to say no more is well overdue. Have you noticed that on every bit of spare land new housing estates are being built? This is due to the population boom that has gone way out of control. We need to reverse this disastrous policy that has been going on for far, far too long. Problems are now arising all over the UK due to this failed experiment. Not that you will read about it in the mass media. Let me not pull any punches on this issue; the media are the most effective method of mass deception and public manipulation. Multi-racial Britain isn't irreversible. The human will and the human intelligence can avoid catastrophic policies, if we decide that we should evade them. A further sign that the government have lost the will to govern, is when people we are accused of hating actually agree with some of our major policies. Think I'm lying? I will explain now. A report in March 2015, stated that voters in every ethnic group want the numbers of immigrants coming into Britain to be cut. Overall, the survey revealed that 79%

thought that immigration levels should be reduced, with 59% wanting 'a big drop'. People from all ethnic groups shared this support for stricter border controls.

We need to give Britain back to the people who built it, who died for it, and to who it really belongs. If this is considered racist then so be it. It all depends what you mean by the word racist? If racism means hating others because they are different, I plead not guilty. If racism means putting your own people first and guaranteeing the survival of our nation and our race, then throw that accusation at me. The only hope of getting Britain back on her feet lies in the emergence of a strong British nationalist party that can gain a majority following amongst the British people of all classes – with the aim of securing a solid voter base on the political scene in Britain.

The important thing is many millions actually believe in these policies. There is a growing army of people in Britain who will never vote for Labour, Conservatives or the Lib Dems ever again as they have seen through their lies. These are no longer the views of a small section of the population. These policies are most certainly what the British public are thinking. The only thing holding them back is fear. But achieving our aims will not be easy. Everything is stacked up against us. However, it is better to cross the line and suffer the consequences, than to just stare at the line for the rest of your life. There must be a national wake up call to put these policies into practice – but unfortunately our people have been programmed not to speak out. We must make people grasp the fact we cannot carry on this way no more and that British nationalism is the future. The oppressor never voluntarily gives freedom; it must be demanded by the oppressed. Stand for something or die for nothing.

In the past the British people have conquered the world. We have invented most of the world's products and we were first in most of the world's discoveries. Our culture has spread throughout the world, but you know what – we are far too polite for our own good. We owe it to our children to aim for something different – for something better. The British public should be aware by now that the parties who have failed us will not suddenly deliver the solutions. The government have no hope of changing course. They will continue to ruin this country as they have in the past. Disaster looms.

The greatest threat to our country is the belief that the people who have betrayed us will save us. We are the only movement with these policies and these are the only policies that can save Great Britain. I made a decision to work for a new Britain – with new hope.

CHAPTER 5

I arrived home from work one night and there was a parcel waiting for me. This would be the NF information and membership pack I had applied for. I can remember opening it up with such great excitement as I had really been looking forward to receiving this. The information pack consisted of the official party newspaper, some leaflets and stickers. Moreover, the membership application form. I filled it in there and then, put my cheque and the membership application form into an envelope and posted it straight away. Within half an hour of obtaining my membership pack I was on my way to becoming a fully paid up member of the National Front. I am going to be dead straightforward from the word go and enlighten you to the reality that the NF in the early 1990's, was a shadow of its former self during its period of greatest strength in the middle to late 1970's. I will also take this chance to give you a little history of the NF – and to make things a little bit clearer to those not so knowledgeable about the far-right in Britain.

A move towards unity on the right-wing had been growing during the 1960's, as patriotic groups worked more closely together. Encouragement was provided at the 1966 general election, when the Conservatives were defeated.

A.K Chesterton, the leader of the League of Empire loyalists, argued that a patriotic and racialist right-wing party could have won the election. Soon afterwards Chesterton opened talks with the British National Party (nothing to do with today's BNP) and discussed a possible deal with the National Democratic Party. The BNP's Philip Maxwell addressed a League of Empire loyalists meeting in October 1966, which brought the merger closer together. A portion of another group – The Racial Preservation Society – then led by Robin Beauclaire, also agreed to join forces. As a result, the National Front was launched on the 7th February 1967. And it was all set to steam roll its way into British politics; British politics would never be the same again.

The main impetus of the party was to oppose mass immigration into Britain. Despite that, do not for one second be fooled into thinking it was a one policy party. It had a wide spectrum of policies like all the other mainstream parties. The NF placed a ban on openly neo-Nazi groups being allowed to merge with them, even though some of the leading figures in the NF had flirted with Nazism themselves in their younger days. The National Front grew rapidly during the 1970's, and had an estimated 20,000 paid up members and over 50 branches nationwide. Its electoral base largely consisted of blue-collar workers and the self-employed who feared immigrant competition in the job market, as the newly arrived immigrants would work for a very low wage. Just like the situation is today. The NF also attracted a few disenchanted Tories who gave the party the much-needed electoral expertise it required. More importantly, it gave the party respectability. The NF contested elections on a platform of opposition to Communism and Liberalism, support for Ulster loyalism, capital punishment for I.R.A terrorists and child killers, resistance to being dragged blindfolded into Europe and the policy that created much support – the compulsory repatriation of the newly arrived commonwealth immigrants. Who in their large numbers were starting to settle into Britain as equal citizens. Additionally, the NF sought opportunities to challenge the Race Relations Act, arguing that the British people had the right to discriminate.

During the rise of the NF it became known for it's marches all over England where it often faced violent resistance from so-called 'anti-fascists', who in turn were the real fascists. The National Front could sometimes raise up to 7,000 members for it's parades, but the crowd trouble always made front-page headlines. Over and above, it gave the left-wing controlled media the perfect opportunity to smear the NF and blame them for the trouble. John Tyndall and Martin Webster were the party leadership at the time. Between 1973 and 1976, the party obtained some huge votes in local elections as well as in several by-elections. Regardless of the huge support that they obtained they never actually won any seats. The problem was the British people may sympathise with the underdog at a sporting event, however, they do not sympathise with the underdog in politics. They incline to fall into line with the mainstream parties. Nevertheless, the membership remained content with how the party was progressing all over the country. In 1974, an ITV documentary exposed the Nazi pasts of John Tyndall and Martin Webster, which resulted in a stormy annual conference. This had a huge impact on the NF's image.

In 1974, a march through central London resulted in major rioting, which resulted in 39 police officers being injured due to clashes with the far-left at Red Lion Square

– who were hell bent on stopping the NF by 'any means necessary'. One Marxist demonstrator was killed whilst attacking the NF march. It was initially believed he was killed after a stampede by a police horse – then later it surfaced his death was caused by a brain haemorrhage resulting from a blow to the head. Either a police truncheon, or more likely a brick being thrown from his fellow anti-fascist antagonizers was the cause of his death. The jury returned a verdict of death by misadventure. The broadcasting services loved the opportunity to blame the rioting on the NF and the party took another laddering in the media. Martin Webster defied a police ban on another NF march through Hyde in October 1977, as he marched alone carrying a Union Flag and a banner saying: "DEFEND BRITISH FREE SPEECH FROM RED TERRORISM". They allowed him to march as one man did not constitute a breaking of the ban. Over 2,500 police officers were present for a one-man march; such was the hysteria surrounding the NF at the time. This attracted more media publicity for the party. By this stage, there was not a household in the country that had not heard of the National Front.

All this was nothing though compared to events in Lewisham 1977, South East London. It was a majority non-White area even back then. The area was like a time bomb just waiting to go off. The NF had promised to: "Smash their way into the media", however, even the NF would never have imagined what would happen on this day. The NF and the far-left had been on a collision course long before the Lewisham march. A full-scale riot broke out started by the far-left, who had managed to mobilise huge numbers of militant Communists. At any rate, 270 Police officers were injured (56 hospitalised) and over 200 marchers and demonstrators from both sides needed treatment. This day saw the first use of riot shields on British soil outside of Ulster. It is often referred to by the far-left as 'The battle of Lewisham' – along similar lines to the previous battle of Cable Street against Oswald Mosley. Without a doubt, the left-wing 'militants' were the tool of a hostile government towards the NF. Whoever controls the streets controls the masses, and whoever controls the masses controls the state.

Also during this period, the NF held many marches in support of the Ulster loyalists in their battle to remain British. The NF stood by their policy that the loyal Britons of the Orange state were fighting a traitorous rebellion. As the I.R.A increased its bombing campaign in Ulster as well as mainland Britain, the NF stepped up their activities against the I.R.A holding many demonstrations against Pro-I.R.A marches and rallies. Just like with their anti-immigration marches, they always resulted in crowd disturbances and a number of arrests.

All this negative media publicity led to a poor showing in what should have been a break through at the 1979 general election. With the name of the NF being associated in the public eye with violent incidents (although orchestrated by the far-left) then a serious threat from a British nationalist party would be neutralised. It was also not helped by Margaret Thatcher promising to do something about immigration on the eve of the election; some things never change. The 'Iron Lady'? Don't make me laugh. Once the Tories got into power, Margaret Thatcher went back on her assurances. The same Margaret Thatcher who signed the Anglo-Irish Agreement, selling out our most loyal subjects – the Ulster loyalists. At the National Front A.G.M of January 1979, over a 1,000 delegates had packed into Seymour Hall in the West End of London as the party were optimistic for the coming election. Prior to the election – opinion polls were looking good for the NF. Thatcher sensing an NF breakthrough, was 'forced' onto national TV to make an anti-immigration speech to sway voters away from the NF. This was known as the 'swamped speech'. The NF were standing in 303 seats nationwide; a huge task for the party which was proof of it's growing membership and support base. Regrettably, Thatcher's false promises were enough to stop the potential NF support that was most certainly out there. All the election deposits were lost; it was a disaster for the NF.

After the depressing 1979 election, Andrew Fontaine challenged Tyndall's leadership although Tyndall saw of the challenge. There was a large belief at the time that Tyndall demanded more power in the running of the party which some other leading party officials did not like. This only resulted in Fontaine and his supporters splitting from the NF and forming the NF Constitutional Movement. The influential Leicester branch of the NF also split leading to the short lived British Democratic Party. Whilst all this was going on the NF membership finally did rebel and ousted John Tyndall, and replaced him with Andrew Brons. After failing in court to keep the rights of the name National Front, John Tyndall would eventually set up his new party that he named the British National Party. Tyndall apparently locked himself away for nearly two years whilst setting up the constitution for the BNP, which in time would become the major players on the right-wing.

The National Front rapidly declined during the 1980's, although it did retain some support in certain areas. The party effectively split again in two halves during the 1980's. On one side were the political soldiers as they called themselves, such as Patrick Harrington, Phil Andrews, Derek Holland and Nick Griffin. They had little time for contesting elections preferring a revolutionary approach. The opposition NF Flag group contained the likes of Ian Anderson, Martin Winfield, Tina Winfield and Steve Brady, who stood candidates under the NF banner at the 1987 general election. During a 1989 Vauxhall by-election, Harrington and Ted Budden both stood under the banner of the National Front for their respective groups, although both were rival organisations. These groups were known as the 'two National Front's'. Confusing? Yes, I know – such were the divisions on the right-wing. They talked about uniting Britain and the White race, however, they could not even unite themselves. Come the 1990's, the political soldiers had fallen out with one another splintering into Harrington's Third Way and Nick Griffin's International Third Position. This led to the Flag group of the NF under the control of Ian Anderson, who was known for his lust of money.

The NF had lost a lot of its support from within due to printing a magazine in support of Louis Farrakhan, who was a Black radical activist. The approach of the NF was to point out they could sympathise with other races who were also concerned about their own people's survival. It was also an attempt to try to soften the image of the party and make it look less hostile towards non-Whites. But it was fiercely rejected by the membership and most of the branches returned the magazines in disgust. An exodus of members and supporters moved onto the British National Party (which was by now the biggest party on the right-wing circuit). Some moved onto the rapidly declining British Movement, whilst some drifted into the Blood and Honour music scene. Membership of the NF was shrinking all the time due to infighting and split after split. I was obviously not aware of all this history behind the NF before I myself became involved in the 1990's. I have tried to be as accurate as I can be with this research, but even to this day you hear different stories from different people. If all this sounds a touch confusing then I fully understand, because it was all so confusing to me. Without digging deeper and making things even more bewildering, this is a brief summary of the splits in the NF – and the damage done to the movement from within.

I had the idea being new to the party that the NF was still the mighty force it was back in its heyday – when it was standing candidates all over the UK – and raising many thousands for it's marches. Why was I to think any different? In spite of this, by the time I got involved it was a very tiny organisation. This was not what I had hoped for; a mass organisation marching on towards political power. If I would have known at the time, I would have joined the BNP that was a far bigger party – but insight is a wonderful thing. This resulted in very poor election results. Gone were the days like in the 1973 local elections, polling as high as 15% in many of the seats they fought. For example, gaining 28% of the vote in Sandwell, in the West Midlands, during the 1976 local elections. The jewel in the crown during the 1976 local elections was in Leicester, where 48 candidates gained 43,733 votes, which rocked the establishment. Leicester had suffered with large-scale immigration into the area, and people said it seemed like the area had changed over night. After 1977, votes began to stagnate and by the 1978 local elections, the percentage started to plummet. I can explain the growth and decline of the party with this short synopsis. At the 1970 general election, the NF fielded 10 candidates. Where at the 1979 general election, it fielded 303 candidates – which was half of the seats in parliament. Then moving forward to the 2010 general election, it fought 17 seats nationwide. The highest ever percentage gained at a general election came in February 1974, when the NF averaged 1,423 votes per constituency – contesting 54 seats.

By the time I got involved, Ian Anderson was running the party which produced a regular newspaper called The Flag. In all honesty, this was an excellent and very well presented broadsheet. Martin Wingfield – did a superb job with its presentation; he was the one who produced it at the time. It really was a good read with its direct message delivered to perfection. I personally think it was the best British nationalist newspaper there has been. I linked up with the West Midlands region of the NF, and the first two people I became close to were Norman Tomkinson, (a through and through Birmingham City fanatic) and an old chap called John Lord (R.I.P). John was a friend to anyone and everyone. He was like everyone's Granddad so to speak. In addition, as well as being a great patriot he was a very decent man indeed with an extremely generous nature. They were two great lads who were a pleasure to know from day one, and made me so welcome in the party.

Norman met me at a redirection point for my first meeting (we used these for security reasons), and then he took me to the hired hall to meet the members. The walls were decorated with Union Flags and all the other flags of the British nations – England, Scotland, Wales and Northern Ireland. I have heard people who have left the party and turned moles for Searchlight (anti-fascist magazine) say they have seen Swastika flags at NF meetings, but that was never the case. The NF was firmly a British nationalist party; nothing else. There was also a table from where you could buy your merchandise like newspapers, badges, leaflets and stickers. When I heard Norman Tomkinson speak at the meeting it was as if someone had switched on a light in a dark room, as I agreed with everything he had to say. I had found my home.

For all the NF's bad publicity, a large part of the membership were decent patriots rightly concerned about the way the country had ended up. At the same time, I will admit to there being some idiots who would show up now and again – total no trainers without a political thought in their heads. These people I quickly distanced myself from because I could see they were holding the party back. The bad image the party had gained through marching in the 1970's –1980's, did help to attract some younger minded males into thinking we were an organisation just out to cause trouble. Most of them would show up and then disappear as quick when they realised we were not what they thought we were.

I remember thinking if the NF did not become an elite movement that it would fail. Ideally, we should have only sought to recruit the dedicated to our movement. Having said that, we did not live in an ideal world, therefore, we must make the best use of the membership and supporters at our disposal. Even so, we must conduct ourselves in a way that it is an honour to be a member of the National Front. The old leaderships tactics during the earlier years – resulting in negative front-page headlines – gave the controlled media a 'trump card' to smear us with. This sadly resulted in scaring off many a decent patriot, whilst at the same time attracting some senseless morons. But it was not only the NF that had these problems; you get this in all political parties – from other right-wing groups, right through to the mainstream parties. I did get the impression though that a lot of members were involved more through habit, than actually believing the NF could make a breakthrough – although the people running the branch were very committed.

A leading figure in the West Midlands region was a man named Andy Carmichael. It later surfaced he was a M15 mole, planted to spy on the party. This happens regular in British nationalist groups; it is nothing new. We were not at all surprised when this surfaced as we had our suspicions about him for a while – just no solid proof. Hence, for all his so-called 'undercover work' he should have chosen another career as we were on to him from very early days. And what did he get out of all his time spying on the NF? A five-minute slot on Sky news saying: "There are some people in the NF I would not want to mess with" – that was it. He had nothing on us at all, and thousands of pounds worth of taxpayers money had been spent spying on a perfectly legal political party. Moreover, I would have loved to have seen his paymasters faces when he informed them he had nothing to report.

Besides that, anyone stupid enough to think we live in a democracy let me tell you this. The trouble we had booking rooms for meetings was unbelievable. You could quite easily book a function room for a Sinn Fein meeting, a Communist rally or for a Muslim convention – but you try booking a hall for an NF meeting. We had to lie about who we were. We had to call ourselves fishing clubs, football teams, historical groups, neighbourhood watch groups – the list was endless. We faced all this pressure just to hold a political meeting in our own country. Tell them you were the National Front and the phone went straight down. That is simply how things were and still are concerning anti-establishment parties. They don't want you to congregate and they certainly do not want you to debate. Regarding the tiny handful of public houses who were previously willing to hire us their function rooms knowing we were the NF, once the far-left and Birmingham City Council found out, they would threaten the landlord with his licence. And in due course, with having to keep a roof over his head and to feed his wife and kids, we would lose those premises.

We would discuss at our meetings what the party had been doing of late. In addition, ways of raising funds and what our plans were regarding fighting future elections. We did fight the odd election hear and there, however, due to party finances we were running things on a very tight budget indeed. I helped with the contesting of fighting elections by delivering leaflets door to door, which initially was a very nerve-racking experience because you never knew whose pathway you were walking up. The fear did subside though with experience. After a while, I learnt how to handle myself to hostile people by explaining we were simply a political party fighting an election on policies we thought were right – and the choice was there to vote for us or not. We were fighting for the indigenous people of our country; everyone who has a vote should know how that right was won. I argued that more was being done for the newly arrived immigrants, whilst many of our own people continue to be homeless and jobless – and that even our own folk were being totally ignored and being forced into poverty. Likewise, many of our ex-squaddies were now living on the streets – left to rot by our government. No one who has fought for their country should have to fight for a roof over their head when they come home from serving overseas. The only thing worse than sending our soldiers to die in wars based on lies, is leaving them broke and suffering from mental disorders when they come back to our shores.

An example of the treachery facing our ex-squaddies is after serving in the British army for nine years, Bournemouth Council denied Matthew Dennis a flat, due to the fact he was not an alcoholic, drug addict or an asylum seeker.

On the subject of door to door campaigning, a lad from the BNP called Michael Davidson actually lost the sight in one eye after a savage attack by a militant left-wing group. In addition, the same scum attacked BNP leader John Tyndall who was an old man at the time and my close comrade Norman Tomkinson, was severely beaten up in Nottingham by a group called Red Action. And they have the nerve to call us thugs. In spite of this, it was the risks I was willing to take to try to save my country.

During my early involvement we stood in three by-elections in the early 1990's, in which all the results were terrible. John Hill stood in Mid-Staffordshire, 311 votes – 0.5%. John McCauley stood in Eastbourne, 154 votes – 0.3%. In addition, Robert Tenner stood in Bradford North, 305 votes – 0.8%. It was very demoralising to say the least. Do not get me wrong, the sympathy for our party was out there – without question – we found that out for ourselves whilst out campaigning. That being said, it never mustered into actual support at the ballot box. The NF's problem was that even with the huge amount of support that we had, it did not automatically mean there were guaranteed NF votes in the bag or a surge in new recruits. As I have said before, we did ourselves no favours by giving the media front page headlines like: "RIOTING NF THUGS AT MARCH" – even though the left-wing agitators caused the trouble. We simply were not looked upon as an electable organisation no matter how much the public secretly agreed with us. Tactical mistakes in the early years had helped to dig our own graves.

Myself, like many others, simply licked our wounds after the depressing election results and carried on with the hope that things would soon change. That's how I was at the time – totally focused and sure that in time the votes would start coming in. My Mom and Dad did not agree with my involvement at all; I suppose for a number of reasons. They had always been Labour through and through, therefore, for me to join the National Front it was a bit of a shock to them. To be honest my Dad was disgusted. That being said, he had been like so many others – brainwashed by the media into believing everything he heard about the NF to be true. Moreover, my Mother had a number of female Jamaican friends who were lovely people. And it is fair to say it was a bit of a disappointment for them both. Nonetheless, it was my choice and my choice alone – no one forced me with an arm behind my back. I had sent off for my membership by myself, due to nothing more than having deep, deep concerns about the decline in everything I held dear in my country.

My girlfriend Karen agreed with what the party stood for but was also worried about the stigma attached to being an active member of the NF. Let me state though, my attitude towards non-Whites never changed when I joined the NF. My resentment was directed at the government for putting us in this position in the first place. My friendship with Lenny from the Engineering factory never changed either. It couldn't – we were too close. The only difference was I was now a National Front member. Even though I had a lot of respect for certain individuals from the ethnic-minorities, I couldn't let that come in the way of fighting for the survival of my race and nation.

I suppose people will point out and say: "Well it's a racist organisation solely for White people?", Well yes, however, so were many other 'organisations' and 'lobbies' set up solely for the advancement of non-Whites. You had the Black policeman's association, the Black Firefighters association, Muslim council of Britain, Operation Black vote, Black history month, Music of Black Origin awards, endless pro-Zionist organisations that spent 99% of their time trying to ban right-wing meetings and rallies. The list was endless – I could go on and on. You also had a huge number of pubs and clubs all over the UK who openly supported and raised funds for Sinn Fein/I.R.A. You had drinking venues in Birmingham solely for Black people – my old mate Tony used one and told me quite frankly I wouldn't have been welcome in there. As I have mentioned before, every single newsagent stocked community newspapers for everybody except for the White British. So let no one tell me I was not doing anything different to what was being done to me and my people. I had the attitude how they dare scream blue murder at me, when they are doing exactly what I am doing. I was simply sticking up for my rights, my people and my country.

I had to develop a thick skin pretty quickly, as being accused of being a racist carried a lot of weight and it sometimes was not easy. For all that, I had a broad pair of shoulders and dealt with it the best I could. Like everything in life nothing stays secret for long and before I knew it everyone knew I was with the NF. It certainly was not something I was ashamed of. Looking at the state of the country I would have been more embarrassed about being known as a Labour party, Lib Dem or Conservative party member. They were the ones who had made a complete cock up of the country not the NF.

Look at some of the criminal convictions of the three-mainstream parties. Let us start with the Tories

– Downloading hardcore child porn, sex attacks on children, abuse of teenage boys, indecent assault, theft, death by dangerous driving, forgery and possession of an offensive weapon. Now onto the Labour Party – sexually abusing young boys, masturbating in public, indecent assault, rape, child molestation, downloading hardcore child porn, drug dealing and sex attacks on schoolchildren. And finally the Lib Dems – sexual abuse of young boys, indecent assault, sex attacks in public toilets, incitement to rape, kidnap, incitement to murder and torture. Also, not forgetting that 'vile creature' Cyril Smith. Not to mention, why do paedophile PM's enjoy immunity from prosecution? Are you aware that leading government officials are subject to health care and hospital treatment that is far more advanced than what's on offer to the every day person in the street? There are very dark forces at work that have been subverting British history for the benefit of financial and political power. Surprised? Well, you shouldn't be!

Admittedly, there were certain people I would have rather not known about my involvement. Birmingham is a rough old place and there were a certain few unsavoury characters about who would not have liked or agreed with my political views. Over my side of town many of the Birmingham Zulu lads did not like the NF – especially if you was Villa. I am not going to lie and make out I was some hard man because I was not. I was simply a run of the mill bloke with concerns for his country. I suppose that I was lucky to a large degree as I got hardly any hassle from anyone – more verbal than physical. That may have been down to my size. I am a fairly big bloke and to people who did not know me that would have worked in my favour. By now, I was fully committed to the struggle of winning my country back regardless of what came my way. From my perspective the fight back had begun.

After the appointment of Ron Atkinson at Villa Park for the start of the 91/92 season, someone from the F.A must have fancied a laugh and gave us the opening day fixture of Sheffield Wednesday away at Hillsborough. The Wednesday fans were furious with Big Ron for doing a U-turn after saying: "I'd be mad to leave here". And you knew that instantly everyone would be out for this one. The Villa lads had some previous run-ins before with Wednesday – a lot more than with their neighbours United. It was obvious lads from both firms would be jumping for joy as this was not a normal first game of the season; this was now a grudge match between two massive clubs. In addition, after pinching their manager off them it simply added to the spice. Our official 7,000-ticket allocation for the Leppings Lane end sold out in hours, but ticket or not everyone would be going. As daft as this sounds, some would say Big Ron's appointment brought the Villa firm back together again; there is maybe a bit of truth in that. It got everybody interested again. Everyone was on the phone to each other and it was all people were talking about.

We were all still travelling in different groups at this stage. If Wednesday's lads were expecting the Villa to bring a firm we did not disappoint them. The day had arrived. It is one I will remember forever – for events on and off the pitch. As Ron Atkinson and the Villa firm both left Sheffield with the results they were looking for.

CHAPTER 6

*I*t was the morning of the game as we all headed to Sheffield in buoyant mood. We had arranged to meet at a boozer about one mile from the ground. The huge Villa travelling army had taken over all the other pubs surrounding the ground. We had all the main faces there that I had got to know throughout the years; lads I had grown to respect. But one-person in-particular and that was a certain lad called Gary Reid. Reidy was the 'rock' we all stood on around this time. He had been around from the C-Crew days and all generations of lads at Villa Park respected him. Even when we had a few seasons with no organised firm, I always looked upon Reidy as the man who should have taken the reins. He could most definitely hold his own as and when needed, as he had proved on many occasions.

Sadly, many years later Reidy passed away on the 18/3/2010, after battling a short illness. It knocked us all for six. He was Mr Aston Villa and it is still crazy to think he is no longer with us after all the years together. The last time I saw him was at Wembley against Man United in the Carling Cup Final just before Martin O'Neil resigned. We all hoped for Reidy that the Villa would have lifted that trophy as we knew it would be his last chance to see the Villa win something as his health was deteriorating by this stage. We lost 2-1 to a late Wayne Rooney goal, and I was gutted not only for myself – but more so for Reidy – because we all knew by then he was very ill.

At his funeral loads of Birmingham City lads turned up to pay their respects; that's a measure of how much he was though of and respected. There was no tension on the day between the rival clubs because this was not the time or place to settle old scores – we were simply there to say goodbye to a bloody decent bloke. All the Zulu lads knew Reidy, but he never had any bother of them. They knew he would not have stood for any shit in the first place. The Villa had lost a top lad and the world had lost a funny, humorous, generous, tough and loyal man; it is still a major loss to all who knew him. However, this season a lad showed up at the Villa called Steve Fowler and he would shortly get the Villa firm proper organised again.

Getting back to the day in question, the weather was red-hot and we were all outside the boozer having the crack. We were chatting away, taking the piss, singing, drinking and taking in the opening day of the season atmosphere – when from nowhere a big firm of Wednesday lads turned the corner and approached the pub. No one was expecting this as it just happened out the blue; there wasn't no mobile phones these days to organise a punch-up. The Villa lads at the time were all a bunch of piss heads (myself included) and once we found a pub we used to stay there. We were not at this stage an organised firm who would go looking for the opposition. It was all rather surreal. It was a strange situation, because for some reason there was no police surrounding the pub. They had problems elsewhere with it going off all over the place as both sets of fans were up for this grudge match; the police really had their hands full on this day.

Like in slow motion, when both mobs clocked each other there was a huge delay, then someone stepped forward and both firms charged at each other. It must have been hundreds a side. The Villa had the advantage of being by the pub and having endless bottles and pint glasses to use as ammunition. We had the superior numbers by far, but fair play to the Wednesday firm as they were well up for it. But fortunately the Villa had a top turnout this day. I have read in some Sheffield United books that Wednesday do not have a firm – well believe me they have. A pitched battle took place and lads from both sides got injured; it really blew up outside the boozer. With there being no 'Old Bill' around due to trouble happening elsewhere, it was a complete free for all. The Villa firm shaded it at this pub but I heard of other Villa lads coming unstuck at other pubs before the game. When the police finally arrived the place was a war zone with glass everywhere and the pub had been smashed to bits. Both firms of lads were still at it hammer and tongs in the surrounding streets. The police made 27 arrests – 13 Wednesday lads – and 14 from the Villa. Some football lads just do not seem to care when the 'Old Bill' turn up – they are so engrossed in what they are doing they just carry on. Being arrested at the football was not my idea of a good day out. Some lads though do not see it this way and end up getting arrested, which happened during this incident.

When the police finally got things under control we were somewhat loosely escorted to the ground. In the distance you could hear fighting going on else where as Ron Atkinson had managed to turn this into anything but a normal season opening fixture. As our firm approached the ground, another mob of Wednesday lads appeared from the right of Leppings Lane, and it went bang off again. The police presence did not stop the two mobs from getting into each other. Because it was by the Villa away end normal fans joined in as well and the Wednesday lads got proper turned over. Although I take my hat off to the Wednesday firm for coming to the away end knowing that's were all the Villa would be congregating. As expected more police arrived and managed to cordon off the two sets of fans. The 'Old Bill' were not messing around by now and forced all the travelling fans into the ground with heavy-handed tactics. It was chaos. It had been a mad couple of hours and the Villa firm had made their mark with two victories before the game had even begun. After the game would be no exception as well as running battles manifested again.

We finally got inside the ground after being baton charged by the 'Old Bill'. The away end at Hillsborough is huge. You get a massive top tier and a smaller bottom tier, which altogether holds around 7,000 visiting fans. It is a good view as well and some lads used to say it was their favourite away game of the season. We all managed to group together in the top tier and the atmosphere was superb. The Villa end was rammed full – not a space in sight. The Wednesday fans were very vocal and they could not wait for Big Ron to appear to let him know what they thought of him. It was a very hostile atmosphere and it felt more like a local derby than a Wednesday – Villa match. You really had to be there to understand what I am trying to get across.

Around 2.55 pm as the game approached, Ron Atkinson came into view in the away dugout, flanked by loads of 'Old Bill'. The Wednesday fans went berserk. He got a frightful reception and cries of 'Judas' from 30,000 Wednesday fans echoed around the ground. It was pure hatred. I have never seen a manager take so much abuse and I do not think many managers would have stood the pressure he was facing. He must have been pleased to have police protection on this day as he most certainly needed it. We were chanting Big Ron's name as he was a high profile manager who had us all positive about the clubs future. We were initially drowned out by the level of noise from the home support; Hillsborough was a cauldron of hate. As the game started we were 2-0 down before any Villa player had even touched the ball – and the home fans did not need any time to remind Big Ron of the score. I was gutted to be 2-0 down so early into the game but it was about to take a massive twist. We dragged a goal back just before half time to give us a fighting chance in the second half. The Villa travelling fans went mental; we were back in the game.

During the half time interval the atmosphere never faded as the fans kept chanting songs to each other. Someone from our firm started singing: "No surrender to the I.R.A", and before you knew it all our lads were singing along; it sounded brilliant – then it spread throughout most of the Villa end. I suppose this day was the start of why we were all of a sudden labelled as a loyalist firm. Skin-head Neil's brother who was a police intelligence officer at the Villa (I know how crazy that sounds) complained to us after the game that the Sheffield 'Old Bill' were not happy with us singing Anti-I.R.A songs as it was offensive and nationalistic. Well my opinion was 'the cheeky bastards'. We were an English/British football team with a majority English fan base who had witnessed all the damage done by the I.R.A over the years and we were being criticised about the songs we were singing. So what if some of our lads hated the I.R.A and supported the Ulster loyalist cause. I also knew a number of Villa fans with republican leanings. That is the way supporting a big club goes. There are also lads down the Villa with Marxist views and nothing is said about that. In such large numbers you are going to have an amount of people with conflicting political persuasions. Would anything have been said if a number of Irish lads had been singing rebel songs? I doubt it. Around this time the I.R.A were very active in Ulster and Mainland Britain, and being a Brummie, I had every right to chant anti-I.R.A songs after they had bombed my city back in 1974. I was also getting more interested in the Ulster loyalism side of things due to my involvement with the NF. Therefore, to hear this chant from the Villa end was music to my ears. This was a stick that some people would choose to beat us with at a later date.

As Big Ron re-appeared for the second half in the away dug out, he was still escorted by loads of 'Old Bill' and nothing had changed – 'Judas' – still rang out from the three sides of the ground holding the Wednesday fans; it was so loud. Pulling a goal back just before half time had given us hope and we started to pile the pressure on Wednesday's goal. The travelling Villa army were again making themselves heard and then from a tight angle our new striker Dalian Atkinson scored an equalizer. We went barmy and we were now firmly back in the game. The Wednesday end fell silent and we could now sense a miracle victory after being 2-0 down at one stage. "Big fat Ron's claret and blue army", bellowed out from the 7,000 plus Villa fans and the game was doing a complete U-Turn – from disaster to victory. We kept piling on the pressure and had some half chances and then as the game was entering its final stages it happened.

We had brought a load of new players close season and I forget now who it was now, but he shot up the wing

– crossed the ball over – and suddenly we saw the net ripple. It was Steve Staunton, and his famous left foot who had given us the lead. Word's cannot explain the celebrations as we had pulled off a miracle. As the full time whistle blew you would have thought we had won the league. It was pure joy and a party erupted in the Leppings Lane end. We chanted for Big Ron to come over to us but he was escorted away for his own safety, therefore, we celebrated with the players. The Wednesday end quickly emptied but not all of them intended to go straight home as their lads wanted to have another pop at us. As we left the ground we were not as organised as before the game, because at this stage we were still all travelling independently. Tucker's coaches had not started yet – that came as the firm progressed. Some had come by train, cars, mini-buses and coaches, and all the pubs were closed surrounding the ground due to the hostile atmosphere and the crowd trouble before hand.

We were all heading in different directions and the police were being very heavy-handed trying to break us up depending on the form of travel you had used. That did not prevent though running battles after the game, but Wednesday shaded it if the truth be told. I did see though another tidy firm of Villa lads turn over some Wednesday lads as we were heading back to Barmy Barbell's car. I suppose depending where and who you were with after the game you had different stories to tell. In any case, I was happy with the two victories before the game and most certainly winning the game after being 2-0 down. As we reached the car to head home – on a more serious note – it was nearly a disaster. Jeensey, C-Crew Clive, Dave Kingham and myself had travelled by car and had jumped a lift with Barmy Barbell. He was well known for his drink driving, so I recommended to him days before we set of why don't he get him self some joints of cannabis and lay off the beer as his job consisted of driving and he couldn't risk carrying the threat of losing his licence. But what a mistake that was. He did bring some joints with him, but as well as smoking them throughout the day he also had about fifteen pints of lager. He could hardly stand up. I am not condoning drink or drug driving but we were young lads at the time and just wanted to get home and carry on the session. Looking back now, I should never have got in the car with him. For all that, I did.

As we set off he was stoned out of his brains as well as drunk, and his driving was a bit crap to say the least. Additionally, he carried on smoking the cannabis all the way back to Birmingham as me and the lads got a carry out to have a drink on the way home. As we came off the motorway after somehow reaching Birmingham in one piece, we had travelled so far and suddenly in the distance I noticed an Island coming up. Not really thinking anything about it, it got closer and closer and I suddenly realised Barmy Bardell had not seen it. His eyes were blood red and nearly shut from all the blow and beer. Being pissed myself I shouted out too late (I was sitting in the front of the car) and suddenly we hit the Island. The car took off like a plane, totally left the ground and shot onto the middle of the Island. Instead of slamming on the brakes and stopping the car, Barmy Barbell just swerved left straight at full acceleration back on to the main road. I looked around at the lads and the sheer look of fright on everyone's faces was something I will never forget. We were holding on to anything as the car left the ground again as he pulled back off the Island. If anything had of been coming up behind us we would have been killed outright.

As the car thudded back onto the main road (how it never fell apart, I will never know) Barmy Bardell turned to me and said with his blood shot eyes: "I think I should have gone around that, not over it". It was not only what he had said that made it all the crazier, it was how he said it like it was nothing more than jumping a red light or something. The lads in the back quickly put their seat belts on for the rest of the journey. As we finally reached home, we stopped off in Sutton Coldfield to meet up with other Villa lads for a beer who had also travelled back from Sheffield. Now I know it was no laughing matter but as we got out of the car and shut the doors, both his front headlights fell out and landed on the ground. We were all in stitches because his car was starting to fall apart and the front and back bumpers were hanging off. We all had a great day out in Sheffield for a number of reasons. Looking back now it was one the best I can ever remember, and it is still talked about to this day. Despite everything, our love for the Villa, beer and having a play up – and being young and naïve, could have seriously finished up with us that day quite easily losing our lives. At the same time, the makings of the new firm had been planted.

This season we had started using the Adventurers pub on match day and anybody who was anybody was using the place. Looking back now we had some right laughs during these years – we were simply one big happy family. Even though we were all die-hard Villa fans we did not always used to go the home games during this time. We were all getting to know each other and bringing all the little mobs from everywhere into one firm for the first time in years. We would all meet up around mid-day, get drunk together and have a laugh and a piss take. This was the real beginning of the Hardcore, even though at this time our firm had no official name. The name Villa Hardcore came about at West Ham away in 1995. I can recall the annual run in with Man United's Red Army at Villa Park. It makes me laugh when people say Man United do not have any lads – it's bullshit. When Man United land you know they are here because they are everywhere. People say with Man United it is a numbers game, but if they can raise the numbers then fair play to them. It's up to you to raise your own numbers and match them – and if you can't, don't go crying about it. That was my opinion anyway. As much as I dislike Man United, I have always admired how they just land at your place and let themselves be known. Where as some other so-called top firms would drink miles from the ground and just go the match. There was trouble all day at various locations due to the huge firm they always bring.

On the political front a general election was called for the 9th April 1992. This would my first general election as a National Front member and I was optimistic for some huge votes to come our way. I know to some people that it may seem an explosive mixture mixing the football in with my politics. Even so, I never combined the two. Yes, I would sing 'No Surrender' at the games, but that's about as far as it went. I never took my political beliefs to the football and I never took my love for Aston Villa into the political world. Neither would have made any sense. I was a young White male who the government had left on the shelf. I was looking for an identity. Something I could relate to; things that gave me a purpose in life. The football and politics gave me that. The government were too interested into making the UK truly multi-racial and multi-cultural to give me a second thought. I had to take it upon myself to give myself an identity; the ruling elite had erased our British culture and British pride.

I waited for the general election with lots of excitement as I thought that maybe things might turn out as a cornerstone for our party. In spite of these hopes, the votes would once again turn out to be a kick in the teeth for the NF and its loyal members

CHAPTER 7

$\mathcal{W}$e held a West Midlands National Front meeting in early January 1992, to plan our target wards for the up-coming general election, as did other regions of the NF who were also contesting seats. We managed to raise fourteen candidates nationwide – which when you consider there were over 600 seats up for grabs it wasn't really that impressive at all. We could hardly be considered a national movement. With the financial side of the party it was about the best we could have hoped for. You see, we did not have the backing of big businesses, or trade unions like the other parties did. Dedicated members and supporters raised all our money in house.

Birmingham branch settled on two wards – Hodge Hill where Eddie Whicker would stand, and Yardley ward where Paul Read put him self-forward. Norman Tomkinson from Birmingham was selected for the ward known as Coventry South East, and John Lord from the Black Country would be standing in West Bromwich East. Our party Chairman Ian Anderson targeted the seat in Bristol East, where as John McCauley put himself forward for West Hertfordshire. In addition, Terry Blackham from Beckenham would stand in Bermondsey ward. Terry at the time was an up and coming activist who would eventually become National Activities

Organiser, who got the NF back onto the streets and marching again –holding various demonstrations against the I.R.A and other anti-British rallies.

Birmingham NF managed to raise the £1,000 deposits to fight the two wards, but that also included the free delivery of 40,000 leaflets per ward from the post office. To a tiny party like ours that was a god send and it really helped our small band of loyal activists as we did not have the manpower to do the leafleting ourselves. We did what campaigning we could and found as per usual loads of support on the doorsteps – which we hoped would end up as votes. Sadly, come Election Day it did not happen. The results were as follows. Eddie Whicker – Hodge Hill ward, 370 votes – 0.9%. Paul Read – Yardley ward, 192 votes – 0.4%. Norman Tomkinson – Coventry South East, 173 votes – 0.5%. John Lord – West Bromwich East, 477 votes – 1.1%. The party chairman Ian Anderson – Bristol East, 270 votes – 0.5%. John McCauley – West Hertfordshire, 665 votes – 1.0%. Terry Blackham – Bermondsey, 168 votes – 0.4%. The two best results on the night were K. Reynolds – Walsall North, 614 votes – 1.2%. And Gary Cartwright – Dudley East, 675 votes – 1.2%.

In addition, the other handful of wards were even more disappointing. The total number of National Front votes over the fourteen wards came to 4,816. I can remember afterwards being very depressed for days as the electorate had completely shunned us. Considering the state of the country, I just could not work out why we had polled so dreadfully. Many different people had many different reasons (and opinions) as to why the votes were so low. But for whatever explanation the electorate had turned their backs on us. It was very hard to take as I could not see what more we could offer the public. As far as I was concerned we had the solutions to all of Britain's problems; politics though does have a habit of kicking you in the stomach.

Now I can guess some people will be asking this question. Would I have been 'comfortable' if the NF had somehow formed a government and my old friends like David and his family, my old pal from school Tony, Lenny from the Engineering factory and the numerous other decent law-abiding non-Whites I had met through the years would have been forced out of the UK? Well, the answer is 'NO'. Still, I saw at the time no alternative due to how the government were turning Britain into a third world country. I know with a forced repatriation policy that loads of suffering would have occurred with the phased resettlement of so many people. Compared though to what was facing us if something was not done about the immigration problem, I found it the only viable option. This was due to the left-wing thinking they could socially experiment with an island nation. All they have done is create a divisive population, the majority being the indigenous British, resenting the mass influx of immigrants. Moreover, in doing so, have sowed the seeds of decades of social unrest in the future of these islands. A very tough decision had to be made – but I did make it.

Over at the British National Party – they were concentrating most of their efforts on two East London constituencies after strong showings in earlier local elections. This proved a wise move as the following year Derek Beackon was elected to Millwall ward in East London as their first ever councillor. The two East London results were as follows. John Tyndall – Bow and Poplar, 1,107 votes – 3.0%. And, Richard Edmonds – Bethnal Green, 1,310 votes – 3.6%. This would set the backdrop for the election victory the following year. Even though I could see for myself that the BNP were now the bigger party, my loyalties lay firmly with the National Front. I suppose at the time it was like my dedication to following the Villa. I had made my choice and for the time being I was sticking to it. I believed at the time that the name National Front would eventually carry us through (being the most recognised name on the right-wing) even though I should have realised that votes speak for themselves. Like Norman Tomkinson and John Lord, I had a blind loyalty to the NF.

The Conservatives won the 1992 general election under the leadership of John Major, but as far as I was concerned whatever mainstream party got in the same would happen. The destruction and the betrayal of the British nation and the British people would continue. All the mainstream parties were welded to the same system with different colour rosettes on. I had the knowledge by now to judge the mainstream parties by their actions and that way you will never be fooled by their words. They had let us down on immigration, unemployment, Europe, the NHS, crime, Northern Ireland etc – and my eyes were wide open as to what was going on.

Before Derek Beackon's victory in the Tower Hamlets ward, he had stood there before with pretty discouraging results. Despite that, the area slowly started began to grow as a centre of support for the BNP. A series of council by-elections in the early 1990's, had seen the BNP gain some respectable votes in the area. Under the guidance of local organiser Eddie Butler, the party had started up a 'Rights for Whites' campaign. Introducing, so I am led to believe a previously used slogan employed by Martin Webster during his days running the show with John Tyndall in the old National Front. It focused on the immigration issue in the area, as well as unemployment and housing. The housing issue was also a vote winner as priority was going to the newly arrived Bangladeshi families. The first sign of real growing support in the Millwall ward came in October 1992, when after a professional campaign BNP candidate Barry Osborne captured 20% of the vote during a by-election. Millwall had long been an area of high unemployment due to the declining docklands in East London. The government had ripped the heart and spirit out of East London. There was a strong feeling in the area of special treatment for Bangladeshi families and the BNP were suddenly becoming a real threat.

Then with support at an all time high, a stroke of luck happened. A Labour councillor resigned in the ward sparking yet another by-election. Derek Beackon was chosen this time around, following the parties policy of rotating its members. A full-scale professional campaign was put in involving leafleting, knocking on doors and stopping shoppers in the streets. More importantly, they had learnt their lesson about holding public meetings where the left-wing 'fascists' would turn up and cause trouble gaining negative front-page headlines. This was rightly considered counter-productive for the parties image. Something is very wrong with left-wing who claim to be open, broad-minded and accepting of difference – but who fly into a rage of intolerance when they encounter a political organisation with a different ideology. After a highly ran campaign from the BNP, on the 16th of September 1993, Derek Beackon became the first elected representative for the party. Derek won the seat with a massive 1,480 votes – 33.9%. Beating the Labour party by just seven votes, with an overall turnout of 44% of the electorate.

The Labour Party looked for someone to blame and they blamed the Liberal Democrats for putting out a leaflet titled 'HOW LABOUR SPENDS YOUR MONEY', highlighting all the money spent on Asian projects in the area. The Liberals sensed an anti-immigration feeling in the ward and attempted to steal the BNP's clothes. All it did was cement the BNP's policies as the leaflet caused anger in the local White community. But the electorate stuck with the party who had been pointing out the immigration issue for years – not just weeks. As expected after Beackon's victory, there was widespread condemnation from all the other political parties. The left-wing rag The Daily Mirror went overboard calling Derek Beackon a 'Nazi', and even the Archbishop of Canterbury – George Carey – publicly made his opinions known of the BNP victory. So much for democracy. Although the Labour Party had other plans to win the seat back when it came back up for re-election in 1994. They moved many more immigrants into the area to try to dilute the BNP vote. There were even rumours of mass vote rigging and people being put down for voting in the area who were not even living there. It is not the type of thing you will ever hear about but it most undoubtedly goes on. Such was the desperation from Labour to remove the BNP from the seat.

When the seat went up for re-election, the turn out rose to 65% (no surprise there) and even though Derek Beackon's poll went up by 561 votes, the BNP lost the seat to the Labour Party. Even after losing the seat the BNP had by now become a household name and it started to attract many more members. This resulted in the party pulling miles ahead of the National Front in terms of membership and professionalism. In recent years, Derek Beackon has re-emerged as a BNP candidate in Thurrock ward, Essex, gaining 17.8% of the vote, finishing 3rd in a safe Tory seat. In addition, more recently contesting Chadwell, St Mary's ward, where he gained a very impressive 811 votes – 20%. He has even more recently stood for the National Front after leaving the BNP due to party infighting. On the other hand, his votes for the NF have been poor in comparison to when he was a BNP candidate.

As well as Derek Beackon's short-lived election victory in 1993, there was also an I.R.A bombing on the 23rd of October of that year carried out by the republican terrorists. Their target was the Shankill Road – a loyalist stronghold in Northern Ireland. It was, and still is, one of the most notorious incidents during the years of the troubles. It was rumoured the I.R.A's intended target was a meeting of loyalist paramilitary leaders which was to have taken place above Frizzles Fish Shop. Even though this was the opinion of many people (still is until this day) it actually was not true. The I.R.A had set out to kill as many Protestants as they could and if they had killed any U.D.A leaders in the process then that would have been looked upon as a bonus.

Two I.R.A operatives entered the fish shop with a time bomb; it exploded prematurely. One of the I.R.A members was killed instantly along with nine other civilians. The Shankill Road had been the target of several other bomb and gun attacks over the years. However, the 1993 bombing had the highest number of casualties, which would result in revenge attacks by the U.D.A. The U.D.A's West Belfast Commanders and its Inner Council were known to have used the room above the fish shop for meetings – apparently it was common knowledge. And the I.R.A used this excuse to try and 'play down' the atrocity. The Inner Council had not held a meeting in months, therefore, it was a total lie that the I.R.A were targeting U.D.A leaders. Their main target was Protestant civilians.

Thomas Begley and Sean Kelly entered the fish shop dressed as deliverymen, with a large bomb hidden under a cover on a plastic tray. They intended to leave the time bomb in the shop where it would detonate once they had made their getaway. It was a late Saturday afternoon and the shop was crowded. As the two I.R.A men made their way through the shop, the bomb detonated ahead of time. The bomb only had an eleven-second fuse. The building collapsed crushing many of the survivors under the rubble where they remained until the emergency services turned up. Many volunteers helped in trying to save the people under the rubble. Over 50 people were seriously injured – not forgetting the nine non-combatants who were killed instantly. One of the I.R.A bombers had also been killed in the explosion but I had no sympathy for him. My only regret was that the other bastard did not get it as well.

At the scene during the rescue operation were several senior loyalists. Do not be fooled into thinking the I.R.A would have considered this as an operation 'gone wrong' – they intended to kill and kill they did. Begley was given a full I.R.A funeral with a huge turn out from his republican supporters. Moreover, Gerry Adams President of Sinn Fein, acted as a pallbearer. Many loyalists saw the bombing as an indiscriminate attack on them directly, but Johnny Adair was convinced it was meant for him. There were rumours that a car load of U.D.A gun men were on their way to attack the Holy Family Catholic Church on Limestone Road, but had to abort the attack due to the high security presence.

The U.D.A launched a number of successful revenge attacks for the bombing over the next week, when they shot dead a Catholic delivery driver after luring him to a bogus call. The U.D.A also executed two workmen who were strongly rumoured to be I.R.A activists and five were wounded at a Council depot at Kennedy Way. The biggest of the revenge attacks was in Greysteel, County Londonderry, where the U.D.A shot dead eight people at the Rising Sun pub on Halloween night on the 30th of October. This was claimed as direct retaliation for the Shankill bombing. The U.D.A were seeking nothing but the elementary right implanted in every man – the right if you are attacked to defend yourself; self defence measures. Little did I know at the time but the Greysteel shootings would also have a bearing on my life in years to come when I got deeper involved in the struggle to keep Ulster British. Now I am not condoning or gloating about murder in any way, shape or form. Having said that, I saw it as the U.D.A using I.R.A tactics against the I.R.A. It was a 'dirty war' and things were done that in a normal country would never of happened; war is never fair nor reasonable. I suppose the simple fact is that the war in Northern Ireland turned normal people on both sides into killers. Sean Kelly the Shankill bomber was released under the Good Friday agreement in July 2000.

For all that, my beloved club Aston Villa were on the verge of having a superb season under Ron Atkinson, and our new firm would officially come together as a proper organised outfit.

CHAPTER 8

*A*fter Ron Atkinson's first season in charge we had finished a respectable 7th place and things were really looking up for the club – on and off the pitch. The start of the 1992/93 season could not come quick enough for us, and little did we know at the time that we would push Man United all the way for the League title. The whole club was on a high. We opened up the season with Ipswich away, which meant a huge turn out for the Great Yarmouth weekend. Thousands of Villa supporters headed to the game and afterwards hundreds of us landed at Great Yarmouth for a major piss up. We found some bar that was a pound a pint (even though it was piss-water) and we totally packed the place out. It was a good drink and a good laugh was had by all – London was to be our next destination.

This was the season that Fowler really stood out to me and rightly so started to make his name as Villa's top lad. However, Reidy was the warrior on our trip to 'The Smoke'. I cannot remember who we were playing, but about 50 of us were on the train heading down south to go on the piss. Someone spotted a similar number of Wolves lads a few carriages up. Our main faces went for a look and Wolves were having a drink on the train. They were as nice as pie telling us how they did not mind the Villa, but hated Birmingham

City. Everything was pretty settled between us at this stage even though there was a bad atmosphere in the air. The Wolves lads got off before London as they were heading to Watford. For the time being, that was the end of that.

As per usual as the day progressed, we had all been split up into little factions. Some had got lost on the London Underground and a couple had been nicked – more than likely Jeensey and skin-head Neil who has more than 30 football related convictions. Our original 50 was now maybe half that. As we headed back from London on the night we pulled up at Watford station and who did we see climb on board. The same Wolves lads with the same numbers that they'd had earlier. When they got on the train they clocked us and noticed our numbers had dwindled and must have now fancied their chances. From being nice as pie earlier, they now started to get a bit funny towards us and you could tell something was going to happen. It suddenly went off and we were backed into a carriage. They were all trying to steam into the carriage to do us over. I fully well admit we backed off – no embarrassment in admitting that; happens to us all. Reidy was holding the front line. He was preventing them from getting through the carriage doors as well as getting a good few slaps in the process. If it was not for Reidy we would have got proper turned over, and only the braveness of Reidy prevented the other lads (myself included) from getting a good hiding. The train driver, or ticket inspector, must have contacted the 'Old Bill' as to what was going on, and at the next station they were there waiting to separate the two mobs.

Reidy that day did us proud and put the other lads before himself – which was not the first time he had done this. From that day, I have always had a personal dislike of

Wolves for what they did. They did not want to know with even numbers, but when we were all split up they thought they would try their luck. But little did they know we had Reidy on our firm who was willing to take the slaps for the other lads. Fowler was also like this – when we were outnumbered he would put himself forward to take the heat off the other lads. I know the older C-Crew lads really rated and respected the older Wolves firm – The Subway Army. To the contrary, this new mob we had came across were nothing but cowards. We had never been a firm of bullies; Wolves showed themselves up for their actions.

The following week we were all drinking as per usual in the Adventurers, when one of the older lads with republican/I.R.A leanings walked in pissed up and started to sing Rebel songs. At the time I knew him personally through the football scene (I will not name him because it is not my intention to name and shame individuals). Fowler walked over and put him straight on his arse and he did not get back up for a good while; he had caught him with a peach of a punch. In all fairness he had it coming for a while as he liked to flaunt his support for the I.R.A. Now before I carry on let me put to bed one of the rumours I have heard from the Noses that Fowler's 'Anti-Irish'. Fowler admits himself his Dad's side of the family are Irish Catholic – and he is known to visit the Republic of Ireland from time to time. To that end, that's one-half of the bullshit about him laid to rest. Even so, Fowler considers himself English as he has every right to. No one in the pub was happy with the Irish Villa lad singing Rebel songs, however, because we all knew him and he had been a good lad through the years regarding standing his ground, no one did or said anything when someone should have – myself included. That was left up to Fowler as he had no respect of reputations. He did not like what the lad was singing and he was the only one with the balls to do something about it. That's how he was from the first time he showed up at the Villa; always ready to take the lead. I instantly had a lot of respect for Fowler.

I could tell he had something about himself which we were sadly lacking at the time before he came along. We had a number of good tough lads, but there was no one willing to deal with the problem directly. He had a certain 'don't give a fuck' attitude, but not in a big-headed way by any means. Now before people jump to the conclusion I am 'bigging him up' because he is a close friend I will explain something now. Yes, I obviously knew the lad, yet we were not best friends or anything. I liked Fowler and got on with him (still do to this day) and he was always sound to have chat with and a piss take. Although, he had his set of mates and I had mine – even though we were all drinking together on match day. He always took the piss in a good way as Reidy did, and he could take it back as well. I had a number of much closer mates at the Villa I could have chosen to 'big up' if I wanted to. I am simply stating what I saw for myself. When he showed up at the Villa, it was what we were missing. He was instantly willing to put himself up front and I was delighted to have him around. We had been crying out for a leader from the old Villa Youth days. Apart from the second division season in 1987/88, we had not really had a proper organised firm. Some will not like to admit that but it was true. Fowler was about to put that right.

The C-Crew who were Villa's top firm back in the early 80's, showed up this season at Spurs away with a firm of about 40 of what we called 'the older lot'. It was looked upon as a bit of a reunion. They were drinking in a pub called the

Park Hotel not far from White Hart Lane, where they had two run-ins with Spurs top lads. The C-Crew were not a firm to be taken lightly as Spurs found out. One tear up happened before the game and one afterwards. The one that happened after the game was a mass pub brawl with one of our older lads getting seriously injured; he nearly lost the use of his one eye. Due to this altercation, Brittle wanted a revenge mission and when we drew Spurs away in the quarter-final of the League Cup, the alarm bell was sent out to all Villa lads regardless of what Villa firm you belonged to. It was a night we all came together and got a major result at a top London club.

This season as the firm got more and more organised we even had the pleasure of beating Man United twice on the pitch. Once in the cup and then at home in the league – with goals by our deadly strike-force Atkinson and Saunders. The Villa took a right good firm again to Sheffield Wednesday, however, it was very low-key trouble wise from the season before. Our firm even had the pleasure of seeing us win away at Liverpool 2-1 – something that never happened at Anfield. I can still recall Dean Saunders scoring the winner up the Kop end, and the celebrations were that crazy I accidentally punched a woman in the face and spent the rest of the game apologising to her for doing so. I know Liverpool was a place highly feared years ago; some of the horror stories from our older lot confirmed this. Having said that, I have never come across a mob of Liverpool home or away. I simply did not rate them at all. Other people though will have different opinions – especially the Black Villa lads who suffered years of racial abuse on Merseyside.

We had the usual piss-take at Coventry on Boxing Day. This lot used to really annoy me. I hated them as they were nothing but a bunch of idiots. If ever there was a firm I did not rate it was this lot. They have always been a joke and always will be. You would simply go there for a drink and a day out – that is it. We ended up getting beaten 3-0, which put a huge dent in our title ambitions. Even after beating us on the pitch they still could not muster a firm at full time. I do not know of anyone anywhere who rates Coventry. We played Chelsea away on the February of this season – took thousands of fans and totally filled the old open end at Stamford Bridge. A goal from Ray Houghton put us top of the table and the party at full time was brilliant. We now firmly believed we could win the title. Nothing occurred trouble wise, but fair play to Chelsea they did have a good little mob in the seats on the side and were beckoning us to come over for a play up. But we were too busy celebrating going top of the table.

Then the crunch game came around at Man United away which some were saying was a title decider as we were neck and neck at the time. The ticket allocation for Villa fans was a major disappointment as they only sent us 1,700, which were snapped up by season ticket holders. If we had been given the tickets we could have taken 10,000 for this game such was the interest. I made my way over to the Leopard pub in Erdington, to watch it there. It's a strong Villa area and you would not have any Blue noses taking the piss if we got beat. The Leopard was totally packed and you could really feel the tension in the pub before the game. This was the game where I got to meet Fordy from the C-Crew. A friend introduced me to him. I did not know many of the C-Crew lads as they were active when I was just a young kid. I had heard of some of the damage they had done to the Blues when they were an active firm, and Fordy's name was one that always cropped up. He was a front-line warrior back in his day. And as well as being well respected on the Villa Park terraces, he was also very well liked as a person – and I could see why. He was dead friendly – a proper nice bloke. Moreover, he was one of those people I instantly got on with.

I pushed him to tell me about some of the old battles with the Blue noses and fair play to him he was not after no personal glory. He spoke very highly of Jimmy Coley, and Brittle. He was mentioning all the other C-Crew lads he had stood with front line but at the same time not bigging himself up. I admired him for that because we all knew he had played a major part in the firm back in its day. Fordy said that apart from West Ham away in the FA Cup in 1980, that for between 2-3 years the C-Crew were as good at their game as anyone. Additionally, that they never gained the recognition they deserved. He added that it was a shame that the C-Crew did not keep the firm going for longer, but situations emerged where most of the firm drifted away for a number of reasons (mostly jail sentences). However, the C-Crew had certainly left their mark on the Villa Park terraces. He was also one who spoke very highly of the Wolves Subway Army and said they were a proper firm who always stood their ground.

Without forgetting events at Upton Park, Fordy said that West Ham were pure evil during the FA Cup tie. Even though West Ham had won the game with a Ray Stewart penalty it was an eye opener for anybody who thought that they were a top lad down the Villa; it was a dreadful game to be at. The hooliganism was as bad as it gets – aided and abetted by West Ham stewards and turnstile operators who were in on it. Fordy had gone on a coach from the Rose and Crown pub in Erdington, and said that getting from the coach to the ground was touch and go if you would make it alive. I'd had that experience myself at West Ham. Once the

Villa reached the ground they immediately realised that the Villa end was full of West Ham and you had no idea who was who; there was serious trouble throughout the game. The Villa lads were wondering how they were going to get out of the ground as the I.C.F had all the exits covered. As the Villa were leaving the ground at full time they were kicked down the concrete steps by the I.C.F. As they were heading back to their coaches it was every-man for himself and they had to run a gauntlet of hate to battle their way back to the coaches. The Villa had been taught a proper lesson about organised hooliganism. It made the Villa realise if they were going to be taken seriously as top firm that they had to become more organised. In many ways West Ham away was a blessing in disguise for the C-Crew.

Villa played West Ham at home in October 1981, and everyone who been attacked in the FA Cup quarter-final was out for revenge. A massive mob of 300 Villa were waiting out side the Holte End, hanging around for West Ham to be heading back towards the Serpentine. Their lads took a hiding and the police had a real struggle to keep on top of things. Without the police it would have been real carnage – a bit like West Ham away in fact. The police made over 70 arrests, 90% of which were Villa fans. The strange thing is that West Ham have never mentioned this in any of their books. Maybe they only want to remember the occasion when they came out on top. Revenge is a dish best served cold.

Getting back to the game at Old Trafford, the ground was packed for this must win game. The atmosphere in the Leopard was nearly as good as being there as the place was rocking. I cannot remember who it was but someone laid the ball out wide to Steve Staunton, and he unleashed a left footed screamer that went flying into the top corner of the goal. The place went mental and hundreds of pounds worth of beer went flying up in the air as we took the lead. We were all going crazy and it would not of surprised me if the Villa players would have heard the roar in Manchester. All the old songs were coming out and we really thought we were going to nick the three points. We were all dancing and going totally wild. It was amazing and I was totally buzzing from my beloved Villa taking the lead. But as the game progressed we sat back and let Man United pile on the pressure.

As the game was approaching full time, Man United did their old special trick of pinching a late goal. From joy to heartache. I was gutted and it felt like a defeat. Getting a point away at Old Trafford was no embarrassment, however, after taking the lead it was traumatic. The atmosphere in the pub took a nosedive and I will never forget even to this day how the gloom descended on the Leopard – as I bet it did in every other Villa pub Birmingham wide. I hated all the so-called 'Brummie Reds' who latched onto Man United because there a big club who win trophies. Not all Villa fans agree with my opinion, but I would rather a Brummie support the Blues as much as I hate them. I firmly believe in supporting your local team.

The next game was a near full house of 40,000 – it was our recent rivals Sheffield Wednesday at Villa Park. They completely filled the away end with their huge allocation. This was the game when the football fan in everyone took over as we went top of the table again. The Villa firm did not give a shit about finding Wednesday's lads. It was mental at full time as the Man United result came in as they had slipped up on their travels. We really believed this could be our year. The after match drink in the Adventurers was one to remember forever. We really thought we had the title wrapped up now.

Next up, we were away at high flying Norwich which brought us crashing back down to earth with a huge bump. With Carrow Road being a tiny ground, they only sent us a small allocation of tickets. Due to my contacts, I obtained two tickets for the away end. One for me, and one for my mate Peter from Stockland Green. Norwich were also having a great season themselves, nevertheless, on the coach on the way there we were all very confident about maintaining top spot; we were all on a high. Sadly, after the four-hour coach journey (which seemed to go on forever and a day) the players did not turn up. We lost 1-0, and with Man United winning it shoved us back down into second place. Let me tell you, the journey home was a very long one and no one on the coach even felt like talking.

After a weeks break for International football we then had Notts Forest away. With the huge end they gave you everyone was up for this one. With the 6,000-ticket allocation, as well as it being a local derby, a top turn was guaranteed. We all met at New Street station Birmingham and had decent numbers out. We were looking forward to the short trip to Nottingham. Now let me put across my opinion of Forest. I know the older lot from the Villa half rated them but in all my years following the Villa I have never seen or come across anything resembling a Forest firm. I know they turned up at Birmingham City in the FA Cup in the late 80's, and gave the Zulus as good as they got – I'll give them credit for that one. That being said, they have never made the short trip to Villa Park. When they came to Villa Park they hardly brought any fans let alone lads. Forest are a club I simply do not rate. I always found Derby a more moody place to visit.

When we arrived in Nottingham we headed for a number of pubs by the ground. Yet to our amazement not a word was said and we just stood in their drinking until the match started. There was nothing in any of the pubs that resembled a firm.

As we arrived at the ground, Fowler and the firm decided to have a look around for Forest's lads but many others like myself went the game. The huge away end behind the goal was full to the rafters. We were on the right hand side behind the goal and the sight of 6,000 Villa fans packing the end out was brilliant. The travelling Claret and Blue army had turned out in huge numbers. After a dull first half, the game seemed to be heading for a draw. Then with the referees whistle drawing near, up popped Paul McGrath with a winner facing the travelling Villa army – we went barmy. The noise coming from our end was surreal and better still Man United had only managed a draw; it put us top of the table again. It was party time again as the players came over to applaud us. I was totally buzzing from the victory. It had been an edgy game but we were heading home with the three points. We all met up again at full time outside the away end and headed off to Burton on Trent for a drink on the way home. But once again – no show from the Notts Forest Executive Crew.

Our next home game was our hatred rivals from Coventry. I can honestly say I nearly detested this lot as much as Blues. They were like an irritating fly you wanted to swat. They have spent years saying what they are going to do to the Villa and have never once done anything of any note. A day out at Coventry away was just a total piss take, where you would take over all their pubs and they could do nothing about it. Always has been – always will be. They had been banding it around for this game that they were coming to sort out the Villa lads. We all arranged to meet up early doors and be ready for them; fuck the game. Even normal fans like myself wanted a pop at Coventry. These idiots needed putting to bed for good. We landed first in town – no sign of them. We then headed to Witton station where the away fans get off – no sign of them again. As the game was approaching we took a walk up to the away end and were clocked by our 'Old Bill'. Coventry were all hiding behind the police lines. It was a joke. None of us were going the game, therefore, we took a walk around Villa Park as Coventry's lads had said they were not going the game either. Being the Villa supporter I am, I kept in contact with a friend inside the ground who said we were playing them off the park – yet we could not break them down. The wankers had come for a draw and to mess up our title ambitions.

As the Full time whistle blew they had held us to a 0-0 draw, and to their fans that was a right result as Man United went back to the top of the table. As the ground emptied we had a right good firm outside the away end firm – between 100-150 lads. The police were on top of their game and kept the Coventry in for about one-hour whilst dispersing our entire firm. That was not the end of it though as we headed straight back into town expecting to bump into them at New Street station. We had heard they were drinking in the rail-bar in New Street station. Nonetheless, they had once again vanished into thin air. Now I know this was a stupid thing to do, but at this stage in my life I saw no wrong in what I was doing. After all their threats about turning up mob handed we never saw them all day, which was lucky for them as there was a lot of anger in our firm on this day; we had a point to prove. How a following of 3,000 managed to get to Villa Park and sneak off home I will never work it out. It was a very frustrating day to say the least. Don't get me wrong, Coventry has some very rough areas. Despite that, it has never been transformed into their football club. As much as I hate Blues at least they had lads I rated and respected, however as for Coventry, I had no respect at all. They try to get involved in the Midlands-rivalry game when they have never done anything anywhere to gain any respect. I know as well the Zulus feel the same about them. Coventry should crawl back into the hole they came out of and stay there – unless one day they do actually get the balls to turn up at Villa Park.

Our next game was Arsenal away. They have always had a decent firm but like most clubs were not as active as they once were. I did not have the money for this one due to all the commuting from South Brum to North Brum; I was stink. As a result, I would be sitting glued to the radio. As always, we sold out our allocation. Our home-grown hero Tony Daley snatched the points with a rare headed goal. He latched onto a cross from Ray Houghton to bang it straight in the net. I can still recall my girlfriend Karen looking at me as if I had won the lottery and not fully understanding how a football result could make me so happy. Although with Man United also winning it kept us in second place. After all, how couldn't a win away at Arsenal be anything but satisfying? We were keeping the pressure on Man United and with four games to go we were still firmly in the title race.

Next up was Man City at home, and the funny thing was loads of the Man City lads had brought flags saying 'Good luck Villa' as they obviously did not want Man United to win the title. Before the game Ron Atkinson had released a statement saying: "ALL I ASK OF THE SUPPORTERS IS TO

CONTINUE TO BACK THE TEAM FROM FIRST TO THE LAST AS YOU HAVE BEEN DOING SO NOBLY. IT IS NOT EASY OUT THERE. I HAVE SAID ALL ALONG THAT WE WONT BOTTLE IT. NOR WILL WE. THERE ARE 12 POINTS LEFT. LET'S GO FOR THEM TOGETHER." For all that, the wheels fell off our title challenge as we lost to Man City, and their fans did not even celebrate when they scored – such is their hatred towards Man United. At full time, the realisation hit us all that we had blown it. It was still mathematically possible to win the title, all the same, we had already given up hope. The fans were numb. I went straight home after the game; I was very depressed. It was a very dark day to say the least as Man United pulled further ahead.

Blackburn away was our next mid-week game and once again I did not have the money to go. I sat glued to the radio yet again, however, high flying Blackburn thumped us 3-0. We had lost our nerve. The players had not kept it together. Our title challenge was well and truly over. Some could use this excuse or that excuse, but Man United were used to the pressure and we were not. I found it very hard to take. I was not old enough to truly respect winning the League in the 80/81 season, or the European Cup the following year, therefore, I was hanging my hopes onto this one. I suppose it was not to be. I was devastated. We had one more game at home to Oldham (who were in a relegation battle) but the game on everyone's lips was QPR away last game of the season. Now we could no longer win the title our lads decided to go out with a bang. We would be taking a full firm to London for the QPR game. We lost again at home to Oldham but by now it was futile even if we had won the game. It was already over regardless of the result.

Skin-Head Neil, Chris Jones and a few more of the top lads had travelled down to London a few weeks before the QPR game, and linked up with some London Villa lads to obtain tickets for the QPR home end. We wanted to make our mark at this game. Skin-Head Neil and Chris Jones had obtained around 200 tickets for the QPR end and all our lads snapped them up as soon as they arrived back – fair play one was reserved for me. They sent us the usual 3,000 allocation that sold out in one day. We did not care though as we had our tickets and were planning on a last day of the season top turn out. Old and new faces were turning out for this one. When the day arrived we all descended on London and headed for Loftus Road. We took over every pub surrounding the ground. Except this was not like Everton away under Graham Taylor when we finished second and took over Goodison Park. The Villa were now an organised firm again. We moved on from pub to pub and they were all jam-packed with the 'barmy' Villa army. QPR were nowhere to be seen at all. All our lads headed for the home end as the game was approaching, but very quietly as not to attract any police attention. We all got in the ground and took our seats right in the middle of the home fans; there were hundreds of us. The Villa away end was totally rocking and as the players came out we let our selves be known; we all stood up to applaud them.

By now QPR knew we were in their end but did not have the lads or numbers to try to move us. They were booing us from all sections of the ground. Yet no attempt was made to have a pop at us. We were simply too mob handed, and even the police and stewards did not know what to do with us. As the game started, Tony Daley broke away and put us into the lead and we all went ballistic hoping for some reaction from QPR lads but nothing happened. I am not sure if at this stage QPR did not have a firm. It was a proper piss take – it reminded me of Coventry away. The Villa fans in the away enclosure could see we had turned up in the home end and were chanting to us and we were chanting back to them. The look on the QPR fans faces was a picture. As the game progressed QPR went 2-1 up – but we had stopped caring about the result by now.

As the full-time whistle blew the league was Man United's – they were away at Wimbledon. I was gutted about not winning the league but it was decided before this game. The dream was already over. Just like under Graham Taylor when Liverpool pipped us during the 90/91 season, my beloved club had twice had that dream cruelly snatched away. You must remember I was a football fan, not a football hooligan. As the Villa players were clapping the travelling fans in the away end some one from our firm gave the nod to invade the pitch. We all climbed over the advertising hoardings and entered the pitch. The stewards and police could not stop us with the numbers we had. Not that this was the plan but when the standing away terrace holding the Villa supporters saw us enter the pitch they followed suit. The other Villa fans in the seating upper tear were going mental and were applauding us. I am sure they would have joined us if they could. We were now taking liberties whilst the stewards and police unsuccessfully tried to restore order.

Having no joy with the home fans the travelling Villa army decided to wreck the goal posts; still no response from QPR. This was a total take over of the ground. It reached such a chaotic stage that even the Villa chairman Doug Ellis came on the loudspeaker asking all Villa fans to clear the pitch as we were giving the club a bad name. However, we were all having too much fun to listen to Deadly Doug. We were here to make a point and we had achieved our aim. Then the Villa fans really took the piss by doing the Conga dance all round the pitch. I am sure if this would have been Chelsea or West Ham away it would have developed into a full-blown riot, as I do not think we would have found it so easy there. Whereas at Lofts Road we had it all our own way. I am by no means condoning this behaviour – I am just taking a walk down memory lane.

We left the ground after a good hour or so, and Villa fans were still on the pitch. There was still no QPR to be seen as Villa's firm walked around the ground. All the local pubs were packed again with Villa, therefore, we made our way to a well-known pub by the away end called The Springbok – where we met up with some more of our other lads. We were in the Springbok for hours after the game drinking away and having a singsong. The landlord that day must have made a fortune; there were about 300 lads in there. When we finally decided to head home late on, as we reached Euston Station and it was full of 'Old Bill' in-case Villa and Man United landed back there at the same time.

The following day I had a phone call from one of the Villa lads based down London who told me some thing that shocked the life out of me. An hour after we had left the Springbok pub a mob of local Black lads not linked up to QPR, had turned up at the pub proper tooled up to have pop at the Brummies. Rumour had it, some Villa fans had been giving some local Black lads some shit after the game and they had got a mob together to seek revenge. They entered the pub with baseball bats, knifes and machetes, and totally trashed the pub. Furthermore, they savagely beat up the landlord – I guess for letting us use his pub. They even forced their way upstairs into his living quarters to see if any Villa fans were hiding up there. Fortunately, we had all left together an hour earlier. If a handful of us had been left behind I dread to think what may have happened. They were about a 100 strong and so I was led to believe they were the local Black gang who ran the area; they were there to teach the Villa a lesson. I still imagine to this day what would have happened if they had landed when we were 300 strong. The lads I was with that day were not bottlers. Nevertheless, how tooled up the other firm were I am certain some of our lot would have been seriously injured as they were not there to play around. It would have been mayhem.

On the ITV news on the night, we made the headlines about our pitch invasion and wrecking the goal posts. Moreover, it even showed the Villa fans doing the Conga around the pitch – much to the embarrassment of the QPR lads. Let me take this chance to say QPR did seek their revenge many years later at a cup game at Villa Park in 2006, when they brought a right mob. This sadly resulted in the death of a steward whilst trying to stop the trouble; he died of a heart attack.

After a great season finishing second and finally starting to get a proper firm together, little did we know that the following season would bring us a trophy under Ron Atkinson. And that Fowler who was now Villa's top lad, would lead the firm for many years to come.

CHAPTER 9

I was now deeply involved in the National Front as well as following the Villa all over the country. Any spare time went on the NF – attending meetings, leafleting, fighting by-elections and council elections. How my Karen put up with me I will never know. Being involved in British nationalist politics hardly left any time for her, then the weekend was match day. Looking back now she deserved a medal for putting up with me for all those years. John McCauley once described the NF to me as a: "Running bath with no tap in it", due to the amount of drop-out members. As soon as say ten new members joined, ten would disappear, therefore, we would never really be making progress concerning membership figures.

I remember thinking that the right-wing would always be weak so long as it based its support predominantly on 'blue collar support'. We needed to broaden our support base. All things must adapt to the environment, and the NF was no exception. Political parties are in the business of marketing solutions. It is our job to identity the problems and to offer the solutions. If our solutions do not sell – it is up to us to improve our message until it strikes a chord with the electorate. Selling NF policy to a British public desperately in need of a British nationalist alternative is our task. In addition, I firmly believed that the NF should present itself with an image of respectability, decency and civilised behaviour. Moreover, when the policy on immigration and racial issues are brought up, to avoid any expressions of hate or insult – common sense really. People on the outside must also realise that this isn't about hatred, it isn't about racism – it is about survival.

The local elections we fought from 1993, to the general election of 1997, were always the same. High hopes on the doorstep that never materialised into votes come Election Day. Without sounding negative, I even started to expect a poor showing because it was happening that often. We were not even attempting to 'update' our party or make us more electable; I was beginning to become a touch concerned about the lack of direction in the NF. I started to get a bit demoralised whilst at the same time casting an interested eye at the ever-growing BNP. The BNP had not managed to win any more seats after the Tower Hamlets victory, however, they were still pulling in some decent votes nationwide. Even a blind man could see they had pulled miles ahead of the NF in terms of membership, votes, seats fought and attendance at meetings. It would not be fair of me to say exact numbers, but the BNP were pulling in more members for local branch meetings than we were for our yearly AGM. John Tyndall from the BNP had put out an olive branch to the NF leadership regarding a merger of the two parties, with the intention of having one British nationalist party instead of two; this was flatly rejected. This would have consisted of the NF going over to the BNP and ceasing to exist. There were people in the NF that wanted to keep the party going. Be as it may it is something I would have personally been in favour of myself.

The attendances at the West Midlands NF meetings were poor. Some new people would turn up expecting hundreds at the meeting, then when they saw the small attendance (not that the meetings were not well organised) we would not see them again. I wanted faster progress than this because at the rate the country was sinking we were not moving forward fast enough. We had the policies that the silent majority were screaming out for but they were not turning to us. I remember saying to one of our members: "If people agree with our policies – but don't vote for us there is obviously a reason? We have to find that reason and change something".

Being good friends with Norman Tomkinson and John Lord who were running the Birmingham branch, I felt a sense of loyalty to those two people – maybe as much as to British nationalism itself. They were not only party colleagues they were two of my best mates. This resulted in me staying with the NF for many more years. How could I leave the party when we had put in so much hard work together? Norman and John were like family to me. We had formed our own little clan running the branch together. Looking back now all these years later, I put personal friendship before the state of the country. It was a choice I made at the time. And that choice was to stay with the NF and not jump ship to the BNP. All these years later, I now regret that decision.

On the football front after finishing 2nd place the season before, hopes were high and we started the season off with a 4-1 victory over QPR. More importantly, the League Cup would draw us against our bitter rivals Birmingham City. After not playing each other since the 1987/88 season, firms from both clubs would be out to prove a point. Before the game at Birmingham on the September of 1993, we were sitting in a pretty third spot in the league so things were going well for our club. When the draw was made alarm bells were sent out as we knew if we did not go mob handed and in one firm we would come proper unstuck at Saint Andrews. Blues would be out to prove a point and anything other than a good strong firm of Villa travelling together would be a suicide mission.

Rewinding the years back a little, my first taste of a Villa/Blues derby came in the old second division season of 1987/88, when Villa gained promotion. The first derby game that season was at Villa Park and fair play to Blues they brought a good firm of Zulus and were in the Wilton Lane seats all through the game. Lads from the Holte End tried to get over the fencing, however, a large-scale police presence prevented anything of any note really happening. The return game at Saint Andrews would see major crowd disturbances as expected. As Peter and I were heading to the ground, unaware to us a mob of 150 Villa Youth were heading through Digbeth, and attacked two pubs en-route – The Old Crown and The Clements. A lad called Gary Lyttle (R.I.P) led Villa's firm that day.

As we were queuing up outside the ground at the Tilton Road end, Blues turned up seeking payback for what the Villa had done to the two pubs. They steamed into us and all hell broke loose. You must remember this was only two years after the Leeds riot and Birmingham were well organised and respected all over the country. The travelling hordes of Villa fans stood their ground as the police franticly tried to restore order. When Peter and I entered the ground the two sections of the Tilton Road they had given us were jam packed with about 10,000 Villa – then you had an empty section to separate the rival fans. It was still the same old shit hole from years ago when my Dad took me down a couple of times. The atmosphere was electric and to Peter and I being our first Villa/Blues derby away we were like kids at Christmas; taking it all in and loving every second of it.

During the mayhem outside the ground some Villa had paid into the corner of the Kop. Not by choice but to escape the fighting going on by the Tilton. The Villa end was that full they should have opened up the empty section next to us which only added to the atmosphere. You could not move in the Villa end. Both sets of fans were up for this one and I could tell just by looking around that Villa had proper lads there. As the game started, suddenly a huge roar went up and the terracing separating the two sets of fans started to fill up as both sets of fans were climbing over to get at each other. All you could hear was: "YOUTH, YOUTH, YOUTH", as fighting broke out with both firms charging at each other, backing off and then charging again. Peter and I both thought this was brilliant as hundreds of police were sent in. The fighting continued until even more back up was called, before the police somehow got in between the two mobs. Lads on both sides had taken a kicking. I am not saying the Villa actually took the end but they most certainly took it to the Zulus and to be fair no one really came out on top. I ain't going to lie like the Zulus do.

The atmosphere by now was pure evil – that is the only word I can describe to explain it. With the game at 1-1, and the fans more interested in each other than what was happening on the pitch, Garry Thompson our centre forward popped up with a bullet header to put us 2-1 up. The Villa end went crazy and a shower of coins from both sets of rained down on each other as the fans made further attempts to get over the fencing. But the police were on top of things by now. As the full time whistle blew the celebrations in the away end only added to the hostile atmosphere – and as the ground emptied it would give the Zulus and Villa Youth another chance to meet up again. Peter and I tried to find the Villa Youth as we left the ground but they had already gone on the hunt for Blues. We decided to take a short cut past the White Towers pub and then back through Aston to head to safe territory as I was stopping at Peter's.

As we approached the White Towers pub we nearly shit our selves because there was a firm of about 200 Blues hanging around out-side. You could tell it was their main lads. I must admit they were a nasty looking bunch – half-White and half-Black. What made Peter and I so scared was we knew if they sussed we were Villa they would have done us over. Even though they were a top firm they were known for doing over any Villa fan; they had a history of this. It did not matter to them if you were a top lad or a fan with a scarf on – you were getting it. They took it beyond rivalry and even admitted in their book Zulus that any Villa fan would do – where as the Villa were not into slapping normal Blues fans; that was the difference. Living over the south side of the city I knew this only to well for myself, as I'd had bad experiences with them before – picking on Villa fans in ones and twos. They even gained the nickname 'BULLY-EM CITY' instead of Birmingham City. I do not know if it was pay back time for all the years the Steamers and the C-Crew had the upper hand over them before those firms faded away. That being said, when they finally did get a good firm together no Villa fan was safe.

Peter and I kept our heads up as not to give the game away as we walked past them. My nerves were shot; this time though we were lucky and they never approached us. They obviously thought we were Blues. I will admit though that they were a mob and a half and deserved the reputation they had gained. As we both headed home little did we know that the Villa Youth had firmed up ten minutes away and would bump into the firm of Zulus we had just passed. They eventually met on Great Brook Street, which resulted in running battles. It would be wrong of me to say who came out on top as I was not there. Although, the majority of lads I spoke to said it was a 50/50 share on the night with numerous arrests as the fighting continued into town. I remember thinking fair play to the Villa Youth as they had turned up against their hated rivals, before, during and after the game. This was no easy result as at this time the Zulus were on top of their game and were one of the top football firms in England. To come away from Saint Andrews with a share of the nights troubles was a major result for the Villa. Despite everything, events during the 1993 league cup game would far exceed this – as the Villa would turn over the Zulus at Saint Andrews. Moreover, at the return leg at Villa Park it would show the Zulus up for the sheer bitterness they hold towards the Villa.

It was a night game at Saint Andrews in 1993. By this stage the Villa Hardcore had come together as a firm, if not yet by name by numbers. Fowler had taken a firm up to Sunderland the round before and had a bang off in a pub by the ground which increased his ever-growing reputation. He had proved himself over the last two seasons and had put himself up front to lead us. Paul Brittle from the C-Crew was back on the streets for this one. Brittle had been a major player in the late 70's – early 80's, in forming and bringing together Villa's best ever firm – The C-Crew – before it faded away around 1983. Paul Brittle was respected and liked by everyone. I personally did not know him but the lads that did never had a bad word to say about him. Most people regarded him as Villa's top lad through the generations and I was one of them. Brittle spread the word to meet at the Ben Johnson pub by the fire station in town and go as one firm. Just having the likes of Brittle there filled you full of confidence, because you knew their would be no backward steps. We had the main faces there from the older lot as we called them and Fowler who was running the latest firm. This was how I believed it should always have been. We had finally learnt our mistakes of the past; being organised and Villa travelling in one firm instead of little pockets of lads here and there.

Come around 6.30pm, we must have had a good 250 lads ready to march to Saint Andrews. Some people have put that figure even higher. Old and new faces were turning up in pockets and the pub was packed solid. Any lingering doubts I had about lack of numbers were put to bed. Saint Andrews is not the type of place you can just turn up with a little mob; you will get turned over. If Villa fans are perfectly honest, Saint Andrews is not a nice place to visit. Love them or hate them, they can pull a good firm together. Blues had been out since early doors and had done over some Villa fans that were drinking in a pub by Aston University which was just up the road from the Ben Johnson where we were congregating. Credit where it's due, we knew the Zulus would be out in force and it was only a matter of time until we bumped into them. News spread about the Villa fans being ambushed, which just made our firm more determined to make a move – start to head towards Saint Andrews and give them some pay back.

As we left the pub I looked around at our mob and knew that second that this would be our night. You have maybe heard this a thousand times but I would have put us against any firm on this occasion. There were too many top lads there to have any doubts. The Zulus were in for a shock. We walked past a number of pubs on the way to the ground and the look on the faces of the Noses that popped their heads out for a look was a picture as they scrambled their way back inside. They were not expecting this turn out from the Villa. The only problem was with a firm this big it was obvious the police would soon latch onto us. As we walked past the Cauliflower Ear pub some lads put the windows through which only alerted the 'Old Bill'. Stupid really when we were trying to keep a low profile, nevertheless, it is what happens at local derbies. Blues knew we were outside but would not come out as they would have got proper turned over – not that they would ever admit to this. Police or not, we were too pumped up by now to let the 'Old Bill' stop us. The police rounded up some of our lads but the majority of our firm stayed together and broke away from the escort. We would shortly bump into the Zulus as expected.

As we reached Garrison Lane, we saw the Zulus in the distance. This is what makes me laugh about Blues. They always have cheap shots at the Villa saying we only throw bottles and bricks, but this is exactly what the Noses did as they came charging towards us. Our numbers were about even. We hesitated a few seconds until the rain of bottles, bricks and glasses ran out. I looked and knew it was their main firm. It was not for the faint hearted and I will admit that if it were not for our front line I would have most certainly backed off. I am not going to lie or try to act the big-man. Our top lads were ordering everyone to stand their ground. We had no weapons at all, however, once the Zulus ran out of ammunition they stopped in their tracks. We had not budged an inch. They were expecting us to run as we had done so often since the Zulus had got it together.

Brittle gave the call and we surged forward. They were not expecting this from little old Villa. Maybe they'd had it easy for too long? Now I ain't going to steal anyone's glory as I was not leading our firm or at the front; there were other much more senior lads to do that job. I was just a number, nothing more. Apart from a few Zulus standing who got walked over, they were off. Little pockets of fighting broke out but by then we had the momentum. Then our firm that had been rounded up by the police suddenly arrived. They saw what was going on, broke free from the escort and charged with us. At this stage the police had lost control of the situation. The Villa were now running the Zulus back up the hill; they had totally folded.

The only thing that stopped us running them back into the ground was the police turned up with the horses and were not messing about. We had without doubt turned them over at their place; our mob was jubilant. As we were shepherded to the ground, the Blues at this stage had not tried to regroup. A highly charged game (but not as charged as the 1987 fixture at Saint Andrews), and a late Kevin Richardson goal gave us a 1-0 victory. A massive police operation was in place to prevent a recurrence of what happened before the game. I knew the Zulus would have been embarrassed by being run before the game. They do not like coming of second best – especially to the Villa. We knew they would be dying to get even; they did not disappoint us.

As we reached Garrison Lane we spotted them again. They were trying to hold back to try to ambush us and outsmart the 'Old Bill'. Seconds later a rain of missiles started again and they surged forward into us. After we had showed them up before the game they had to try to do something to salvage some pride. Fighting broke out everywhere and regrettably normal fans from both sides were caught up in it. This was something I was always dead against. The police were well organised by this stage and baton charged the Zulus back up the road. Then another set of police officers rounded up our firm to take us off in a different direction. We were then escorted us all the way back to Aston in what can only be described as a 'human chain'. Just as I thought the nights events were over, we heard the cry 'ZULU' fill the air. Suddenly a firm of Black lads appeared from nowhere. I am sure they were up to the old Blues trick of picking of pockets of Villa fans. They must have only seen the front of our firm and did not perceive how big our mob actually was. Either this or it was their last chance of making up for getting ran before the game.

They did not have the numbers this time and the look on their faces told us they did not see how far back our firm was stretching. I will give that to Blues – they hate the Villa so much they always travel to seek us out. Once our firm saw the Zulus, they broke through the chain of 'Old Bill' and got stuck into them. The firm of Black Zulu lads could not handle the size of our firm and after a few getting slapped they were off. That being said, this was no major scalp as it was simply a numbers game. They had come unstuck against a far bigger mob.

The police started to force us off into different directions to break the firm up – which they did. I then headed back through Aston as I was stopping at Karen's in Stockland Green. The next day though the bullshit started to flow from the Zulus saying how it wasn't their firm that we ran. We had ran normal fans, attacked innocent people; they ran from the police not the Villa firm – the list was endless. Excuse after excuse. The Zulus do not like admitting when they get done. That's the thing about the Zulus – especially if it's the Villa. Their resentment towards Aston Villa goes beyond belief. You only have to read their book to see the bullshit that's in there. I honestly think they believe their own lies.

In any event, the return leg at Villa Park would show how deep that hatred ran as me and four other friends would find out for ourselves.

CHAPTER 10

*A*fter our result at Saint Andrews, the lads from over the south side of Birmingham where I was from were saying how they were coming to Villa Park to prove a point in the return leg. I found this hilarious after claiming we only ran their normal fans and they had ran from the police not the Villa firm. The Blue Noses have always had this thing about selective memory. The Hardcore met at the Adventurers pub with people turning up from about 3pm on-wards for the night game. This is another thing with the Zulus. They claimed we used the Adventurers pub because it was close to Queens Road Police station. It is the nearest pub as you leave the main Villa end; the Holte End. It has always been a major Villa pub going back many, many years way before I even stepped foot inside Villa Park as a child. The 'Noses' purported we used the pub to have protection from the 'Old Bill'. Does anybody with half a brain actually believe this? My own personal opinion is the Zulus used this as an excuse for never showing up at the Adventurers – even during their glory years as a top firm. They use any flimsy excuse to have a sly dig at the Villa – always have done, and always will.

Come around 6.30pm, we had a good 200 lads in the Adventurers. Something though I could not understand was after our victory at Saint Andrews, that the older lot were meeting up in Perry Barr. Now this may have been because at the time Brittle from the C-Crew had brought the Little Crown pub. All the same, I could not work out why we had not met up again as one firm. We had fallen into the old habit again of not meeting up as one mob; it has always been a bit of a problem down the Villa. I may be wrong in saying this but I have always found the Villa to be more organised for Blues away, than when we play them at home. The Zulus had been on the phone to the Adventurers and both the Big and Little Crown, saying they were on their way. We left for the ground about 7.15pm, and anybody who was anybody was there.

As we reached the Holte Pub – which at the time had been closed down for years – suddenly we spotted a mob of lads in the distance. Initially, no one knew if it was another mob of Villa or the Zulus. As we got closer we knew it was the Zulus by the majority Black faces in the firm; it was their top boys. The roar went up from both firms and both sets of lads charged forward. We clashed by two burger vans – although I must admit it was a poor showing from both sides as only a handful of lads actually stepped forward to have a go. It was quite funny, because lads were grabbing hot dogs and burgers from the stalls and throwing them at each other; pathetic really. I admit that we had the superior numbers but did not take it to them. I could lie through my back teeth and say we turned them over but that's not my style. For a Birmingham local derby I expected a lot more from both firms. I admit I was as much to blame as anyone, as no one seemed to want to get into each other. It was simply one of those.

The 'Old Bill' forced us down Witton Lane, where we bumped into the older lads. We asked if any Blues had showed up at the Big or Little Crown, however, they had not. The firm Blues had out was the one we had bumped into – as like I said – was very disappointing. We won the game 1-0, through to a goal from Dean Saunders our super striker; the fans worshipped him. It was one of those games I cannot remember much about – due to circumstances that happened after the game. Word spread on the Holte End terrace that the Zulus had been in contact again with our older lads, and were definitely making a show after the game at the Big and Little Crown. On that account, we all headed there after the game. I never foreseen the danger I was about to put my friends and myself under. Both pubs either side of the road were jam packed with Villa lads; top faces everywhere you looked. The phone calls kept coming from Zulus that they were on their way. Villa waited and waited but no show from the Zulus and people started to drift home. About mid-night me, Jamie, Noel, Tony H and Stickman decided to call it a night and left the Little Crown to head home. By now it was pitch black.

The streets were deserted which only added to the creepy atmosphere as we headed to a late night chip shop just down from the Big Crown. Unexpectedly, a Black geezer walked up to me and said: "What was the score mate?" Not thinking nothing of it I replied: "1-0 Villa mate", and it was then I noticed his head drop back ready to head-butt me. It was a pathetic attempt for a head-butt as I had plenty of time to step back – a blind man could have seen it coming. We were all in shock as he never approached us in an aggressive way. Just as we were about to make a move on him we heard a huge roar of "ZULU" fill the air. It was actually like a scene from the film Zulu as about 40 Black lads appeared from the car park of the Big Crown. I admit I was instantly in sheer panic mode as any person would be – especially against such large numbers.

We all fled in different directions, knowing if they caught us we were in big trouble. Stickman, Noel and Tony H got away – and who could blame them. Anyhow, Jamie and I were not so lucky. Around ten of them threw me up against the chip shop window and started to attack me with fists and boots. I curled up in a ball and was waiting for the knifes to come out as I knew they would be carrying weapons as this is what they were known for. As I glanced out the corner of my eye I saw Jamie lying on the ground and witnessed all the other Zulu lads beating him with baseball bats and spraying him with CS gas. The boots and fists kept raining down on me, yet it was surreal because watching Jamie being attacked somewhat made me shut off as to what was happening to myself.

All of a sudden, I saw a number of the Zulus pull out blades on Jamie and start to slash at him indiscriminately. To anybody who has never been in a situation like this it is some thing you never forget. Seeing a close friend lying on the ground getting slashed stays with you forever. To make matters worse he was calling out my name for help; there was nothing though I could do. Regrettably, he copped the bulk of the attack. I was the lucky one attacked by the smaller mob and I only received a good kicking without any weapons being used on me. During the attack they were shouting things like: "You dirty Villa bastards", and it seemed like it lasted for about half hour – when it was maybe only five minutes or so. The attack suddenly stopped after some one from the Zulus gave the orders to go, then as they ran off I could hear them laughing. This was their revenge for being turned over at Saint Andrews.

I got up with my face plastered in blood from the boots and the fists. The chip shop window they had thrown me against had shattered; I think they had planned to throw me through it. More importantly, Jamie was lying on the floor motionless. My first reaction was to call an Ambulance then check on Jamie. He was lying in a pool of blood on the floor and his face was that beaten if I did not know who it was I would not have recognised him. He was mumbling something but not making any sense – he was in a bad, bad way. His back was sliced open and the wounds were pouring of blood. He could not even open his eyes due to the CS gas that had been used on him. I felt guilty for not helping him although there was nothing I could have done. The Zulus had fled away from the scene of the crime like the cowards they were. I have always considered them a 'dirty firm' as do all Villa lads.

The Ambulance arrived and rushed him to the accident and emergency department at the hospital in town, where after cleaning him up they stitched up his slash wounds. Even though I was covered in blood from my kicking, I looked a lot worse than I actually was and never needed any hospital treatment – apart from being cleaned down by the nurses. I had been very fortunate. I informed Jamie's family which made me feel even worse as our adventure had totally backfired on us. Seeing the horror on his Mom's and Girlfriend's face when they arrived at the hospital made me feel I was to blame – as without me suggesting let's head to the Little Crown we would of more than likely gone back to the Adventurers. I was solely the one responsible for this happening.

When Jamie arrived home two days later his face was still so beaten that his own son who was only a child at the time did not recognise him. That only added to my guilt for not helping him out. He eventually received a big pay out from the criminal injuries board, however, that was not the point. To look at his scars to this day it looks as if a pack of wild animals attacked him. Let me get one thing straight though. We went to the Little Crown with the hope of the Zulus turning up, therefore, some might say you put yourself in that position in the first place – which is true. Be as it may be, can anybody honestly say that this was anything other than a savage attack? It went way beyond football violence. It was a perfect example of how low the Zulus will stoop when it comes to the Villa. If you would have witnessed what I did, I still think to this day they could have killed Jamie; maybe they intended to. He is lucky he fell face down otherwise I am sure they would have slashed his face open or worse still stabbed him through the heart. They were nothing but cowards.

The simple fact is the Zulus knew that Villa had firms in both the Big and Little Crown, however, they would not show up there. They waited until both the pubs had emptied to pick up a few straggling Villa fans to do over. They did not care who it was. In addition, they do not mind admitting it either; it is pure Villa hatred. They have always been like that regarding Villa. For a firm like the Zulus who are rated nationwide why did they have to stoop so low that night? I found out the following week that they had been waiting in vans around the corner from the Big Crown – sitting tight until nearly everyone had gone home to carry out their attack. When the word spread about the Zulus I had some of our lads on the phone, and even though they were disgusted at what had happened it came as no surprise to them. This was how the Zulus operated. You see, a lot of the silly name-calling they direct at the Villa they are guilty of themselves.

They call the Villa a racist firm and love to hang the right-wing tag around our necks and label Fowler a racist. Is Fowler a 'racist'? Well NO. And if anybody ought to know it should be me. He has never had any connections with right-wing groups, yet this does not prevent the bullshit from being spread about him. I have heard all sorts of stories from Blue noses about how the Zulus have turned up at a NF or EDL march and ambushed Fowler and he has had to run and hide. Moreover, a majority of the Blues lads all believe it and take in everything they hear as the truth – it's total bullshit. Yes, people in our firm did have right-wing leanings – some obviously more than others. But Fowler was not one of them; he was in it for the fighting. It was an easy way to throw some mud at him that would stick and the Zulus used it to their full advantage.

I know a number of White Birmingham City fans who are supportive of right-wing groups to this day, yet they still travel with the Zulus come match day – even though they are known for having a large number of Black faces in their firm. It's just how it is. Back in the 1970's, Blues had the biggest National Front following in the UK apart from maybe Leeds or Chelsea. I know this to be a fact as some of the NF old timers have told me who were around at the height of the National Front. The old NF newspaper used to be on sale at Saint Andrews come match day and Birmingham City would always be in the top three regarding paper sales, until the firm did a huge U-turn and became multi-racial.

Big Tony, who runs the doors on match day in Aston, is one of Villa's most respected and liked Black Villa lads – and believe me he can look after himself. Do people really think

if racism was an issue down the Villa that the likes of Big
Tony would have travelled with Fowler and the Hardcore?
Big Tony is no idiot and he would not have stood for in your
face racism. Despite the fact it was never an issue. Then again
– this was nothing new. When the Zulus pulled together a
majority Black firm around 1985, some of the Villa Youth
were discredited as being NF because it was a majority White
firm. People automatically assumed that because the one firm
was Black and the other firm was White that there was a
racial issue between the two clubs – it's nonsense. With the
Hardcore it was just history repeating itself.

Unfortunately, some of our older lads did not take to
kindly regarding the rumours about Fowler and believed the
bullshit that was being bandied around, and suddenly for no
reason had a problem with him. It was bad enough the Blue
noses using the racist tag but then he had it from some of his
own. Fowler took it on the chin and took it in his stride –
but I know he was not happy about his own turning against
him – especially when there was no evidence pointing in
that direction; just sheer rumours. It got so bad with one of
the older Villa heads that on his web site he even refused to
recognise The Hardcore as a Villa firm, whilst at the same
time mentioning our rivals The Zulu Warriors, which I
found very strange. My own personal opinion is people
could not throw stuff at Fowler like he has no balls or he
doesn't stand his ground; they had nothing on him because
he had proved himself. The racist tag fitted him perfectly. It
gave them something to smear him with and discredit what
he had done for the Villa. On the subject of the word 'racist' I
would like to take a closer look at some elements of the Zulus
and point out a few facts.

During the mid – 1980's when I started following the Villa away, it is correct that for a number of years when the Villa arrived back at New Street station the Zulus would be waiting for us – sometimes with numbers ranging from 200-300 lads. I will give them credit for that. It did not matter what numbers we had we were terrified of them; I am being perfectly honest. The Villa had some good lads but weren't a match for Blues when they got proper organised; to say otherwise I would be lying. I will never forget the one year when we were coming back from Leicester and there must have been a good 600 Villa on the train; not all lads but still 600 in numbers. As we arrived at New Street and left the train we heard the cry 'ZULU', and you have never seen 600 people scatter so fast in your life; myself included. That is how much they had the edge over us as no one even stopped to look at their numbers – we just fled.

As I left New Street station by going up the escalators I saw little pockets of Black lads who were affiliated to the Zulus – stopping and mugging Villa fans who were all White and very young. The young Villa fans were terrified of them. They were the types who would go in a hat or scarf and take a packed lunch; easy prey so to speak. I remember a game at Villa Park when I about fifteen and the Zulus literally walked around Villa Park with a mob of 300 plus before the game and proper took the piss. They had a right firm and Villa simply could not match them. Some of these lads considered themselves Zulus when in reality they were nothing more than 'Townies' who latched onto the Zulu name when it became fashionable to be associated with them. It gave them a reason to make a 'few bob' when Villa 'scarfers' were heading back into Birmingham after following the Villa away. This happened on a number of occasions and I witnessed it first hand for myself. I know what I saw and no one can tell me any different.

The majority of the muggings or 'taxings' as they called it were carried out by young Black youths, and the victims were always predominantly White. Didn't this show a racist element to their firm as it did to me any many others? They terrorised us. I was very young at the time and I was shit scared of the Zulus. Fortunately, I was one of the lucky ones who always managed to get away in time, however, many others were not so lucky. I even know of Villa fans who stopped following the Villa away by train and instead went by coach due to the consistent bullying from the Zulus at New Street Station. You see I do not mind admitting that 99% per cent of worldwide serial killers are White – that is a fact and one I admit to. Then again, it needs pointing out that 99% per cent of muggings of innocent, defenceless White Villa fans at New Street Station (and the surrounding streets) were carried out by Black lads associated with the Zulu Warriors. I am not one to be politically correct; I say things as I see it.

The timing could not have been more perfect for the Zulus, as the Leeds riot in 1985 gave them the reputation they yearned for. It also followed suit with the rise of the Black culture in Birmingham. This promotion came from all angles, most notably with Black musicians becoming a force in the music industry and it was suddenly fashionable to be Black. This resulted in a huge recruitment drive in Birmingham, and everybody wanted to part of the Zulu Warriors. Black lads who had never even stepped foot in Small Heath were suddenly calling themselves Zulus, and lads who couldn't even name what the ground was called, or name a player, were calling themselves Zulus. I knew of a number of Black youths who supported Liverpool, Man United, Arsenal etc – yet on match day would link up with the Zulus to try to make a bit of money. Even some Villa fans turned to the Zulus when they came to force. Maybe they could not handle them or just wanted to look fashionable and part of the new 'in scene'. I felt so disgusted at these people; you do not change your club for no reason. It suddenly became very dangerous being a Villa fan in or around town. If we went for a drink in the city centre we had to be very careful where we went; it is fair to say I hated Birmingham City Football Club and the Zulu Warriors. Still do to this day.

The Noses really did have things sown up. In addition, many White lads were scared of Black lads because of their reputation which resulted in the Zulus having the total run of Birmingham City centre. Anyone who says any different is a liar. The C-Crew down the Villa had disbanded and apart from the second division season in 1987/88, the Zulus to my knowledge faced little if any opposition. I sometimes wonder if the C-Crew would have kept it together for longer would the Zulus of had it so easy. But the fact of the matter was the Villa could not handle them when they had managed to recruit a large part of Birmingham's Black youth. To some people this is a taboo subject that should not be raised, nonetheless, it needs pointing out. I am not saying Blues did not have many Black lads who were passionate about the club as they did. A number of them were Birmingham City through and through. With what we faced up town for a number of years I am surprised that not every White Villa fan ended up in a right-wing group. The Blue noses if anybody set the racial divide between the clubs – not the other way round as they like to have people believe.

Getting back to their sheer bitterness towards the Villa you only have to read their book Zulus to see right through them. As well as calling The Hardcore a racist firm, there was a comment from a leading Zulu saying that the C-Crew were also a racist firm. This was a cheap shot at the C-Crew who had no way of preventing this lie from going down on print. Anyone with half a brain knows the C-Crew had a large number of Black lads in the firm. You only have to mention some of the leading faces in the C-Crew to know this was a lie. Black Danny was one-half of the leadership with Paul Brittle. Now I am sure his name Black Danny gives away his racial background. He eventually became public enemy Number 1 in the eyes of the Zulus when they got it together. The Blue noses really scrapped the barrel with this lie and showed themselves up for the hostility they hold against the Villa.

Another annoying, but not surprising habit with the Zulus is their selective memory when it comes to Villa turning them over. They fall over each other lying about numbers and only want to remember things in their bitter, twisted eyes. They claim to have spent many seasons in the Holte End 'Taking the piss' – it's their words not mine. This belongs in the fantasy section at a children's book-store. The Holte End back in the late 70's – early 80's, during the height of hooliganism, held 28,000 fans and it was a rough end back in its day. They claim to have gone in the Holte End one season only twenty handed and came out unhurt. Does anybody really believe this? They also professed one Blues lad walked across the Holte End wearing a Blues hat and nothing happened to him apart from Villa fans throwing hot pies at him. I actually found that quite funny and it gave me a laugh – so thanks for that one.

One thing though that did stand out to me was they were forced into admitting whilst the C-Crew were around

Villa had the better firm. Believe me knowing Birmingham City this must have killed them. Although, it was a fact and one even the Noses could not avoid admitting. The lads running the C-Crew at the time were the likes of Brittle, Black Danny, Jimmy Coley, Andy Brown, Fordy, Joycey, Jimmy Ryan, Dewar and many more I did not know by name or face. They were a proper stand on front line and many of them were top boys as well outside of the football – without going into their private lives. They most definitely had the psychological edge over the Blues for a number of years as they were a proper organised firm.

During the 1982 season, tensions were running high between the clubs as Villa had lost their manager Ron Saunders to Birmingham City. It was one of the biggest ever shocks in British football history after Ron had guided us to a number of trophies; including the league title the season before. He resigned his post just after the Villa had qualified for the European Cup Quarter-Final. It was a huge shock as it happened so close to our European victory; to move to our local rivals was a killer. We worshipped Ron Saunders as he had turned our club around. I was only about eleven at the time but when my Dad told me we had lost Ron to Birmingham City, I am sure I cried? The game at Saint Andrews would see a full turn out from the C-Crew.

The C-Crew had plans to make their mark on this day and pulled off a major result at The Sty as some of us called it. The C-Crew met at a pub in the Highgate area of Birmingham to outflank the 'Old Bill' and were 250 strong; all top lads. Previous seasons had mostly resulted in them being rounded up by the police and escorted to the ground, but on this occasion things would be different. When the C-Crew reached the ground they paid into Blues home end

- The Kop. Their plan had worked and the police were none the wiser as to who they were. Villa firmed up in the Kop and were waiting for everyone to get in. I was told by a very reliable source that before all the C-Crew had managed to get in the home end the Blues and the 'Old Bill' had sussed who they were – in any case, Brittle had to make a decision to make their move now. The C-Crew charged right across the Kop, and the travelling Villa fans in the Tilton Road end still describe it to this day as total chaos as the Blues retreated. They clashed with Cuddles and his firm as hands on fighting began. Jimmy Coley was doing a lot of damage to the Noses (as per usual) as they scattered Blues across the Kop. The police eventually managed to round up the C-Crew up and threw them out of the ground but the damage had been done. This was a major result by a top firm and sweeter still at their hated local rivals.

I have mentioned this for one reason and one reason alone. Instead of the Birmingham lads holding their hands up and admitting Villa got the result, they played it down with what can only be described as blatant lies. They claim the C-Crew were in there too early. I never realised there was a set time you could take someone's end? Some of the older Villa lads told me the players were out warming up, therefore, it was not early at all. The Noses also claim it did not go off – it is enough to make you laugh. To that end, every one of the thousands of Villa who were in the Tilton away end who witnessed it for themselves are making it up? They have never done anything even close to this in the Holte End, so to save face they have done all they can to play it down. Moreover, they insist Blues did not have a firm in the Kop during this period, yeah right! Would there have been any embarrassment in giving the C-Crew credit for this one. It is not as though the C-Crew were not a rated firm. The Blue noses just cannot bring themselves to see past the hate filled venomous they have always held for the Villa.

Something though I will give the Zulus credit for is when they were on top of their game from 1985 onwards, they would show up at Villa Park even when Blues weren't playing there. This was during the years Villa had no proper organised firm, nevertheless, they still deserve a mention for doing this. Not many clubs would have had the nerve to do this. It was hard being a Villa fan around this time as the Zulus were so big in numbers as well as being very well organised. It seemed that when they really came into force all our top lads had disappeared for one reason or another. The rise of the Zulus really came at a bad time for the Villa and fair play to them they took full advantage of the situation. I am not saying Villa did not sneak the odd victory hear and there, however, they were very few and far between. We knew in our hearts that they were the better firm at that time; it was just one of those things. We learnt to accept that – I do not mind admitting I hated the Blues for way they used to bully us. They were animals when it came to the Villa; they really despised us.

The Zulus would always travel to seek out the Villa as they did at an England-Scotland game years ago when they knew Fowler and his boys would be up there; fair play to them. They took a good mob up to Scotland of Black and White lads and done the business. Unlike them, I do not mind giving them credit when it is deserved. I also remember another occasion at Coventry away – it was around 1985-86. Cuddles took his firm over to Coventry early doors to wait for the Villa Youth and had spotters at New Street station waiting for the Villa lads to board the train. When the Villa arrived, Blues were straight into them and ran the Villa everywhere. Like I have said , the Villa were scared of them and the sheer cry of the word 'Zulu', would have most Villa fans running for cover. That's how bad it was with them. They made our lives hell for a number of seasons.

That is why I could not understand it when some people did not like it when Fowler showed up. Villa had been going along for years with no top lad. Fowler had a fresh approach and a more fearless attitude towards the Blues and other mobs. When the C-Crew first hit the terraces many of the Steamers did not like them being around as they were stealing their glory. I felt this happened with Fowler. I heard on numerous occasions: "Who's this Fowler guy, never heard of him and he's putting himself up front as Villa's top lad". People who were no longer doing anything did not like somebody new coming along and doing something. Maybe it was because Fowler had made his name in a couple of seasons. That being said, he had earned his stripes by his actions not just words. Fowler had balls of steel and would stand on against any firm. He was not one to go around shouting about what he was going to do – he just did it. He tried to install into the Villa lads a bit of confidence and tell us we were as good as any mob. He totally rejected that the Zulus were too much for us. He would be forever saying: "Were as good as they are", and trying to build team spirit.

To the handful of people who did not like Fowler showing up I ask you this: "Was you happy with the Villa having no firm, and for a major second city club having no organisation ?". Fowler was just what we needed. Someone to re-shake the Villa back up and wake up a firm that had gone to sleep. I like many others, sat around for years waiting for one of the older well-known lads to deal with the problem

– but they never did. They had grown up and moved on; fair play to them. But we were crying out for a leader. From being a laughing stock he put the Villa back on the map. You only have to read rival firms books to see Fowler ruffled a good few feathers. I admit at the time there were lads who I would have put in front of Fowler to run the firm – old Villa faces that had been around for years that I had seen in action. For all that, none of them had the balls like Fowler to try to change things. He got people talking about the Villa again. He got the Villa that organised that we even went to Upton Park looking for West Ham. We came unstuck, however, it was a measure of how far he had took the firm forward. He also got Villa talked about on the England scene, and for many years took a mob of Villa to most England games. He deserves credit for this because putting yourself up as Villa's top lad your there to be shot down. Like Black Danny and Paul Brittle years ago he became a target for the Zulus – which was to be expected being Villa's main face. Yet fair play to Fowler – he took it in his stride. I am only saying things as I saw it myself. Some people may have seen things differently, nonetheless, I am just being as honest as I can be.

If Fowler had any faults (in my opinion) it was that he would be willing to work with small numbers – which I personally found a bit on top. If there were a mob up the road of say 100 lads he would be willing to face them with only 30-40 of our lot – sometimes even less. I called them 'suicide missions' but Fowler did not want anyone to take the piss out of the Villa. Even though I did not agree with this myself you have to take your hat off to Fowler for having such trust in the lads around him. Another Villa lad who deserves a mention is Tucker. When we started using the Adventurers, he was the one who got all the little clichés talking and looking upon our selves as one firm – instead of little factions. Tucker is also a decent lad to have a conversation with. My wife Karen met him up Sutton years ago and we had a few beers with him and his missus; she said herself what a nice lad he was. She hates all that football hooligan stuff, however, after meeting Tucker she could not sing his praises high enough. I know to some people he is just a football yobbo – but he's very easy to get on with and has time for everyone. Another lad who I have a lot of time for is Dandy. He is a cracking lad and it is always a pleasure to bump into him on match day. He's a proper decent bloke.

Other lads who I respected a lot – as I have mentioned before – were Reidy, skin-head Neil, Fat-Stan, Chris Jones and Luddy (just to name a few). They were the first Villa lads I got to know really well as I have already pointed out and they made me feel part of the firm even though I was not a top lad or anything. They were not the type of lads to look down on anyone. If you were Villa through and through, they accepted you. If you were not a front line hooligan it did not matter. The lads understood some people were not as up to the job as they were – it was never a problem. I must make it crystal clear not all these lads endorsed my right-wing views; they were football lads, not political activists. When Gary Reid died it knocked me for six. He was a cracking bloke and a hard fucker, but had a heart of gold. He would never see any of the lads without a drink, and you knew if he was there if any trouble came your way he would be the first to back you up. He was truly one of the best people you could have wished to have known. I cannot find the words to praise him enough. I am just glad I was one of the lucky people who had the pleasure of knowing Reidy before he sadly passed away. Even the Noses respected him. He was truly the best of British. I could go on and on naming all the decent lads I have met; it would take me forever. These people did not only become part of my life, Aston Villa was my life.

A close friend of over 25 years who deserves a mention is Ripper. He has been a good lad over the years and if he caught you with one of his hay-makers you were going down. He was one of the lads who could have maybe led the firm but he never took it upon himself too – he was just happy doing what he was doing. I have lost count the amount of times he has bailed me out money wise whilst sitting in the pub broke and we have ended up going home after a 12-hour session on his expense. That is what he is like – a proper bloke's bloke. He has also borrowed me money for holidays before; you cannot knock people like that. Mate's you know if you hit a hard time you can truly rely on. He is one of those mates who you know is only a phone call away and he will be there to help you in whatever way he can.

Even after all the bullying we faced during the height of the Zulu Warriors, two Blues lads deserve a mention. For a man who pulled together one of the UK's best firms at its peak and more or less kept it together for the best part of 25-30 years he deserves credit – and that is Cuddles. He really got the Blues together and achieved what he set out to do. You only have to read encounters from Britain's top firms and nine times out of ten, the Zulus will get a mention. I would never try to take this away from them. After the Leeds riot of 1985, this put the Zulus on the map and a large part of Birmingham's Black youth flocked to them as I have explained. They really took the piss out of the Villa for a number of years. Some Villa lads will try and point out Villa had no firm then. Even so, the Zulus did what they had to do.

In addition, under Cuddles leadership they had full control of Birmingham City centre and were a feared outfit.

Disregarding the savage attack I faced at the hands of the Zulus, I would not attempt to have a 'cheap shot' or play down that nationally they were a much-respected firm. My mate Paul a Villa lad from South Birmingham, went trough school with Cuddles and admits he's 'the real deal'. And 'Cud' as he is known for short, deserves a mention for getting the Zulus so widely acclaimed. Another Blues lad I had a lot of time for in the late 80's - early 90's, was Craig; a Black lad who was one of the Zulu Juniors at the time. I could not believe in the Zulu book he didn't get more of a mention as he was a right game lad and very active. But knowing Craig he was not the type who was in it for the glory like others who want their names plastered all over the book to bump up their ego. There are lads today at the Villa who have never heard of Craig, and I have to put them in the picture and tell them what a top lad he was as well as a decent kid.

For a while during those years I was using a place called The West End Bar, which was located on the outskirts of Birmingham City centre. Like many bars at the time the Zulus used the downstairs room on a Friday night; it was a good night out. The music was good as well, therefore, some friends and I would head there for a night out. Like always I never took my Villa badge off no matter where I went and quite stupidly left it on going into known Zulu pubs. It is just how I was – young and naive I suppose. It was only a matter of time until the wrong person spotted it and said something.

One night I was standing on the stairs having a beer when a mob of Black Zulu lads walked in and noticed my badge. The one lad instantly put his face right up to mine and was looking for trouble. I had brought it on myself by wearing my colours – as loads of Villa fans had advised me not to be so bravado in the city centre. They all surrounded me as the Zulus liked to intimidate any Villa fan. Fair play though to Craig, he stepped forward and told them to leave it out and that I was OK. He said: "He's been using here for months and he's no bother", and moved them on. Thank fuck for that.

Later on that night we bumped into each other in the toilet and I thanked him for helping me out. Not knowing him at this point, I did not know how he would be talking one to one with a Villa fan. But I must admit he was a spot on lad. He did not seem to have that deep anti-Villa hatred like the rest of them – if he did he never showed it towards me. He said to me as well: "If any of my lads come up giving you shit or telling you to take your badge off, come and see me and I'll look after you", and he then shook my hand. He had no attitude about him at all, however, at the same time lots of confidence. We actually built up a friendship for a few years until the bar closed and everyone moved on. We would always stop and have chat and he would always be on the look out for me. He was a proper decent Black Zulu lad who I ended up having a hell of a lot of respect for. I heard years later that he had moved up to being one of Cuddles generals which did not surprise me at all. In a strange sort of way, I was happy for him when I heard this because he was a spot on lad. So thanks Craig, even though it is now so long ago that he has maybe forgot what he did for me.

Some people may say I have no right to comment on the hooligan scene as I wasn't one myself or a top lad, but over the years I saw enough to know what I'm talking about. I have tried to be as honest with this chapter as I can be. Some may say it's bias and some may say it is full of bullshit

– which it is not. I have tried to be as fair as I could be without bending the truth. Even though these are obviously are my own personal accounts and other peoples will differ.

CHAPTER 11

*D*ue to my involvement with the NF, I was now a fully committed Ulster loyalist and had very strong views on what was happening in Ulster; Ulster loyalism is part of the NF ideology. Pretty much the same how the I.R.A had links to the A.N.C and hard-line communists and Marxists – one name Brian Keenan springs to mind. I suppose it would be fair in saying that to some people the NF was a gateway into loyalism. Whereas, I was aware of the situation in Ulster from a very young age. From my Dad telling me about the Birmingham bombings, then seeing IRA supporters placing posters all the way from Digbeth into the City centre – as well as not forgetting the endless bombings and shootings of innocent folk and the endless slaughter of British soldiers and police officers, I had developed a deep-rooted hatred for Irish republicanism.

Northern Ireland was something I had always found interesting due to it involving my nation – Great Britain. I was not an expert on the Ulster conflict, nonetheless, I certainly knew who's side I was on. I found it so heart warming that a land just across the water was so loyal to Great Britain and would do anything to remain part of the Union. Whilst at the same time the British government wanted to wash their hands of Ulster and showed them back no loyalty whatsoever. The government to be quite blunt were on the side of the Provisional IRA. No one will ever tell me any different. When I looked at how the majority of immigrants had no loyalty towards Great Britain, it filled my heart with joy as well as pride that the Ulster loyalists were so proud of their British roots and British sovereignty. I do not mind admitting by now I had developed an admiration for the loyalist paramilitaries and not only for their loyalty towards Britain – but for also taking the war to the republican movement. I also supported the Orange Lodges, but to take on the evil I.R.A more was required than a bowler hat and an Orange Sash.

Now before anybody throws the sectarian tag at me let me point something out. My mother was a Roman Catholic and my wife Karen is a Roman Catholic. All the more, Karen is an English Catholic – not an Irish Catholic. Would I have settled down with a practising Irish Catholic? Well, who knows if the right girl would have came along before Karen. But with my views regarding the Ulster conflict maybe it would not have worked out. I have had, and still have, a large number of friends who are Roman Catholics. I was never anti-Catholic. Some of the staunchest British patriots on the mainland are Roman Catholics. However, it would be fair to say I hated everything and anything Irish nationalist and most certainly republican. It is how my views had developed; I will not lie. The British government were not doing anything to crush the I.R.A; they were actually holding private talks with the Provisional I.R.A. As a result, I started to lean towards the loyalist paramilitaries.

Events in Ulster made world news again in a small village called Loughinisland, in County Down. The Ulster Volunteer Force carried out the operation. The U.V.F were the first loyalist paramilitary group to spring out of the Unionist community. The Loughinisland decimate showed how far the loyalists were willing to go to strike back at the republican movement. On the evening of the 18th June 1994 – 24 people were in the Heights Bar watching the Republic of Ireland v Italy game during the World Cup. Just after 10pm, a unit of U.V.F volunteers walked into the bar armed with assault rifles and opened fire. Six people were instantly murdered and five others seriously injured. The U.V.F had received intelligence that republican terrorists had been using the bar for meetings. The U.V.F claimed responsibility within hours of the attack.

The attack on the Heights Bar was in response for the shooting dead of three U.V.F members by I.N.L.A volunteers on the Shankill Road. This was how things were in Ulster. If the loyalists got wind that the I.R.A were using a bar they would touch for it. Sometimes their intelligence was right – sometimes it was not – but to both sides of the conflict it did not make a difference either way. The I.R.A had gained a lot of support from the nationalist community by killing innocent Protestants, therefore, the loyalist paramilitaries adopted this stance. I shed no tears for the victims of the loyalist paramilitaries as I knew most certainly no tears would have been shed for my people. The loyalist paramilitaries sent out a message to the I.R.A that for every Protestant/ loyalist that was murdered – retaliation would take place. Now I know this was brutal though the ends did certainly justify the means. Many loyalists simply looked upon this as retaliation which intensified the killings on both sides.

I was not supportive of the Ulster Protestants because I was a religious nut. Even though I'm Church of England, I do not live strictly by my faith. I supported the loyalists because they were fighting to remain part of Great Britain – it is as simple as that. But I must make it clear, I was never trying to take away the 'Irishness' of the republican/Catholic community. I considered the Catholics in the north as much Irish as I considered the Catholics in the south. Being an Ulster loyalist never meant to me that everybody resident in Ulster was British – how could you even dream of labelling the republicans anything other than Irish when that was where their loyalties lay?

Obviously, I leant towards the Protestant side of things, nevertheless, that only played an insignificant part in my eventual involvement. I was a firm believer in the Union and there would be no Union without Northern Ireland. I supported Ulster because it was a British cause, and I found it only right to side with my kin-folk. I know it is brutal and no one should support or carry out murders of any kind in the modern age. However, Northern Ireland was not a normal country. It was a country at war and because of this people will sadly be killed by accident as well as desire. To me the I.R.A did not seem to give a damn who they butchered and I ended up adopting that attitude.

After the attack on the Heights Bar, I am led to believe that the Mid-Ulster Brigade of the U.V.F had carried out the shootings with out clearance from the leadership in Belfast who were all for the loyalist ceasefire/peace process. Although, in the event of an 'enemy attack' the U.V.F units were given the freedom to retaliate against what they deemed to be 'appropriate targets'. This did not go down well with the Shankill Road hierarchy (the Brigade Staff). David Ervine from the Progressive Unionist Party, said that there would never again be another attack such as Loughinisland. He also added: "It was the worst day of my life". In October 1994, the

U.V.F and all other paramilitary groups did eventually call ceasefires. In July 1996, Wight's unit broke the ceasefire and carried out a number of operations – Billy Wright wanted to go on a full out attack.

Additionally, Wight's unit had previously 'pierced' the republican stronghold of Cappagh, County Tyrone. On 3rd March 1991, the Mid-Ulster U.V.F assassinated three Provisional I.R.A men in an ambush outside Boyle's Bar. Wright was quoted as saying: "I would look back and say that Cappagh was probably our best". The Cappagh killings in particular shattered the morale of the I.R.A East Tyrone Brigade, in a village that was a seemingly impenetrable I.R.A 'fortress'. Billy Wright took personal credit for this boasting that his Mid-Ulster unit had put the East Tyrone Brigade of the I.R.A on the run and 'decimated' them.

Wright was a political militant within the U.V.F and he publicly disagreed with the U.V.F. ceasefire, being sceptical of the I.R.A's motives behind the Northern Ireland peace process. Wright had also apparently denounced the U.V.F leadership as 'communists' for their left-wing inclinations and their public statements about reconciliation with the republican community. All the more, Wright had attracted considerable media attention at the Drumcree stand-off, where he supported the Orange Order's desire to march its traditional route. The U.V.F leadership eventually stood down Billy Wright and his Portadown Unit. He was expelled from the U.V.F and threatened with execution if he did not leave Ulster; Wright ignored the threats and remained in Northern Ireland. In response, Billy Wright took with him the majority of the Mid-Ulster U.V.F and formed the break away Loyalist Volunteer Force, who some people nicknamed 'The Loyalist Drug Force' due to their involvement in large scale drug dealing. They operated outside of the Combined Loyalist Military Command structure.

Shortly afterwards, Wright was back in jail serving eight years in the Maze prison. On the morning of the 27th of December 1997, the Irish National Liberation Army assassinated Wright inside the Maze prison. Three I.N.L.A volunteers armed with hand pistols undertook the operation. It was confirmed at a later date that the prisoners had escaped onto a roof to attack Wright and reach his part of the wing. The three I.N.L.A activists were imprisoned on the same block as Billy Wright. He was murdered as he sat in the back of a prison van whilst waiting on a prison visit. Rumours were circulating that Wright was set up for his murder as how could hand pistols have been smuggled into a top security prison. It is led to believe they were smuggled in inside childrens nappies.

An I.N.L.A statement read: "Billy Wright was executed for one reason and one reason only, and that was for directing and waging his campaign of terror against the nationalist people from his prison cell in Long Kesh". This brought Northern Ireland to boiling point again as revenge attacks were imminent. The L.V.F carried out a wave of sectarian attacks in retaliation. L.V.F gunmen opened fire on a disco in the republican area of Dungannon. Four civilians were wounded and a former I.R.A activist was killed. Police believed that the disco itself was the intended target with the intent to kill as many civilians as possible. Little did I know at this stage I would eventually visit the Maze prison myself to support a loyalist prisoner from the U.D.A/U.F.F. And after seeing for myself the security measures put in place, I firmly believe that Billy Wright was most definitely set up for his assassination.

Over at the National Front we stood two candidates during 1994 – fighting two by-elections. In June 1994, we fought for the Barking seat down south where Gary Needs stood against all the major parties. I had realised by now not to build your hopes up as results had not been very impressive during earlier elections. We obtained 551 votes – which was 2.9%. An improvement but still pretty poor considering the area. Then in December of that year we fought for a seat in Dudley West, in the West Midlands. As always we were promised many votes on the doorstep – but again we were let down by the electorate; we obtained 561 votes – 1.4%. The BNP fought an election in Dagenham, in June 1994. They put forward party leader John Tyndall who gained over 1,500 votes and a very exceptional 7%. The results spoke for themselves as to which party was on the up. The funny thing is a lot of us at the NF could see this for ourselves. Although, sometimes a loyalty to a certain party can be more solid than your loyalty to your nation. It's wrong as the country should come first, but many members were of the same stance.

I myself used to slag off the BNP, but at the same time secretly admire how they were pulling in some very decent results. I had a very strong attachment to the NF and to its name. In its former years it had been a huge party that had scared the living daylights out of the Tories prior to the 1979 general election – before the NF vote collapsed. I know of people who left the NF in 1982 to form the BNP, who were hell bent on pushing the BNP forward, even though at that stage the NF were the bigger of the two organisations. Party loyalties play a big part in this. Sentiment can play a big part in staying with a party you can see is on the decline. It is how things are.

At Villa Park even though our league form had dipped under Ron Atkinson, we had happened to reach Wembley against the mighty Man United in the League Cup final. However, let me rewind a little and explain about our exploits leading up to the final. We had drawn Spurs away in the quarter-final and everyone was going. A number of our older lads had experienced some trouble with Spurs before, therefore, this was a kind of 'revenge mission'. Tucker took a coach to this game and even though we were only 50 handed it was the bulk of the main lads we had at the time. By now, we were a very tight unit and all good friends. Gone were the days of little clichés here and there. We would also be meeting up with all the other Villa lads at Tottenham. When we arrived at the Park Hotel, it was full to the rafters with Villa's older lads. We had really come out of the woodwork for this one – there was a number of old-heads there who I had never seen before. I remember saying to skin-head Neil: "I don't recognise any of the lads in here". Neil said: "Neither do I and I have been coming down from the 1970's". This spoke for itself at the firm we had managed to pull together. Spurs had sent spotters down and would be turning up before the game.

As we all left for the game our firm stretched back for ages. We had hundreds of lads there. As we were approaching the ground, Spurs appeared from the dark of the night, however, they must have had the shock of their life to see the numbers we had pulled together. Spurs like the Zulus in the earlier round must not have been expecting Villa to pull together a firm like this. Moreover, once we grouped up and charged them Spurs were off. They never even put up a fight. We entered the ground really charged up. The atmosphere was fantastic like it always is at Spurs, and we won the game

2-1. There was about 6,000 Villa there that night and it was electric all through the game with rival fans taunting each other. Spurs had a firm in the stand to the right of us. Despite that, nothing happened inside the ground. At full time, we had reached the semi-finals and we were all ecstatic.

As soon as we left the ground running battles started straight away along side Park Lane. The police were out in huge numbers and tried to force the Villa off into a different direction away from the ground. We broke away from the escort and headed back to the Park Hotel which was closed on police advice. We all mobbed up again outside the boozer and decided to make our move. We headed back towards where we had bumped into Spurs before the game and we timed it just right as Spurs came into view. The confidence in us that night was brilliant. We were on a roll. Just like before the game when we charged at Spurs they folded and scattered everywhere. I could not believe this from Spurs because they were one of the best mobs to come out of London at that time. No hands on fighting really occurred, because both times Spurs just simply lost their bottle. They did not like being turned over by little old Villa. Maybe it is one of those nights they are trying to forget about; mission accomplished.

For the semi-final draw we had the easier of the two ties – Tranmere over two legs. We had fortunately avoided Man United. The first leg was at Tranmere. Just like Spurs away Tucker took a coach and the same 50 lads were on it. We really came together this season. Everyone trusted everyone and you were with lads you knew would not leave you. There were running battles before the game with the Villa coming out on top. Then the ticket-less Villa fans went to the home end during the game and ran a firm of Tranmere lads who had gathered there. We had now really developed as a strong unit. There were reports of trouble going off in all the surrounding pubs during the game, due to ticket-less fans from both sides having a piss up. The Villa lost the game 3-1, and Wembley now seemed a million miles away.

We mobbed up after the game and started to head back to Tucker's coach. A load of our lads had been arrested. We were all very down about the result, when suddenly a pub came into view. Skin-head Neil was not in the best of moods after his beloved Villa had been beaten – then what he did next I will never forget. He looked at me and said: "I'm going in – you up for it?" Now I know this might sound a bit far fetched but believe me every word is true. Neil threw open the doors of the pub and ran in. He was going mental and I was watching him through the pub windows; he was on a one-man mission. The Tranmere lads must have thought: "Who the bloody hell is this nutter?", and there he was all by himself steaming into pockets of lads. Neil's one of those lads when he gets put down he gets back up and charges in again. By now, our main faces had all realised the situation and our coach load of lads entered the pub to bail Neil out. Fighting started, however, it did not last long before Tranmere got proper turned over. It was a similar night to Spurs away; we had really done the business. Before we headed home we had to wait for the lads who had been arrested to get bailed. The laugh we had on the way home was brilliant, with everyone taking the piss out of each other. We all took it in turns abusing each other and I also got my fair share of stick. That's what I loved about The Hardcore away days – no one was above having the piss taken out of them – top lad or not.

In the return leg at Villa Park, we beat Tranmere 3-1 over 90 minutes, therefore, it went into extra time and penalties. The atmosphere at a packed Villa Park was as I have never experienced it before. These were the days the Holte End was still a standing terrace, and words cannot explain the tension in the crowd. We won the penalty shoot out and the Holte End entered the pitch – myself included. We had reached Wembley and the celebrations were crazy. We never gave a thought about Tranmere or their fans who were there in large numbers. This was our party day.

The after match celebration drink in the Adventurers was led by Gary Reid who was blasting out all the old Villa songs from way back before I stepped foot in Villa Park. If there was anybody who knew every single Villa song, it was Reidy. He really knew how to get the pub rocking. We were buzzing – Aston Villa at Wembley. The final would be against the mighty Man United. However, little did we know after our firms victories at Sunderland, Birmingham City, Spurs and Tranmere – we would truly come unstuck against Man United's Red Army.

CHAPTER 12

With Wembley now here our run up to final could not have been worse. We had lost the last three league games and confidence was terrible. The players had the Wembley jitters as some would call it. Nevertheless, to all Villa fans and lads alike this was the one that mattered – Man United at Wembley. No one likes Man United and us lot at the Villa were no different. Man United were on for the bloody treble and all that stood in their way was my Aston Villa. We all headed down on the Saturday morning because the game was on the Sunday. Me, Etch, Pip and Harold landed in some right shit hole bed and breakfast. At any rate, it was just a room to get our heads down after a good drink. We all met up in London – hundreds of us – and were soaking up the atmosphere and having a good beer or two. It was not like a normal meet up because everyone just seemed happy to be at Wembley. It felt more like a carnival atmosphere.

On the Sunday morning though I heard some of our lads had been turned over by Man United. They had been stabbed; that put a bit of a downer on the day. I should have known Man United's Red army would not have been lying low. You see, to Man United visiting Wembley it's nothing. However, to Aston Villa it meant the world and the occasion took over us. We made the mistake of taking the event too lightly as we would find out before the game. We were in a pub god knows where in London with a right party atmosphere going on when pockets of lads started to drift off to the game. I would have thought the best idea would have been to all leave together – but some wanted to get the game early and some wanted more beer. It is how it is on Wembley day; there is a real buzz in the air. As I was at the time, I stayed behind with the stragglers to get as much beer down me as you do before I headed to Wembley. Most football lads in their early twenties could relate to this. When we decided to leave for the game our numbers were very tiny – the bulk of our firm had gone. There must have only been 30 of us left behind.

We boarded the tube to Wembley all very drunk as you do on cup final day, and all in good spirits. The tube stopped at Dollis Hill station – its two stops from Wembley. Instead of it pulling off it remained there for a while. Some United fans were in a carriage just down from us and we could hear them singing. The tube had still not moved. We stepped off the tube to look how many United were in the carriage. Some verbals were exchanged and fighting broke out on the platform. We were holding our own at this moment in time, however, we were not aware that Man United's Red Army had firmed up at Dollis Hill. Suddenly, I heard this almighty roar – one I will never forget. What I witnessed I have never seen before, nor since, as hundreds upon hundreds of the Red Army poured down the stairs of the tube station. I have never seen a firm so big in numbers. There must have been a good 400 of them. It was as if it was never ending and I stood there open-mouthed knowing we were now in big, big trouble. We tried in vain to shut the tube doors as we knew by now we were in for a good hiding. They started to enter the tube and they were coming from all angles. We had nowhere to run if we wanted to. We were getting obliterated. There were that many Man United on the tube it reached a stage where no one could move. I do not mind admitting I had totally lost my nerve by now. As well as the hundreds on the tube you had the same numbers trying to get on. They were like a pack of wild animals. We could do nothing in retaliation. It was every man for him self as they gave us a good hiding. I instantly received a black eye.

The tube was that full the Man United lads realised they could not actually give us a beating anymore, therefore, they changed tactics. People were screaming – I was more than likely one of them. These were big lads in there late thirties; they knew what they were doing. They started to grab us and try to gouge our eyes out – it was horrific. Some lad who got hold of me I will never forget the look on his face – he really wanted to kill me. These were no drunken football fans – these were Man United's Red Army and they were on a mission. I remember seeing Carl Clinton on the floor with bodies all over him. It was unbelievable. Then skin-head Neil who was only yards away from me got his ear bit off. I witnessed this happen and it honestly knocked me sick. The anger on the lads face was shocking as he sunk his teeth into Neil's ear and tore it off. As all this was going on, the Man United lads outside of the tube who could not get on were trying to put the tube windows through. Not that if they had done so there was any room to get on. I just folded my head in my arms as the nightmare continued. I have never been so scared in my life. It was even worse than when the Zulus turned us over at Villa Park.

I cannot honestly say how long it went on for, but it seemed like an eternity. Then suddenly the tube started to move off. The hundreds of Man United on the platform missed the tube because it was so full. As it left the station it was total mayhem and I was lucky I still had my eyes in place. Neil was not so lucky with his ear missing and blood gushing from the wound. Someone from the Man United Red Army then shouted something and like magic it all stopped. I guess they could see we had already had more than enough. They had destroyed us. From a total full-blown attack they suddenly stopped. The lad who gave the order was obviously in charge. This will sound crazy but he even started talking to one of our lads as if nothing had happened. It was all very surreal. I can remember me and Carl Clinton looking at each other as if to say did this really happen. I was in total shock – so was everyone else.

When we arrived at Wembley, I fully well expected a good kicking as we left the tube as the atmosphere was still moody. But as Man United's lads left the tube it was as if nothing had happened. Some of them even shook our hands. I watched them walk off and Christ what a mob it was. They had no passengers with them on this day. Admittedly, we did not have the numbers, nonetheless, our full turn out would not have handled this lot. To anybody who says they do not rate Man United, try meeting this firm that we bumped into.

We walked up Wembley way still not talking after what happened; we were not expecting that. Skin-head Neil went off to try to get his ear sorted. It was only then I realised the inside of my mouth was cut and it was bleeding heavily. But no time to get that sorted as the Villa were at Wembley. The bleeding eventually slowed down but I had to keep swallowing the blood that what was building up in my mouth. I did not go and get it looked at because I did not want to miss the game. For the second time this season I had put myself in very dangerous situations – first with the Zulus and then Man United's Red Army. I knew deep inside this had to stop. We won the game 3-1, and it was brilliant to see the Man United end empty before the full time whistle had even blown. No one gave us a chance – Ron Atkinson had pulled off a miracle. The celebrations were superb. Even in the pubs afterwards there were no Man United fans about. It was as if they had sloped off home sulking because Aston Villa had stopped their treble. After what had happened before the game I was happy just to have a drink with a couple of mates. I was still shook up; I do not mind admitting.

When I arrived back in Birmingham on the Monday afternoon after stopping the night in London, Karen had somehow found out about what had happened before the game. My black eye didn't help either. I sometimes wish I had settled down with a dumb-ass bird as Karen is one of those girls where nothing gets past her; she is very switched on. You can't get away with anything. She was furious about me putting myself in such a situation again as she had every right to be. She said how would I have felt if it had been her. She reminded me of what happened to Jamie with the Zulus, and was I that stupid to forget that. I could not argue back as I knew she was right. I know a lot of people will relate to this and admit you do things and take risks at a certain age, which when your older you would not do. I would however in the next year or two finally realise what I was doing was wrong.

By now I had climbed the ladder in the NF and was trusted with responsibilities. Norman Tomkinson had appointed me Birmingham Branch Organiser. I was living for the party and pushing everything else aside including my family. It's how its gets you. Let me state though I never considered myself a football hooligan. I was a political activist who just travelled to Villa games with the main faces. My roles consisted of writing to people sending in for enquiries, contacting members asking for information, meeting up with new members, arranging leafleting sessions and booking halls for meetings – the list was endless really. This was always under the guidance of Norman. He has given his life to the British nationalist cause. He has been a member of the NF for nearly 40 years.

The one letter of enquiry around this time stood out to me from the rest and showed the uphill battle we faced as patriots. Norman passed onto me a letter from a man in Bristol who wanted the NF to give him a call due to receiving nightly trouble from a local gang of Black youths. I was asked to call him urgently as he had also been onto our headquarters, which at the time was in London. I called him on the night and I was amazed how the phone call went. He started by telling me how this local gang was making his life hell and he wanted something doing about it; he guessed the NF was his only option. I then asked him would he like to receive an information pack, or attend a meeting nearest to his home at one of our local branches. He shouted down the phone a very firm: "No nothing like that". As a result, I questioned would he like to donate to our party. Once again, he replied: "No you don't understand". I started to ask what he actually wanted from us after explaining some of our policies.

He wanted us to send a gang of lads down to protect his property during the night. I explained that we were a political party and not a vigilante group, even though we sympathised with his problem. I put forward to him why didn't he stand for us at the next wave of council elections and express his concerns through the ballot box. His answer knocked me for six. He said: "I don't agree with the National Front and I certainly would not stand or vote for you, but I thought on this one you could help me out. I have always voted Labour and always will". I just hung up the phone. This man wanted us to do his dirty work without even supporting us back, then go and vote for the party that had brought the problem to his doorstep in the first place. Everyone I told about this was gob-smacked but to be honest looking back now it should not have been surprising. People never cease to amaze me.

Another occasion that I still recall to this day was booking us a hall under a false name for a Birmingham branch meeting. We had to book our meeting venues under false names due to no one would allow us to hire their premises; so much for democracy. The funny thing is the same halls that refused us were only too pleased to allow the I.R.A and their communist supporters to hold meetings there. This was a fact – and one we tried out for ourselves. The halls and function rooms who had denied the NF were phoned up by a bogus caller from the NF making out we were the I.R.A wanting to hire their premises for a republican fundraiser. We were never refused, nor questioned about what would be happening during the meeting. Moreover, let us not forget all this was happening in good old democratic England. We obviously never booked the halls but this is an example of what we were up against. Therefore, we had to resort to using cover names.

Getting back to the meeting, we used the name of a fishing club as cover and everything was going to plan. It was upstairs in a community centre. There was nothing going on downstairs as we headed upstairs. During the meeting we heard voices downstairs and gathered the downstairs room had also been hired out. There was a huge staircase and two doors separating us, therefore, there was no chance of them seeing us or even knowing we were there. We did not really take much notice of it to be honest. As we left after the meeting had finished we had to walk through the downstairs hall and a huge group of mainly Black and Asian kick boxers were training away. They were all very big fit lads – obviously not knowing that upstairs the NF had been holding a meeting. I dread to think what would have happened if they would have known. Not that we were there for trouble, having said that, I am sure if our presence would have been known it would certainly not have gone down too well; we got away with that one.

At the next meeting though things would take a turn for the worse. We hired the upstairs room again and every thing was going to plan. Suddenly, there was a knock on the door. I instantly thought it was the kick boxers who had found out we were the NF. I do not mind admitting my nerves went; so did everybody else's. Norman and I went the door and thankfully a little old White man was standing there – relief. Although, we had made the mistake of booking the hall as a local fishing club. Little did we know that the manager who ran the hall was a keen fisherman himself and now wanted to attend our meeting. The problem was none of us knew anything about fishing to try to lie our way around it – I quickly put on my thinking cap and told him it was strictly members only. He carried on the conversation standing in the entrance of the door telling us where he had fished and what he had caught.

He must have noticed we were totally lost in the conversation. The walls were all decorated in Union Jack flags, St George flags and an Ulster flag, which he could certainly see by now. Our cover story was falling to pieces by the second. If only I would have used any other name we would have been all right. It was typical of our luck with booking halls for meetings. We eventually managed to nudge him out the door to finish the meeting. You could tell from his face our cover was blown and not only that, we had the kick-boxers downstairs to worry about. I did not want to play the big hero and put our members under any threat, therefore, we ended the meeting and made our move to get away. Except for we still had to walk downstairs and get past the kick-boxers. I wondered if the manager who ran the hall had tipped them off as to who we were but there was no way out apart from this one exit.

Heads down, we walked down the stairs quietly and thankfully we could tell the kick-boxers were none the wiser as to who we were. Some of them even politely nodded their heads as to say goodbye and I was only too grateful to do it back. We had got away with that one again and had a chuckle to our selves as we reached outside. Despite that, we were now in the same situation as before – having nowhere to hold our Birmingham branch meetings. This carried on for years –finding a place then losing it. It became normal. We eventually found a place in Dudley Port in the Black Country who knew who we were and did not mind renting us their upstairs lounge. To them it was a night's taking at the bar and we brought them no hassle. The sad thing was we now had to drag our Birmingham members over to another part of the West Midlands to hold a Birmingham branch meeting. All other avenues had been exhausted. Now do not forget Birmingham is a big place and Great Britain likes to preach it is a free country. Why did a perfectly legal political party have to move out of its home city to hold meetings? Why was the I.R.A who had actually bombed Birmingham more welcome in Birmingham than the NF? The BNP had the same problems years ago. I used to call this the 'democracy of hypocrisy'.

Our masters had put us in this position where being proud to be British was regarded as a sin, and to oppose your nations murder was looked upon as a crime. Even though we still operated as Birmingham NF we had been effectively forced out of our own city.

CHAPTER 13

*D*uring the years involved in our patriotic movement I have spoken to many people, to try to find out what their thinking – and you know something. The majority of people do not like what's going on. I have never known a time when there was so much distrust towards politicians. Such a feeling that our country was heading in the wrong direction. In addition, that something has to change. If all these people I were speaking about where prepared to act – things would change. And the crowd of traitors that have been ruining this country would not be in power much longer. However, most of these people do not act and the country continues to decline. You may be one of these people I am referring to. You may feel as British nationalists do that things have gone very wrong in Great Britain. Perhaps you are one of the millions who do not think it is your job to do anything about it. That it is somebody else's job? You may feel that you are not 'cut out' for politics. You may feel that after years of being sold down the river it is not something you would ever bother with. That it is a 'dirty' occupation and you do not want to dirty yourself by getting involved. You may also feel powerless. What can I do to change Britain's course? That the people in power are too strong and that they have it all sown up. What can everyday people like yourself do to fight back? All these attitudes are understandable, as I was once in that position myself – not feeling it was my duty to get involved.

When I was growing up in Birmingham the place back then was a nice place to live. It was clean, safe to a large degree and had tight-knit communities. There seemed to be none of today's problems like poverty, high unemployment, race riots and crime. In the 1970's, and up to the late 1980's, Birmingham was a city with character and pride – today it's bland and soulless. I always had an interest in politics but only to a certain degree. I was too much into my fixation for Aston Villa to care about politics. At school, there were never political debates. I always looked upon politics as it was for 'other' people. I remember though as a kid watching the news and seeing British soldiers fighting in the Falklands, as well as being murdered by the I.R.A. I can recall seeing them in their uniforms and realising that they were fighting for our country. In addition, I guess that triggered me off to becoming aware of my country and what it stood for. I frequently watched the news as well as reading my Dad's newspapers, and even though I was very young, I knew something was not right. This never came from my parents as they were staunch Labour. The more information I took in the more I could see was wrong. This was solely my own opinion; I was never pushed into this way of thinking. At this stage, the last thing I ever thought about was getting involved in politics; I was too young for a start. It seemed confusing and frightening. The problems I could see where still problems for the politicians to sort out whilst I got on with following the Aston Villa results on match day.

As I started to grow up the problems I could see just started to get worse. I was by 'natural instinct' very patriotic and I could see we were in rapid decline. I thought though that someone would come along from the main parties – take control of the country – and change course. I waited and waited thinking surely these clever politicians could see what's going on and they will soon put it right? Nevertheless, it did not happen. And as time passed by things just got worse. I started to examine the main political parties and the more I looked the more I became concerned. It soon became obvious that no one from the main parties was going to do anything about Britain's problems. They all struck me as the same party with different colour rosettes on. As I left school and started work, I knew that something had to be done. I looked back on Birmingham when I was a child and how it had declined, and I realised that it was time for me to try and help change things. Even though that thought seemed out of character and a touch uncomfortable back then. I could not any longer hold my anger back at what had happened to our great nation. Having said that, I did ask myself – what could I do? To that end, I do understand people being hesitant about getting involved as I was once in that position myself.

I eventually joined the National Front because they shared my concerns and wanted to change the things that I wanted to change. It was as simple as that. It was not as though I had not given the other parties a chance – I had; they had failed us miserably. I have never regretted taking this step. Our struggle has been hard with set backs along the way, and victory as it stands is still nowhere near in sight. In spite of this, we have managed to awaken from their slumber a huge number of our fellow compatriots. Moreover, do not be fooled by brainwashing communists. This number is growing every day – every-week. More and more people now agree with us than ever before. Maybe more that in anytime in our history as a nation. Being involved in British nationalist politics you no longer feel the frustration of seeing everything in Britain fall apart whilst doing nothing. It gives you that sense of pride that you are doing something. You are fighting back for your country. I did not start out in life intending to get involved in politics – situations made me get involved. I felt a duty to act and to save my nation. I have never regarded immigrants as the problem. To me the problem was the politicians who had betrayed us. And I will say it again – it is not the immigrant that is the enemy. The immigrant is just a victim – a tool of the whole process. The enemy is the White traitors who rule us today. The true nationalist fights not because he hates the one in front of him but because he loves those behind him.

We had fought two world wars apparently for our freedoms, yet now governments have surrendered that freedom to Europe. The European superstate is a farce; national identities remain stronger than a common European identity. No one can honestly tell me that there is not an anti-British and anti-White agenda to halt our growth and keep our people down. I will stand by this until my dying day. The media have poisoned our people's minds about being proud of who they are. And at the root of it all lies past and present governments who claim to represent us. They are all the same – they are all to blame. Our masters would like us to think we are powerless and to roll over and die. The reason we face such a hostile media is that we refuse to do that. Do not expect the ruling parties to put us over in a good light when we threaten to rise and replace them. If people are determined enough, they can make their voices heard. If we organise together and take action – we can make a difference.

If your one of those people who assume that say maybe the Tories will come around and look after Britain's interests – I will tell you this. The rot in this party – like the other mainstream parties – is too deep. Those at the top whose lives are comfortable will never try to change things. Do not expect a rebellion against the system from within the system. There are too many people whose bread is buttered to give a damn. Too many comfortable careers at risk. They have opted for the quiet life and they simply will not change. Why bother to actually govern when you can just brainwash people into thinking you do? I will give you an example of this. Michael Fallon from the Conservative party made a comment about certain parts of the UK being 'under siege' and 'swamped' by immigrants; all well and good. However, after speaking his mind he was forced into retracting his statement and said he had been 'misquoted'. These orders without a doubt came from the Conservative leadership. Shortly afterwards David Cameron said he looked forward to the day that Britain had an Asian Prime Minister; are you getting the picture here?

It is an absolute certainty we get hammered in the media because the system fears our potent and appealing message. If we were not a threat they would leave us alone. Another point I must make is how we get the racist tag thrown at us, and how the media condemn us for labelling all immigrants under the same banner – which in modern British nationalism is no longer the case. Nonetheless, lets look at this another way. When the media print an anti-NF/ BNP story they do not just single out just certain members in our party who may have made a silly statement years ago –they print a story condemning us 'all'. They don't just say certain things about certain individuals – they have a go at the entire membership calling us 'Nazis','fascists','racists' and 'yobbos. Isn't this doing exactly what they accuse us of doing? They do not personally know the whole of our membership, despite that, it does not stop them from putting us all under the same 'racist' banner. It is the double standards of the people in control of the media and the government. The only people who are mad at you for speaking the truth are those people who have been lying to the electorate.

Now I will touch on a very taboo subject. Maybe even more taboo than the immigration issue itself – the slavery days. Yes we all know Black people where put on ships in chains and sold to the highest bidder; that was wrong. On the other hand, some facts need pointing out. Jews ran most of the American slave ships and American slave-markets. However, no one points the finger at the Jews because to do so you are immediately accused of being 'anti-Semitic'. When the transatlantic slave-ships docked at the African slave markets to buy slaves, they purchased slaves who were already slaves. It was the Arab Muslims and Black Africans themselves who captured members of rival tribes and took them to the coastal slave-markets to sell to the Whites and the Jews. White people did not go into Africa and kidnap free Black people. They barely needed to get off their ships to buy the already captured slaves. The slaves were already at the slave-markets in chains.

White people throughout history have also been used as slaves, but hardly anyone knows about this as it does not fit in with the anti-White agenda. Africans enslaved 1.5 million White Europeans in the Barbary slave-trade. African Muslims raided up the coastlines of Europe, particularly the British Isles, but even as far away as Iceland kidnapping and enslaving White European Christians. The men were used as galley slaves and the women were used as sex slaves. This was far more brutal than working on a plantation farm or as a domestic servant. Wealthy Black people also had Black slaves themselves. In addition, the Black rulers from these nations sold on their own people. This is another example of having a pop at the White man and making us feel eternal guilt for something that was not entirely our own doing. It is another method to silence all resistance to immigration and to make the White man look evil. Britain and the Royal navy led the global fight to stamp out slavery, and we were the first country to abolish it. The Muslim slave trade in Black Africans was far greater in numbers and longer lasting than the transatlantic slave-trade. But despite this, it has been erased from history. In Mauritania, slavery was only made a punishable offence in 2007.

Due to all the anti-White slavery propaganda, some young British born Black men are brought up through no fault of their own with a 'bee in their bonnet' regarding the slavery era. For all that, the truth is if you go back to the 16th, 17th, and 18th century, there were far more English people sent from this country and used as slaves. Additionally, slavery was not strictly a racial institution; it was an economic institution. Moreover, if you were bottom of the heap, whether you were Black or White, you were likely to end up as a slave. The slavery propaganda gives some Blacks the attitude that British society owes them a living and 'special privileges'. Until the truth about slavery is out in the open you are always going to have an unstable multi-racial society.

Some people will not get involved or even vote for a British nationalist party because for example they have a good job, even though they 100% agree with us. People fear they may risk losing their job by getting involved in British nationalism. I have myself spoken to thousands of people who have directly told me this themselves, therefore, I know this to be true. At the same time, my opinion is that most of the time people use this as an excuse for not getting involved. It is their trump card out. They want the benefits of British nationalism but do not want to do anything to achieve them. If you really want to do something you will find a way, if you don't you will find an excuse. There are laws in our country against what is called 'unfair dismissal'. Moreover, most employers do not want to end up in court over this. The working person does have rights. There is actually more fear that people will lose their jobs, than there actually is real danger of it happening. This is once again another example of how the system has trained our people not to speak out.

Never let yourself be gripped by this fear. And do not let any employer intimidate you by playing on it. Despite that, yes there are certain jobs where it actually could land you in trouble. The police force, the prison service and the fire service for example – public sector work. But doesn't this make you realise that things must change in Britain? Why in a so-called democracy are certain things not allowed? Why is it acceptable to be a devout Muslim in the police force but not a British nationalist? Why not, if you leave your politics at the gate? Is there any point anyway of chasing a career however rewarding, if the country is heading for the scrap heap and there is nothing worth living or working for anyway. If you believe in something and you keep putting one foot in front of the other, and don't get caught up in having to defend your beliefs or worry about what other people may think of you because your saying something that's different. Then if you keep putting that one foot in-front of the other you will eventually get somewhere.

I had adopted the attitude by now that you had no right to moan about the state of affairs in Britain if you were just sitting by letting it happen. I have never changed my stance. The vast majority of our activists are not paid or in it for the glory. We do it because we want to save our nation. I have lost count of the amount of people I have spoken to who say they agree with most of what we stand for, however, they find us too 'extreme'. Although, when you ask them to single out what is extreme about our policies they are usually lost for words. Moreover, at the end of the day they cannot really provide an answer. I would like to explain this. Anything, and I mean anything, which challenges the existing government will be labelled 'extreme'. If you are trying to change the course of a country, name-calling like 'extremists' will be aimed at you. After all, by calling people extremists you avoid having to deal with their arguments. Consequently, they can frighten people off from looking at what we have to say. It is a clever trick but it works. It is all very simple really – just call someone an extremist and the debate is over; end of discussion. Our people fall for this trick every time.

Looking at things from another perspective perhaps there are certain parts of our manifesto that to certain people do look extreme. To a large part these would be the people who have been consistently lied to over the years and having the wool pulled over their eyes. People who run away from Britain's problems instead of facing them. There are two ways to be fooled. One is to believe what isn't true, and the other is to refuse to accept what is true. Anybody who stands up and says we cannot go this way no more will be shot down with the cry 'extremist'. We are saying we must take action and change course, therefore, some elements of society will look upon us as extremists. Our people have been quietly sleeping so do not expect any opposition or name-calling when we are trying to wake them up from their slumber. We have simply sounded the alarm bell in a country heading for disaster. In a lesser crisis, our policies may be considered extreme. Be as it may be, in the state we are in now they are essential. If we were to tell you otherwise we would be lying to the electorate like all the other parties have over the years.

Now let us look at word 'extreme' from a different angle. What Tory, Labour and Lib Dem have done to our country is extreme. Surrendering our cities and towns to the third world is extreme. Holding talks with Sinn Fein/I.R.A is extreme. Allowing British industry to collapse is extreme. Having our laws imposed from Brussels is extreme – with the majority of the British people still under the misconception that decisions are brokered in parliament. I could go on, and on and on. Living in Birmingham, I have seen over the years many organisations and institutes set up solely for non-White people. And they are never criticised or have the 'extremist' tag aimed at them. It is looked upon as the norm in a city where British people have been put to the back of the queue.

The only thing stopping millions standing up and saying no more and getting involved in British nationalism is 'fear'. Fear of being called names and upsetting some soaking wet left-wingers. Let me make another point perfectly clear. The Asian or West Indian does not by being born in England become an Englishman. By law, they become a United Kingdom citizen by birth, when in terms of realism they are still Asian or West Indian. Nationality is what people think they are – race is what they really are. The sooner immigration is stopped and large-scale repatriation is brought into play, the sooner will our people regain the will and purpose to take back our country's future. At any rate, how will we afford these resettlement grants? By stopping ALL foreign aid. Nigeria for instance has been awarded £1.5 Billion over five years. Yet, their oil revenues are enormous whilst their own people live in poverty as the British people pick up the bill once again. Africa has been receiving aid from Britain since 1929, and they have still not advanced. So where does all the money go? To the African war-lords.

Now getting onto 'diversity'. Diversity is a code word for 'White genocide'; pretty much so like the word 'anti-racist'. Those who claim an 'anti-racist' position in reality have a bigoted 'anti-White' agenda. This is backed up by the United Nations, which clearly states: "In the present convention, genocide means any of the acts committed with the intent to destroy in whole or in part, a national, ethical, racial or religious group, and deliberately inflicting on that group conditions of life calculated to bring about its physical destruction, in whole or in part".

People have been driven out of their areas due to mass immigration. We have lost our right to exist as a culture and a race in our own country. If multi-culturalism is something our people really want then why do we have 'White-flight' from every single area that the immigrants move into? In 2012, the UK government spent £8.5 Billion on foreign aid, yet in the same year 1.8 million of our pensioners were living in poverty and a further 1.2 million people were on the edge of hardship. Were well on the way now to spending, or should I say donating, more than £12 Billion annually in foreign aid. To make matters worse our government have withdrawn the breast drug Kadcyla from being used widespread on the

NHS because it is deemed too expensive. Shouldn't we should be looking after our own? There seems to be plenty of money obtainable for everybody else apart from the British people. Were not ashamed as patriots to appeal to people's feelings and to utilise those feelings into turning them into British nationalist voters and supporters.

There are even no-go areas for the police nowadays. If areas are too rough for the police to venture into imagine what it is like living there? People are forced to having to live in these areas due to financial problems in today's society. For the unfortunate few who have not fled the areas it must be a living nightmare. Even if our chances of gaining power were zero, it would still be our duty to get involved as our cause and fighting for your country's survival is only right. The future of our nation depends on us and us alone. If we fail, Britain will surely turn into an Islamic state. Anybody with their eyes open can see this. Let's face it – Europe is not an Islamic homeland. Muslims are not part of the ethnic make up of Europe but have arrived through mass immigration. Yet they demand that we indigenous British must obey their culture and Stone Age beliefs. We need to show the Muslim community that if they are to live amongst us, that any who actively support Islamic terror groups that they will be treated under the Treason Act.

History has always been made by brave people in sometimes small numbers, whilst the rest of the sheep sat back to see who comes out on top. All of us if were honest seek a deep satisfaction in living. Even so, the longer we live in a materialistic society that is going nowhere, the more most of us fail to truly find that satisfaction. Has there ever been a time when technology has been so advanced, including all the home comforts – yet really lacking in real contentment to make living all worthwhile. This is what happens when your nation has no direction or identity. Speak to people and truly ask them how they feel and I bet you I know the answer. We all have to get old and we all have to die. Nevertheless, are our people happy just growing old and watching the collapse of our country. I honestly do not think so. But we have chosen action instead of just sitting around grumbling. It gives us purpose, it gives us direction and it makes us comfortable to live with ourselves; knowing that we have chosen the path of honour. Above all, we are a family bound by blood ties – united in our common ancestry of a race who have given so much to the world. A warrior culture that has seen us prevail over our enemies for a thousand years. Today, you and I stand on the front-line. We owe it to our forefathers for every sacrifice they made to secure our native homeland. Our flag doesn't fly from the wind moving it – it flies from the last breath of every soldier that died defending it.

It has brought us together in a comradeship that we would never have found on the outside. One of the most important things in life is to have good friends who share the same ideals and same goals. We have found that in British nationalism.

CHAPTER 14

After our League Cup victory under Ron Atkinson we followed it up with real poor league form just as we had before we lifted the trophy. The four games following the cup win we never scored a single goal, and the great day out at Wembley now seemed a million miles away. The final game of the season was Liverpool at home, which would be the last time that the Holte End would be a standing terrace. The three games before Liverpool at home we faced three straight defeats; the team had gone to absolute pieces. Regardless, Liverpool at home was not just a normal occasion – it was to wave goodbye to the Holte End. Even writing this now it still saddens my heart that this standing terrace is no longer there. This was where I had spent many a year cheering on my heroes in claret and blue. This was where I had virtually grown up over the years and seen many a Villa player come and go – some good – some not so good. Nevertheless, my love for the club never faded. I'd had some great times and some low times. This was where you would meet up with your mates and have the time of your life chanting and swaying with the crowd. It gives me goose bumps even now to think back of the times standing on the Holte.

Many teams claim to have taken the Holte End. West Ham and Chelsea are two clubs I could mention; it's pure bullshit. They may have showed up in there for five minutes but as for taking it – well it's pure fantasy. Even the Zulus when they were 'on top of their game' never showed up in the Holte. The Holte End back in its day held 28,000 fans, so anybody with half a brain can work this out – it was too big of an end to ever be taken. It made Liverpool's Kop and Man United's Stratford End look tiny in comparison. That being said, Glasgow Rangers had taken it in the 1970's. It was a pre-season friendly and Glasgow Rangers brought about 25,000 fans. They arrived the day before and not only took over Aston but most of Birmingham City centre. The local newspapers for two days jumped on this invasion and it made headline news. I was told the Rangers fans were simply unstoppable.

The problem was on the day of the match when the Villa fans arrived to enter their beloved Holte End, it had already been taken over by the Glasgow Rangers fans. This obviously did not go down to well with the Holte Ender's. However, there was nothing they could do to move them on. Rumour had it that thousands of Rangers fans had got into the Holte End during the night to take up shelter. The standing terrace was awash with empty whisky bottles and empty cans of beer. Word spread about this, and the Villa lads had to take up position in the Trinity Road end to try to make a stand. The Villa had managed to get together a little firm to try to do something when all hell broke loose. A Villa fan suddenly opened up the flag of the Irish tricolour to try to stir up the Glasgow Rangers fans; he got his wish. This was like showing a red rag to a bull and the Rangers barmy army invaded the pitch via the Holte End. It was total carnage and the game was abandoned. But this trouble did not end here.

After taking over the Holte End and getting the game abandoned, the Rangers fans then went on the rampage around the ground. Local homes and businesses were attacked. A bus full of Villa fans was ambushed and people were stabbed during the mayhem. The Rangers fans eventually advanced into Birmingham City centre where the rioting continued. They had most certainly left their mark. I am not happy about no one taking the Holte End, but if it had to be anybody, I am glad it was Glasgow Rangers. Every club has had their end taken at some stage. Do not get me wrong, my love for Rangers comes a million miles behind my love for the Villa. At the same time, more for political reasons, I do have a soft spot for Scotland's finest. Glasgow Rangers have strong connections to the loyalist people of Ulster, so I'm sure you can understand my attachment towards them. Nonetheless, I will state this again – this is the only time the Holte End has ever been taken.

Getting back to the Liverpool game at home – with it being the Holte End's last time as a standing terrace some of us decided to go in the seats in Trinity Road so we could look at a packed Holte End for one last time. Sounds a bit corny but its true. Loads of our lads went in the Holte End, but myself, Kev Jeens, Barmy Barbell, The Clinton brothers, C-Crew Clive, Dave Kingham, and many others went in the seats. We did not intend to really watch the game; we were there to watch the crowd chanting and swaying. This brought me back to my childhood when from the Trinity Road seats as a young ten year old kid I fell in love with the club. Les wouldn't take me in the Holte End as he said it was too rowdy. It still gave me that same old buzz watching this huge terrace fill up – god what a stand it was. You can keep Liverpool's Kop. This was going to be our last time seeing the Holte End full to the rafters and it was a very emotional day. The game pulled in a season record crowd of 45,347. Villa won the game with two goals from Dwight Yorke, and to see a packed Holte End going barmy for the last time was brilliant. Other football lads will know what I mean about their own ends. It becomes part of your life.

As the game ended people would not leave the ground straight away as they wanted to hang onto their beloved turf for just that minute longer. We hung around in the ground for as long as we could until the stewards escorted us out. To say it was poignant would be an understatement – I was gutted. To be perfectly honest when they ripped down the Holte End, it totally killed the atmosphere at Villa Park; like at every other ground. A perfect example is Arsenal's Emirates Stadium. It holds over 60,000 fans, yet you can hear a pin drop. I think when they ripped the Holte End down they also took part of me with it because it has never been the same since. You no longer get those goose bumps, and you are lucky if the fans even sing when you score. All seater stadiums killed football, nonetheless, I suppose I am lucky in a way that I knew the Holte End when it when it was a standing terrace. Some kids will never know what its like to stand on the Holte End with 28,000 people swaying and chanting. I feel sorry for them as it was a life changing experience for me. Time moves on but even looking now at packed all seater Villa Park its just not the same. Football fans have now become nothing more than the controlled atmosphere decoration to help sell the TV product, as normal fans have been priced out of the game.

Like always at the Villa Park, winning a trophy heralded the beginning of a slump for the club. Our league form under Ron Atkinson had been terrible and had been carried over into the 1995 season. The only thing that stopped a fans revolt was he had brought us some silverware. But this was not enough for our Chairman Doug Ellis, and Ron Atkinson was sacked after losing away to Wimbledon 4-3. I was devastated to lose Big Ron, although Doug was more than right to relieve him of his duties as we were heading for relegation. Our new manager was soon announced. It was Villa hero Brian Little from Leicester City. Our fans were delighted as he was looked upon as a legend at Villa Park. At any rate, the Leicester fans were disgusted at him for walking out on them. The Villa fans had a song for him: "Brian Little walks on water". He was a hero to us as a player. Moreover, guess what was one of our first away games under Brian Little? Leicester away. The timing could not have been more perfect to make it a very hostile day – not only for Brian Little but also for the Villa Hardcore.

Leicester was always a rough place to visit. I can remember going there with the Villa Youth as a very young kid and seeing trouble all day. It was around the 1986/87 season. The Villa had a firm in the seats on the side and were fighting with the police during the game and ripping out all the seats. I can remember at full time a mob of very angry looking Villa fans breaking away from the police escort – it was the old Villa C-Crew who had turned out for this fixture. In addition, nothing has ever changed at Leicester. If you are looking for trouble you will find it.

On the day of the match as Brian Little walked out of the tunnel, it reminded me of the Ron Atkinson situation a few seasons earlier at Sheffield Wednesday. Brian Little had the whole ground on his back, with flags and banners telling him exactly what they thought of him. This was to be expected.

The 3,000 Villa fans were chanting his name and winding the Leicester lads up. The atmosphere for this game was as I have never witnessed it before for Leicester-Villa. It had a certain edge to it. It was very intimidating and at boiling point at all times during the game. The game finished 1-1 after a Villa goal by Guy Whitingham. It was a real moody atmosphere, and fair play to Leicester they made their little ground very menacing.

Most of our lads had not gone the game and Fowler and his mob had stayed in the city centre drinking. At full time Fowler and his lads walked back to ground and bumped into Leicester's Baby Squad in and around the terraced houses that surrounded Filbert Street. It was one of those places Filbert Street. If you did not know the lay out of the ground and the surrounding area, it could be dangerous and easy to get picked off. A huge punch up developed and a number of the Villa lads were arrested. The police were straight onto them and threw in the back of the meat wagon; no messing. As we left the ground little pockets of Leicester were everywhere and you could cut the atmosphere with a knife – especially when it was pitch-black come 5-30pm. This would not be the Hardcore's last run in with Leicester. Over the next few years if any club had the edge over the Hardcore it was Leicester. Home and away the Baby Squad always turned out for the Villa and had some victories along the way.

I remember a League Cup semi-final first leg at Leicester when they landed on a pub full of Villa and well and truly turned us over before the game. Leicester are well known for this. I can remember Fowler going mad at all the lads for not standing their ground; he really let the lads know what he thought of them. They used to also travel in numbers to Villa Park, and I can remember on more than one occasion them turning over the Villa lads at our place. I have a little soft spot for Leicester, because for a tiny club they have always had a little firm willing to give it their best shot against the bigger boys. They are a lot better outfit than their neighbours Derby and Forest that's for sure. The return league game at Villa Park was a nightmare. We were beating Leicester 4-1 with minutes remaining, when Leicester bagged in three goals in two minutes to make the final score 4-4. The whole ground emptied in shock – it was such a kick in the stomach. Everyone was that downhearted no one gave a damn if Leicester had any lads there or not. Everyone just went home.

Events happening over at the National Front would see our already tiny party split in two. This would leave the NF financially crippled. This happened during a bitter and corrupt split in the party in 1995. Our party Chairman Ian Anderson had been pushing for a name change from the National Front to the National Democrats. A majority of the membership wanted to keep our long-standing name and had not taken to this very well. A loyal member who had passed away had left the National Front £100,000 in his will to help advance the cause of our party. When this surfaced about the legacy, Ian Anderson started again his campaign for a name change. He claimed that by changing the name to the National Democrats we would avoid all connections with the NF name. And that we would shift the negative tag from around our necks.

To an outsider this maybe all makes sense, however, it was not all that it seemed. We had other suspicions as to why he wanted to change the parties name. I never trusted Ian Anderson and I was not on my own. From early days I could see right through him. Although I kept my opinions to myself as I did not want to be seen as troublemaker. It was well documented he had severe financial difficulties, and he used the NF to siphon off as much money as he could. And how did I know this? He had ripped me off a number of times regarding NF merchandise. He was the proprietor of Freedom Books which stocked all the NF merchandise, with every penny made going into his pocket – not the NF funds. Anderson was well known for accepting cash and cheques for goods that were out of stock – and for which he had no intention of replacing. A number of times I would phone him up asking where my order was and he would swear blind he had sent it out; it never arrived. Moreover, I was not the only one who was left out of pocket by Ian Anderson. To put it in a nutshell he was a money-grabbing bastard. He was running the party for his own ends.

A date was set for a postal ballot which not surprisingly would be sent to a loyal activist supportive of Anderson and the name change faction. Nearly everyone we spoke to wanted to keep the name National Front, and there was no way the name change faction of the party stood a chance; or so we thought. We wanted to get this over with then move forward under the name National Front with the help of the financial windfall that had fortunately came our way. A date was set for the ballot and when the results came in 72% of the membership had voted for a name change. We could not believe it. This was not what we had expected after talking to the membership and we could most certainly smell a big fat dirty rat in the background. All hell broke loose from the different factions as to how the vote was fiddled. John McAuley who was the deputy chairman, took with him the NF old guard and kept the name National Front; he saved the NF from going under. I liked John. He was a good British nationalist and had been around a good while. He was a Watford fan from Hemel Hempstead, and could deliver a good speech in his crisp, sharp southern accent.

The problem now was the £100,000 left to the National Front. You must realise that the money was left was to the National Front and not the National Democrats. The member who had sadly passed away had made it perfectly clear who the money was for. Ian Anderson took the money with him to bank roll his new adventure – and more than likely to ease his financial problems. Norman Tomkinson put the overall figure at £160,000. The people loyal to the NF did get some solicitors to look into challenging it and we had a strong case. But we simply did not have the money to fight it. We had been left without a penny to our name. I still think to this day what we could have done with that £100,000 windfall. Credit though to the likes of John McCauley, Norman Tomkinson, Tom Holmes, Steve Rowlands, Bernard Franklin and Terry Blackham and anyone else who I forgot to mention. They managed to save the National Front from going under.

Do not underestimate though how much damage this did to the NF. It totally split what was left of an already tiny party in two. With one half walking away with a nice little cheque in their back pocket and the people loyal to the NF having to start again from scratch. Looking back now this is the time that the NF should have ceased to exist and gone over to the BNP; that's my personal opinion. It was too much of an uphill battle after the split with the National Democrats. We were simply 'pissing in the wind'. The National Democrats as expected never really took off, and after fighting 21 seats at the 1997 general election (with very poor votes) they were already on the slide to oblivion. Its only little strong hold was the West Midlands, but all the leading figures left to join the

BNP in 1998. It never even put candidates forward for the general election in 2001, and by the beginning of 2002, the National Democrats had ceased political activity.

They reformed as a pressure group called 'Campaign for National Democracy'. The party officially dissolved after the death of Ian Anderson in 2011. Another situation arose from within the right-wing in 1995. Nick Griffin, the ex-leader of the old National Front who had been running the I.T.P (International Third Position) – a tiny pressure group – decided to put his support behind the BNP. Nick has had many fans as well as a huge number of critics. People who knew him from years ago had many stories to tell about how he had ruined every organisation that he had been involved in. Not being the type of person to listen to rumours, I ignored all the warnings I had heard about Griffin. As far as I was concerned he was a good experienced British nationalist and was a good appointment for the BNP; or so I thought. Griffin was also an excellent speaker and most certainly could hold his own in political debates. Nick Griffin would eventually become leader of the BNP and take the party to new heights before his eventual expulsion in 2014.

As the end of the 1994/95 season was coming to an end, Villa were off to Norwich and facing the threat of relegation. Even though the fans loved Brian Little this was the situation we were in. We all headed first to Great Yarmouth and had a good play up as you would expect. The highlight of the weekend was when Kev Jeens, C-Crew Clive and myself, shaved of Barmy Bardell's hair when he was pissed up asleep in the bed and breakfast. It was hilarious when he woke up with hair all over his pillow – but fair play to the kid he took it well. At the game itself the Villa end was rammed solid, and at one stage if the scores remained the same the Villa were down. Steve Staunton unleashed his famous left foot and scored a screamer to make the final score 1-1 – which was just about enough to keep us up. We celebrated at full time as if we had won the league.

The first game of the following season 1995/96, was Man United at home which would see me put my relationship to Karen on the line – and facing a football related trial at Birmingham Crown Court. I was about to take Karen and myself on a journey to hell and back.

CHAPTER 15

*T*he football season had started again and Man United at home it was – what an opener. I was now eager for the season to start again and being annihilated by Man United's Red Army at Wembley now seemed nothing but a distant memory. It's strange how quick you forget things. We all met up as per usual at the Adventurers – it was packed solid – wall-to-wall; you could not move. Man United had brought a huge following and would obviously have their Red Army somewhere about. We all went the game and it was brilliant. We thumped Man United 3-1, and the atmosphere was superb. We do not beat Man United very often at home, nor away for that matter. We really played them off the pitch. At full time we all met back at the Adventurers and it was party time. You cannot beat that opening game of the season buzz, especially beating Man United. We were all in high spirits after the game and I will admit I was very drunk. So was everyone else.

Suddenly I heard: "Man United are here". As I looked out of the pub window a coach had pulled up outside of the Adventurers and must have thought it would have been OK to drop in for a pint. It was not that type of a pub – especially for the likes of Man United. The pub emptied and both sets of fans clashed on the car park of the Adventurers. The fighting had already started and people were struggling to get out the tiny doorway as it was bottlenecked. How I wish I had been one of the lads who did not get out. I cannot remember who was getting the better of who, when a bottle thrown from the Man United mob landed by my feet. I was about to make one of the most stupid mistakes of my life. I was unaware that the police were now on the scene as I picked up the bottle and threw it back in the direction of the Man United mob. Next thing was I felt this almighty whack from two police truncheons on the back of my legs. I collapsed on the floor. Being drunk it did not take a lot to put me down. I was arrested and thrown in the cells overnight to sleep off the beer; I fell to sleep in no time. When I was released the following morning I had been charged with affray. Not being arrested before I thought it was a silly little old football charge which would be an insignificant punishment. How wrong was I?

When I received the police statements I could not believe what I was reading. The arresting officers had stated I led the Villa firm out of the pub and was the ringleader who pointed out the Man United fans for our fans to attack. They also claimed I kick started 'a full blown riot' which resulted in injuries. However, it got worse. They then proceeded to claim I picked up a house brick and was in the process of going to smash it over a police officers head, before the two arresting officers knocked me down with their truncheons. I was totally in a state of shock over this. I was planning to throw my hands up to whatever charge I was guilty of as I knew deep down I was stupid and in the wrong. The statement from the police was total fabrication. There was no way I could admit to all this.

I rushed up town to see a top solicitor and took my documents with me. We sat down talking and I asked if I was found guilty of this trumped up charge what would it carry. I informed my solicitor it was my first offence, however, he knocked me for six when he said to me: "Even with no previous, if you're found guilty it can carry about four years". I knew lads like skin-head Neil and Kev Jeens who had been arrested at the football dozens of times and had received just a slap on the wrist. Without my knowledge, I was unaware that times had moved on and the courts were now clamping down on football hooliganism and dishing out heavy prison sentences as a deterrent.

I was god-smacked. As I said, I was willing to hold my hands up to being in the wrong but I had to fight this. There was no way I was admitting to everything that they had tried to frame on me. I had a good chat with my solicitor and said there and then that I was going 'not guilty'. I could not believe the two police officers were actually willing to get a man sent down on a trumped up charge. I was not the first and I most certainly will not be the last. The two officers were willing to put me in a position where I could have lost my job, lost my freedom and most certainly lost my Karen. However, they did not care. They were as corrupt as you could get. And these are supposed to be the people who are upholding the law and meant to be leading examples for our communities. I know the police force faces a very tough job, and to a large part I respect them and support them – especially when you consider the politically correct handcuffs they have to work under. Additionally, my Mother and Father had brought me up to respect the police. But there was most certainly some bad eggs serving in the West Midlands Police Force and I had unfortunately came across two of them.

I kept on being sent to court and it kept on being adjourned. It was all ever so stressful and caused my depression and anxiety to sharply increase. It put a right strain on my relationship. All the same, it was my own doing. It was only a matter of time at the football before I got myself seriously injured, arrested or both. Eventually it went to the magistrates court and my case was transferred to the Crown Court as I had wished. A date was eventually set for the trial. On the day of the trial I kept it quiet from Karen and made out I had the day off work. Karen had told me if I was sent to jail we were over for good; can you imagine the pressure that had placed me under? I was terrified of being sent down. I am not going to lie – I have never been more scared in my life. With my political views I knew inside I could become a target. I stuck on my best suit and headed up town. When I arrived at court I met up with my legal team and had a final chat. I was very impressed with the team fighting my corner. The main man seemed to really know his job. My fear was why would the jury decide to back me over two so-called law enforcers? Police officers are largely respected from all sides of the community, apart from a section of the ethnic minorities.

I cannot remember which officer was up first, but I can remember they both put their hands on the bible and swore to tell the whole truth. That made me cringe as they was both hoping their lies would get me sent down. I suppose to them that it would be one less yobbo on the street. As they started to give their evidence they were obviously lying through their back teeth and my defence spotted a chink in their story and totally tore apart their web of lies. It reached a stage where they were saying different things about the same incident and were most certainly tripping each other up. I am certain to this day they never met up to get their stories straight. Anyone could tell they were making it up as they went along and my defence was onto every little slip up that they made. It actually became enjoyable to watch them make fools out of themselves and took away some of my severe tension.

I also had two character references to help me fight my corner – The landlord of a local pub I used and my boss at work Johnny Cass, who gave me a real glowing reference to the jury. When it was my turn to go in the dock I tried to stay as level headed as I could as not be drawn into anything that may put me in the frame. Anyone who has ever been in the dock will tell you its the loneliest place in the world. The prosecutors tried all they could to make me out to be this monster that the police had me down as. I honestly think by now the jury had already made their minds up. The police officers web of lies had been my biggest defence and the jury could see this.

At the summing up I had a good feeling about the result and after a short while the jury came back out and returned a 'not guilty' verdict. I was ecstatic. I congratulated my legal team on doing a fine job with my defence. The 'Old Bill' looked gutted; they had totally messed up. If they had played it fair I would have been only to willing to throw my hands up and admit to my charge, and save all the ball ache of Crown Court and the pressure of a trial. Nonetheless, they wanted their pound of flesh and fell flat on their faces. As I left the court, I went to meet Karen on her way home from work and surprise her with the good news. I caught up with her by the bus stop I expected to see her at and broke the good news. Even though she was happy at the outcome, she was still upset at what I had put her through – and rightly so. I knew this had to stop. It was not fair on her to keep putting her through crap like this. I had suffered months and months of depression and anxiety due to waiting for this trial to come around. Did I really need this any longer? Karen had forgiven me but she certainly had not forgotten. Who was I to judge her ill feelings towards me? Many other girls would have said by now it's over. I was not exactly being a good partner bringing her consistent worry whilst attending the football. I took a good hard look at myself and said is this the road I wanted to carry on going down? I also felt I wasn't setting a good example as a British nationalist, as how could I knock on doors come election time claiming we needed to be tough on crime when I was getting myself attacked and arrested at the football.

As for why lads like myself got involved with the football? Well, it was a lifestyle choice. A lot of people became indulged in the match day scene without necessarily going down the violence route – which kind of blurs the real meaning of what a 'hooligan' really is. I hate that term; it is so ancient. People have many stereotypes about the lads that engage in football violence, that for the most part is complete crap. Besides, the main reason that lads do it is because of the adrenaline rush that you do not get doing anything else. After all, most the time it is not even about the fighting – it is more about being around your mates having a laugh and taking the piss out of each other. Nine times out of ten when you attend the football, nothing happens. Some people have the assumption that if you travel with a bunch of football hooligans that there is trouble every week – nothing could be further from the truth. Most people that try to understand how hooliganism works focus on the fighting and hating the opposition. When to the majority of football lads it is about close friendships, trusting your mates and backing each other up as and when the situation occurs.

Do not get me wrong the lads who I was travelling with were known troublemakers, but that does not mean to say I didn't think of them as good people. Some of them would do anything to help the lads out. Even though, they liked a punch up at the football on a Saturday after working all week. They were not into attacking normal fans like the Zulus. They liked to battle with rival firms of lads. Many lads like myself got involved in the football because it gave you an identity and a sense of purpose and belonging. I will not lie – the days out were a good crack with the beer flowing and ripping each other to pieces. Landing at someone's pub early doors and taking it over; it all added to the match day atmosphere. No one can deny it doesn't give you a buzz – it does. But for me it had gone far enough. Just attending the games with the Villa Hardcore, I'd had two serious run-ins with the Zulus and Man United. Both times the situations had got way out of hand. I finally realised it was way over my head and I was not really cut out for it. I certainly was not cut from the same cloth as Fowler and Reidy.

If I had been sent down for four years it would have totally ruined my life. I still kept in contact with the lads who I had become close to, still do to this day. Additionally, I still regard them as good people. As the firm had become more organised the situations had become more dangerous and more regular. Not to mention, with the football intelligence being on top of things most of the time as soon as we landed at an away game we were rounded up by the 'Old Bill – which took the fun away as we could not shake them off all day. I had taken enough risks, therefore, I decided to put all my energy in saving my nation. This was not to say I still did not go the football any more as I did. Although, I would be content to go with just a couple of mates and have a quiet drink, and if I bumped into some of the lads better still. I no longer had any intention of going around with a mob knowing trouble was maybe only seconds away.

I am also not knocking the lads who carried it on. I was pleased that that Villa had got an active firm together under Fowler – which I will not deny. After many years of being bullied by the Zulus how could I look at things any different? But I no longer wanted to be putting myself in these situations. The Villa Hardcore name would carry on for many years, and even now Villa's younger new firm call themselves the Hardcore Youth. And they have carried on the tradition of being pro-loyalist. As the years progressed the Villa Hardcore became more and more organised and they had many high profile incidents that resulted in a number of its leading figures getting dished out heavy prison sentences – including ten-year football banning orders.

This season would also see us bring some more silverware to Villa Park, again in the form of the League Cup. Moreover, over at the National Front we would be making plans and pulling out all stops to fight the 1997 general election after our crippling split with the National Democrats.

CHAPTER 16

*B*rian Little had completely turned the club around after flirting with relegation. People talk about the 'golden era' under Marin O'Neill; don't make me laugh. This was a golden era for our club – we never won anything under O'Neill – and the highest we ever finished was 6th. Under Brian Little, we finished a healthy 4th place in the league which would now get you into the European Cup as I still call it. We had also reached the FA Cup semi-final where Liverpool beat us 3-0 at Old Trafford; oh well, you can't win them all. For all that, on the 24th March 1996, we beat Leeds United at Wembley to claim the League Cup yet again.

Rewinding a little, at Arsenal away during the semi-final first leg, major crowd disturbances had developed before the game at a pub where Villa fans had congregated. A mob of about 100 Arsenal lads attacked the pub which resulted in a 'pitched battle' taking place with around 30 Villa supporters. Lad's who were there said it was absolute carnage as the Villa managed to see off a firm that was three times their size. It is still talked about down Villa Park to this day. It proved to me you only have to be in the wrong pub at the wrong time, and then you are stuck in the middle of this mini-riot with bottles and glasses flying everywhere. You do not know if

209

some of the other lads are carrying knives or worse. Getting back to the final against Leeds United, I had travelled down with two mates; I just wanted a quiet drink. All our top lads were down there for the weekend in large numbers. I knew Leeds who had a fearsome reputation would have a firm out looking for the Villa, and it would only be a matter of time before they bumped into each other. Before the game, I was tucked away in a quiet little boozer miles from the ground. However, at the Green Man pub at Wembley it was about to explode.

One-half of the pub was Villa and the other half of the pub was Leeds – a recipe for disaster for a late 5pm kick off. The pub was rammed to the hilt and it was only a matter of time before hooligans from both sides would want some action. The mood suddenly changed and bottles started to be thrown from one side of the pub to the other. I heard it was just a shower of broken bottles and glass as the pub got thrashed. It took the police ages to arrive as the missiles carried on from both sides. News reports said around 200 fans were involved in the trouble at the pub, which resulted in 50 arrests – half from Leeds and half from the Villa. Though I was led to believe, Leeds shaded the pre-match violence. That was not my idea of a good day out anymore. In addition, after what happened against Man United two years earlier I just wanted to soak up the atmosphere this time around with no bother. There were flashpoints all around Wembley before the game, all the same, I never came nowhere near to any myself. I was simply down there to see the Villa lift the trophy – which we did after playing Leeds off the pitch; we thumped them 3-0. Brian Little's name echoed all around Wembley. It was amazing. This was what dreams were made of. It had been a great season for the Villa on the pitch and the club were on the up again. Moreover, more importantly, I now had my court case out the way and I could relax again. Happy days.

By now every political party had started making plans for the up-coming 1997 general election, and over at the National Front we were no different. The problem was we were left pot-less from the split with the National Democrats and raising money was very hard. None of our members or supporters were rich people, so we had to rely on what little donations came our way. We were not like the major parties; funded by big multi national businesses. To be perfectly honest to say we were struggling for funds would be an understatement. John Tyndall from the BNP had released a statement saying the BNP would be contesting over 50 seats at the 1997 general election, and targeting some wards they looked upon as BNP strongholds. We also knew the National Democrats would have money to fight the election after the split with the NF – money that was ours. Even though we had the most recognised name on the right-wing, we had the least money to put into the campaign. It's simply how it was.

Despite that, before the general election itself a by-election was called in Uxbridge, that would give all political parties a chance to see how their support was with the general election looming. John McCauley, who was now Chairman of the NF, put himself forward to show the country that the NF (even after all its problems) had not gone away. Then the shocking news hit us. As well as all the mainstream parties putting candidates forward, so had the BNP and Ian Anderson's newly formed National Democrats.

That hit us for six. The votes were going to be hard enough to obtain anyway with the apathetic British public – but now three right-wing candidates were fighting for the same seat. It was stupid. It has always been the same with the right-wing; putting candidates forward just too mess up a rival British nationalist party. I am not saying the NF were also not guilty of this – we sometimes put candidates forward just to try to stop the BNP getting a good vote. Its suicide. The BNP put forward a lady for the seat named Ms F Taylor, and the National Democrats put forward our old chairman Ian 'money bags' Anderson.

Come election night it was very depressing results for all three British nationalist parties with not even one of us even reaching 1% of the entire vote. The BNP came out on top with 205 votes, then the National Democrats with 157 votes, then John McCauley from the NF with 110 votes. We were all way behind the three main parties. I spoke to John McCauley on the phone the next day and he was very disappointed with the result. We did not like getting beat by the National Democrats, as that was a kick in the stomach. But results do not lie and these were the facts we were faced with. Nevertheless, before I get onto the general election itself, let me take you back to February 1996, and explain the run of events that made me take the decision to get involved with the loyalist paramilitaries of the Ulster Defence Association.

On the 9th February 1996, the I.R.A brought to an end their seventeen-month ceasefire with the Docklands bombing in London. It killed two people and injured dozens of civilians. It was total carnage and was intended to do as much damage as was possible. It also created an estimated £100 million pounds worth of damage. Thirty-nine people alone were treated in hospital for injuries sustained from the shattering glass. This was a message from the I.R.A to the British government that they wasn't happy how the talks had been going, and also showed that their army was still in place and ready to strike as and when needed to make themselves heard. The explosion left a ten-metre wide – three-metres deep crater. Three near by buildings also suffered from the blast which resulted in one being totally demolished and the other two needing complete rebuilding. As per usual, the I.R.A described the deaths as 'regrettable'. Heard that one before.

On the 28th of the same month, the Prime Minister's of the United Kingdom and the Republic of Ireland announced that all party talks would resume in June. John Major's decision on dropping the demand for I.R.A decommissioning of weapons cemented my opinion that the I.R.A were bombing their way to the negotiating table. The British government were once again showing themselves to be the weak and feeble people I had them down to be. I saw this as another slap in the face to the victims of the bombing, and another act of betrayal to the loyalist people of Ulster. Moreover, what happened the next day would start me on the path to getting involved in the struggle to keep Ulster British. I had always been a supporter of the loyalist paramilitaries but now was the time to get actually involved.

The day after the Docklands bomb, I had booked in an appointment at a newly opened tattoo parlour that had opened up just around the corner from my work place in Digbeth. I left work and arrived there early. He was running a bit behind schedule and told me he would be ready in about one hour to start on me. He suggested why didn't I go and grab myself some food or a drink whilst I was waiting. I said OK and left the tattooist. I actually fancied a pint of lager, but all the surrounding pubs in the area were Irish republican bars – the area was well known for this. The closest pub was literally two minutes away which was a very well known

I.R.A supporting shit hole of a pub. I suddenly thought to myself: "I'm going in for a look". And its fair to say I was curious as well as wanting to see what these scum got up to. As far as I was concerned this pub was in Birmingham, not Ireland, and I had every right in my own country to nip in for a pint – as much as I would not like the clientele who would be in there.

As I walked in I was obviously a bit on edge as I did not know what to expect. As soon as I entered the premises the Irish music was blasting out, which I worked out to be Rebel music by the lyrics. It was one of them bars where you could tell everyone knew everyone. I just grabbed my pint and sat down with my copy of the Birmingham mail. Whilst supping on my pint and reading my paper, I casually glanced around and all the walls were decorated in republican regalia. Framed pictures of ex-I.R.A volunteers were on display which I found very insulting considering this bar was only a five-minute drive away from where one of the bombs went off back in 1974. Despite that, it only got worse. The money on the jukebox ran out and some old guy put some more money in. When he had selected his records he sat down and they began to play. It seemed like the whole pub was joining in apart from me. Not that anybody was fortunately taking any notice of my presence. These were deep Rebel songs glorifying the I.R.A and mocking dead British soldiers. The whole pub seemed to come alive when they came on. It was sickening, nevertheless, I just tried to casually read my newspaper and hide my anger. You could feel the passion in their voice and their faces; they really hated any thing British. This was a proper I.R.A sympathisers bar without a doubt.

Then as the five O' clock news came on they had a giant TV screen on the wall. The music was suddenly turned off and someone shouted to turn it up as it was about the Docklands bombing the day before. I sat there just casually watching it like the rest, trying not to give away the pure hatred I was feeling. When the reporter showed the damage the bomb had done, as well as mentioning the deaths and injuries, they started to shout vile pro-I.R.A statements at the screen. This was serious shit. Nearly everyone in there was shouting something or the other and they were openly mocking the dead and injured. I was totally numb by now. Over and above, all this was happening in my home town of Birmingham. I remember thinking if they loved Ireland so much why don't they fuck off back there! I'd had enough by now and my worst dreams and about this bar had come true.

As the news ended the Rebel music came back on and the singing started again in full swing. Now was the time to leave – I had seen enough. I had just came across the most repulsive anti-British people you could have wished to meet. They were more than likely not I.R.A activists themselves, however, they supported the killings that were brought about by the republican war machine; not forgetting the ethnic cleansing of the Ulster loyalists. The people using this pub would have most certainly helped to fund their bombing campaigns – that did not take much working out. As I left the pub I said to myself that after the general election was out the way and I had done my campaigning, that I was going to try to get into contact with the loyalist paramilitaries of the U.D.A or the U.V.F.

Such was my anger, when I reached the tattoo parlour I changed my tattoo from a skulls head to a U.F.F Red Hand of Ulster tattoo. (Which was quite funny as the tattooist informed me he was a Roman Catholic). The following morning on the way to work I could not stop laughing as someone had sprayed on the front of the pub a huge 'U.F.F', in red spray paint. I obviously wasn't the only one who knew about this bar. My viewpoint on the republican movement was only further cemented by another I.R.A bombing in Manchester on the 15th June 1996. It cost local insurers over £700 million pounds and over 200 people were seriously injured. The police investigation revealed it was the biggest bomb ever detonated during what they considered 'peace-time'. The cowardly I.R.A released a statement claiming responsibility for the bombing. Yet again, coming out with their shallow call of 'we sadly regret injury to civilians'. To me this was bullshit. You only plant a bomb with one sole intention and that is to kill and cause as much destruction as you can – just like the Shankill bombing.

The total cost for the rebuilding work was completed by 1999, at an eventual cost of £ 1.2 Billion. That was why the British government were so eager to talk to the I.R.A without them decommissioning. It was costing the British government too much money when the bombs went off. And the I.R.A knew this only too well. The Downing Street declaration of 1993, had allowed Sinn Fein to participate in talks about the future of Northern Ireland on condition that it called a cease-fire. On the 31st August 1994, the I.R.A had announced a 'complete end of military operations'. However, as I have stated that had ended with the bombing of Canary Wharf. Regardless, my mind had already been made up to fight back against the I.R.A; the time had come.

At the general election of 1997, at the close of nominations the National Front had somehow raised the money for six parliamentary seats. Now I know this was not very impressive. In spite of that to know our financial situation after the split we'd had, we had done well considering. The National Democrats, who we knew would have a war chest to fight with raised 21 candidates. Over at the BNP they surpassed their target of 50 seats by fielding 54 candidates. I had not forgotten the earlier by election in Uxbridge, where none of us did any good. I used my head and did not try to build my self up only to get disappointed again. We had the usual media attacks that most certainly lost us votes. After all, with the far-left being in control of the media you sadly do not have any control over that. Whenever there's a big story in the media, look for the story they are trying to distract you from.

We had done all the campaigning we could have done for a tiny party and we had to work hard for every single vote we achieved. Little did we know at the time we also had another spy in the West Midlands NF who had been following our every move during the election – hoping to unearth some terrible story. It later surfaced he was working for ITV; for a programme called The Cook Report which was headlined by Roger Cook. Apart from some 'sloppy' and 'stupid' comments made from some of our less prominent members they had nothing on us. Nick Griffin from the BNP also had the same happen to him, and at the end of the programme Nick Griffin and Roger Cook had a political debate on a car park after Roger Cook confronted Nick Griffin about the BNP's policies. They additionally had nothing new on the BNP apart from the same old out dated claims of 'racism' and 'holocaust denial'. Moreover, Nick Griffin more than held his own when confronted with the state sponsored set up. Nick Griffin had his answers and gave Roger Cook as good as he got in what can only be described as 'ambush journalism'.

I was right not to set my hopes too high regarding our votes. Even after how active the I.R.A had been on mainland Britain during the run up to the general election – with the NF and the BNP campaigning partly on the Northern Ireland issue – the votes largely, especially for the National Front yet again failed to come in. Our party Chairman John McCauley stood in Beckenham ward, gaining 388 votes – 0.7%. Our two West Midlands candidates polled as follows. Walsall North – Alan Humphries, 465 votes – 1.1%. Dudley North – G. Cartwright, 559 votes – 1.2%. In addition, the other three NF candidates polled even worse. It just was not our night. The National Democrats who had the money to put forward more candidates with much better election addresses, failed miserably – so much for the name change. Ian 'money bags' Anderson had for a while fancied his chances of taking British nationalist politics into Northern Ireland, and he had put himself forward for the seat in Londonderry East. The result was terrible with only 81 votes – which was 0.2%. That was the National Democrats first and last venture into Ulster politics.

Closer to home, the National Democrats stood in Birmingham Ladywood, gaining 685 votes –1.8%. The rest of the National Democrats votes were also very poor and they were already on the road to oblivion; every single deposit was lost. It simply had not worked out for Ian Anderson and his name change party. Over at the BNP, even though they had also obtained some very poor votes they did extremely well in three target wards. Ms F Taylor, who had previously fought for the seat in the Uxbridge by election, was put forward for Dewsbury ward, and gained 2,232 votes – 5.2%. Party leader John Tyndall put himself forward for the seat in Poplar and Canning Town, and gained 2,849 votes –7.3%. And the best of the night was in Bethnal Green and Bow, where David King gained 3,350 votes – 7.5%. Those three votes saved the BNP their £500 deposit for gaining over 5%. Which was a little victory in itself as British nationalist candidates hardly ever managed to save their deposits. This only further secured the BNP position as the main right-wing party in Great Britain, as they had pulled further and further ahead of the National Front and the National Democrats. Even though the results for the NF were yet again very disappointing, now the elections were over I did not intend to just sit around. The time had come to do something for loyal Ulster.

Even though I had finally realised that travelling the country with a firm of football hooligans was not a good idea, or my cup of tea, I was about to foolishly embark on a nightmare trip to Poland with the England national team. It was a trip I will never forget – for all the wrong reasons.

CHAPTER 17

I was still following the Villa but admittedly not as much as I had been due to the general election. When the election was over a friend from Erdington phoned me up and asked if I fancied travelling to Poland with a few lads for a World Cup qualifier in Katowice. Being a British nationalist, I had always wanted to follow my country abroad – but for one reason or another it had never happened. Now let me state I was going to Poland for the experience and to support my country; trouble was the last thing on my mind. However, when I arrived there trouble was something you simply could not avoid – even if you wanted to. I had been duped into a trip from hell. We booked the flights from Birmingham to Berlin in Germany with the overland train to reach Poland. I had been told only a handful of us were going. I heard a rumour from another mate that some of the Hardcore lads may also be on the flight. For all that, when I arrived at the airport all the main faces were there – we had virtually the whole plain to ourselves. My mate had outsmarted me. He had well and truly stitched me up – he found it hilarious. It was not as though I wasn't pleased to see them, nonetheless, I knew by now this would not be a quiet few days away. Regardless, my intention was to have a good beer and a good laugh, and not get myself into any situations. If only.

The flight over to Berlin was free beer and we had drunk the plane dry before we even landed in Germany. When we landed, we all headed to a well-known drinking establishment and settled down for the day. Most of our lads were off their heads on ecstasy tablets. As soon as we got in the bar some of our lads had words with some Leicester fans which I suppose set the tone for the trip. We'd had a lot of history with Leicester. Fortunately, that was somehow smoothed over before it got out of hand. But the German police were not messing around. They sprayed some of our lads in the face with tear gas and arrested them for stepping out of line. The German police were just waiting for trouble and were sat outside the bar ready to arrest any England fan who stepped out of line. As the day progressed into night, the police had enough of us in the bar steaming drunk and playing up – and forced us out of the bar and to the train station. The German 'Old Bill' would stay with us to the Polish border. It was a while before the train to Poland, therefore, we all headed for the bars in the train station to top up our drink. At least the Berlin police had us off the streets so to speak. As we boarded the overnight train to Poland, little did we know at the time that the police waiting there for us would be even more violent than the Polish fans themselves.

As we got on the train a large group of Huddersfield lads were on there and there was this one lad from their firm that stood out from the rest. He was fronting their mob. I had noticed him at the train station and he was a proper little cocky Black geezer who was walking around as if he was in charge. I knew I was not the only one who had noticed him and that something would give on the train. I knew some of our top lad's would not take too kindly to his arrogance. As we left for Poland, the inevitable happened and a scuffle broke out with Huddersfield on the train. We were not the only lads on there. There were different firms of lads from everywhere. Villa and Huddersfield were at it straight away. The train walkways were very narrow so the fighting with Huddersfield never really took off as you could not really get to each other. One of our top lads Gary Reid, had a word with the Black lad fronting Huddersfield's firm, and a meet up was arranged when we got to Katowice in Poland. I do not think this would have happened if the Huddersfield lad had not been so full of himself and so cocky. The Huddersfield lad brought the attention on to himself. The story being flung around was Villa's lads were all 'neo-Nazis', and singled out this idiot because of his race – some things never change.

Before we left for the train to Poland, loads of our lads had brought canisters of CS gas that you could buy from normal shops in Berlin. Its sold in Germany mainly for women as an anti- rape spray which is all well and good, but its obviously also used for the wrong purposes when it falls into the wrong hands. Loads of the Villa lads had brought it in bulk, boxed it up in Berlin, and had it sent back to Birmingham by mail; some got through and some never. Because of it being legal to purchase in Berlin our firm were armed to the teeth with CS gas as we headed to Poland. Getting back to the train journey – we had been travelling for what seemed like days when we reached the Polish border. This is where the police would change over. During the early hours of the morning Polish hooligans attacked the train. I could not believe it. Nearly everyone was fast asleep and not expecting this. These Poles were crazy and they totally trashed part of the train before clashes with the England lads started on the station platform.

Some of the Poles were severely beaten, but they kept coming back for more. They were unreal – real fighting machines.

Even though I had sworn to stay away from the football and the danger it brings, I was now in the middle of a war zone. I started to regret coming and we had not even reached our destination yet. Then the nightmare really did begin. I was about to enter a real trip from hell. I cannot remember where or why due to amount of alcohol drunk and broken sleep, but suddenly loads of Polish police were on the train dishing out beatings. Me and my mate Ripper locked ourselves away in a toilet to escape the beatings the Polish police were giving out; they were animals. The German police who had boarded the train from Berlin were strict, however, some of them were all right if you showed them some respect. But the Polish 'Old Bill' were something else. Someone from the Villa firm had let off some CS gas – more than likely at the Huddersfield lads who were further up the train. The police were battering everyone, thugs and fans alike. They then started banging on the toilet door where me and Ripper were hiding. Like a fool, I opened the door and the police dragged us out. My mate Ripper pretended to have an asthma attack and they left him alone. There was mayhem going on everywhere, and for no reason at all the police threw me off the train as it was moving. I had done absolutely nothing wrong.

As I was being thrown off the train all I could hear were lads screaming from the police batons. The train was only moving very slowly and then the reality hit me that I was in the middle of nowhere on my own. My mate Ripper stuck his head out the train window and saw me standing there stranded on my own. Fair play to him, as not many would have done this, but he opened the train door and jumped off before it pulled out of sight from the station. During this, he twisted his ankle the way he fell. He did so because he did not want to see his mate stranded on his own. That is what you call a true friend. And who was leaning out the window taking the piss as the train pulled off? Yes, the Black lad from Huddersfield. After all, it is only what we would have done if it had been roles reversed. However, the knight-mare had only just begun. Before we knew it we were in this police hut on the train station and it was like a scene from a film. It was like being transported back into the 1970's. A police officer walked in and did this gesture of a knife being dragged along the throat. I honestly thought we were in for one hell of a beating. Unknowingly, it was not our blood they were after any more – it was our money.

Minutes later, they brought in a Wolves fan from the Black Country. He was only a very young kid and even though I do not like Wolves I felt sorry for the lad as he was petrified. They sat him down with us and he kept asking me if we were going to be all right; I did not have the answers. You could tell he was not the type to have caused trouble. Like with me, they must have thrown him off the train for nothing. There was one officer sat in a chair watching some film chain-smoking his head off. In addition, every now and again he would look at us and start grinning and laughing in a crazy manner as if to say you're in big trouble. Well it worked if he intended to frighten us. The main man then walked in and pulled up a chair next to us. He had this almighty cosh that was made of rubber and you could tell it was flexible.

He made sure we saw it. It was the same as the ones they had been using on the train. He could not speak a word of English but he made it clear he wanted our pockets emptied. Little did I know at this stage why? I thought maybe he was after some I.D to charge us and then he started to go through our wallets. I think we all then started to realise it was money he was after as he pulled all our notes out of our wallets. He was looking at us grinning as if to say you cannot do anything about it – and he was right. He took most the money from my wallet, put a little back in, and then gave it me back. The same happened with Ripper. What's more, regarding the Wolves lad, he took from him every penny he had to his name. This left him totally broke. I still am not sure to this day why he did this to him. The Wolves lad was close to tears but I was simply relieved we had not been beaten half to death as it was what we were expecting. I told the Wolves lad not to worry now as we were safe from a beating; he started to calm down a little. The Polish police were as corrupt as you could get, which we would find out again at a later stage of the trip.

My mate Ripper then enquired about the next train to Katowice. You could tell they were not going to arrest us now. They had got what they were after. They showed us a map of where we were and how to get to Katowice – but in very broken English. We were literally in the middle of nowhere. The next train from the station was in seven hours time. It was a long depressing night. There was nothing open on the train station at all and it was totally freezing. Picture your worst nightmare then multiply it by ten. Due to my sheer boredom during the night I went for a little walk outside of the station, however, I only lasted about a hundred yards until I turned back. Christ what a dark depressing place. It looked that rough as I left the train station my better instincts told me to turn back. It was just a mass of grey tower blocks and you could see no one there had anything at all. We were better off inside the train station away from anyone's attention. Ripper some how fell to sleep, but the

Wolves lad and myself sat up all night chain smoking and exchanging stories about our days out at the football. It was so depressing. We were all very hungry but there were not any shops around at all. I do not think no one around there had any money to spend anyway even if the shops would have been open. We just sat there and waited for the clock to slowly come around. What a long horrible night. It was one of those situations where you would have given anything to be back home at this stage.

As the night progressed into morning, we could smell some food in the air and wondered for obvious reasons where the smell was coming from. We all jumped up. We were hoping this was some kind of local train station cafe doing a morning fry up – how wrong we were. When we found the place it brought it all back to me how poor this country really was. You had two huge steel containers simmering away; it was Polish soup. The one was very cheap for a bowl and some bread and the next one nearly double the price with some bread. We opted for the more expensive one because it was still cheap. There was no chance of a fry up here – this was dark and depressing central Poland. You could sense the feeling of poverty and lack of hope in the air. It was horrible. Therefore, we sat down for our morning soup. Believe me, nice or not, we all cleaned up two bowls in five minutes flat. A local man obviously short of money opted for the cheaper version and you should have seen it. It looked like flavoured water. It must have been disgusting but the poor bloke maybe did not have much option. If we would have had more money I would have treated him but we had to watch our pennies. As I said, the Wolves lad was skint – but me and Ripper sorted him out. We would not have seen anyone going hungry after that experience.

Next plan, the train was in half hour. I felt dirty after being stuck on a train station all night and would have given anything for a shower. We headed for the train out of hell to link up again with the Hardcore lads somewhere along the way. Ripper made contact with Fowler and there was a stop arranged at some point to meet up again. The next hurdle was we had no tickets for the train we were on and money was very low. We did not even know if the money we had would cover the train fares but this was the situation we were in. Suddenly the doors to our carriage swung open and this very sharp tempered little Polish ticket inspector was standing there looking at us in a very aggressive way. I do not know if the police had wired him off, but he was certainly expecting us and wanted some money for the train tickets – and more than likely a few quid for himself. After he had finished his rant he took the money for the three fares and finally left us alone. We were down to our bare bones but fortunately we would be linking up soon with the lads and have access to cash machines in Katowice.

I will never forget to this day some old Polish guy got into our carriage on the train and we had such a laugh with him. He was a barmy old chap but was game for a laugh even though we could not understand each other; he really entertained us for the rest of the journey. We all had our photos taken with him sitting on our laps. He was only a little chap maybe in his late 70's, but he loved having a play up on the train and I suppose we made each other's day. We had now finally reached our destination to link up again with the Villa lads and head into Katowice after our nightmare. I found out through my mate Harold that trouble had been going off on the train all throughout the night, with the Villa Hardcore doing all the damage. I was not impressed with this myself because apart from Huddersfield coming the big one the Villa firm had been dishing out slaps to anyone and everyone. We had never been a firm of bullies, but I think the occasion, and having the biggest firm out there got to the lads heads a little. Although, this was nothing compared to when we eventually arrived in Katowice.

We caught the connecting train and after god knows how long we reached our destination. We left the train mob handed and we most certainly had the biggest firm out there by far. Moreover, in the distance I caught sight of the arrogant Black guy fronting Huddersfield's firm. Let me tell you this straight with no ifs or buts. He had a cheeky look around and after seeing our numbers, him and his boys were off in a shot. They didn't realise the numbers we had due to the narrow train we was all on and they were not hanging around to find out if our lads were still upset with them – which they were. You have never seen a mob of lads vanish so quickly into the morning Polish sunrise. That was the last we saw of 'Mr Gobby' all trip. I know fully well if he'd had a straightener with Reidy, there would only have been one winner.

After getting hold of some money we started to head for the bars so we could start our drinking session. After our night at the train station stuck in the middle of nowhere, Katowice was like a dream come true even though looking back it was still a dull depressing place. It had bars everywhere, McDonald's, cash machines, KFC and loads of restaurants. At least now I was back into some sort of normality. We had other Villa lads over there who we were meeting at the Hotel Katowice as a link up place. Rumours of trouble were already circulating of baseball bat gangs of Poles roaming around looking for the English. This was confirmed when some English lads walked in beaten to a pulp. These Poles were proper aggressive lads. But the Villa Hardcore were itching to carry on what they had started. More English fans walked in beaten black and blue by the Polish police for just walking the street. This was one crazy place and the day had not long begun.

The Katowice Hotel was full of normal England fans but no other firms. As a result, the lads decided to move on for some excitement. I knew they were on the look out for other mobs which I myself wanted no part to play in. But I was not willing to risk being left on my own after what had happened the night before. We entered a bar and Newcastle's firm was in there. They did not stay long as they could tell something was about to happen. The Villa simply had superior numbers to all the other England firms out there. Then suddenly the Polish police turned up. They were animals 'whack, whack' off peoples legs – mine included; god those batons hurt. The batons they had were so many feet long, and flexible and they left such a sting and a bruise. The police loved wading in. They hated the English.

They rounded us up together and sent us away from the bar we had just entered and forced us over the road. Some more Polish police turned up, stood us up against a wall and took money off us. I could not believe this was happening again. They were not satisfied with just beating us senseless. Once they had taken our money and given us a few more whacks with the batons they let us loose again. The corruption in this police force was shocking. They were beating and mugging England fans. We headed back to where there was a number of bars and loads of English about and found a bar to settle down for a drink; the Police had followed us. More and more police turned up and you could tell it was about to get nasty as the English fans were now getting steadily drunk and dying for a play up. Suddenly, some tables and bottles from outside were thrown at the police line. It was about to go off big time.

The England fans were now taunting the police. I was tucked right inside the corner of the bar simply watching events unfold. The police suddenly charged and as fans were trying to get back into the bar the doorway got bottle necked and three lads were stuck in the doorway with their arms sticking out; I will never forget this. The Polish police started to whack their arms with those rubber batons. The screams were horrific as we all knew how sharp these batons come. The police just keep hitting them and hitting them. There was simply nowhere for the England fans to go until after a few minutes they somehow got back inside, as the front of the England firm forced the doors shut. These lads arms were beaten like you could never imagine possible. By now, the police had surrounded the bar with a ring of steel. I thought they were planning at any time just to storm the place and beat the living day lights out of anyone they could get hold of.

There was a little side door out of the bar which led into the restaurant side of the premises which was not being surrounded by the police. We all went into the restaurant and out the main doors into freedom. I was expecting any second for the police to spot us but we had been lucky on this occasion. Some of our lads had been split up and we were now in two firms. Its what happens on trips away. You always lose people but mostly end up getting back together again at some stage. At the next bar, a little mob of our old rivals Birmingham City walked in. I fully well expected them to get turned by our lads and to be honest even though I would not have played any part in this it would have been exactly what the Zulus would have done to us. They were petrified as they only had tiny numbers – but fortunately one of them knew Fowler and they were spared. It was good though to see the old 'bully boys' have it on the other foot for a change.

Next breath Fowler had a word with some West Ham lads over an incident that happened with them a few years earlier and it went off. West Ham had linked up with Carlisle who also had a firm out there. Fowler wanted a one on one with Carlisle's main boy but he bottled it. Suddenly, it turned into a pitched battle, with chairs, tables, glasses and bottles flying everywhere. The Villa Hardcore were coming out on top but I do not think the other lads were looking for trouble to be perfectly honest. It was just how our mob was behaving on this trip. They were taking no prisoners but I did not like what I was seeing to be perfectly honest. Everyone and every firm was fair game for the Villa lads. Next breath, we heard this almighty roar and up the road in the distance there was a mob of about 300 Polish hooligans steaming down the road. What a sight to put the shits up you. They were all tooled up with all types of weapons. Although, there was no chance of the England fans standing together because they had just been fighting with each other; we were in big trouble now.

Then out the blue the Polish police turned up again in large numbers. That was the only time all the trip I was pleased to see a Polish copper. The Polish mob would have destroyed us. Half of the police charged at the Polish mob and the other half attacked us again with their rubber truncheons. We all scampered and ran off in different directions. We were all spilt up again. We all regrouped again at a pub full of normal English fans, but yet again it didn't stop the police from making the most use of their batons as they could. They were totally out of order. Any England fan was looked upon as a target – troublemaker or not.

We eventually headed for the game knowing the Poles would have firms surrounding the ground and that any English would do – so we all stuck together in a tight unit. It did not take long for the Poles to find us. The police had given us a poor escort, therefore, when a mob of Poles appeared the Villa lads just went into them and fighting broke out. The sound of that old police truncheon filled the air again. What a noise it made when it connected with the body. I have never seen a mob with more bruises in my life. The Polish had little mobs everywhere but we were more organised at the ground and went for a little walk around the stadium. Some high-ranking police officer must have had a word and said get these English lads off the streets and into the ground. And that is exactly what they did – with brute force.

As I entered the ground it was just like the country as a whole – very grey and depressing. No wonder these Poles loved fighting so much, they had nothing else. There were about 3,000 English fans there and it was bitterly cold. Harold from Erdington decided to take his trousers off in the ground but anyone who knows him will know this is just his normal behaviour. The Polish end next to us was filling up and then suddenly a huge fight erupted in it. Swarms of people were running at each other – creating gaps in the terraces and then the gaps would start filling back up again as the various mobs met. We found out this was the rival firms in Poland settling differences – and by god, they knew how to do it. It was crazy and as per usual the Polish police stormed in and gave anyone who was unfortunate enough to be in their way a good hiding.

I had spent years travelling the whole UK following the Villa and been to some rough and moody places like Middlesbrough, West Ham, and Leeds – but these Poles were on another level; they were lunatics. All they wanted to seem to do was fight. The Villa Hardcore were looking out for Huddersfield in the ground but they could not be found. The match was pretty dull even though we took a 2-0 lead, but the cold night air was too much for everyone. I have never felt so cold in my life. The concrete grey stadium just added to the freezing conditions. We heard that a train was leaving back to Berlin, but it was before the game ended. Due to the temperature a decision was made to leave for the early train. It was just too cold and I think our firm had had enough of those Polish coppers batons by now; well I had anyway. As we left for the train Polish lads were milling around, and fighting once again broke out all the way back to the train station. We eventually got on the train and went to settle down for the long journey back to Berlin. It was an old-fashioned train, like something you had in England in the 1970's, with endless carriages that were very basic and shabby. Nevertheless, that was not the end of the trouble. Fowler had spotted some Carlisle lads getting on the train. It was the same lads who they'd had the bang off with earlier and it was inevitable that something would happen.

After about half an hour the Villa lads went looking for Carlisle – smashing their way through the carriages to find them. I took no part in this myself as I was knackered and I'd had enough by now of all the rioting going on. When the Hardcore reached the Carlisle end of the train they had barricaded themselves in. They knew the Hardcore were on the train and with our numbers they would not have stood a chance. When the Hardcore reached their carriage they would not come out, so our lads who had brought some CS gas from Germany sprayed it into the cabin. They were all coughing and spluttering as this CS gas was dangerous shit.

After a while some of our lads forced their way into the cabin and fighting broke out. After giving the Carlisle lads a bit of a slap the Villa firm decided to leave them alone as it was a no contest. In all fairness we had been out of order on this trip. I will speak the truth. I am not going to lie; the Villa had been beyond the limits of acceptability and fairness. I know other Villa lads agreed with me on this.

As we eventually reached the German border after our long rest, we were all ready for a good drink again as you do when you're away. As soon as we arrived in Berlin the police followed us everywhere and we had our own personal police escort wherever we went. The high light of the return trip to Berlin was when we went the red light area and paid in to see a live strip show. We were all roaring drunk and having such a laugh when suddenly a huge cheer went up. As I looked over Harold had stripped off and was about to enter the stage before the show was brought to an abrupt end. The minders then threw us out but we just moved onto another pub. That was nothing new from Harold; it's what you expect from the kid. He's crazy but very entertaining to have around as you can maybe guess.

We flew home to Birmingham after all the events and everyone was totally knackered. It had been such an experience for all the wrong reasons. I was disappointed by how the Villa Hardcore had conducted themselves with other England fans. Since that trip to Poland, now the lads have got older they admit that they were out of order. It was one of them. That was the first and last time I followed England abroad due to how our firm had behaved. I knew later on down the line there would be pay back when we did not have the numbers. Moreover, my opinion was proved right at a later stage. That being said, the Hardcore were out in Poland to show that the Villa were back on the England scene. In addition, they had achieved their goal.

Despite everything, let us never forget out of all the firms out there in Katowice from Carlisle, Huddersfield, Leicester, Newcastle, West Ham, Villa Hardcore and the Polish hooligans, that there was only ever one firm really in charge...................... And that was the baton happy Polish police.

CHAPTER 18

I was now ready to get involved with the loyalist paramilitaries but where did I start? I knew they were not openly advertising like the BNP and the NF, and they certainly were not in the Yellow pages. I knew of people in the right-wing movement who were in Orange Lodges in the West Midlands but for the impact they had they may as well have been on the moon. Something more was needed. I knew some NF lads who had visited loyal Ulster, nonetheless, I just did not want to walk up to them and say: "How do you get into contact with the U.D.A". Not everyone who visits Ulster actually gets involved with the paramilitaries. The majority go for the marches and to take in the proud British culture. However, I wanted to go that step further. Then at one West Midlands NF branch meeting the chance fell my way.

A member from Birmingham NF had invited over a lad from East Belfast and he was selling a loyalist magazine that had just been released. I purchased the magazine from him as you do and took it home to read. I could not believe what was in there – an advert from the Loyalist Prisoners Aid. This was a wing of the Ulster Defence Association. The L.P.A was a fund raising wing for the U.D.A, which raised money by a number of methods for the prisoners inside the

Maze who had been imprisoned whilst fighting in the war against the I.R.A. This was exactly what I had been looking for. If this magazine had been in support of the other loyalist paramilitaries – the Ulster Volunteer Force – then I would have contacted them. But I had came across the U.D.A first and this would be the organisation I would be making contact with.

There was a PO Box address in the magazine that you could contact; I instantly wrote a letter to enquire about getting involved to some level. I later found out after all these years that the West Midlands L.P.A had finally decided to come out in the open to try and get more people involved – which for me was brilliant news. I sent off my letter with my phone number and waited for contact. I told some close friends who said I was taking things too far but my mind had already been made up; fight fire with fire. Then after a short while contact was made. But before I carry on let me give you a little insight into the U.D.A/U.F.F. The Ulster Defence Association is the largest of the loyalist paramilitary groups in Ulster. It was formed in 1971, and it took on an armed struggle for many years against the I.R.A and its republican allies. It used the cover name Ulster Freedom Fighters as for many years the two claimed to be separate organisations. Due to this the U.D.A were somehow able to remain legal until 1992.

The U.D.A/U.F.F position was to defend loyalist areas from Irish republican attacks. Some of the organisations high profile attacks were the 'Milltown massacre', the 'Castlerock killings', and the 'Trick or treat' murders at the Rising Sun pub in Londonderry. The nickname given to the U.D.A by their rivals the U.V.F was the 'Wombles' – aimed at the furry fictional creatures from children's television years ago. The motto of the U.D.A/U.F.F is 'Quis Separabit' which means in Latin 'Who shall separate us'. At its peak it had an estimated 40,000 members. The U.D.A operated a structure of leadership, each with a Brigadier representing one of its six Brigade areas. The Brigade areas were, North Belfast, East Belfast, South Belfast, West Belfast, South East Antrim and North Antrim and County Londonderry. It officially ended its armed campaign in November 2007.

I answered my phone one day and it was a bloke with a strong Liverpool accent who asked for me. His name was Stan. I would later find out that he was a huge Liverpool fan. He then proceeded to tell me he was now running the West Midlands L.P.A, as the person before him was no longer around. I did initially find it a bit strange a Scouser running the West Midlands L.P.A – for all that, he informed me he had been living in Birmingham for years and the West Midlands was his base. The phone call went very well with us just having a basic chitchat. In addition, he seemed a dead friendly lad. Little did I know at this time we would become very close friends, and years down the line Stan would end up getting twenty years for terrorist offences. He asked where I would like to meet up for a chat and as I was over at Karen's at the time in Stockland Green, we arranged for the Greyhound pub in Erdington. It is a nice little quiet pub where you ain't got people on top of you listening to your conversations.

I told a few mates from the Leopard pub that's just up the road from the Greyhound in case things went tits up for any reason. Karen knew about it all, and even though she was not happy she understood my strong views towards the Ulster cause. I started to make my way to the pub. As I walked in the pub I was looking for some strange faces and spotted a table of three lads who I did not recognise. I knew it was them straight away. I did not know at that time if they were going to slam a gun on the table and tell me to go and do this or do that. I did not know what to expect. My mind was racing. I approached the table and asked for Stan. I sat down and we started to talk.

Stan explained why the L.P.A had finally came out in the open. It was to try to generate some more supporters and raise some more funds for the prisoners. He explained they regularly held fund raising nights where you would have on a disco and guest speakers from different parts of the UK. You would pay an entrance fee and buy things like raffle tickets and so on; fund raising nights. Likewise, he said that once I was settled into the L.P.A that he would give me a prisoners address to write to him in the Maze prison and become his sponsor. I liked what I heard. It was nothing too heavy but I would still be doing something for the U.D.A – now matter how little it may have been.

I could never have foreseen the emotional roller-coaster ride I was taking myself on getting involved with the U.D.A. Let me state that me and Stan hit it off straight away and we had a good feeling about each other from the word go. Stan suggested that whilst I was finding my feet there was a social night coming up in Liverpool and why didn't I come along. He offered to take me and mate who was also interested. Stan would drive and introduce us to the people there. That was an offer too good to refuse. A night out with like-minded loyalist people, listening to some traditional loyalist music and knocking back a few beers. I'll have some of that. Not forgetting the chance to make some more contacts.

It was a brilliant night and far exceeded what I had expected. There were people there from all parts of the UK. It was a proper Union of the British people and I loved that.

All the walls were decorated in Ulster flags and the flags of the loyalist paramilitaries and I was instantly hooked. There was a normal disco early on and then a loyalist disco blasting out all the old songs about victory over the I.R.A; I was alive with excitement. Stan then introduced me to Frank, who I had heard about over the years. Frank had been around for ages. He was a London lad – a Spurs fan –who was very easy to talk to and very sharp when it came to having a laugh. Moreover, I felt at ease in his company. As many people have said throughout the years, if it was not for Frank there would not have been any type of organised loyalism on the mainland. Frank's involvement with the U.D.A started in the mid 1980's, with him taking over the London Brigade in 1988.

It soon became clear to the other English Brigades that Frank intended to introduce a more militant line as he proceeded to alienate any volunteers who he deemed had become complacent. His own militancy led him to be arrested at the Crown and Cushion pub in Birmingham in May 1993. The funny thing was I sometimes used the pub on match day as its only a ten-minute walk to Villa Park. A bag in his possession contained seven handguns and ammunition. Frank and two other men were held on remand on the Category A wing in Birmingham's Winston Green prison. One of the men – Eddie Whicker – was eventually released from custody due to lack of evidence. Frank and a Belfast colleague eventually appeared at Birmingham Crown Court. At the time, Frank was looking at a sentence of 10-14 years, but thanks to a late change of plea and a deal with the prosecution – his co-defendant received a sentence of two and a half years. The judge could not hand down the sentence he had planned for Frank, as it would have been disproportionate in comparison to the other defendant.

Subsequently, he only received a sentence of five years – which for Frank was a right result.

Further on down the line, Frank would form a loyalist umbrella group called the British Ulster Alliance. The night made a lot of money for a prisoner, but more so it really cemented my friendship with Stan. There were foot lads there from all over England but no sign of any tribal friction which made me happy. It was just one happy gathering. Stan drove us there and back, never had a drink himself, and never even charged us petrol. That was his way of introducing me into the L.P.A. He deserved a pat on the back for that. When he dropped me home he asked if I had liked what I had seen and I replied with a: "Yes, yes, yes, I want to stay in contact". I had only attended one function but I knew that from then on I would be a loyalist for life. I had finally made my connections with the U.D.A. Stan explained to me that once I felt settled in he would be taking me over to Ulster to meet people in the U.D.A.

Initially, Stan invited me to Southport in England to celebrate the Battle of the Boyne, which is celebrated every 12th of July. A mini-bus of us travelled to Southport on a real sunny day. I was unaware at this stage the friction between the loyalist paramilitary groups of the U.D.A and the U.V.F. However, I was soon to find out. The U.V.F was the first loyalist paramilitary group to spring out of the loyalist community in the mid-1960's. During its years at war against the I.R.A, its deadliest attack in Ulster was at McGurks Bar, which killed fifteen people. It was reported the I.R.A were using the bar which was the reason behind the bombing. The U.V.F also carried out some attacks in the Republic of Ireland. The most deadly of which were the 'Dublin and Monaghan bombings' which killed 33 civilians. The no warning car bomb attacks had been carried out by units from Belfast, and Mid-Ulster. Even though the U.V.F whose nickname was the 'Black Necks', due to the uniforms that they wore, were a lot smaller structure than the U.D.A – they were still a very dangerous paramilitary organisation.

The Battle of the Boyne celebrations had been going on now in loyalist circles for over 300 years, and it was very steep in Ulster history and tradition. When we arrived in Southport we set up in a pub and put our U.D.A/ U.F.F flags on display. I noticed other lads walk in who were linked up to the U.V.F, who did not like our U.D.A flags being on show; I sussed this out straight away – even with my minimal knowledge. Now I know to an outsider that this must sound crazy as we are both fighting the same corner – keeping Ulster British. Moreover, both organisations hate the I.R.A and both celebrate the Battle of the Boyne. Regardless, that did not matter – the atmosphere was there when the U.V.F lads saw our U.D.A flags on presentation. We did not stay long and moved on from that particular pub.

The streets were heaving with thousands of people here to celebrate this day of historic British culture. All you could see were thousands of Union Jack flags, Ulster flags, Rangers flags and Rangers football tops. It was such a brilliant sight. I remember thinking this is how it should be on Saint George's day. Having said that, most of the English have had the pride knocked out of them – but not me. All these people were waiting for the loyalist flute bands to start playing and when they came into view I could see why. The sound of the bands filling the air was superb and I knew I had made the right choice by getting involved. There were people here from all parts of the UK; everywhere you could name. None of this England – Scotland hatred you sometimes get. We were all one together. Although, later on in the day things would get a bit nasty to my dismay.

We moved on for a little pub-crawl and eventually finished up in a pub on the sea front. Every pub was full of loyalists but a majority of them were affiliated to the U.V.F. It is just how it was on this day. As far as I was concerned we were all loyalists out to celebrate the same occasion, but some of the U.V.F lads had different ideas. We had our U.D.A flags out in the pub and were getting some right funny looks from the large group of U.V.F lads. I knew something was going to happen shortly. The U.V.F lads said some thing to one of our crowd and Stan made the decision to leave the pub; they were seconds away from filling us in. As we sharply left the pub, the U.V.F lads followed us out as we made a run for it. We were heavily out numbered. It was crazy. Loyalists wanting to attack other loyalists just over waving a different flag. We made our get away although the U.V.F lads were trying to trail us. We somehow lost them which was very fortunate. We finished up in a pub a few miles from the main area, where Stan sat me down and explained about the rivalry between the U.D.A and the U.V.F. I was very disappointed to say the least as I could of quite easily got involved with the U.V.F myself if they had came my way first. I could not believe the hatred between the two loyalist organisations. But fair play to Stan, he saw the situation developing and got us out of there just in time.

This was only the beginning of my involvement in the U.D.A, and throughout the year we attended fundraisers all over the U.K. We used to take a mini-bus of lads from Birmingham L.P.A. Some were sworn in members of the U.D.A and some were not. After all, it did not matter either way because we were all there for the same reason – to do our bit for Ulster. Some of the socials I attended I fully well admit that I did not know where the money raised was going. I heard whispers it was going directly to the loyalist paramilitaries to purchase arms – but to be perfectly honest that suited me just fine. My friendship with Stan just kept growing from strength to strength; we really formed a strong bond. We became more than just political associates, he quickly became one of my best friends. Many of the lads at the Villa did not have much time for Scousers, nonetheless, Stan was a brilliant bloke who had such a similar sense of humour to me. We were always laughing and playing up. And I was ever so grateful to him for showing me the ropes and getting me involved with the L.P.A. He finally arranged a trip to Scotland to watch Glasgow Rangers play at Ibrox, and I jumped at the chance.

After a long 6-hour journey our mini-bus arrived in Glasgow and we headed for a well-known Rangers pub for a loyalist karaoke. It was called Bingham's Bar – named after a U.V.F member from Ballysillan in North Belfast, who was shot dead by the I.R.A in 1986. We were advised to keep our U.D.A connections quiet in the pub as it would not have gone down too well. After what happened at Southport we did not want a re-run of that again. The pub was rammed with Rangers fans and the atmosphere in there was brilliant. We all took turns singing well-known loyalist songs; the place was rocking. The landlord of the pub was a big nasty looking Scottish U.V.F bloke – but he made us ever so welcome and even got a round of drinks in for the lads. As we headed the game I did not know what to expect, but when we reached Ibrox what a sight. It was just a sea of Red, White, and Blue and the streets were heaving with people. There was such a buzz in the air. We landed in another pub right by the ground which was packed wall to wall with everyone singing loyalist and Rangers songs. I will never forget when some Scottish lad stopped me at the bar for a chat and I spent half hour just nodding my head to everything he said. His accent was that strong I never understood a single word. The other lads found it highly amusing as you do. We then headed to the game.

We arrived there late and the ground was full by then; what an experience. Thousands of Union Jacks filled the stands as well as Ulster flags, and obviously Scotland and Rangers flags. It was such a sight. This was a perfect example of having an identity and a culture you could say was yours and yours alone. It made me so proud. Then the crowd started to sing: "God save our Queen" and: "No surrender to the I.R.A". This made the hairs on the back of my neck stand up. Being surrounded by over 45,000 people of the same mind was such an experience. It converts you for life. Rangers actually lost the game, despite that, it did not matter that much to me about the result. I had gone for the Rangers experience and really enjoyed the whole day. I was like many English lads regarding Rangers. We had our own English teams we supported – my self Aston Villa; we supported Rangers as a second team. Not so much for the players – I could not even name the players – moreover, what Glasgow Rangers stood for politically. Supporting Rangers to a large part was a political statement. After the game, we headed back to the U.V.F karaoke bar to finish of the night and got very drunk in there. The Scottish lads made us all very welcome again. That is why I hate it when some English lads say they hate the Jocks. They do not understand how much we have in common with the Rangers lads.

The following week I got a phone call of Stan asking me how I enjoyed the day out in Glasgow. I told him it was brilliant. He then said to me: "Now you have found your feet would you fancy a trip over to Ulster with me to meet some of our people?". I did not need asking twice. Stan suggested just me and him go over so he could show me around the place without worrying what the other Birmingham lads wanted to do, as being my first time over it would be easier for us to travel alone; I was buzzing. He said it wouldn't be for no special event like a march or a fund raising event. It would be just to get me introduced to the people he knew and to slowly pave my way into the U.D.A in Ulster. This made a lot of sense as having a low-key trip was maybe the best thing. The flights were booked and Stan being Stan paid for my flight from the Birmingham L.P.A funds .That's what Stan was like, always helping me out and looking out for me. He was a very giving person and looked after his lads. He explained to me that I would be visiting an estate in County Antrim, called Rathcoole – which fell under the South East Antrim Brigade of the U.D.A/U.F.F.

South East Antrim was the biggest of the Brigades of the U.D.A/ U.F.F. It was under the control of an Ulster loyalist named John 'Grugg' Gregg, who Stan said I would more than likely meet when I was over. Grugg was a hero in loyalist paramilitary circles due to the attempted assassination of Gerry Adams (president of Sinn Fein) back in 1984, which resulted in Adams needing treatment at the Royal Victoria hospital in Belfast. I was informed that Grugg and his unit were apprehended almost immediately by a British army patrol that opened fire on them before placing them under arrest. Apparently, the law enforcement agency had known about the attack in advance. Adams survived the assault due to the security forces replacing the Rathcoole U.D.A weapons dump with low velocity bullets, which unfortunately resulted in Gerry Adams surviving the ambush.

Following his release from prison Grugg returned to Rathcoole, where he once again became an important figure in the organisation. When John Gregg was asked if he regretted anything about the shooting of Gerry Adams, he replied: "Only that I didn't succeed". Under John Gregg the South East Antrim Brigade were prepared to ignore the terms of the loyalist ceasefire when they voted 'NO' to agreeing to the suspension of the armed struggle. Grugg had a fearsome reputation, however, this was not the perception I got of the man when I eventually met him. Grugg played the bass drum in a U.D.A band called the Cloughfern Young Conquerors, who I would eventually march with myself on a regular basis. The reputation of the band grew after a mass brawl at the annual apprentice boys of Derry march after an altercation with a rival U.V.F band.

Moving forward many years, Grugg like other leading loyalists in the U.D.A/ U.F.F inner council were lacking in enthusiasm for the Belfast agreement when it appeared in 1998. I was led to believe Grugg's Brigade continued to be active – sometimes using a 'cover name'. Republican enemies described him as a man driven by 'pure bigotry'. But that was an accusation that you could label all people on both sides of the Ulster conflict. Loyalists had seen demographic shifts in traditional Unionist areas that had now become republican areas, and Grugg and other leading loyalists were hell bent on this not continuing. Grugg was concerned about the 'Greening' of loyalist areas which meant once loyalist areas becoming strongholds for Sinn Fein/ I.R.A. There were also rumours of John Gregg's links with so-called neo-Nazi

English organisations, which was a total lie. If anybody should be able to answer that it was me. It was total fabrication. Grugg was a loyalist full stop. Even so, it does not stop these same old recycled lies from popping up all the time.

During the year 2000, despite the continuing activity of his South East Antrim Brigade, Grugg shared the concerns of other Brigadiers about what he seen as a coming war between the rival U.V.F and West Belfast U.D.A Brigadier and drug dealer – Johnny Adair. At the time, Grugg was not keen to antagonise Adair or fellow U.D.A colleagues and his Brigade accepted Johnny Adair's invitation to attend a loyalist day of culture organised by Adair on the lower Shankill. There was a stage there where members of West Belfast 'C' Company 2nd Battalion took to the stage hooded up and let of a volley of shots. It's what is known as a 'show of strength' in Northern Ireland. Loyalist hero Michael Stone was also introduced on stage to a huge applause from the crowd.

Old tensions were about to resurface with the U.V.F during a provocative march when supporters of Johnny Adair displayed a flag of the L.V.F – the Loyalist Volunteer Force – a break away group from the U.V.F. The U.V.F had detested the L.V.F since its foundation. The L.V.F had by now forged strong links with West Belfast U.D.A/U.F.F 'C' Company. As the march passed the U.V.F controlled Rex Bar on the Shankill Road, hundreds of U.V.F members were standing outside and as the last band walked past an L.V.F flag was on display. A commander from the U.V.F attacked the march and tore down the flag from person who was carrying it and then proceeded to attack him. Hundreds of U.D.A members were walking behind the band and a mass brawl broke out in the street.

Due to this altercation, Johnny Adair gave the orders for shots to be fired at the Rex Bar. The new breed of U.D.A men were very different from the original U.D.A that emerged during the formation of the organisation. The U.D.A leaders enjoyed a lifestyle far beyond the means of ordinary Protestants. This led to questions being asked by the wider loyalist community. Certain leading loyalists would flash around thousands of pounds in the bookies which did not sit nice with ex-prisoners who were struggling to muster up a few quid to put a bet on .This annoyed a lot of old timers who were struggling to make ends meet. I think I am right in saying that the U.D.A resembled by this period a succession of paramilitary factions, rather than an Ulster wide organisation.

The U.V.F had been informed that no L.V.F regalia would be on display on the day of the march, however, this promise was not kept. The was a plan to antagonise the U.V.F; which worked. After the attack on the Rex Bar, some members and supporters of the U.D.A then went on the rampage in the Lower Shankill, attacking homes of known U.V.F members and their families. This would obviously bring revenge attacks. The U.V.F struck back 48 hours later, shooting dead two Adair associates as they sat in their Range Rover car on the Crumlin Road, which neighbours the Shankill Road. Adair was returned to prison on the September of 2000. The feud with the U.V.F continued with more killings on both sides. It also triggered a spate of executions in North Belfast. As one senior loyalist said to me: "This feud did more damage to our community than the I.R.A ever managed to do in over 30 years". Both the U.D.A and U.V.F leadership were anxious to contain the feud within the Shankill area, where hundreds of families had been displaced. Within the Shankill area, both

'A' and 'B' Company of the West Belfast Brigade U.D.A, had refused to get involved in the feud which had angered Adair. Eventually both sides to prevent an escalation of any future problems between the two organisations, reluctantly agreed an official ceasefire.

After all this loyalist blood shed, worse was to come as people under the control of Johnny Adair would eventually murder John 'Grugg' Gregg in 2003. This feud would tear the U.D.A/U.F.F apart and would lead to the demise of Johnny Adair's grip in the U.D.A.

CHAPTER 19

*S*tan and I were now at Liverpool airport and I was all set to go on my first adventure to Ulster and to visit the well-known notorious Rathcoole estate. I never slept the night before such was my excitement. We had flown from Liverpool because we had gone to visit some of Stan's family before our trip. I did a bit of research on Rathcoole before I headed of on my travels and I found out that Rathcoole fell under the control of South East Antrim Brigade U.D.A. Other areas that also fell under South East Antrim were Rathfern, Monkstown, Glengormley, Whitewell, Shore Road, Greenisland, Ballymena, Larne, Antrim, Carrickfergus, Ballyduff and Whitehead. The U.D.A South East Antrim Brigade was reported as being the most powerful and dangerous Brigade in Ulster. It was also stated in one newspaper that it was 'the most bloody and murderous' unit operating within the U.D.A. The six counties that make up the Province of Ulster are County Antrim, County Armagh, County Down, County Fermanagh, County Londonderry and County Tyrone. I was a tiny bit nervous about visiting Rathcoole estate, but at the same time could not wait to get there as I knew I would be meeting people who had actively been engaged in the war against the I.R.A.

As we landed at Belfast, Stan and I grabbed a taxi and started to head to Rathcoole. I was bursting with a feeling inside I had never had before – it was hard to explain. After a short while Stan then told me that Rathcoole estate was only five minutes away. However, Stan needed a cash point machine so asked to taxi driver to pull over at the nearest bank. As Stan left the taxi, the taxi driver turned around and said to me: "Are you sure you want to go here, its a very dangerous place". I told him we had contacts there and he once again said: "If you know people here that's alright, but you don't want to be walking round here if you don't know anybody". I assured him we knew people there, nevertheless, he still looked concerned for me. This further cemented the reputation that the area had.

Stan got back in the cab and we entered Rathcoole estate. The very first thing I noticed was a mural on a wall with an AK47 assault rifle and next to it the words 'Ulster Freedom Fighters – Simply the Best'. It was so eye catching and it astounded me. I was now in deep U.D.A territory. We have all seen these murals on TV and in the papers and so on – but to see one for yourself was brilliant. The presentation was amazing – you could not have asked for more detail if you tried. Then I spotted another one of a loyalist gunman and the words ' Rathcoole U.D.A'. I felt like a kid at Christmas and we had not even left the taxi yet. Stan then pointed out to me to look at the kerb-stones. They were all running concurrently, painted in Red, White and Blue. It was so amazing. I heard this is what the loyalists did many years ago to stamp their mark on Protestant areas. I then noticed a row of shops on the estate and next to them some more U.D.A/ U.F.F murals. I remember thinking to myself how these murals were not just put up in certain out the way side streets. They were as much part of the community as the shops on the estate themselves. Moreover, they were as much part of the estate as the people themselves. Not to mention, nearly every lamp-post was flying a Union Jack flag, an Ulster flag or a loyalist paramilitary flag. If ever you had second thoughts about the loyalty towards Great Britain from the Unionist people (which I never doubted for one second) then your mind would have been made up by seeing this.

Rathcoole estate was built in the 1950's, to house many of those displaced by the demolition of inner city housing in Belfast city. It was also built to reduce underlying sectarian tensions in Ulster. It included a huge cinema, a shopping centre and schools; the population of the estate grew rapidly. The cinema was eventually shut down and a new bar built on its premises known as The Alpha – alternatively, its official name the East Way Social Club. A taxi firm also operated from the same building. Other housing developments were built near Rushpark and Rathern. Other estates in the district included Merville gardens and Fernagh. Since the late 1950's, Rathcoole and the above estates have been an integral part of Newtownabbey. By 1977, Newtownabbey was given a Borough status. A prominent feature of the community is its Christian churches including all main Protestant denominations. Notably, it has never featured a Roman Catholic Church within its boundary.

Towards the end of the 1960's, civil unrest in Ulster brought about what was known as 'ethnic cleansing' from a number of areas – and from both sides of the population. Rathcoole became a new home to many Protestants displaced from Belfast itself. During the 1970's, the family of Bobby Sands – the I.R.A hunger striker – moved out of Rathcoole to the republican area of the Twinbrook estate in Belfast. They were one of the many Catholic families to leave the estate to be replaced by similarly displaced Protestants. The estate was well known for several sectarian murders and other violent crimes during 'The Troubles'. In October 2010, there was serious rioting in the U.V.F controlled part of the estate after buses were hijacked and set on fire. Police also claimed a U.V.F gunman was sighted at the scene of the rioting. The unrest in the U.V.F part of the estate was a reaction to police raids on selected U.V.F homes in Rathcoole. Those who take time to view Belfast from its surrounding hills, can never fail to identify Rathcoole's location, as it is home to one of the most prominent and distinctive features of the Greater Belfast skyline. At the centre of the estate are four high-rise apartment blocks that stand out from an otherwise low-level landscape – in much the same way that the giant Samson and Goliath cranes of the old shipyard characterise the landscape of the east of the city.

As we pulled up on the car park of the club, the first thing that struck me was the size of the building – it was huge. Then I noticed (which you could not miss) that in bold lettering across the front of the club was the wording 'South East Antrim Brigade'. These people were not even trying to hide who they were. I knew then this would be a proper U.D.A controlled bar. It also had a memorial plaque outside the club dedicated to all South East Antrim's fallen members who had died during the troubles. It was very impressive as well as being very moving. To that end, we went to enter the club. There was a big steel gate separating the entrance of the club that you had to access through a buzzer. This was obviously in place during the height of the troubles to prevent any republican gunmen from attacking the place, as the club would have been known as a U.D.A bar to the I.R.A

– and I guess a legitimate target for attacks. You had a camera inside the club where someone would look to see who you were then buzz you in; the people obviously recognised Stan.

We entered the club and I was nervous but excited at the same time. It was a very dimly lit place which I found only added to the atmosphere. There were two levels to the downstairs bar and a pool table in the middle. It was not that busy at the time, although as I have said it was only a casual visit as no function was on this weekend. We approached the bar to be served and what I noticed was a banner hanging over the bar saying – 'Ulster Freedom Fighters – We rose in dark and evil days', with a Red Hand in the middle of the banner. I loved it. This said it all, and what the place was all about. We got our drinks and went to have a chat with some lads in there that Stan knew. I shall not name any of them but they were all sworn in U.D.A members. I quickly came to realise there was no such thing as strangers in the Alpha – just friends who I had yet to meet.

We sat down with our drinks and Stan introduced me to the hand full of lads in there. They were dead friendly and instantly made me feel at ease. They knew in advance that I was National Front; I suppose Stan had filled them in before I came over as to who he was bringing. Now let me take this chance to make something perfectly clear. For endless years there have been reports of right-wing groups and Ulster loyalists working hand in hand. Anyhow, I want to put this rumour to bed – for the last time. This has never been the case. Yes, of course, some loyalists hold some right-wing views – a selection of people from all parts of the UK from England, Scotland, Wales and Ulster will hold right-wing views. That being said, it has always been one-way traffic regarding the connection with the right-wing and Ulster – with the right-wing supporting Ulster – not the other way around. Ulster loyalism is part of British nationalist ideology which we campaigned on for many years – and rightly so. Despite the fact, there are no right-wing leanings in loyalism as their struggle is solely to remain part of the UK and to defeat the I.R.A and its allies.

In spite of this, enemies of Ulster have used this false accusation as a stick to beat the Ulster loyalists with. As the saying goes 'throw enough mud and it sticks'. Admittedly, I was never put down or condemned for being a member of the NF whilst I was over in Ulster. This was more out of respect for me supporting their cause than for them holding the same views as me regarding immigration issues on the mainland. The loyalists had their own war to fight and it was the Ulster policies of British nationalism that brought us together – nothing else. Besides, the Unionist political parties were dead against the NF/ B.N.P as much as Sinn Fein, and they did everything in their power to distance themselves from us. This needs pointing out.

We started chatting, and the lads from Rathcoole gave me a little run down on some of the past stories from the estate. In addition, I was amazed to find out that years ago there was even a Rathcoole NF branch in the 1970's. Even though it faded away as quickly as it was formed when the war with the I.R.A increased and the U.D.A became a real force in County Antrim. (None of the people I ever met were involved in the Rathcoole NF). As I have said, the need for the U.D.A in Ulster was far more needed than British nationalist politics. Stan took me around in someone's car to look at all the murals on the estate and I was well and truly stunned with the professionalism of the paintings. They ranged from U.D.A/ U.F.F murals to portraits of the Queen and the links between Ulster and mainland Britain. I was so fascinated. If I did not know in advance that the locals had painted these murals themselves, I would have honestly believed a professional company had been hired to do them; such was the detail. This was what I considered real displays of patriotism and loyalty to Britain and it made me feel so proud to be British. It was a life changing experience to see the murals for myself for the first time. Although let me state this was not only the case in Rathcoole, as every loyalist area had their own selection of murals. We then headed back to the Alpha and after being buzzed back in, Stan pointed out to me that John 'Grugg' Gregg was in there; Stan knew him well.

I looked over and he was a mountain of a man – heavily tattooed and someone you would most certainly want on your side. To look at him he looked very intimidating and I knew that seconds from now I would be introduced to him. Then it finally hit me who he was again – one of the U.D.A Brigadiers who had been involved in the attempted assassination of Gerry Adams of Sinn Fein/ I.R.A. This was no normal situation by any stretch of the imagination; I was about to meet the legend known as Grugg. Stan sat us down and Grugg noticing Stan walked over to our table. I was a bag of nerves as what do you say to such a leading figure in loyalist paramilitary circles? At any rate, my assumption of the man would prove to be wrong. He sat down at our table and Stan introduced us. He instantly showed interest in me being over in Ulster and made me really feel at ease in his company. Stan told him it was my first time over and he carried on talking to me as if he had known me for years, as my nerves began to settle. He thanked me for coming over to support his people; I was well chuffed. I am not going to make up a fabricated story as I so easily could do and say we became close friends who always stayed in contact through the years as we never. But throughout the years whenever I was over in Rathcoole, Grugg always gave me half hour of his time to say hello and to thank me for coming over and supporting his people people. That made me feel very humble from such a leading figure like Grugg. He could have quite easily walked in the Alpha and gone and sat with the locals – but he always gave us English lads a bit of his time to say hello and thank us for our support. For that and that alone, I liked Grugg.

I also had the pleasure of him showing me his back piece tattoo of the Grim Reaper that covered his whole back. What a tattoo it was with Ulster flags and Union flags either side of it. He was known for having this tattoo, and even though I hardly knew him I had my own personal viewing of it. My parents had always brought me up to have manners and I really respected Grugg for the time he gave me. After a good drink in the Alpha, Stan and the lads suggested we go to another bar a small taxi ride away. It was called the Cloughfern, which was just up the road from Rathcoole in a place called Rathern, which still came under the South East Antrim Brigade of the U.D.A/ U.F.F. As we arrived at the Cloughfern, the mural on the side of the pub once again caught my attention. This was where the band the Cloughfern Young Conquerors were based. Moreover, the mural at the side of the bar was actually of the band itself. It was different from all the other murals. They were considered a very militant U.D.A band who were known throughout the whole of Ulster. The mural was done to perfection as usual. However, because it was a U.D.A affiliated band the mural also had the U.D.A emblem on it; amazing artwork to say the least. We went into the bar and just like in the Alpha, I was instantly made at home. The warmth from the people was second to none as we steadily got drunk and exchanged a few stories as the night progressed.

The Cloughfern Young Conquerors flute band were established in 1966 during the peak of the troubles. Throughout the years the band became bigger, stronger and better – creating a band of loyalist brothers and new supporters and friends. The C.Y.C had come through thick and thin by being penalised by the security forces and other bands. The bond between the band was never broken and that is why it is still here today. Grugg once released a statement about the band stating: "We don't need to shout about it anymore, we don't need flags or banners, as everyone knows who we are". When I got deeper involved in the U.D.A this would be the band that I would march with myself – and what an honour. They really knew their stuff.

Next to the Cloughfern pub was an Orange Hall from the Cloughfern district of Newtownabbey (Lodge 535) where I would eventually be sworn into the Lodge; it was one of the proudest moments of my life. By doing so, I could march on the 12th of July celebrations. I can remember the one year during the 12th of July parade that the Orange Order were not happy about the C.Y.C waving an Ulster Freedom Fighters flag at the event and some argument broke out. Not all loyalists supported the paramilitaries and some looked upon them as a 'stain' on the Unionist community. On the other hand, my opinion was you could not fight back against the I.R.A with flags and bowler hats as much as I supported and respected the Lodges – that was my opinion anyway.

Unless you're willing to pick up a gun and defend Ulster, I believed that people should never criticize those who are and be thankful for their sacrifice – whether you agree with their actions or not. Grugg was not too happy about the argument breaking out with the Orange Order and later on in the day sent down some masked U.F.F gunmen to let off a round of shots in defiance at the Orange Order. I guess this was Grugg's way of letting people know who was in charge. He actually in advance warned me this was about to happen and not to be frightened as the gunman turning up were from his Brigade – and as a result I had nothing to worry about. Despite that, seeing masked gunmen for the first time firing off a volley of shots was a shocking and alarming experience if I am perfectly honest. By now, I had well and truly started my journey into Ulster loyalism – and to say I was addicted would be an understatement.

Like all English lads I had heard a lot about the Shankill Road in West Belfast because of its near location to the I.R.A strong hold of the Falls Road. Every English loyalist wanted to visit the Shankill at some stage – if just to tell your mates you had been there. It was deep in history and fell under the West Belfast Brigade of the U.D.A/ U.F.F. Stan agreed to take me there the next day which was a Saturday. He also knew a few main people from over that way. After our night at the Alpha and the Cloughfern, I woke up with a terrible hangover. Even so, the excitement of visiting the Shankill soon sobered me up. We let Grugg and all the other lads know we were going for a visit and they were OK with that. At that time the U.D.A were one big happy family, and the tensions and murders that followed on years from now were nowhere in sight. We were 'advised' to stay out of U.V.F controlled bars as if some of the U.V.F lads would have found out we were affiliated with Rathcoole U.D.A they may not have been happy with us using their clubs.

We headed off in a taxi on the Saturday morning for the Diamond Jubilee Bar in the location of the Lower Shankill. During the 1970's and 1980's, the West Belfast Brigade was heavily involved in a series of killings as the troubles escalated. The Brigade reached the peak of its notoriety during the 1990's, when a certain Johnny Adair emerged as its leading figure. Under Adair's direction the West Belfast Brigade and its unit 'C' Company in particular became associated with a killing spree in the neighbouring nationalist/Catholic districts of West Belfast. Eventual feuding with the rival U.V.F and other U.D.A/U.F.F factions would eventually bring Adair down. His Brigade also suffered due to a number of its leading U.D.A gunmen serving lengthy prison sentences. Their main hit man was called Stevie 'Top Gun' McKeag, who had gained himself a feared reputation spreading far and wide. I would have the honour of meeting Top Gun during our visit to the Diamond Jubilee. Top Gun's reputation had risen so high that he was said to have carried out at least twelve separate operations for the U.D.A, although other loyalists put that figure even higher.

Top Gun's killing spree flourished under Adair's leadership. There were reports of details of known republicans being passed on by some sections of the security forces which were then used by 'C' Company – and in particular Top Gun who carried out the executions. I also heard well-believed rumours that because of the jealousy of his achievements, his own Brigade eventually put Top Gun 'out of favour'. Top Gun's murder campaign continued with a series of major hits on known provisionals as well as the republican/nationalist community in general. During 1994, Adair was imprisoned although he still reportedly sent out his orders from his prison cell. 'C' Company meanwhile continued to mix freely with the L.V.F – a splinter group from the U.V.F – and a bitter rival of the bigger U.V.F. They were seen together at the Drumcree conflict which only cemented their relationship. As I have already mentioned, under Adair, 'C' Company moved closer to the vicious feud with the U.V.F.

The militancy of 'C' Company brought Johnny Adair many admirers at one point in loyalist circles and especially from us lads on the Mainland. We worshipped him for his apparent no nonsense approach to the I.R.A. – even though we were later to find out that none of the murders were actually carried out by Johnny Adair himself. Little did we know at the time what road he was taking his Brigade of the U.D.A down? How were we to know just being occasional visitors to Ulster? To us English lads he was looked upon as a hero. Just like the hero status we held for Grugg, Top Gun and Michael Stone – and so on. But in years from now that was all to change as the U.D.A would tear itself apart from within.

We arrived at the Diamond Jubilee in a taxi from Rathcoole. We were now in the heart of 'Johnny Adair territory'. The murals on the Shankill were just like in Rathcoole – very breathtaking; the Shankill had an assortment of murals. The murals stretched the whole of the Shankill Road. These were murals of all the loyalist organisations that had at some stage operated during the troubles. Some murals like the U.V.F and the Y.C.V were one of the same organisations, pretty much like the U.D.A/U.F.F. We entered the Diamond Jubilee. As we walked in a lad named Tommy walked over to say hello; he knew Stan. He was a dead spot on guy and instantly put me at ease after buying me a drink. The pub was empty at the time as we started to have a little chat and he was delighted being my first time over that I had took the time to come and visit his area.

It was still very early on, so Tommy offered to take me to the loyalist souvenir shop up the road. It sold everything you could name from pens to coats, all with loyalist paramilitary slogans on. You name it they sold it, badges, towels, clocks, mugs, jumpers, t-shirts – everything. I honestly could not decide what to buy I was that excited and I was grabbing everything I could. Tommy and Stan waited outside and had a fag as I was fixated like a kid seeing Farther Christmas for the first time. A mate of mine from Birmingham NF was a U.V.F supporter and I brought him a U.V.F badge. As we left the shop Tommy asked me what I had brought and I showed him. All the merchandise was U.D.A/U.F.F apart from the U.V.F badge for my mate – and I remember Tommy telling me nicely: "When were back in the Diamond don't get that U.V.F badge out, the lads would not like it mate". He said it with a grin on his face. I did not need telling twice and put it in my pocket out the way.

We headed back to the Diamond Jubilee with my bag of goodies. As we walked in the pub had now started to fill up and guess who was in there – only Top Gun. However, he had not so long ago been involved in a very serious motorbike accident. He loved his motorbikes but had sadly suffered a number of broken bones and had to have several operations, including pins in his legs. He was still in a very bad way when I met him. To be honest he looked ill and frail and not the man I had pictured in my head for obvious reasons. Top Gun always used to win the award for 'C' Company U.F.F volunteer of the year, which like I have stated, some other members of 'C' Company became jealous over this. Although, he most certainly deserved the yearly award and it is sad to think other people in his Brigade took this stance with him. Me, Stan and Tommy sat down at Top Gun's table but he wasn't saying a lot really. You could tell he had most certainly not recovered yet from his accident. Other members of West Belfast Brigade walked in and joined our table and we had a really good afternoon all laughing and joking as well as some of the lads giving me a history lesson about some of the past events on the Lower Shankill. In addition, I was informed about an interface area called Lanark Way; some of the stories regarding Lanark Way were breathtaking.

I noticed Top Gun liked his gold as he had a gold miniature gun around his neck and loads of gold chains. He had numerous loyalist paramilitary rings on his fingers which really caught my eye. I'm not saying for one minute he didn't make me feel welcome in his company because he did, however, I had met him during a bad time in his life. Additionally, it was still an honour to spend an afternoon with such a loyalist hero who had more than played his part in the war against the I.R.A. Sadly, this was the first and last time I would meet the legend Stevie McKeag, as family members found him dead at his home in September 2000. I would like to take this chance to point out it was not at the hands of republican terrorists; it was reported it was from an overdose of painkillers. The U.D.A had lost one of its most dedicated and honourable soldiers ever to have passed through the ranks of the organisation. Top Gun was buried at Roselawn Cemetery in front of thousands of mourners. Due to his hero status a mural was painted of Top Gun on Hopewell Crescent, just off the Shankill Road, with the words on the mural saying: "Sleeping where no shadows fall".

After topping ourselves up from last night's drink, Stan suggested a U.D.A pub-crawl around the Shankill area.

The lads in the Diamond Jubilee were begging us to stay although Stan explained being my first time over that he wanted to show me around as much as he could – which they understood. It still saddens me to this day how after the West Belfast Brigade had made us so welcome, that in years from now the Brigade me and Stan were representing – South East Antrim – would end up in a bitter and vicious feud with 'C' Company with the loss of Grugg and Rab Carson from our base in Rathcoole. At the same time, I will speak as I find – they were brilliant with us during our afternoon get together. We all shook hands and they wished us all the best and said your welcome over at any time. Before I left, I wished Top Gun a speedy recovery and he thanked me and patted me on the shoulder.

We left the Diamond Jubilee to head for some more U.D.A controlled bars. We went to a further four bars but by now we were very drunk to say the least and I have completely forgotten the names of the establishments that we used. Even so, like always once they heard our English accents they made us ever so welcome. In addition, we met some more great people. Suddenly, Stan was looking a lot worse for wear and he could hardly stand up, therefore, I suggested should we head back to Rathcoole estate. I had never seen Stan this drunk before and he could not even speak, so I was left with the job of getting us a cab and getting us back to home base. Even to this day, Stan and I still laugh about how on my first trip over I was the one who got him home when he was supposed to be looking after me; hilarious. Consequently, when we landed back at The Alpha the night was to take another funny turn regarding Stan.

Stan somehow got into the club with help from me holding him up, and me and some of the lads lay him down on the seats to have a sleep and to try to sober him up a bit. I had another drink or two then fell to sleep myself in the club. Its one of those places where you know you are safe if you are smashed. All the lads have got your back and would always make sure they got you to bed. Little did I know at the time that Stan had woke up and got a second wind and was break dancing all around the down stairs bar. I woke up feeling so ill and all I could see was Stan jumping about all around the club like a young kid; I could not believe the recovery he had made. I felt terrible with a splitting headache and decided to go back to Sammy's flat as the night was over for me. Stan carried on drinking until 4am in the morning – and fair play to him after his early showing he got himself back together and had his own little private party in the Alpha. We had both had a superb day. Moreover, jokingly Stan reminded me the next day that he was the real party animal and Stan most certainly had the last laugh.

We both woke up in Sammy's flat about mid-day on the Sunday morning – both suffering from terrible hangovers. But we had some people to meet in the Alpha who we had not yet bumped into during the weekend. Therefore, a shower, a couple of headache tablets, a bit of breakfast and we were both raring to go again. I was still only about 25 years old at the time and I could handle my drink a lot better then I do nowadays. Sunday for some reason is always a big drinking day in the Alpha and it was packed in there. As Stan and I walked in he was the brunt of jokes for his dancing last night. We had such a laugh at Stan's expense. Shortly afterwards Stan introduced me to a middle-aged man who had been active in the U.D.A/U.F.F South East Antrim Brigade. As we started talking he said something to me that made me really understand that getting involved with the U.D.A was no joke.

He told me about all the people they had lost throughout the years at the hands of the I.R.A. Then he said to me: "Listen Tony, its great to have to over and I'm delighted for your support, but you must be aware that when you're in Ulster you only have to be in the wrong place at the wrong time – someone puts a gun to your head and it's game over". He followed it up with "The I.R.A would look upon you as a target as much as anyone else, because you're drinking in our clubs and bars."

That sobered me up. Up until then I had treated the weekend as just a piss up, however, talking to this person it hit home that there was a serious side to our visit as well. These people were under attack on a daily basis from evil men and women who did not care who they murdered. That chat struck a chord with me and it hit home what I had became involved in. For all that, my choice had been made – it was the risk I was willing to take. Now some people may ask why I stopped the football because of the trouble it was getting me into and then get involved with the U.D.A that was obviously far more dangerous. My answer is this – the match day scene was based on clashing with lads from different clubs from different areas, and apart from the team you support you was all pretty much the same kind of people. Most were hard working lads who worked all week and liked a play up at the weekend. If you come out on top at the football it has no real meaning. It wasn't as though there was any long-term goal you was aiming for – apart from getting yourself seriously injured or facing a lengthy prison sentence – which later on down the line did happen to all the leading Hardcore lads.

I am not knocking the lads who carried it on, that was their choice. Moreover, as well as realising I was not really cut out for the football scene, I had seen a bigger picture and a bigger prize at the end of the day by fighting for Ulster. We were fighting for our country – and even though I am an English man, Northern Ireland is our country. Over and above, it needed defending. I considered Ulster the most loyal part of the British family of nations; people of the same blood. Fighting back against the I.R.A who had killed endless of my people from the mainland and Ulster seemed a good enough reason to put your neck on the line. I felt the need to get involved far out weighed the risks it may bring. If I was going to continue putting my self in harms way I wanted it to be for a valid reason. And what better way than fighting to keep Ulster part of Great Britain.

As the day progressed it was soon time to start making arrangements for our cab to the airport and so we started to say our goodbyes. Fair play to Grugg, he popped in to wish us a safe journey home and once again thank me for coming over. I was delighted by his gesture. I had made many new contacts and met real people who had actively been engaged in the war against the I.R.A. This is what I had been after for years. I had met many people who were to become friends for life. One person in particular who deserves a big thank is Sammy who always put me up in his flat. From the first time I met Sammy he took me under his wing and treated me like a brother. He was always there to help in any way he could and I will forever be grateful for that. We have remained in regular contact ever since and he is truly a top bloke and a very close friend to this day. Sammy was not involved in the paramilitaries like many of the lads – he was a dedicated member of the local Orange Lodge, and our friendship has lasted ever since. In all my years, I have never met anybody as proud to be British as Sammy; he is fiercely patriotic.

As I boarded the plane home I remember thinking how welcome I had been. I had felt more British over in Ulster than I ever could have in Birmingham. Visiting loyal Ulster only confirmed my belief that the people there were more proud of our Queen and our Union than anybody was. It was truly amazing some of the gestures that people made and that is what made it such a fantastic trip. As I landed back in Birmingham with a large part of my heart left behind in Ulster, I knew then that the I.R.A would never break us – never.

I had instantly fallen in love with the country and its people. After just one trip I knew that I would never be completely at home again in England. But I suppose that's the price you pay for the richness of my visit to the Province. Like I have said, my Dad's side of the family were English from Crewe, and my Mom's side of the family was part Welsh. Although, I considered myself 100% English and proud of it. For all that, I felt that I would have been proud to be an Ulster man myself more than anything else in the world. Only being my first trip I still had the 12th of July celebrations to attend as well as the Remembrance Day parade, which were also life-changing experiences. Moving on from here, I was on the verge of making another contact soon in Ulster – a young lad by the name of Steve who was serving eight life sentences in the Maze prison for the Greysteel shootings. He would become like Stan, one of my dearest and closest friends.

I was also on the verge of changing jobs, that would prove to be a wrong move and showed some of the bitter people involved in the right-wing movement. My change of job would also prove to me how having a different political opinion in today's Britain was not allowed, as I lost my job for being a member of the National Front.

CHAPTER 20

*D*uring early 1998, a job offer came my way at a huge multi-national engineering company which was based in South Birmingham – not far from my Mom's and Dad's home in Kings Norton. Even though as this particular stage I was spending most of my time over at Karen's in the Stockland Green area, is was not a problem as the cross-city train only took about thirty minutes. A friend from the Navigation pub wired me of about some vacancies so I applied, went for an interview and got the job. After working at the factory in Digbeth, I had learnt a hell of a lot about engineering due to Chris Butler (R.I.P) training me up over the years, and I could tell the interview went well; the money was brilliant. It was ever so emotional to leave the factory in Digbeth after working there straight from school and making real close friends. Lenny was gutted I was leaving but I promised to keep in contact which I did. It was very hard leaving Lenny behind. It was like saying goodbye to family, nevertheless, the chance had come to better myself so I jumped at it. As I started to work there, being a multi-national company its work force reflected that. There were all races and religions working hand in hand – and I would be a liar to say any different. It was a very happy shop floor I worked on and I always said our crowd was the best bunch out the lot. The financial turnover at the company was running into the many millions; it was a great company to work for.

After a short while I became very close friends with a Roman Catholic guy known as 'Irish John' from County Mayo in the Republic. What a fantastic man he was. It was actually a pleasure to turn up for work and see his big smile and friendly face. He knew I visited Ulster for political reasons, although he never held it against me or showed any bitterness towards me. In addition, I most certainly never shoved my views on the Ulster conflict at him. We worked together – got on really well – and that was how I liked it. I would be safe in saying he was my best mate at the company. Irish John had no republican leanings – I had sounded him out on that without directly asking him so to speak. He considered Birmingham his home and called himself an 'adopted Brummie'. On the other hand, like the majority of Irish people who had moved to England, he talked fondly about Ireland and was very proud of his Irish roots. He was one of those people you could not help but like. He had a deep County Mayo accent that resulted in him being the brunt of many jokes – but it was all in good fun and he took it well. We still to this day meet up every Christmas time for a drink to talk about some of the laughs we used to have.

After working there for nearly two years the one morning I was called into the Manager's office; it was not a manager I directly worked under. It was just before Christmas. Now I wondered what this was all about as I had never lost any time, hardly ever late, knew my job inside out and mixed with everyone; I left my political views at the gate. I was told there was no longer a job for me; I was shocked. He never gave any reasons. He said it was not my work rate or time keeping, but that they were letting me go. Last in, first out – short, sharp, and simple. All the same, he stated they would supply good references for the future, which they did to their word. I loved it there – I was heartbroken. I really was. But the truth had not yet unfolded.

As I was packing my things up to leave my line manager approached me. My sacking had not been that clear cut after all. He told me out of the way of other people that someone had sent the manager of the company a letter stating that they were employing a National Front member and included some photos of me at NF branch meetings. I instantly knew who it was. Now it was all falling into place. My line manager had told me off the record and for that reason I was not going to kick up a stink about it. He said he had put me straight out of respect for the work effort I had given him over the last two years. He was a smashing bloke and I would not have got him into any sort of trouble by letting them know I knew the reason behind my dismissal.

The scum-bag who had put me in it, I'd had problems with him before – so had many others in the NF. You see, he had a jealousy over me that was deep rooted. He was from the Black Country branch of the NF, and I must admit he did a fair bit of work for the party. That being said he despised how popular I was. I will not even give him the time here to name him as he simply is not worth the publicity he would crave. I lost count the amount of times Norman and I had abusive phone calls of him when he was drunk. What's more, he would also leave silly threats on our voice mails. I wanted him expelled from the party – so did Norman. But the NF leadership allowed him to stay in the party because he was the only one doing any political work in Wolverhampton. He even once phoned our headquarters in Kent, and left a drunken message on the answer machine and was still not thrown out the party. It was due to the size of the NF and its lack of activists. Nut-cases like him were allowed to remain in the NF when they should have been expelled from the word go.

What had finally made him crack was when I was backed over him for an election we were both fighting. We were both putting candidates up and my ward in Birmingham got the backing for a leaflet distribution over his ward in Wolverhampton. He did not like that and must have sworn to himself to seek revenge. If his idea of revenge was getting me the sack then unfortunately for him it worked. After ho e sent in the letter and photos of me, he squirmed away from the NF as he knew I would not ignore this one as I had before. He knew this would not be taken lightly, and he vanished into thin air. Norman agreed with me that at the first sign of trouble he should have been expelled. A loose cannon was allowed to roam around doing what he liked; I paid the price.

Many years later he was spotted at a BNP meeting in Dudley where I only found out the following day. In all honesty, I am glad I was not there as trust me I would not have walked over to him and shook his hand – if you get my drift. This regrettably would not be the last time I would have problems from people inside my own movement. Its strange but true, but over the years I have had more problems from within the right-wing than from any ethnic people or the I.R.A. The right-wing has always been racked with infighting and even though it does not change your political opinion, it does make you second think about some of the people you are working with – and is it really worth the hassle. I know personally that many other people feel the same way. Consequently, it did not turn out too bad in the end as I went back to the factory in Digbeth that was expanding by the year – was given a promotion – put through my driving and landed a company car. And additionally, a good wage to go with it.

Nonetheless, let us look at my dismissal. I was a good worker who showed everybody respect. I was also a good timekeeper and polite as my references showed. Despite that, because at the time I belonged to a perfectly legal political party – the National Front – I lost my job. I never once brought my politics into work and had made a number of non-White friends. As the old saying goes: "You can vote for whoever you like as long as its not the NF/BNP". I know that some of the main gaffers even said to my line manager that they fought to keep me because I was a good worker and a nice helpful chap – although the main man at the top had the final say on matters. An executive of the company even walked up to me, shook my hand and said: "I'm sad to see you go, they are making a mistake". Therefore, I had left with my head held high. This just made me more determined to carry on fighting for British freedom – as in this Marxist state we were now living in you cannot have your own opinion on the state of your own country. The Government had most undoubtedly turned its back on its own people. But I'm going to be perfectly honest here. Cultures that don't think that they themselves are worth saving, deserve to be replaced. My political beliefs had cost me the job that I loved.

What's more, two months before my dismissal a top managers job had come up for grabs due to an employee leaving. It was a very important role in the company with a huge salary to go with it. I didn't apply for the position as I never stood a chance as there were people way ahead of me in the pecking order. The position eventually went to a

Black lad called Trevor Bunter; there were numerous White applicants with far more experience and knowledge than Trevor. Trevor had been 'fast-tracked' into the position in what is known as 'positive discrimination', which gives preferential treatment to minority groups. He even told me himself face to face that he had landed the position because he was Black. In modern day Britain it seems that only White British people can be accused of the crime of 'racism'. This evil left-wing world-view is an inevitable result of decades of enforced 'diversity', 'tolerance' and out of control immigration.

Now I had found my feet in the U.D.A, Stan asked me if I would like to sponsor a prisoner. This would mean writing to him, even helping him out now and again financially and sending him in books etc. In return, he would keep in contact with me by phone and by mail from the Maze prison in Ulster. This is what I really wanted from the beginning – to support a lad who was inside serving time for the U.D.A/U.F.F; this was what the L.P.A was all about. Stan gave me the address of a lad named Steve Irwin who had served in the North Antrim and Londonderry Brigade of the U.D.A/U.F.F. He was serving eight life sentences for the attack on the Rising Sun bar in Greysteel, County Londonderry. The attack was in retaliation for the I.R.A bombing of the Shankill Road a week earlier, which resulted in the death of innocent loyalists – it was known as the 'Greysteel massacre'.

Even though as some may say that the I.R.A were already on the way to the negotiating table, the Greysteel shootings made the I.R.A realise they could never obtain a United Ireland by bombs and guns alone. The pressure from the republican community being put onto Sinn Fein after the Greysteel shootings played a 'major' part in bringing the I.R.A to the negotiating table. The threat of loyalists carrying out more pub attacks was simply too much for the nationalists/republicans. There was undistorted fear in every republican bar that they may have been the next target for a U.D.A/U.F.F hit squad. At this particular time, the loyalist paramilitaries had the I.R.A on the back foot – no question about that.

On the evening of the 30th October 1993, three gunmen arrived at the Rising Sun bar. They would use two cars for the operation. Brian McNeill had driven the 'scout car' in front of the car carrying the U.D.A volunteers. He was to use a pre-planned signal of tapping his brake lights three times to warn of any police checkpoints which may have lay ahead. The U.F.F had been watching the Rising Sun for a number of days. They knew that the I.R.A used the bar and had information that high-level republican ex-prisoners drank in there. To that end, as far as the U.F.F were concerned it was a legitimate target. The U.F.F wanted to hit the I.R.A somewhere they would not expect it as republican Belfast had 'gone to ground'. A number of targets had been considered, however, Greysteel would be the one eventually chosen. It was rumoured that this order came from Belfast, when in reality North Antrim and Londonderry U.D.A. had carefully selected the Rising Sun. Every U.F.F unit in Ulster was on stand by after the Shankill bombing; retaliation was imminent. The provisionals had 'struck first' and the U.D.A would most certainly 'strike back'. That's how it was in Northern Ireland.

The guns had earlier been test fired at a forest in Ballykelly. The unit of U.F.F volunteers had surveyed the lay out of the pub prior to the attack. They had undertaken a surveillance of the bar to check out the security system in place – and to suss out its blind spots. They checked out the lounge and the bar and decided that the lounge was the better bet. The gunmen wearing boiler suits and balaclavas were to enter the lounge. There was a Halloween party going on inside. Initially, some punters thought it was a Halloween 'prank' until the U.F.F started shooting into the packed crowd. Steve Irwin, who was the number one gunman, shouted the now infamous line 'Trick or Treat' before he opened fire. He used a VZ 58 (similar to an AK 47). The scene was chaotic as people inside the lounge began to panic. The second gunman – Torrens Knight – stood outside the bar with a sawn off shotgun in-case any one tried to follow the gunmen out of the lounge after the shooting had finished. The third gunman – Geoffrey Deeney – only shot once with his 9mm pistol before the gun jammed which resulted in many people surviving the attack. Steve Irwin had taped two magazines together for his rifle as to save time reloading. When the shooting was over the gunmen fled the bar and drove off towards Eglinton, where they set fire to the car and again linked up with Brian McNeill, who would be driving the 'clean car' to the pick up point after the shootings.

The following day the U.D.A claimed responsibility for the attack using the cover-name 'Ulster Freedom Fighters'. The U.D.A statement also claimed that the nationalist electorate had been targeted after last Saturday's slaughter of nine innocent Protestant civilians. All four men were eventually arrested and charged with the murders. In his sentencing remarks, Judge Carswell LJ, commented on the merciless and barbarous nature of the offences committed by the defendants: "You have pleaded guilty to a series of offences which appalled and disgusted all the right thinking people in this community. In your various ways, you were concerned in or connected with one of the most callous and cold-blooded massacres in the catalogue of so many heinous crimes committed in this Province. Comparing atrocities would be as fruitless as it would be painful. It is sufficient to say that on the scale of barbarities which have been perpetrated by cold-hearted practitioners of violence over the last quarter of a century, the Greysteel murders rank very high. There is nothing that can be said by way of mitigation in the case of those directly concerned, that they have now faced up to their responsibility for what they did, pleaded guilty to their crimes and publicly expressed their regret".

The U.D.A had ordered the Greysteel massacre as part of its strategy of utilising the I.R.A. The U.D.A would have argued that their ability to achieve a balance of terror was instrumental in the I.R.A declaring a cease-fire. To put it concisely, the point had been reached where the loyalist paramilitaries would not only replicate the tactics of the I.R.A – they would take it one-step further. As far as I was concerned if there was no I.R.A war machine there would be no need for the U.D.A. The I.R.A had brought this terror onto their own people by the Shankill bombing.

Stan calls me up and gives me Steve's address to write to him. Little did I know at this stage that Steve would become a major part of my life as well as becoming a close personal friend – where we would help each other out the best we could through all periods in our lives – good and bad. I wrote my letter and kept it brief and simple. I obviously did not know Steve at this stage and due to his past, I did not really know what to put in the letter. I seemed to conquer up all these images in my head of how he would be and I was really stuck for words at the beginning. But trust me this was not the case for very long as we both had the same sense of humour and the letters just got more and more bizarre. I admit some would even say we had a sick and twisted sense of humour, nevertheless, that was how we had our laughs along the way. I know it helped Steve whilst he was serving his sentence to have me available for a play up and it helped me as well. I was 'buzzing' that I was now supporting a U.D.A prisoner. I used to wait with such delight for his letters to arrive as they were always full of the banter we used to throw at each other.

In the one letter Steve asked me to put my phone number in my returning letter so he could call me up – so I did. He wrote back with a date and a time he was calling me up for our first chat. He could not just call unexpectedly, because in the Maze prison you had to apply for someone's name to go on your call list and have it cleared. I will never forget to this day as I sat there waiting for the call. I was a bag of nerves. Who he was, and what he had been imprisoned for all suddenly got on top of me. Daft really, when you consider I had met the likes of Grugg and Top Gun. Even though for months we had been having letters coming and going to each other, I got that nervous I recall I was going to go out so I missed the call; silly but true. Then as promised at 7pm the phone rang.

I picked up the phone and it was Steve. I remember thinking how compared to most of the Ulster lads I had spoken to before that his accent was very soft. Some real deep Belfast accents were very hard to understand, whereas coming from Londonderry Steve's accent was a lot softer. We started chatting and I do not mind admitting I stammered all the way through the conversation. This was not a normal phone call by any stretch of the imagination. I was talking to one of the U.F.F's top activists who was serving eight life sentences. What's more, something that made me feel so good inside was how Steve kept on thanking me for my support

– just like Grugg did and all my contacts from Rathcoole. The loyalists never for one second took our support for granted and it really made me feel at peace knowing inside I was at last doing something that was of benefit to the L.P.A, no matter how little it may have been.

As the phone call ended Steve once again thanked me for my support and that was the start of a life long friendship. He used to call me up about every two weeks, however, the phone calls like the letters got more and more hilarious as we talked nothing but crap – joking and laughing at anything. Meanwhile, Stan invited me over for my first 12th of July parade and suggested that we go and visit Steve in the Maze prison; I did not need asking twice. The Maze prison held the most notorious terrorists from both sides of the Ulster conflict, and this was something I would have never turned down; I was actually going to meet Steve in person. The flights were booked and about fifteen of us from the West Midlands L.P.A were heading over for the march. Moreover, myself to visit the Maze prison for the first time.

We arrived in Rathcoole, and we all set up in the houses we were staying on the estate. You were never short of a bed in Rathcoole – the people there were only too pleased to put you up. Come the day of the march I had the pleasure for the first time of marching with the Cloughfern Young Conquerors. What a fine band they were. After marching with this band I swore to myself that even though my support for the U.D.A didn't start and end in Rathcoole, that I would never march with another band bar the C.Y.C – and this has been the case ever since. However, his was no march where you could just turn up in your jeans and a football top – you had to look the part, therefore, we had all taken our best suits over with us.

On the morning of the march we all looked the business even if I do say so myself. As the parade was about to start, there were hundreds of bands and thousands upon thousands of people lining the streets. This was the most open display of British pride I had seen in my life. It was amazing and I felt like crying with pride. I then spotted Grugg who played the base drum in the band and he walked up to me with a clenched fist as to suggest were in for one hell of a day. I had been to Southport before to watch the 12th of July parades, although Southport was nothing you could compare to this. This was so much bigger.

Sammy from the Orange Lodge was a Marshall on the day and as we were marching I will never forget him saying to me: "Tony if we don't march in line it ain't worth marching at all. Now get back into line" – and he was right. The majority of the marchers including myself were wearing the sash. They were all slightly different depending on the area or district you were affiliated to. The noise generated from all the bands was truly fantastic as flutes and drums filled the air. At the front of our band a standard-bearer carried a flag of the bands name the C.Y.C with a Red Hand in the middle – which displayed the bands connection to the Ulster Freedom Fighters. For the first time in my life I felt like a true loyalist as I was marching for Ulster and its people. It was a long day but truly worth it. At the end of the parade we all landed back at the Alpha for one almighty piss up.

The Remembrance Day parades were the same. Although, for this occasion you had to be on your very best behaviour. It is a very dignified event. I will never forget my first march for Armistice Day. As the parade set off around Rathcoole estate it was that huge you could not see the beginning or the end of the march. It seemed like the whole estate had turned out for this. It was such a sight and an honour to be involved in such a huge event. They were always really touching episodes and after the march we would all gather on the car park of the Alpha to listen to high-ranking members of the U.D.A/U.F.F deliver their speeches on the sacrifices made by Britain's war dead. A man named Tommy Kirkham was a leading figure in Rathcoole, who always addressed the crowd. In addition, followed up by the playing of the last post, then a two-minute silence in honour of our fallen comrades. It was so moving. Just like on the 12th of July, I would regularly attend these marches throughout the years. The good thing as well about Remembrance Sunday was the huge upstairs room in the Alpha would be opened up for this event to cope with the demand of people at the club. The upstairs room in the Alpha had all the standards on display which fell under South East Antrim Brigade's control.

The one-year Stan had me on such a wind up on Remembrance Day. We were all as usual sitting in the Alpha and there were hundreds of people in there. It was rammed solid – standing room only. Stan approached me and said: "On Remembrance Day every body gets a round in for all the lads and its your turn Tony". I looked around open mouthed and said to Stan: "But I only have £70 pounds on me. I bet the round will come to near on £800 quid". Stan proceeded to tell me I could get into a bit of trouble if I didn't get the round in, therefore, I started to try and tap up the lads for some money as I thought I was in for a kneecapping or even worse. Don't forget I was still new to it all at this stage and a bit naive. After about ten minutes Stan walked up to me and said: "Have you got the money for the round?" – which I had not. Seconds later Stan started to laugh his head off as this was a wind up invented by Stan and the Rathcoole lads. I sat there with my head in my hands, even though I still saw the funny side of it eventually. Grugg found it highly amusing which was only right. They had me right in the nett.

Grugg then pulled me to one side and called me outside. I was obviously wondering why? There was a car waiting outside and he took me to a secret location and showed me where the local lads were sworn into to the U.D.A. Words cannot explain how interested I was. I wondered exactly how many people had been in this room and had committed their life to defending Ulster from the I.R.A. I know without a doubt if I had been born in Rathcoole, I would have also pledged my life to the U.D.A and served in South East Antrim Brigade under John Gregg. It would have been an honour. I have no reservations about admitting this. This was once again another nice gesture from Grugg. When we returned to the club it was a brilliant lively afternoon get together. The laughs we had in the Alpha were unforgettable. Even writing this now it brings back such happy memories. I would also at times now and again stay behind in England for the National Front Remembrance Parade in London which was equally as moving but attended by much smaller numbers.

The day had finally come to visit Steve Irwin in the Maze prison. As per usual Sammy was on hand to give Stan and I a lift. As we arrived at the Maze prison there was a little coffee hut on the car park – but Sammy advised us not to go in there as it was mostly used by the I.R.A waiting to go in to visit their people. As we headed into the Maze prison, Sammy arranged with us a place to meet up afterwards for our lift home to Rathcoole. The top-level security measures inside the Maze only confirmed to me that Billy Wright of the L.V.F had most certainly been set up for his murder; there was no way anybody could of smuggled handguns into this prison. You booked in first with your visitors pass and then had to wait in a tiny room before you came out into another room to be searched. You then had to wait in another room for the prison bus to take you to another building. In addition, you then waited on the prison officer calling out the name of the prisoner you was going to visit. The security was well on top of things. The I.N.L.A terrorists who had killed Billy Wright, had somehow been helped to get those weapons into the jail – I will stand by this until my dying day.

We finally reached Steve's wing of the Maze prison, then had to sit in a waiting room until we were called. I would be a liar to say anything different than I was nervous but excited to finally be meeting the lad I had become friends with. Steve was already sitting there waiting, with a load of chocolates and crisps from the prison canteen. We shook hands, hugged and smiled. After meeting Grugg who was a monster of a man, I think in my mind I expected every loyalist prisoner to somehow look like him – but Steve never fitted into this stereotype. I had heard he used to be a bulky lad before he was sent down for the Greysteel shootings, however, he had most certainly lost a good few stone. In all honesty, he was a very good-looking lad; just not the type you would picture of doing what he had done. Not that it takes a certain type of person to do anything in life, all the same, I am sure you will understand what I mean when I say he never fitted the bill. I instantly noticed he was a very switched on lad and was most certainly on the ball. A shrewd lad who did not let anything get passed him – as I would find out throughout the years. He listened to every word you had to say before carefully answering. You weren't getting one over this kid. You could tell if he had not got himself into this situation he most certainly would have got somewhere in life apart from jail, I am sure about that. But in the cold light of day this was the situation he was in because his country had been at war with the I.R.A.

While the majority of the loyalist paramilitaries identified Sinn Fein/I.R.A as the enemy, some Brigades of the U.D.A (and the U.V.F for that matter) were prepared to countenance 'strategic strikes' on the wider republican community in retaliation to attacks against the loyalist population. As I have already stated, the U.F.F strike on the Rising Sun was in retaliation for the no warning I.R.A bomb on the Shankill Road. The scenes were truly horrific following the Shankill bomb, with people trying to get through all the rubble to reach the dead and injured. During the war in Ulster morality played little part in the politics of terrorism and the U.D.A/U.F.F would argue that their ability to hit back against the I.R.A played a major part in the provisionals declaring a ceasefire. The I.R.A ceasefire was announced following the attack on the Rising Sun pub – therefore, the strategy of the U.D.A/U.F.F most certainly worked – however brutal it may have been.

We started talking and having a play up as you do, before I asked Steve about where he grew up and his reasons for getting involved with the U.D.A. Even though I knew the basics about the lad, just like he knew the basics about me, being the first time we met it was obvious we were going to open up to each other . With Steve being from Londonderry, I questioned him about the rumours I had heard from people in Rathcoole about his home city. The city of Londonderry had been severely affected by the troubles over the years. The 'Ulster conflict' is widely considered by some people to have emerged in the city with many regarding the battle of the Bogside as the beginning of the troubles; other people may have different opinions about this. The 'Bloody Sunday' incident in 1972, also occurred in Londonderry – an encounter that Sinn Fein/I.R.A have played on to their full advantage.

Steve was from the Waterside – which is a part of Londonderry on the east bank of the River Foyle. Traditionally, the Waterside ends at Caw roundabout near Foyle Bridge. The Waterside is a mainly Protestant area, however, the surrounding areas are mainly Catholic/republican strongholds. During the troubles the Waterside's Protestant population grew, due to Protestants moving there from the west side of the river. The conditions the Protestant people had to live under were stomach churning. There were places you simply could not go if you were a Protestant. All the local amenities were totally out of bound for the Protestant people, including a majority of the pubs and clubs. The loyalist people of Londonderry were under attack day and night from the I.R.A, and yet people wonder why lads like Steve ended up joining the U.D.A. The Protestant community were living under a 24-hour 'siege mentality'.

I then brought up the conversation regarding the border areas in Ulster, which stretched over 360 kilometres from Lough Foyle in the north to Carlingford Lough in the North East. There was a policy in place from the I.R.A by forcing Protestants from rural border areas. This was looked upon by the I.R.A as part of their 'long war' and was a strategy to force the British government into doing an eventual deal with Sinn Fein. Protestant farmers were at the forefront of the war being waged by the provisionals. Protestant farmers could not carry out a days work without having a shotgun by their side; such was the threat from the I.R.A. A large number of farmers from border areas had been murdered whilst simply carrying out their daily duties. A number were ex-U.D.R and ex-R.U.C officers, all the same, a large number were just ordinary Protestants. Then when the land came up for sale no Protestants would think about buying it due to the repercussions – in what can only be described as 'ethnic cleansing' of border Protestants. The relentless bombings of Protestant owed businesses and the burning out of Protestant farmers had gone completely unreported in the media; some things never change.

It is very common when reporters mention the war in Ulster, to see it in terms of the Protestant majority against a Catholic minority, nonetheless, this was not the case along the border areas. Let us make no bones about it 'ethnic cleansing' was exactly the right label for what was, and is still going on to this day. Although, to the outside world little knowledge was known about this; the people there suffered alone. During this period, a place named Castlederg suffered more than its fair share of atrocities due to its location in County Fermanagh. It is a staunchly Protestant area close to the Irish border. The Town is surrounded by a mass of country roads and unsecured borders leading to a 'safe haven' provided by the Irish Republic. The network of roads meant the I.R.A could attack Castlederg with ease and then make their escape without any chance of being caught.

Steve and I also spoke about family matters as our families had their fair share of problems along the way – and it was good to get some things off your chest. We also touched on the Greysteel shootings that had got him incarcerated at the time. Nevertheless, this was a private conversation between two friends and now is not the time or place to tell the world about what was discussed. Steve informed me that for the last 30 years members of the Orange Order returning home from the 12th of July celebrations in Coleraine, had their buses and coaches attacked by republicans in Greysteel, and had their windows put through; it happened every time. Likewise, they stopped reporting it in the media after the Greysteel shootings so they could keep making out that it was an innocent and mixed village; like hell it was. The one thing I can tell you though is that at the time in question Steve had no regrets about carrying out his orders as a soldier. He was honoured to have been selected to 'hit back' for the Shankill bombing. Chilling words but something I understood as most people do not realise Northern Ireland was not a normal country – far from it. It was a totally divided country with deep divisions running through both communities.

As the visit ended it was very emotional to have finally met the lad who I had become close friends with through simply writing to each other and speaking on the phone. We hugged at the end of the visit and as always he politely thanked me again for my support. As Stan and I watched Steve walk off to head back to his cell, I remember thinking again what a bright young lad and how if he had been born in England instead of Ulster his life would have took such a different road. As we left the Maze prison my eyes were full up as Sammy was ready to take us back to home base in Rathcoole.

Now on the subject of supporting Steve, I need to put something across very clear as I know some of the questions people not supportive of the Ulster cause will put forward. Yes, I was supporting and backing a man guilty of eight murders, however, I will now explain why. Being a British nationalist standing by your own people is part of the make up of what were all about. Every other nation adopts this stance, therefore why should it be any different for the

British? Look at some examples here. Nelson Mandela was a convicted terrorist, charged and sentenced with planting bombs at train stations. Despite that, he was looked upon worldwide as some kind of hero. On his release from jail he was made President of South Africa, and he is hailed by the majority of Black people world wide as a freedom fighter – not a terrorist.

Digging a little deeper, Nelson Mandela was the head of the terrorist wing of the A.N.C, and the South African Communist party. At his trial he pleaded guilty to 156 acts of public violence. This included mobilising terrorist bombing campaigns where bombs were planted in public places, as in the Johannesburg railway station massacre. Many innocent people including women and children, were killed by Nelson Mandela's terrorist wing. In my eyes he was the Black version of Gerry Adams. His history of planting bombs with the intent to kill innocent people was never looked upon as a crime as it fits the Marxist/communist agenda to portray him as a good man. There are even two statues in London glorifying this communist terrorist. It is time to remove the statues of Nelson Mandela from Parliament square, because it glorifies a man who believed in violence and terrorism.

Moving on from here, look at how Sinn Fein/I.R.A have been accepted by the British government as normal politicians and not terrorists. Yes, it is correct I was rubbing shoulders with the loyalist paramilitaries, then again, don't forget the British government were holding secret talks with the I.R.A for many years – even after everything that the I.R.A had done to the British people – including directly targeting the British government themselves. What is the difference? Look at the powerful positions that Sinn Fein have now been handed in government in the so-called quest for peace. With the goal of a United Ireland still at the top of their final agenda. The acceptance of Sinn Fein/I.R.A by the British government is one of the most disgusting acts of betrayal in British history. How dare people question what I was doing? Let us not forget the Queen herself actually had a private meeting with Martin McGuinness, and even went as far as shaking his hand. The same hand that had been responsible for thousands of deaths, including a member of her own family.

On the subject of Sinn Fein/I.R.A you only have to look at their votes at every single election in Ulster to see the support they have from the republican community. It does not matter to them one bit the innocent people they have butchered along the way in their pursuit of a United Ireland. Why is supporting the loyalist paramilitaries any more of a crime? Here in England the support from people of Irish descent for the I.R.A is immense, and to a large extent they do not make no bones about it or even try to hide it. I am not saying every Irishman supports the I.R.A; I know many who do not. Nevertheless, it made me adopt the attitude why should it be any different for me. In addition, a point that most people forget to take on board is that by the loyalist paramilitaries forcing the I.R.A into a ceasefire it made England a safer place to live. With the I.R.A no longer bombing England we were less prone to republican attacks on the mainland. That was down to the U.D.A/U.F.F taking the war to the I.R.A.

Let us once again take a look at the British government. Look at the crimes committed against the British people by the British government. The crime of surrendering our country to the immigration invasion. The crime of speaking directly to the I.R.A and selling out our most loyal subjects

– the Ulster loyalists. The crime of handing over lock stock and barrel our rights and laws to Europe. The crime of ignoring our young children being used as sex slaves by men of Pakistani origin, due to the fear of being called 'racist'. The crime of covering up known paedophiles such as Jimmy Saville, Cyril Smith and many other public figures. I could go on and on. Look as well at the support worldwide for Islamic extremists especially here in England, with the likes of Anjem Choudary free to spread his hate for the west and our Christian way of life.

Another example of our feeble government is how long it took to finally extradite Abu Hamza. It took eight years to finally get rid of this evil man even after preaching 'hate speeches' from his Finsbury Park Mosque. He should have been on the first plane out of here, but due to legislation and the UK signing up to the European Convention on Human Rights – this Islamic terrorist was allowed to stay in our country. How did this make our country look worldwide? After looking at all these illustrations do I really have anything to answer to – I think not. I was a British patriot supporting my own people in a war against the I.R.A who had bombed my home city of Birmingham. I was simply standing by my own kin-folk as everybody else does. Moreover, my attitude to this day has still not changed.

The Good Friday Agreement was a major political development in Northern Irish politics known as the 'peace process'. The agreement was made up of two inter related documents both signed at Belfast on the 10th of April 1998. It was a multi-party agreement by the majority of Northern Ireland's political parties and an international agreement between the British and Irish governments. The D.U.P was the only major political party to oppose the agreement. The Belfast agreement set out a complex series of provisions relating to a number of areas, including the future status and system of government within Northern Ireland and the relationship between Northern Ireland and institutions in both the Republic of Ireland and the United Kingdom. In addition, the principle of respect for both of Northern Ireland's communities and their traditions, the decommissioning of arms held by the various paramilitary groups on both sides, and the one that caused so much uproar...the release of the members of terrorist groups. I wanted to see the loyalist prisoners get back home to their families, however, to also see the republican child killers set free was going to be a bitter pill to swallow.

The agreement was approved by voters in Northern Ireland at a referendum held on the 22nd May 1998, whilst on the same day voters approved the agreement in the Republic of Ireland. The agreement came into force on the 2nd of December 1999. The present constitutional status of Northern Ireland as part of the United Kingdom and Northern Ireland's devolved system of government was based on the Good Friday Agreement – as well as the 2006 St Andrews Agreement. The voter turn out in Northern Ireland was 81%, with 71% of the people voting 'Yes'. In the Republic of Ireland the voter turn out was much less with 56% turning out to vote and a huge 94% also voting 'Yes'. I myself was dead against the agreement due to my hatred for the I.R.A, but if it meant the loyalist prisoners getting released then I suppose there was a little part of me that could understand why people had agreed to it. I am not saying I did not want peace in Northern Ireland, although not peace at any price; the republican terrorists walking free. My idea of achieving peace was to smash the I.R.A from within, regardless if the tactics used were from within side the law or outside of the law; cut off the head of the snake.

Due to this agreement the majority of prisoners would be set free in July 2000, which included my close friend Steve Irwin. I actually had it planned to go and surprise him when he got released and meet him outside the jail. But I thought I might be getting in the way as he obviously had family to go and see first and to get himself settled. Therefore, I put our meet up on hold. Nonetheless, I would finally be able to meet up with him on the outside instead of just relying on letters, phone calls and visits at the Maze Prison. And when we did finally meet up for a weekend together what a weekend it was; it was pure chaos.

As I have said me and Steve loved nothing more than a play up, so when I first booked my flight over to Belfast I brought myself a blonde wig to surprise him when I landed at the airport. When I walked out after getting my luggage the look on his face was a picture as it took him a minute or two to recognise me. That just set the tone for the weekend. Steve at the time was living up a place called the Woodvale. The Woodvale area begins after Ainsworth Avenue, when the road changes from the Shankill Road to the Woodvale Road. As well as extensive housing the Woodvale area also contains the Woodvale Presbyterian church – a building on the corner of the Woodvale and Ballygomartin Road that dates back to 1899. The area takes its name from Woodvale Park, which is a public gardens and sports area that was opened in 1888. Steve was living with his missus, and she had also become a very good friend of mine and I was made ever so welcome whilst in her company. She's a smashing girl and very easy to get on with.

We started of the day heading to a Glentoran football game in East Belfast, and as you do took in a few bars around the ground where I met up with some of Steve's mates from North Belfast. Little did I know at the time these North Belfast lads would also become very close friends of mine as the years progressed. We had a great day out at the football and I was pleased for Steve as Glentoran scored a very late winner which sent all the fans home happy. I met some great lads on the day and spent most the game chatting away rather than watching the football. After the game we headed into town and went to a good few bars and had a play up. Then one of the funniest things I have ever witnessed in my life happened. A man suddenly appeared into view with a beard and a moustache, but wearing a women's top, a mini skirt, stockings and a pair of ladies shoes. He was obviously a cross dresser or a transvestite and me and Steve could not breath we were laughing that much. It was hysterical and is still a talking point to this day. Like with Stan, it seemed like all we used to do was laugh.

We then headed back to his flat on the Woodvale, where we stocked up with loads of alcohol, weed, and ecstasy pills. I am not condoning abusing drink or drugs, however, we were young lads at the time and with Steve being in jail so long we wanted a proper play up. What I can only explain now is a night of total madness. We were totally on another planet as the night progressed and then Steve suggested we go for a 'walkabout'. In other words, wondering the streets having a laugh; and by god didn't we half. We both went out in fancy dress and had the one of the best laughs of my life – if not the best night I have ever had. I won't even go into some of the things we got up to but all inside the law. We had both totally lost our minds and the carry on that followed was totally crazy. I actually witnessed the second when I saw Steve lose his mind and go into overdrive. You had to be there to understand it. We were both on another dimension. The following day we were the talk of the Woodvale, as people had seen us out and about, walking around like two men possessed. It was a night to always remember. The following day we both felt that rough we never left the flat until it was time for my flight home. The laugh we had brought us even closer together. We were two of a kind.

At a later date we also attended a coach trip from Rathcoole to Londonderry, which was organised by Frank from the British Ulster Alliance. It was to visit locals from a loyalist enclave called the Fountain estate. What an experience that was. I could not believe the conditions that these people had to live under. They were under attack 24 hours a day from the I.R.A. Many of these attacks came from the Nailors Row area. They had nothing – and I mean nothing. They were living under a 'siege mentality'. All this is carried out under the guise of 'Irish freedom'. The generation of republicans who carry out these attacks have had their heads filled with anti-Protestant, anti-Unionist, anti-loyalist and anti-British hatred by the likes of Adams and McGuinness. These people have sown the seeds of hatred throughout the nationalist community, and this is the way in which it manifests itself. On the way back to Rathcoole after drinking all day, things got a bit out of hand on the coach between a few of the lads, including myself. What started of as a play up finished up with Frank having to put us back into line which was only correct as there were women on the coach. In spite of that, it was a great day out and I made more contacts in Ulster as well as getting a history lesson about Londonderry from the locals.

When it was my turn to invite Steve over to Birmingham, I brought him over for a National Front AGM as a special guest. I was going to ask him to give a speech on the Ulster troubles, however, with all the bad press he had received in the past I decided against it in-case it leaked out. I was also going to present him with an award for serving his time for the U.F.F and Ulster, but once again I stayed on the side of caution as I did not want him all over the papers again. I am sure it would have emerged; there were a couple of people in the NF I had my doubts about at the time. My assumption proved correct as these people were eventually expelled from the party.

Not forgetting the 'walkabout' we had around the Woodvale, now it was our turn for one in South Birmingham. Like before we hit a load of pubs and bars before we decided it was time for another play up – this time sadly without the fancy dress. Steve was hungry so I took him to a local Chinese takeaway where he had curry sauce and chips. I have actually mentioned this for a reason I will get onto in a bit. After eating his Chinese in the street, we were both steaming drunk by now and had just taken a load of speed, therefore, we started our 'walkabout'. We looked at each other and I knew then that the madness was about to start. We were walking the streets acting the fool and then we started to dare each other to do things. I knew an NF member who lived up the road so we headed to his house (it was after midnight) for a mess around. We agreed on knocking his door a load of times and posting a pound coin through his letterbox before running off. I know to some people this will sound stupid, nevertheless, it was our way of playing up and we both found it so funny. We then ran off for our next play up.

We were walking up some alley when Steve dared me to eat some leaves of the floor which had fallen from a nearby tree. It was raining at the time and we were both ringing wet but we did not care. The speed had also started to take effect by now. We were both in that type of mood now to do anything for a play up. I eat a hand full of these filthy leaves of the floor and swallowed them. We were both rolling around laughing; it was brilliant. Now it was my turn to dare Steve to do something. As we carried on up the road I noticed a drainpipe that was leaking water from the heavy rain and I dared Steve to put his mouth under the leak and drink the drain water – which he did. He took a good few mouthfuls as well. We were on a mission and once again having the time of our lives; it was crazy. After messing about for another hour or two, we headed back to my house to carry on the night. Karen was resigned to the fact it was going to be one of those weekends – fair play to her. Steve's missus was the same when I was over in Ulster. They looked upon it as two long lost friends coming together and they just let us get up to whatever we wanted to get up to without getting in the way. They both deserve a mention for this.

Steve suddenly alerted me that he had bad stomach cramps and had to run the toilet. He had severe diarrhoea and he was in so much pain; he was in agony. It was running out of him like water and he was looking at me begging for help. Deep down inside I was dying to crack up laughing, except for the look on his face said it all. The funny thing to come of it all we were blaming the beer in the pubs and the Chinese takeaway. We were even on the verge of going back to the Chinese and having it out with them that they had served us rotten food. It never even entered our heads the drain water had given Steve the diarrhoea. This situation actually ended our night prematurely as I searched Karen's medicine box for Imodium tablets. I know to many people this will sound like two stupid lads not acting our age – but we were like two peas in a pod. Once we started playing up there was no stopping us and no boundaries. It was just how we were

On my next flight to Belfast I found out something shocking, although at the same time not surprising. I got a pull at the airport from Special Branch who like to monitor British nationalists and Ulster loyalists. They told me they knew where the NF had held the AGM conference and named the hotel as well as the false name we had booked it under. They'd had someone trailing me and Steve all weekend to see what we was up to; this was obviously because of Steve's past. For all that, this was of no shock to us as we had spotted a Special Branch operative during the weekend sitting in a bar casually reading a newspaper. I recognised his face from a pull I'd had from him before at the airport. Steve walked over and offered to buy him a drink – he did not stay long after that. On the subject of Special Branch, they had stopped me on a number of occasions during my flights to and from Belfast and had approached me to work for them as an informer. They said it could be financially rewarding for me. Due to my links with Steve and South East Antrim U.D.A/U.F.F, I suppose they thought I could be a useful man to have onside and give them information. Anyhow, I told them abruptly I work for my country and my people, and no one else.

They tried all kinds of approaches to try to get me to talk. They tried the 'scare approach' by telling me I was looked upon as a 'very dangerous man' and it would be wise to have them on side to protect me. I cracked up laughing at that one. They even tried to soften me up by telling me how brave they thought Steve was for his attack on the Rising

Sun bar, and they admired him for his courage. I knew this was only being said to try to get me to open up and talk. I also had Special Branch knock at my door on six occasions trying to get me on side but after slamming the door in their faces those visits soon stopped. After many years of harassing me they finally gave up; I now no longer now get a pull when flying to Belfast. Although it did make me think if they were that interested in me who was a virtual nobody, how many high-ranking people over the years they have managed to get onside and work for them. I bet that figure is really high.

But it was not to be all fun and games for Steve and I as we were about to find out. I had invited Steve over for a National Front Remembrance Day march in London. I mostly used to go to Rathcoole for Armistice Day, but I thought for a change and to get Steve a weekend away I would go on the NF's march this time around. We were only going for a drink or two and to pay our respects to the fallen. Steve and I went down on the train together, where we met up with all the other lads down there and had a few beers and a good chat with everyone. There was no sign of any trouble and a good day was had by all. The march passed of peacefully as always, apart from a few 'loony lefties' shouting insults at us. The march was attended by just over a 100 National Front members.

I was a steward on the day. Steve was on the march and why shouldn't he have been? He was an Ulsterman whose people had paid the ultimate sacrifice at the Battle of the Somme and he had every right to pay his respects as anyone else did. In spite of that, in the following few days the media had somehow found out about his presence at the march. Steve and I had our own idea how the media had found out about this, though that's another story in itself. We know for a fact he was set up by someone on the right-wing circuit to take his photo standing outside the pub we were using. To this day, I blame myself for taking such a high profile loyalist on the march knowing what the consequences may be; I did not see the danger at the time.

As per usual the media latched on to him attending the event and slaughtered him as well as printing lie after lie about the occasion. I have never read more bullshit in my life. There were headlines stating a loyalist killer linking up with 'neo-Nazis' in England and a photo of Steve standing outside a London pub with two of my mates. Well, I am certainly not a neo-Nazi. I am a British nationalist – full stop. I find it very insulting when I am labelled a Nazi or a racist. The media have no right to label me anything as they do not know me as a person. However, it only got worse. Steve was accused of standing near The Cenotaph and giving Nazi salutes and shouting offensive right-wing slogans in short distance of the Queen and Tony 'traitor' Blair and other VIP guests. This was a total lie. We had simply attended the march then headed off for another pint or two before we headed home to Birmingham. But why let the truth get in the way of a good story as some would say.

Following Steve's front-page headlines, there were calls to revoke his licence and send him back to jail for something he had not done. I felt terrible over all this as I had put him in the firing line by taking him on the march. After him being in jail for so many years I wanted him to take in the experience of a NF memorial march as he had so much of life to catch up on. All the same, my decision was the wrong one. Nevertheless, Steve was about to get himself in serious trouble. Steve eventually did have his licence revoked after he was arrested and charged after an altercation at a

Glentoran football match in Ulster. He was handed down a prison sentence of four years for the football charge, which meant he then had to serve the eight life sentences he received for the Greysteel shootings.

I was devastated I had lost my mate once again. The strange thing was I actually had a flight booked over to go and stop at his again, not thinking he would be sent down as I was expecting him to get bail. I still ended up visiting Ulster and stopping at my base in Rathcoole. Steve's missus arranged a visit for whilst I was over but it was not a good visit; you have these from time to time. There was no laughing and playing up as with him being sent down it had put us both on bad downers. It was horrible to see him back in jail again. I will admit I was disappointed with Steve for putting himself in this situation in the first place after getting a 'golden ticket' with the early prisoner releases due to the Good Friday Agreement. He had not only let himself down, he had also let down his missus, his family and his friends. Disregarding that, mates are mates and even though I was beside myself about his return to jail I would be there to stand by him again. You don't turn your back on your friends for whatever reason. Steve would serve his prison sentence in HMP Maghaberry, Lisburn, County Antrim, where my support for him would continue.

However, over at the National Front an appointment was made that would get the NF back on the streets and marching again – gaining nationwide publicity for the party. We were about to smash our way into the headlines once again.

CHAPTER 21

*A*t the National Front AGM (Annual General Meeting) down south a clever appointment was made. A young, but very keen activist named Terry Blackham was handed the role of National Activities Organiser. Terry had been around for a good few years, was a trusted British nationalist and had bags of energy in him. I remember thinking myself what a good appointment it had been – I couldn't think of anybody more suitable for the position. He reminded me of Joe Pearce who had been around in the 1980's; totally dedicated to the cause. His job was to get the NF back on the streets and marching again. At the AGM, he announced he was applying for a march in Dover against the recent arrival of asylum seekers being dumped on the people of the town. The locals in Dover were outraged over this recent invasion and we took this opportunity to get the NF back on the streets and back into the media – and to let the country know the NF were still around. After lengthy discussions between Terry Blackham and the police, the march got the go ahead.

On the day of the march we all had to be escorted in from outside the area by the Dover police. There would only be around 50 NF on the march but the numbers did not matter; gone were the days the NF could raise thousands for their marches. The media were well up for this and waiting for us to show up. I will never forget that before we headed into Dover we all had to stand in front of a police camera and give our names and addresses. This was to gain intelligence as to who was who in the National Front and to put our names on file as so called 'right-wing extremists'. We headed into Dover in our mini-buses with an escort of endless police cars and police wagons. They were not letting us out of their sight. When we arrived in Dover I will never forget the amount of media that was there; it would gain us nationwide publicity. There were hundreds upon hundreds of police officers to control a march of only 50 NF members. It was well over the top, although this order had come from the top – I had no doubt about that.

We all formed up on the eastern docks to march the half mile to the western docks. The media were snapping away at us as if they had never seen British nationalists before – but we did not mind as this would give us the publicity we were craving; getting the NF back in the papers and the TV. As the march started every single NF member was carrying a Union Jack flag. We were here to make a solid point. The police that had been drafted in for the march had dogs, horses, riot vans, riot gear on and video cameras to get us all on film. The police presence made it seem more like a Villa-Birmingham football match than a small bunch of patriots walking the streets of their own country waving our British flags. People were out on their balconies clapping us and waving Union Jacks as we marched along the sea front. Even though I would have liked more NF on the march we were still making ourselves heard with our tiny numbers.

Then as we reached so far up the sea front I noticed a similar number of people gathered just up from us. I initially thought it was more NF supporters to join our march, however, my assumption would prove to be incorrect. It was the so-called 'anti-fascists' – an off-shoot group from the Anti-Nazi League called Anti-Fascist Action. The same group who were later to be connected to one of Lee Rigby's killers. Make no mistake, they were there to stop and attack our march. Do not be fooled for one second thinking these were your normal student types. They were all hooded up and had their faces covered by scarves. They were known for violently confronting their opponents – and had strong sympathy and links to the I.R.A. As the marchers and demonstrators got closer to each other, the police started to panic as Anti-Fascist Action were trying to break through our lines. Bricks, bottles and other objects rained down on our march as the police really had their work cut out. Was I scared – you bet your life I was. I am not going to lie.

The anti-fascists were attacking us from all angles, and it did get a bit on top a couple of times. The police were very concerned about a full-scale riot breaking out. The police charged in to the anti-fascists with their horses to disperse them, which worked short term until they regrouped again. The majority of the Anti-Fascist Action thugs had been known before to violently attack NF/BNP supporters, therefore, they were not to be taken lightly. They had some hard lads in their ranks that would without a doubt would resort to extreme violence. As we carried on marching singing Rule Britannia, some more Reds came out of a side street and I could tell some of our people were getting a bit concerned – myself included. Now it all made sense to have so many police officers on duty.

The strange thing was even though the anti-fascists had their faces covered up and were openly attacking our march and throwing bottles and bricks at us, the police never arrested any of them. It was as if their job was to keep them away from the NF as best as possible – but at the same time not to make any arrests. We were on our best behaviour as John McAuley and Terry Blackham had warned us at a briefing before the march, that Dover police would have been very quick to arrest us for the smallest of things – unlike with the anti-fascists. We kept our heads held high against all the odds and the pressure from outside and kept our flags flying high. Anti-Fascist Action were flying all sorts of flags, and even an I.R.A flag to really wipe our noses in it. This was what we had come to expect from these people – nothing surprised us. Due to the consistent attacks from the Red rent- a mob, it took us over half an hour to complete our march. When we finally completed the march, we had a rally at the end of it where John McAuley gave a speech about the never-ending immigration floodgates still being open for the world to come and settle in Britain.

As we all headed away from Dover in our mini-buses – once again under a huge police escort – we put on the radio and we had gained the publicity we were yearning. Every radio station was mentioning the NF march, although as the left-wing media do they had us down as the agitators – not Anti-Fascist Action; no surprise there. When the police finally left us to head back to our home regions, we all stopped of at a local newsagent and we had made the front page of every newspaper. The coverage was as per usual anti NF, all the same, we had smashed our way into the headlines. If anybody had thought the NF were dead and buried by now they would be thinking otherwise. On top of all this, we were on all the headline TV news bulletins – Sky, BBC and ITV. Moreover, to this day I still think its amazing how such a small number of British nationalists could generate such huge publicity. Our job had been done.

This was the first of our three marches in Dover, and even though the second two marches did not generate as much publicity as the first, the people of Dover and the UK knew that the NF was back on the streets again – and ready to fight for their rights. We also had a number of more low profile marches during this time, as well as regularly opposing any pro-I.R.A marches that would spring up around England. Whenever the I.R.A marched in England, the anti-fascists would always be there to support them. To me this was sickening as the majority of the anti-fascists had no Irish connections at all. It was simply a march for everybody and anybody that was anti-British. You had all types on these pro-I.R.A marches; Black and Asian people, mixed race people and other White European people. It was simply an excuse for all the vermin of our society to get together and show their hated for a country they were all too pleased to live in.

At these pro-I.R.A marches the NF used to turn up with flags of the U.D.A/U.F.F and the U.V.F, and even though our numbers were always fairly small, it's safe to say our loyalist paramilitary flags most certainly got the reaction we were looking for from the Troops Out movement. We would chant: "U.F.F, U.F.F, U.F.F", at the passing I.R.A filth, and it gave me great delight to see them as wound up as I was. We may have only been small in numbers but by god we were a dedicated little bunch of activists who under Terry Blackham were out most weekends fighting back against Britain's enemies. To my delight, our anti-I.R.A demonstrations even used to reach the media in Ulster which made it all the more worth while as my contacts in Ulster knew I wasn't only fighting for Ulster whilst over in Ulster; I was a full time 100% committed loyalist and proud of it.

Moving on from here, Frank from London had decided to form a loyalist umbrella group. It was to be called the British Ulster Alliance, which brought together all British patriots from the NF, BNP, U.D.A, U.V.F, L.V.F and other pro-British organisations. This move brought us some solidarity. I thought this was a good idea after all the tensions between the various groups throughout the years. This made us all come together under one loyalist banner and put aside petty squabbles of the past which had occurred on the mainland. We were all just decent patriots who had come together from various groups who supported Ulster. Some loyalists in Ulster had shown some hostility towards people on the mainland who were involved in 'right-wing' groups. The B.U.A and Frank in particular, were quick to remind these people that many a good loyalist had come from these so-called 'extremist' groups. In addition, that their sacrifice and support should not be treated any less than others who had played their part throughout the years.

The B.U.A also raised money for the loyalist areas that had given us so much warmth over the years. It was our way of giving something back to the people that had made us so welcome. It was something I was very supportive of. The B.U.A even eventually set up their own band. The B.U.A still operates to this day, however, now under the name E.L.P.A – The English Loyalist Prisoners Association. Additionally, in 2015, after many meetings and conversations on the mainland an agreement was made to proceed with a formation of a new pro-Unionist pressure group called 'Defend the Union'. Credit must be given to Frank as he was determined to give us a loyalist voice on the Mainland – and that he did.

However, over at the BNP a leadership challenge was emerging. In October 1999, Nick Griffin who was supported by Tony Lecomber, stood against John Tyndall to gain control of the party. Griffin would eventually destroy the BNP from within. As with all political parties both campaigners would tour the country telling members why they should be elected as leader. Some lads I knew from Birmingham BNP who had been pestering me for years to join them invited me along to listen to both Tyndall and Griffin speak. Like all campaigns it got a bit personal at times and underhanded rumours from both camps were flying around. This was to be expected. I agreed to go and listen to what both men had to say – even though at the time I was fully committed to the NF. I found it interesting as Griffin was stating he had all kinds of plans to modernise British nationalism. I was not as though I was being disloyal to the NF, as I was only going along as an observer from a friends invite. I was just popping along to another patriotic meeting, even though I would not have a vote on the leadership contest as I was not a BNP member at the time.

I would first hear John Tyndall speak. Tyndall could deliver a cracking speech – no question about that. He made the hairs on the back of my neck stand up. I was one of his biggest admirers; I could listen to him all day long. Despite that, as some would say he was very much old school. Tyndall was a great man and great leader who had given his life to British nationalism, although I had personally been thinking myself for some time that something new was needed on the right-wing circuit to make it more appealing to the voters. Tyndall gave a good account of himself and his speech was sheer class, nevertheless, the word was that Griffin had some great ideas to take the BNP into the main stream of politics.

I was obviously with the NF at the time, nevertheless, looking back we did not really have the calibre of people to try to change our direction – myself included. The majority of our members were happy just standing a few candidates here and there and holding our marches and demonstrations. Likewise, so was I for a number of years, even though I was politically getting a bit frustrated about the lack of real direction the NF was taking. This is not by any means criticising the people running the party; they were giving their all. In spite of that, at the rate the country was sinking we were not moving forward fast enough.

Therefore, I went to hear Griffin speak in the West Midlands. I will admit as a speaker I preferred to listen to John Tyndall as I though he had a certain style about him that made you rise of your seats. Griffin did not draw you in as much as Tyndall, however, he had some great ideas to move British nationalism forward; all of which I agreed with. Don't get me wrong Griffin was and still is a great speaker, however, I was more interested in what he had to say than as to which speaker I preferred to listen to. Griffin had a whole range of ideas to modernise the party with a new image and fresh ideas to pull in all the voters who agreed with us, but who still would not vote for a British nationalist party at the time. As I left the meeting, I said to myself that if I had been a BNP member I would have been voting for Nick Griffin. He had impressed me, yet as I have already stated I also had a hell of a lot of respect for John Tyndall and his dynamic speeches.

Nick Griffin won the leadership election as expected and set about modernising the party. I refused to listen to all the bad things I had heard about Griffin. The main policy on repatriation had already been changed from compulsory to voluntary, which I thought was a clever move as it gave the enemies of British nationalism less mud to throw at the BNP. In addition, it made the BNP policies more acceptable to the British voters. It was obvious to me the old way of putting our message across had failed and this was what was needed. The National Front still to this day have not changed or adjusted any of their hard line policies. Some may say fair play to them for sticking to their core beliefs, but deep down inside I realised that to become electable you needed to soften your parties image. Moreover, to accept a few policy changes that were going against the grain so to speak. For all that, at the time I did not have it in my heart to leave the NF.

Even though I had drifted away from the football due to all my time being spent on the NF and the L.P.A, on the 20th May 2000, my club Aston Villa had once again reached Wembley in the F.A Cup Final against Chelsea. Our manager at the time was another old Villa player – John Gregory. It was to be the last ever F.A Cup Final to be played at the old Wembley with the twin towers. Due to the sentiment of the occasion everyone was going and more importantly even though through the 90's we had picked up some League Cup wins over Man United and Leeds, this was our first F.A Cup Final in 43 years. Season ticket holders quickly snapped up all the tickets and they were like gold dust for the rest of the fans trying to obtain one. Lads who had been following the Villa for over 40 years could not even get one, nonetheless, with it being such a huge event everyone was still going for the day out.

It was like all the other times at Wembley – more like a carnival atmosphere. Reaching the F.A Cup Final captured everyone's imagination. We had a steep history in the FA Cup and it was about time we stamped our name on the trophy again. The Villa Hardcore took their firm down for the weekend even though there was no sign of trouble anywhere, I am sure Chelsea had a firm out – but the two firms never came into contact all day. Besides, I was only down there for a drink and to somehow try to get a ticket. Try as you like no tickets were available unless you were willing to pay between £300 - £500 pounds off the ticket touts. There were many very disappointed Villa fans down Wembley. We had to face facts – we were not going to get in.

Rumour had it loads of Villa were meeting up in some pub by Wembley to watch the game on a giant screen and that suited me just fine. As we walked in the pub the game was about to start; perfect – we had timed it just right. Having said that, as well as loads of Villa fans being in the pub there was also the same number of Chelsea lads in there and my first though was that this would not stay quiet for very long. But strange as it sounds we all sat together to watch the game. There was no sign of any trouble which was great as I could just relax now and watch the match. We sat there chatting and drinking and they were good lads to be honest. Bull shit afterwards was flying around about Villa 'neo-Nazis' and Chelsea 'neo-Nazis' linking up together to watch the game; this was pure fabrication. Some people though wanted to believe this rumour. They know who they are – I don't need to mention any names. At the same time, the people who were there know the truth. There was obvious banter going on between us but no sign of any ill feeling at all.

The first half was terrible and the Villa players simply did not show up. The second half was all Chelsea and it was only a matter of time before they took the lead. Then on 73 minutes, Roberto Di Matteo, scored what proved to be the winning goal – capitalising on an error from Villa goalkeeper David James. After the goal Villa could simply not get back into the game; we were dreadful. Our F.A Cup dream was over. We were all devastated at full time as the Villa players had not even tried for such a big occasion in the clubs history. Even though it was still a good day out with no sign of trouble, I was that upset about the result I shot off early back to Birmingham and had a good drink on the train on the way home to drown my sorrows. It was not meant to be I suppose. All the more, the NF were about to smash our way into the headlines yet again.

After our successful marches in Dover, the next hot spot for dumping newly arrived asylum seekers was the seaside town of Margate. It reached such a stage where regular holidaymakers could not book a hotel or bed and breakfast. The locals and tourists were in uproar. Terry Blackham – had two marches planned to show our disgust at this further betrayal of the British people. These marches were to take place on April 2000 and June 2000. As per usual, we took a mini-bus from Birmingham NF and had to once again meet up with the police to escort us in. Once all the different NF branches had arrived at the re-direction point, a special train was laid on to take us into Margate. The sight that greeted us when we arrived there was amazing. It seemed like the whole town had turned out to support us. The locals were not only there to support us but to join our march. In addition, for a change the police were going to allow the locals to join our procession. This was something I had never witnessed before. Depending on where you were marching, the police could sometimes be very strict and just looking for any reason to arrest you – the London Metropolitan police were the worst; it's fair to say I disliked them. However, I will speak as I find, in certain parts of the country the police could also be very friendly towards us and not show us any hostility. Credit must be given to the police on this day as they were very laid back towards us and even stopped and chatted with us; fair play to them.

There was just short of a 100 NF members there for the march – but that was bumped up by between 200-300 locals. The locals I spoke to were furious at how these asylum seekers had been put up in top class hotels, whilst their own people were struggling for decent housing. Moreover, their kids were attending crumbling out of date underfunded schools and the hospital waiting lists were getting longer and longer. It is safe to say the people here were very angry, and this march gave them a chance to express their feelings. As the march set off the streets were also full of local NF supporters who had also come to cheer us on. It was brilliant. They were all waving Union Jack flags, and it showed to me that deep down inside we were speaking on behalf of the silent majority. It also showed the local people that the NF were willing to take to the streets and stand with them, as this mass invasion of asylum seekers had shook Margate's society to the core. Just like in Dover, the media were there from all over the country and we were sure again to grab all the headlines.

As the march neared its completion, the anti-fascists had formed a human chain in the road to stop us finishing the march. Although, they were not as militant as the ones we had faced in Dover; these were more your lefty students and schoolteachers. True to form, the BBC broadcasted that only 50 NF members were on the march but the local media were more honest about the day's events and printed the real numbers who had attended the parade. It was the best NF march I had ever been on due to the support from the local people. We made all the front-page headlines and all the prime time national news UK wide – mission complete; the NF back in the spotlight again. At the end of the march, Terry Blackham gave a speech to thank the locals for their support and we even gave a round of applause to the police who had been brilliant with us.

The second march was not as successful as the first with maybe only half the numbers turning up, even so on the day we still grabbed all the headline news as expected. Nonetheless, religious riots were about to sweep over our country stirred up by the far-left, as militant Islam was about to finally show its strength in numbers. My beloved Britain was about to go up in flames......yet again. !!!!!!

CHAPTER 22

On the 21st of April 2001, a mugging and severe beating upon a 76-year-old White Christian world war two veteran would be the spark that was needed for Islamic riots to spread across the north of England. However, these riots were to be of no surprise to me as I had contacts in Oldham and other northern towns who had been telling me for years about attacks on Whites and non- Muslims. These Muslim extremists were setting up Islamic zones in the areas of Great Britain where they had settled. Slightly diverting for a moment, further proof of their evil plot to take over British society surfaced in Birmingham, June 2014. It was known as the 'Trojan Horse' case involving Birmingham schools, where a campaign by hard-line Islamists was exposed. Music and Christmas events were cancelled, and a school trip to Saudi Arabia was only open to Muslim pupils.

For more than two centuries, Wahhabism has been Saudi Arabia's dominant faith. It is a chilling and unforgiving strand of Islam that insists on a literal interpretation of the Koran. Strict Wahhabis believe that all those who do not practice their form of Islam are infidels and enemies. Critics say that Wahhabisms rigidity has led to misinterpret and distort of Islam, pointing to extremists such as Osama

Bin Laden and the Taliban. Wahhabisms explosive growth began many years ago when Saudi charities started funding Wahhabi schools and Mosques. In addition, it is this form of Islam that is being promoted in British schools – funded by billions of pounds from Saudi Arabia. Should we be worried? We should be petrified.

Getting back to the Birmingham schools, children were also being taught that western women were 'White prostitutes', and they were encouraged to sing anti-Christian songs. Moreover, forced segregation of boys and girls was imposed upon the children in what was labelled a 'narrow faith- based ideology' – which included fear and intimidation against their opponents. An Islamic state is ideological. People who reside in it are divided into Muslims who believe in its ideology and non- Muslims who do not believe in it. Responsibility for policy and administration of such a state rests primarily with those who believe in the Islamic ideology. Non-Muslims therefore cannot be involved to undertake or to be entrusted with the responsibility of policy-making. This situation had been allowed to flourish in Oldham and other northern towns.

Walter Chamberlain was approached by a gang of Muslim youths as he was walking home after watching a local rugby league match. What then occurred was a vicious attack upon a non- Muslim who dared to walk through 'their area' which resulted in Walter receiving fractured bones as well as other injuries. His battered face appeared on front page of every national newspaper. Anyone with half a brain could work out this was a religious attack – not a racist attack. If Walter had been a Muslim convert this attack would not have taken place. By now, there were many of these no go areas for Whites and non-Muslims all over the

UK – including my home city of Birmingham. This attack on an old world war two veteran came as no surprise to the National Front. Following a long period of religious tension in the Oldham area, the National Front applied for a march to highlight the attacks on innocent non-Muslims who were being regularly set upon for going into the wrong areas. At the time I was all for the application of the march as I saw no other way of emphasising the issues that were facing our people. The spineless mainstream political parties were burying their heads in the sand yet again – therefore, it was left up to us to highlight the problems that had arisen in Northern England.

The religious tensions in the area stemmed from the Muslim community setting up home in England, whilst their social and cultural attitudes where still those of Pakistan, Bangladesh, etc, which they strictly imposed on all their children. They wanted the benefits of living in the UK, whilst at the same time taking no part at all at integrating into the British was of life. This was a fact, not just opinion. The government have promoted division in our society. Additionally, the high birth rate of Muslim children is being funded by welfare payments. We are in fact subsidizing the racial and religious destruction of our own people. No two totally different cultures have ever been able to live together for long once their numbers have grown enough to become a force – as what had happened in Oldham – and whose holy book promotes violence to non-believers. One of the verses that may be quoted to support this warped ideology is Qur'an 9:5: "And when the sacred months have passed, then kill the polytheists wherever you find them and capture them and besiege them. And sit in wait for them at every place of ambush". Over and above, a verse that should chill every

British person to the bone – Qur'an 9:29: "Fight Christians and Jews who do not believe in Allah – until they submit".

We have said to people you can come here from any part of the world and carry on your own traditions and cultures. Do not bother to learn our language, do not assimilate in any way at all. And you can take over our towns and cities and we will all say it has made us a wonderful diverse nation; if only that was true. We were never asked or voted on an Islamic invasion into our Christian homelands. Christians would not be allowed to do like wise in an Islamic state, so why should we accommodate our demise with Islam. Without a shadow of a doubt, Islam is the greatest ever threat to our culture and way of life – a far greater threat than even Nazi Germany. We had actually been warned about the take over of our country by the former President of Algeria – Houari Boumediene – when he stated: "One day millions of men will leave the southern hemisphere to go to the northern hemisphere. And they will not go there as friends. Because they will go there to conquer it. And they will conquer it with their sons. The wombs of our women will give us victory".

Members of the Indian community are far more successful, financially and academically than the Pakistanis or Bangladeshis – and to a large part have integrated into British society. The Indian community are known for their loyalty towards Britain and have stood shoulder to shoulder with Britain in two world wars. You do not hear of Indian drug gangs pushing heroin onto our youngsters to get them addicted and you do not hear of Indian grooming gangs targeting our young vulnerable girls. This is a Muslim problem, not an Asian problem. The Sikh ethnic minorities occupy the least amount of prison space. They occupy the least amount of council housing. They pay the most per capita in income tax. They employ the most people per capita in the economy and they claim the least amount in state welfare. To be integrated into a population means to be for all practical purposes to be indistinguishable from all its other members. The Indian community have gone a long way to achieving this.

The majority of Muslim parents banned their young schoolchildren from having White, or non-Muslim friends. Some even force their kids not to listen to 'western music', or to wear western styled clothes. They were completely segregating themselves from British society – and anyone who says or thinks any different is fooling himself or herself. Nevertheless, the NF march was banned – with a three-month ban on all marches in the Oldham area, with the aim of keeping order and preventing further increases in religious tension. The NF looked upon this as appeasing the Muslim community yet again, and bowing down to the dominance of radical Islam and trying to sweep the issue under the carpet.

Due to the attack on Walter Chamberlain, what followed were several skirmishes occurring in the town with a mob of Stoke City football hooligans going into a Muslim area looking for some pay back. This resulted in running battles between the two sides. Even though the National Front were banned from marching in Oldham, it did not stop us from turning up on the day of the planned march for a leafleting session in a majority White area. I can remember putting a leaflet through a Muslims door and he approached me for a chat. If I had known a Muslim lived there I would have avoided in doing so; I certainly was not there for trouble. In all fairness, he was very courteous and we began to talk politics. Nonetheless, what he said knocked me for six. He brought up the subject of homosexuals and said to me: "Even though we differ on many issues, my religion says we can stab homosexuals through the heart. At least we have that in common". I could not believe what I had heard. Even though I do not agree with the promotion of homosexuality, his opinion and my opinion were certainly not of the same. He then began to tell me that England would be a better place under Sharia law, however, I had my reply for him and said: "If Muslims prefer Sharia law, then the NF advise them to go and live in those places where that's the state law". After having the final say, I then walked off to carry on my leafleting session.

As word spread about the National Front's arrival, tension built up in the town. A mob of Muslims estimated at around 400 strong, started to make their way into the city centre where the NF had congregated. When I heard this on a police radio I admit that my bottle started to go; this was serious stuff. The NF had defied the banning order due to stating it was an affront to our freedom of speech and right of assembly. Five hundred police were deployed to keep the two groups separate. By now, the whole town was at boiling point. You could feel an atmosphere in the air that I had never felt before in my life – it was frightening. Oldham was about to go up in flames. Over a dozen National Front members were arrested for simply displaying a Union Jack flag and singing Rule Britannia. They were held over the weekend and charged with breach of the peace. Oldham magistrates were told the NF had defied police warnings not to turn up in Oldham. The NF were described as 'outside agitators' which made me cringe. Would they have dared used that language to describe the Muslim community? Not a chance.

The riots that were about to emerge were the worst religiously motivated riots the UK has ever seen. As I have previously said these were not race riots, as Islam is a religion not a race. Enoch Powell's famous speech many years ago was being proven right – yet again. The Oldham riot was the first in a series of major riots during the summer of 2001, which only proved what the NF had been warning about for years was now a reality. The NF had an old slogan many years ago 'Repatriation or riots' – how correct this slogan turned out to be as the riot swept through Oldham and neighbouring Chadderton. In the Glodwick area to the south of Oldham town centre (a strong Muslim area, and a no go area for Whites and non-Muslims) it reached its peak with the use of petrol bombs, bricks, bottles and anything else they could get their hands on. A full on battle raged on between the rioters and the police. Fifteen police officers were severely injured and 37 rioters were arrested. These riots continued for three days solid and further divided the divisions between the already fragile, Muslim and non-Muslim communities. Let me make this perfectly clear yet again – these were not Asian rioters – they were Muslim rioters. Moreover, they were now flexing their muscles due to their ever-increasing numbers and loyalty to their warped religion.

The Oldham riots had a knock on effect just as the riots did back in 1985, and copycat rioting also broke out in Leeds and Burnley. For all that, the worse was yet to come in the city of Bradford. The Bradford riot which was to blow the governments claim of a multi-cultural utopia out of the water was actually kick started by the far-left and their communist allies. The National Front had applied for a march in Bradford, which was once again banned by home secretary David Blunkett. Unlike in Oldham, the NF agreed to stay away from the Bradford area after lengthy discussions with the police – which we did. The far-left though had been allowed a rally in the city centre and started a rumour that the NF were in town; there wasn't a single NF member in Bradford. Why on this day after the NF had been banned were the so-called anti-fascists allowed a rally?

Like in Oldham, Bradford had seen lots of religious tensions between the non-Muslim community and the Muslim community, and the myth spread by the far-left that the NF were in town was just the spark that was needed. During the course of the anti-fascists rally, a lie was spread that the NF had set up base in a pub in Bradford city centre. A confrontation then occurred outside a pub where innocent White lads were attacked. A young White male was attacked by a large group of Muslims and stabbed; they had singled him out as being NF due to his short haircut. This what was known as 'racial stereotyping' - and was seen on every national TV station.

The riot that started was estimated to have involved up to a 1,000 Muslim youths. At the start of the riot there was around 500 police officers on duty – but as the riot increased that number was made up to nearly a 1,000 officers; such was the extent of the anarchy. What began as running battles with the police turned into the targeting of businesses, setting fire to cars and burning down shops and properties. A fire-bombing of a Labour Party social club of all places, resulted in a Muslim man receiving a 12-year prison sentence for the attack. The most notable attack during the riots was an arson attack on a BMW dealership, which destroyed the building and all the cars on the forecourt. The riots were yet to continue for many days. When the rioters finally stopped more than 300 police officers had been injured – and there had been 297 arrests in total. In addition, 187 people were charged with riot offences, 45 charged with violent disorder and 200 jail sentences totalling 604 years were handed down. The number of convictions was unprecedented in English legal history. The total damage to the Bradford area was estimated at around £7 million pounds – obviously to be settled by the British taxpayer yet again. If the far-left had planned to burn Bradford down to the ground by their lies spread about the NF – they had got their wish.

As per usual, the media and the government instead of blaming the Muslims who had been the ones stockpiling the petrol bombs, attacking innocent local non-Muslims, as well as burning down buildings and businesses – they pinned the blame entirely on the National Front. How could this be when we wasn't even there? It had not been the National Front who had promoted mass immigration into these areas and forced through policies that could not work. The blame lied solely with the Muslims and the lies spread by the 'far-left' which was intended to stir up the angry mob of Muslims. The Red rent- a mob had intentionally thrown a match on a huge keg of gunpowder that was ready to go off. It seemed in the media the rioters could do no wrong, when I knew myself this had been simmering for years.

Nearer to home in Birmingham, an area called Alum Rock that had become a strong militant Muslim area through the years had been sticking up posters in the area stating – 'No Whites after 8 pm'. The National Front had found out about this and had applied for a march in the area to once again high light the problems local people were facing in and around the Alum Rock area of Birmingham. I myself was actually against the march – and let my feelings be known to the NF leadership, as I knew if it kicked off the NF would get the blame and get us even more bad press coverage. When the police found out about our intentions to march, they released a statement saying the National Front would not be tolerated in the area and it would be inappropriate for the NF to congregate in the city during this time of religious tension.

Due to the recent riots in the northern towns the police force were already planning another banning order on the march. In addition, Birmingham City council who are maybe the most left-wing council in the UK, were also against the march and supportive of the proposed ban. As the date for the proposed march was getting nearer, the National Front decided to call it off after lengthy negotiations with West Midlands Police. The NF had called off the march amid concerns for the safety of local people and the police – who would have been in the firing line if a full-scale riot had started yet again. I was pleased with this conclusion, as like I said I was dead against the march from the word go.

The decision to cancel the march came only hours before the police were due to hear from home secretary David Blunkett, who himself would of most certainly banned it anyway. By simply stating our intention to march in the area it gained us yet again blanket coverage in the nationwide media. But I was beginning to ask myself was this really the kind of media coverage that was doing our party any good? Tensions in the Alum Rock area were at boiling point. However, unlike in the northern towns the day passed off peacefully due to the police visiting the homes of the Muslim community assuring them that the National Front would not be congregating in Birmingham. Dozens of NF members – myself included – had visits from the West Midlands Police who handed us letters banning us from Alum Rock on the day of the cancelled march. This really infuriated me as I did not intend to go to the area anyway. It was me who had pleaded with the NF leadership to not apply for the march in the first place. I let my feelings be known as I ripped up the letter in front of the 'Old Bill'. I saw this as just another way of appeasing the Muslim community.

After all the religious unrest in the UK, the BNP were about to make huge grounds at the up and coming general election with some amazing votes. Over at the National Front, I was getting closer and closer to leaving the party due to situations that were unfolding. During this chapter in my life it was a busy time for Karen and I. We got married in Cyprus and I felt like the luckiest man on the planet as she had stood by me after all I had put her through over the years. We also finally decided to buy a house together, and after a lot of looking around we settled for a home in Bournville, South Birmingham. Where Karen was from in Stockland Green, North Birmingham, the area had really declined and had become a densely populated immigrant area with lots of crime going on including muggings and drug dealing. Local police had also admitted that the wider Stockland Green area had become a burglary hotspot with issues of anti-social behaviour. Additionally, they added that there was a high turnover of troubled residents moving into the area – many of who had criminal records. Therefore, I wanted to get Karen away to a better area where she would be safe. We really pushed the boat out moving to Bournville, as it was one of the only nice places left in Birmingham due to the immigration invasion. I was willing to take out a huge mortgage to give Karen the house that she deserved.

After getting my personal life sorted we had the general election coming up – and my focus was now on trying to save the country that I loved.

CHAPTER 23

*A*fter all the riots in our northern towns the general election of 2001, was now just around the corner. What an opportunity to capitalise on the recent unrest in the UK .The NF had been front page of all the tabloid newspapers in the riot towns, and every national news channel had broadcasted our marches. In addition, the true British people certainly knew we were out there. The communities were completely divided in two by now and the abandoned British people needed a party to speak up for them. Nonetheless, like I had been thinking for a while – YES – we had grabbed all the headlines nationwide – but despite that it was always bad publicity like 'NF riot again' – when in fact it was the Muslims and the far-left causing all the trouble. There was a saying that 'there was no such thing as bad publicity', but I no longer agreed with that.

The BNP had also been very active in the riot torn towns, however, they had approached it with a more subtle way of electioneering; all suited up and talking directly to the people about their problems. The BNP had dropped the street marches as they said it gave our enemies less mud to throw at them – which I had by now started to realise was the correct approach. We were gaining all the negative press and being accused of kick starting every riot. With the BNP's new modernisation of the party they were on the verge of some breathtaking results.

Looking back now, however I thought the NF could have made a break through I do not know. We were giving of the wrong image with a section of our membership dressing unaccordingly whilst we were in the public eye. I am not for one second having a pop at skin-heads – I was once one myself. Even so, the image most certainly scared of would be potential voters. I knew this by talking to people. I thought for many years it was correct the way that NF were going about things but no wonder the votes had not been coming in. I had concluded by now that giving of the wrong image and not putting across sensible political solutions was our downfall. This was my opinion and my opinion alone – some people will agree and some will not.

The BNP had abandoned the old image which was holding back the right-wing. I was supportive of this new image being pushed forward as I knew it was the right road to go down. I suppose I had politically 'grown up'. Some of the Birmingham members coming into the NF were treating it as a drinking club and were not taking it serious enough. They were more interested in the confrontations with the Reds than winning seats at council level and were doing more bad for the party than good. Small sections of the younger Birmingham members had also aligned themselves with Combat 18 and the neo-Nazi Blood and Honour music scene, and were becoming more and more radical; they had most certainly had their heads turned away from the NF by now.

What pushed me further towards my inevitable exit out of the NF was at the close of nominations for the 2001 general election, the NF had not put forward a single candidate in any of the wards where we had been gaining front-page headlines during the Islamic riots. I could not believe after all the publicity we had gained we had totally abandoned putting candidates forward in any of the 'hot spots' as I called them. I remember thinking what a waste of time after all the travelling to Oldham. The candidates we had selected were put forward in wards that had not seen any religious uprising and lawlessness. I was annoyed at missing out at such a good chance for the party to finally obtain a good vote. This could have made people sit up and really take notice of us. However, that was about to go to the BNP.

The final wards selected were in Erdington – Birmingham, Bermondsey, Wolverhampton and two in Thanet. The two wards selected in Thanet were neighbouring areas to Dover and Margate, where we had previously held a number of marches. Even though the NF had grabbed the headlines in these towns a while ago they had not seen the rioting as we had in the northern towns. In addition, yesterday's front-page news is old news. You have to strike whilst the irons hot; we had selected the wrong target areas. I was pleased to have the one in Erdington, Birmingham, as we had been doing some work in that ward. In spite of that, I would have been more than happy to drop it for a ward in Oldham, Burnley, Leeds or Bradford.

The BNP's main target wards were in Oldham East, Oldham West and Burnley. Party leader Nick Griffin, put himself forward for Oldham West after earlier fighting a by election in West Bromwich in 2000, gaining 974 votes – 4.2 %. I phoned up a lad called Mick from Hinkley, who was running the NF enquiry line at the time and told him of my dismay that we had not targeted a 'hot spot' for this election. Moreover, I told him I was thinking about leaving the party. After a lengthy discussion he talked me out of resigning, however, I knew deep down inside it was only a matter of time before I left the NF – my heart was no longer in it. I am not knocking the good people that were involved in the NF – but we were lacking direction. In addition, we were defunct of new ideas. I began to realise we were not going to achieve our goals. Politically, we were little more than a poorly organised pressure group.

Come election night the BNP pulled in some results that would rock the establishment to the core. As the elections had loomed, the BNP had put themselves into a position to speak up for the abandoned White communities and to draw advantages on the troubles that everyone knew they had been warning about for years. Nick Griffin pulled in a breathtaking 6,552 votes – 16.4 %, and only a few votes behind the 2nd place Conservatives. In Oldham East, Mick Treacy, pulled in 5,091 votes – 11.2 %. Amazing. In addition, the other target ward in Burnley, the candidate Steve Smith gained 4,151 votes – 11.3 %. Other high results were in Pendle, Barking, Dagenham and Canning Town. These were record-breaking votes for a British nationalist party. Over at the National Front our best result of the night was in Erdington, Birmingham, where we gained 681 votes – 2.2 %. A huge difference to the BNP votes as you can see for yourself; we had missed an excellent opportunity to make our mark in this current climate of unrest. The results for the BNP gained all the headlines so much so that you would of actually though they had won the seats. The media went into overdrive asking why the BNP votes were so high – as if that needed answering. Nick Griffin was on every news channel due to the fantastic vote secured in Oldham. Even though, for the time being I was staying with the NF against my wishes.

However, there was to be more shocking news coming from Oldham – the hot bed for Islamic extremists. In the early hours of February 9th 2002, a Muslim gang from Oldham beat Gavin Hopely, a 19-year-old White lad to death. After this murder extra police were drafted into the area amid fears of more riots following the unprovoked attack. As we all know, Oldham had been the focus of severe rioting the summer before and the police feared the National Front would once again apply to march in the area following the incident. Gavin Hopely had been murdered because he had mistakenly wandered into the towns strong Muslim area called Glodwick – an area well known for attacks on local White people and non-Muslims. The anti-White, anti-British media knew about this but kept it quiet. Anybody who believes that the media are not bias are simply living on another planet. Are you aware that the Government – as and when needed – are able to take control of the media and withhold any news they deem to be 'inappropriate'.

Gavin, who worked for a security firm, was out with two friends when the ambush happened. They were looking out for a taxi to take them home. They were suddenly surrounded by a crowd of Muslim youths – some armed with lumps of wood and clubs and other dangerous objects. Gavin's friends escaped leaping over a garden fence before being rescued by a very decent Muslim man named Mohammed Umar, who allowed them safety in his home. This must be pointed out that there were also decent Muslim people living in these areas. Nevertheless, it still does not change the colonisation of the Oldham area. Gavin was found by a passer by and taken to the intensive care unit of North Manchester hospital; he failed to regain consciousness. He died late on the following Friday night. The teenager lived with his parents in

Whitworth. At the time of the attack a police representative said: "The racial aspect is an open question at the moment. Clearly it is one of the strands of the investigation, but we cannot nail that down at the moment". This was a clear insult to Gavin and his family, and once again an appeasement to the Muslim community. Imagine a police spokesperson saying that about the Stephen Lawrence case?

After the slaughter of Gavin, three Muslim men from Glodwick were arrested and charged with grievous bodily harm – not murder. Another police statement read: "We hope people will let the police deal with this. It would seem that Mr Hopely and his friends had enjoyed a night out when they got involved in a dispute with a gang of Asians. We don't know what sparked the attack". Well I did. They were White Christians in the wrong area at the wrong time and deep down so did the police. But the police could dare not say the truth in this Marxist state we are living in. One local resident though said it all: "The police claim there is not a no go area in this town. But if you put a foot in the wrong street – you could easily end up like young Gavin". At last a bit of truth and honesty.

There are 1.2 billion Muslims in the world today. Of course, not all of them are radical. The majority of them are peaceful people and deserve to be shown respect and allowed to practice their religion without interference. The radicals are estimated to be between 15-25% of the Muslim population, which leaves 75% of them as decent law-abiding citizens. However, when you look at the 15-25% who are radicals, you're looking at between 180-300 million who are dedicated to the destruction of western civilisation. Some may ask why worry about the radicals who are in the minority? Because it is the radicals who behead and massacre.

Therefore, that makes the peaceful majority irrelevant. It is time to take political correctness and throw it in the garbage where it belongs.

Likewise, this was not the only no go area for Whites and non-Muslims in the UK. My mates mother was a police constable and told me the police knew of similar areas in Birmingham, Bradford, Derby, Leeds, Leicester, Liverpool, Luton, Manchester, Sheffield, North East London and East London. And I am sure all these years later that many more areas can now be added to that list. The strange thing to come out of all this tension in the Oldham area was that the BNP failed to ever win a seat on Oldham council, even after putting in loads of intensive campaigning. To this day, it is still a question that bewilders all British nationalists. My own personal opinion is that large-scale vote fraud took place to stop the BNP winning a seat on Oldham council to prevent any more riots; I stand by this statement. The support for the BNP in the Oldham area was too high for this not to have happened.

There were also two other murders of White lads around this time. Unlike in the Stephen Lawrence case that has stayed in the spotlight for years, what followed was total silence from the media. The further two victims of Muslim violence were Andrew Holland from Bolton, and Sean Whyte from Pendle – just outside of Burnley. Compare these two murders to the murder of Stephen Lawrence. His mother Doreen was handed a life peerage in the House of Lords, and was given the title Baroness Lawrence of Clarendon – as well as being awarded an OBE for services to community relations. In addition, Doreen Lawrence was also involved in the opening ceremony of the Olympic Games. She has also received an achievement grant at the 14th pride of Britain awards, and in April 2014, was named as Britain's most influential women in the BBC Women's power list. Since his death, there have been music concerts in remembrance of Stephen Lawrence. There is a building that includes a gallery and a TV studio named after Stephen at Greenwich University – not forgetting the memorial gardens nominated in his memory. We have the Stephen Lawrence charitable trust – the Stephen Lawrence education standard – and memorial lectures all over London every year.

Have you ever heard of Gavin Hopley, Kriss Donald, Ross Parker, David Lees and Charlene Downes? I bet not. If I carried on naming all the White people killed in known racist attacks I would need to write another story. These are just some of the names of innocent victims of anti-White murder in Britain. You will not see their names in the mass media – and you will not hear of concerts being held in their memory. No memorial gardens and no charities opened in their names. The media cover up over these murders was, and still is, one of the greatest ever insults to the White people of the UK – and it is still going on to this day.

Further on down the line in the 2002 local elections, the new modernised BNP were about to make a breakthrough at council level in Burnley. Burnley as I have stated, had been a target ward for the BNP at the last general election. After intensive campaigns by the BNP and its opponents the BNP gained three seats on Burnley council. As expected, the party grabbed all the headlines. These were only seats on a local council, however, it was still a huge victory in itself. It was also a sign of loosening loyalties of traditional working class communities to the Labour Party. This was partly due to bad housing, appalling social effects of mass slum clearances, and high-rise council housing that had initially been introduced in the 1960's. It was also partly to do with rising unemployment and the huge decline in the Labour Party membership. Once again, we are back to the collapse of the two-party system and the steady fall in the number of electors who vote Tory and Labour. Although, as the Liberal party has found, it needs more than the erosion of the two main parties to achieve an electoral breakthrough in Britain. What is needed is a real collapse, which was what was beginning to happen in the North West of England.

The BNP tuned into the sullen continuity of economic crisis wining them support and leading to that collapse. Rising unemployment discredited the trade union leadership in the eyes of the local people, which made the BNP's penetration all the more easier. Racial and religious tensions were sky high and the BNP were there at the right time. The behaviour of some sections of the Muslim community had provoked a White backlash. A number of issues had given the BNP a base for gaining wider support in all parts of the North West. The NF were still standing the odd candidate here and there but still with very low votes; I wanted a piece of the glory that the BNP were getting. Being a member of a political party is not like supporting a football team – you can change who you back and my exit from the NF was drawing near. It was now only gaining the courage to make that break and leave behind good friends. At the local elections of 2003, the BNP contested a superb 221 council seats gaining another five seats on Burnley council and two seats on Sandwell council in the West Midlands. In addition, seats were gained in Calderdale, Dudley, Stoke on Trent and Broxbourne. This is what British nationalism had been striving towards for years and I wanted to see a change for all the hard work I had put in. Nick Griffin at the time was being hailed as the new messiah of the right-wing.

Whilst I had been campaigning with the NF for a seat on Birmingham council, a situation developed that finally made my mind up to leave the party. A small team of party activists assembled at Birmingham New Street station to head to our target ward to do some campaigning. A small number of the newly recruited Birmingham NF lads had been spending a lot of time attending the Blood and Honour music events and were having their heads filled with all this Combat 18 and Hitler crap. Moreover, they were being lead astray from the National Front. I was not happy about this as I could see they wasn't any good for the party and were holding us back. I would like to state not all the new recruits were bad – but some were simply not up to scratch. They had been sucked into the most extreme form of neo-Nazism which was not what the NF was about. They were dressing in such a way that they frightened the living daylights out of anyone who came our way. We were trying to obtain votes not give the public heart failure.

Whilst we were on the train a young respectable looking Black woman got on with her young son who was about seven years old at the time. Her son was reading a book, and as we reached our destination one of our members threw at him a Combat 18 calling card and said: "Use this as a book marker" – I was disgusted and embarrassed. Even though I'm a British nationalist and certainly not politically correct, I had been brought up to have manners and respect for people –regardless of my political views. This was a step too far in my eyes. I knew where they had obtained this calling card from their links in Combat 18. The BNP had earlier themselves had problems with Combat 18 in the early 19990's, but had weeded them out and proscribed them from the party. In the cold light of day I should have said something, nonetheless, they were beyond control by now and their loyalty was no longer with the NF. Also, if I am perfectly honest, I am not one for confrontation if I can avoid it. With my anxiety and depression, I try to avoid conflict as it only makes my condition worse. I am not saying by any stretch of the imagination that these people were encouraged by the NF leadership to act in this was as they wasn't. At the same time, they were loose cannons that were getting deeper and deeper into all that Combat 18/Hitler scene.

It is something I have never related to myself. Why admire a dictator who fought against your own country and failed. If ever you wanted people not to vote for you this was the perfect reason. We were simply allowing in too many 'wrong' uns' and did not have the strong leadership to put them into line. This incident finally confirmed my decision to leave the party. Maybe it was the excuse I was looking for as for a good while I had been trying to pluck up the courage to leave the NF. I would be staying with the NF for this election and then I would be writing my letter of resignation. I had simply had enough of going around in circles trying to revive a political corpse.

A small number of us in the NF actually agreed with the BNP's new approach as it had not only cleaned up its image – it was now winning seats. A few of us had previously tried to implement some ground rules into the NF at branch level in Birmingham. After a deliberation one afternoon regarding the image and direction of Birmingham branch, myself and a member called Alan (who was the branch secretary) had pushed forward a proposal regarding dress code for Birmingham branch meetings. This was only a tiny step but we proposed this motion for two reasons.

Firstly, because we could never keep hold of a function room for our meetings, we thought that by improving our dress code we would have more chance of keeping hold of the premises for further meetings. Nine times out of ten, some of our members choice of clothing gave the game away that we were the NF; it did not take much working out. Don't forget, we always had to book the function rooms under a false name due to who we were. Secondly, when new members or supporters attended their first branch meeting it looked like everything they had heard about us in the media was true; about being a skin-head organisation. You would see them once, maybe twice, then they would disappear and more than likely end up with the BNP.

When I arrived for the one branch meeting I had a number of the Combat 18 supporters waiting outside the hall for me, shouting insults and dressed even more militant than usual. I now know they had been put up to this. They were saying things to me like: "Who are you working for?" – when all Alan and I were trying to do was bring the party a little up to date and make us more appealing in the public eye. People who had been involved for five minutes had the nerve to point the finger at me – with the encouragement from the people they had linked up with. I was accused of taking orders from above my head from HQ, but this was not the case. This was solely an idea from Alan and I. We had plans to slowly bring into the branch some rules and regulations that had been needed for years. People were just too blind to see we needed change to move forward. I could see by now things were not going to change.

After the elections of 2003, I wrote my letter of resignation to the party. This was one of the hardest decisions of my life as I had been with the NF for many years, put in a lot of hard work and made many close friends. Norman Tomkinson was not only a party comrade – he was one of my best friends as well outside of the party; I considered him family. Moreover, I felt terrible sadness and guilt for leaving him behind after working together for so long. Everything I had learnt from holding meetings to fighting elections I had learnt from the eminence of Norman; it was very hard. Regardless of what right-wing political party you belonged to, Norman was liked and respected by everybody; and rightly so. (Norman now lives in America where he is still an ambassador for the National Front). The NF had been my life for many years and I had a huge sentimental attachment to the party. The party Chairman at the time of my resignation was Tom Holmes from Great Yarmouth, who had taken over the leadership when John McAuley had stepped down for personal reasons. Tom was a lovely old chap who you could not help but like.

Tom had been involved in British nationalist politics for over 40 years, but told me himself that he was too old to go around the country speaking at meetings. I got the gist from Tom that he only agreed to become Party Chairman because there was no one else willing to take over the position. Tom had fought in three general elections standing in Great Yarmouth, North Thanet and Halifax. Bernard Franklin and Steve Rowlands, were also good people who I had a lot of time for. The old Chairman John McAuley, who had saved the party from going under had stepped down from front line politics. John had also faced many problems at work due to his involvement in the NF. John McAuley was a good man and someone I looked up to from a young age. My other close friend John Lord (R.I.P) had sadly passed away a few years earlier and it was like losing a Granddad we were that close; it broke my heart when John died. I loved that man like one of my own. After he had passed away the Birmingham branch was never the same – the hole could never be filled. And as for Terry Blackham, talk about dedication and staying power. For many years Terry was the unofficial leader of the party, holding his demonstrations and marches all over the country. Even though I was very active myself it was nothing in comparison to the workload Terry put in. He was a shining example to all members young and old.

I wanted to leave the NF on good terms, therefore, I wrote my letter of resignation to Norman Tomkinson, and Tom Holmes, explaining my decisions for leaving the party. I would not have just walked away without explaining why and thought honesty was the best policy. I had to get somebody else to post the letters as I could not bring myself to do it. Eventually when the letters arrived Norman texted me saying I was making the wrong decision, all the same, I held to my guns on this one – however awkward it made me feel. I couldn't have met Norman for a 'one to one conversation' as I knew he would have talked me out of it. Making the break was not easy believe me. As things do word travelled fast and everyone in the NF knew that I had left the party.

Unfortunately, I lost a couple of good friends due to my resignation but that was their decision not mine. But that was not the end of it. I suddenly started receiving abusive text messages sent to my phone from numbers I did not have registered. I knew these were from the small section of Birmingham NF lads who had a bee in their bonnet with me – it did not take much working out. A certain individual was stirring them up to give me hassle; I later found out others were as well. I will not give them the pleasure of naming them. So much for all the years service I had given the National Front. For all that, it must be made clear that these were only a very tiny faction from within the NF who were acting alone – the hierarchy would never have encouraged or supported anybody carrying on like this.

I suppose really that I should not even label them as being NF as their loyalty was no longer with the party. You get the more extreme right-wing groups promising you the world if you take the more 'hard- line' approach and a quick route to success. And to the more vulnerable and naive it can sound appealing. You get this from time to time. A small number of people will join the movement and refuse to toe the line. Then eventually after causing a whole lot of trouble will splinter off to join hard-line neo-Nazi groups, or you will never see or hear of them again. It's nothing new.

These pathetic messages carried on for a while. I had numerous offers from friends and associates to sort this problem out as I knew directly who was behind it all. Some of the people who offered to help you would most certainly not want knocking on your door. And even though there were comrades in the U.D.A who told me to use their names, this was not the road I wanted to go down. I was not interested in revenge or getting involved in a silly game of sending messages back – I choose to ignore them. I did not have a 'hard-man' image I needed to uphold. I was never one to try and make out I was something I was not. They were not worth worrying about. This just made me more convinced that I had made the right decision to leave. These people should not have been allowed into the party at the beginning; I knew that. Nevertheless, this situation had manifested by allowing anybody to join the NF. In the same breath though, when your a tiny party struggling for members I suppose we couldn't be picky over who was willing to get involved with us. And we certainly wasn't big enough or professional enough to have any kind of vetting operation in place. Despite that, it was no longer my problem.

In all honesty there had been little if any leadership from the higher ranks of the NF for years, apart from Terry Blackham. I personally thought Terry should have been Chairman of the NF, but it was something he wasn't interested in taking on. Don't get me wrong the people we had available at the higher realms of the party were doing the best job they could have possibly done. In spite of this, it wasn't enough to have built a strong British nationalist alternative able to take on the establishment. Some people won't like to admit this but it was the truth. I am not free from criticism myself – I never pushed hard enough for change. The party had been running on the enthusiasm of the street level activists, with little organised guidance from above. For too long the NF was operating as no more than a scattered political group, kept afloat by a little team of dedicated members. It had its chance in the 1970's and the 1980's, and it was unfortunately no longer a threat to the administration ruining our country. The BNP was now our only hope.

Moving on from here, some very close friends of mine would be being sent down for some of the worst football related violence seen in Birmingham for many a year. Additionally, some of the longest ever banning orders from football grounds were about to be handed down. I knew years ago that this would eventually happen as the Villa Hardcore got bigger, more organised and more dangerous. This was a pre-arranged battle arranged by both the hooligan firms of Aston Villa and Birmingham City. Dozens of fans were hauled before the courts for their part in what was dubbed 'The Battle of Rocky Lane'. The game at Saint Andrews gave the firms from both sides the chance to rekindle bitter rivalries as the two clubs had not played each other since 1993, when the Villa had turned over the Zulus on Garrison Lane. I was asked by some old friends to come along as all the old lads were turning out and the Villa were going to take it to the Zulus. Fowler's firm would be meeting up at O'Reilly's in Aston, and the old C-Crew were meeting up in Moseley at Sensations nightclub. The Villa were going to surprise the Zulus by landing with two firms.

I knew the police would be out in force for this one and looking to hand down long prison sentences and banning orders. I never even gave it a second thought about going as I knew what lay ahead. And through past experiences I knew what the Zulus were like regarding the Villa; if your caught on your own your in big trouble as the Zulus are known for turning over any Villa fan regardless of your numbers. On the night of the game about 150 lads from the Villa Hardcore and about 60 Zulu Warriors, clashed on Rocky Lane where the police filmed it all on camera. No arrests were made at the time. Rival hooligans were armed with CS gas, batons, knifes, spring-loaded coshes and snooker balls in socks – someone was even swinging around part of a car engine. The Zulus were heavily outnumbered but they stood their ground even though they were backed off a couple of times.

A month after the game the police mounted a series of dawn raids after going through the video of the hooliganism. The old C-Crew had also clashed with the Zulus by McDonald's Island and turned them over which required a 'robust' police response. However, as per usual the

Zulus played it down saying it wasn't their firm; some things never change. The Villa had hit the Zulus with not only one firm, but two. I would be a liar to say I did not think: "Fair play lads", even though I was no longer into it myself. For a number of days following the clashes the newspapers printed stills of people involved in the orgy of violence (I instantly recognised most of them) and a large number of the lads handed themselves in.

The return fixture at Villa Park exploded into more scenes of shocking football violence, which resulted in over 40 arrests mainly from Aston Villa. If anyone thought for one second that the inclusion of CCTV at football grounds could dampen the hatred running between Aston Villa and Birmingham City they were wrong. The two games this season were not throw backs to the 1980's – it was much worse. Villa Park was a cauldron of hate. In all my years following the Villa, I have never witnessed Villa Park like this. I was only there as a fan but it was pure evil. Everyone was looking out for Blues fans that may have been in the home end. Such was the callous atmosphere, I phoned Karen to pick me up ten minutes before the game ended as I knew what would follow as the ground emptied and I did not want to be caught up in any of it. Besides, the following morning I had to drive to Manchester to visit a customer from work.

At full time it took over 300 police officers to bring the rioting under control in Witton Lane, as the Villa hooligans bombarded the Blues fans leaving the ground. It was absolute chaos. Every Villa fan – young, old, White, Black, tall, short, fat and skinny seemed to be involved. Never before have so many normal people turned into hooligans for the night. A mate of mine who's a Blues fan phoned me up the following morning and said to me: "I have never known Villa Park like that before. I was shitting myself at full time. It was proper moody". Moreover, when the Villa hooligans could not get at the Blues fans, they turned on the police which resulted in running battles. Just like the game at Saint Andrews, the local newspapers printed pictures of fans that the police wanted to talk to. The assortment of people was amazing – the one hooligan must have been about 70 years old. It was just one of those crazy nights, made worse by Birmingham City winning the game. The one thing that came out of all this was the pure, pure hatred that still to this day exists between Villa and Blues. And no amount of prison sentences, banning orders, police officers or CCTV will ever change that.

After all this, I was about to receive a phone call from Stan who would have the horrific news that John 'Grugg' Gregg had been murdered on his way home from a Glasgow Rangers football match in Scotland. This would tear the U.D.A/ U.F.F apart, leading to Stan receiving a 20-year prison sentence.

CHAPTER 24

*I*n May 2002, Johnny Adair was released from prison yet again. Once free he was a key player in an effort to forge stronger links between the U.D.A and the L.V.F. People I knew had told me that the L.V.F were up to their necks in drug dealing. This went a long way to understanding Adair's affiliation with the L.V.F. The most open declaration of this was a joint mural in West Belfast linking up Adair's 'C' Company and the L.V.F. Other elements in the U.D.A strongly opposed these actions which they saw as an attempt to gain external support in a bid to take over the leadership of the U.D.A. Stan had been advising me not to visit the Shankill when I was over in Ulster. All the more, for whatever reason he had not told me the full story about what was going on within the U.D.A leadership. Unknowingly, I did not have a clue what was simmering away in the background.

Another loyalist feud kicked off again and ended up with several people dead and scores evicted from their homes. Adair was expelled from the U.D.A in September 2002, along with his close friend and sidekick – John White; Adair's removal was well overdue. The organisation was once again at war with each other. Adair's West Belfast Brigade then split from the mainstream U.D.A. John 'Grugg' Gregg (who I had great admiration for) had been a strong supporter of Adair's expulsion. What followed were numerous death threats and attempts on Adair's and White's life from Grugg's South East Antrim Brigade. Adair was returned to jail in January 2003, when his early release license was revoked by the secretary of state for Northern Ireland on the grounds of engaging in unlawful activity. Bad blood had been simmering now for a while between Adair and Grugg. Grugg had a bomb placed under his car by allies of Adair, and had other attempts made on his life. In retaliation, Grugg allegedly responded with an attack on Adair's home two days before Adair was returned to jail.

In spite of this worse was to come. I will never forget the missed call I had from Stan in the very early hours of Sunday morning. It will stick in my mind forever. I do not mind admitting it made me sick with shock. I was fast asleep at the time. Stan had left a voice mail on my phone with his voice breaking up in tears saying: "They have got Grugg". At the start I could not work out exactly what he meant so I put on the teletext as it always reported the latest news from Ulster. It never directly named Grugg, but I gathered by reading the news on teletext and Stan's voice message that Grugg had been killed. Therefore, I called Stan. Stan answered the phone and said: "Grugg's been shot dead, can I pop over and see you". Stan was very upset and I was too much in shock at the time to have any emotions.

When Stan arrived at our home we hugged and he explained what had happened. Late on the Saturday night of February the 1st, Grugg and another Rathcoole lad Rob Carson, had been shot dead on Nelson Street in the old Sailortown district near Belfast docks whilst returning home from a Glasgow Rangers game. I did not know Rob that well, however, I knew his Dad Bobby and really liked the bloke – he always made me welcome in Rathcoole. Additionally, I was also very good friends with Rob's sister Lynn. Grugg's movements were some how known to Adair, who ordered from within his jail cell for a hit team to attack Grugg's taxi as it took them from the port in Belfast. There were strong rumours that someone close to Adair spotted Grugg on the ferry returning home. Other rumours have also circulated as to how Grugg's movements were known. To this day, no one really knows the truth.

When Grugg's taxi stopped at traffic lights close to the motorway, another taxi that had earlier been hijacked on the Shankill road by Adair's 'C' Company – rammed the taxi taking the lads back to Rathcoole. Masked gunmen immediately opened fire with automatic weapons; Grugg was killed instantly. Rob Carson died in hospital later and the taxi driver was seriously injured. Another close friend of mine – Monkey from Rathcoole and Grugg's son Stuart (who I had also become friends with), were also in the vehicle. Fortunately, neither sustained injuries in the attack. Stan and I phoned up Sammy from the Orange Lodge to find out if he knew any more than we did. He was dumbfounded as we started to speak. I asked Sammy why Grugg was allowed out of the estate knowing that he was a wanted man by Adair's faction after earlier attempts on his life. I could not work out why Grugg had not taken more precaution with his safety. Sammy told me that Grugg refused to be intimidated by Adair and his drug-dealing cronies and choose to carry on as normal. He was not the type of man to be intimidated; which he wasn't. Grugg was a warrior – a loyalist legend – and would not go into hiding for nothing or no one. Nonetheless, more pain was to come for Grugg and Rob Carson's family.

Somehow scum bags from the media were at the scene of the ambush within minutes, and took photos of Grugg lying dead slumped in the taxi. It was absolute gutter journalism without a thought for the families who would be grieving. The photo of Grugg made front page of all the newspapers and that photo still haunts me to this day. I could not look at it; I was totally sickened. It was disgusting how low the media sunk. However the families got through this I will never know. Word's cannot explain how low I felt as the U.D.A had once again torn itself apart from within. We asked Sammy to keep us informed of the funeral arrangements as the lads from West Midlands L.P.A would be going over to show our respect for our fallen comrades.

Stan knowing Grugg and the other lads involved in the incident for far longer than I did, flew over in the next day or two to give his support. He said he would phone me once the funeral arrangements were made – which he did. I could not make Rob's funeral due to work commitments, however, I could make Grugg's. Nearly everyone you could think of from the English loyalist movement headed over to Belfast to say good-bye to the loyalist hero. Stan had arranged for me to be picked up from Belfast airport and then taken to see Grugg's body in the chapel of rest. As I walked in I was horrified to see the man I had grown to respect lying there. I only stayed in there a minute or two as it was too upsetting. It was as if it was not really happening – had we really lost big Grugg? I could not come to terms that this had happened at the hands of so-called fellow loyalists. If Grugg would have been murdered by the I.R.A I could have accepted that, because that was the risk you was taking getting involved with the loyalist paramilitaries. Although, to this day I still find it hard to accept that he was taken from us due to a loyalist feud from within the U.D.A. I most certainly had not got involved with the L.P.A to experience situations like this.

After all the loyalist feuds in the past I had hoped all this was behind the organisation – but it wasn't. I found the earlier loyalist feuds between the U.V.F and the U.D.A gut wrenching, even though my obvious loyalties lay with the U.D.A. Although, this latest feud was internal. I do not mind admitting I had really fallen in love with Ulster and its people – and the U.D.A itself. I considered myself a U.D.A man even though I was not 'sworn in'. It really broke my heart to see its people turn on each other again. How can you promote and defend an organisation that keeps turning on itself? Some of my mates on the Mainland had said to me years ago that they were nothing but a bunch of gangsters – how could I now disagree? It made the U.D.A motto of 'Quis Separabit' seem nothing but a pipe dream. I had contacted the U.D.A to somehow help in it's war against the republican movement – not to see them turning their guns on each other. It really made me question if it was really worth all the heartache as it had really knocked me for six losing John Gregg. Deep down I wanted to walk away from it all, all the same I was in too deep. From the highs of getting involved in the U.D.A and meeting all the top people – to attending Grugg's funeral – I had been on such an emotional roller-coaster.

On the day of Grugg's funeral all the leading faces were there from the U.D.A/ U.F.F, and the streets were awash with thousands of people to say good-bye to the man that we all looked up to and respected. An estimated 7,000 people lined the streets. There were even floral tributes sent from all the other loyalist paramilitary groups as a mark of good will and respect. I suppose it went some way towards easing past tensions between the rival organisations. I was then approached by Stan and other Rathcoole U.D.A lads and asked if I would be a coffin bearer – I felt highly honoured by this gesture. During all my years involved in politics this was the highest accolade I could ever have imagined. I suppose it was the Rathcoole lad's way of thanking me for my support throughout the years.

As Grugg's body left his Rathcoole home, two masked U.F.F gunmen from South East Brigade fired a volley of shots over his coffin; this happens at the majority of loyalist paramilitary funerals. A number of people took turns in carrying his coffin and when my turn come I was so nervous about letting the occasion get to me – whilst at the same time fighting back the tears that were running down my face. I still could not believe all this was really happening; finally saying good-bye to big Grugg – the man who had made me so welcome in his club. A lone piper led the cortège to Carnmoney cemetery, where John Gregg was laid to rest to the U.D.A/ U.F.F song 'Simply the Best'. I remember watching his son Stuart and seeing the pain he was going through and could only imagine what a terrible time this must have been for the young lad. But Grugg's death was not to be the end of events.

The murder of John Gregg would be the undoing of Adair and 'C' Company. Grugg was the most senior U.D.A Brigadier to have been killed since John McMichael was blown up by the I.R.A in 1987. Due to Grugg's attempted assassination of Gerry Adams of Sinn Fein/I.R.A, it had gained him hero status within the ranks of the U.D.A. This was a step way too far by Adair and his allies. Hundreds of U.D.A men heavily armed – launched an invasion on the Lower Shankill to attack and remove all the people that had remained loyal to Adair. All of the murals that had been put up from Adair's orders were defaced. This resulted in all of Adair's supporters being driven out of Ulster by force. Due to the attack and removal of Adair's associates, the West Belfast Brigade was brought back under the control of the mainstream U.D.A. I knew a U.D.A member who I had met years ago from 'C' Company, who had told me that all Adair's Brigade were worried about was making money from drug dealing to racketeering.

I can remember once whilst up the Shankill Road many years ago during the height of Adair's reign, and seeing him and his associates in huge Range Rover cars worth a hell of a lot of money. No one dared questioned his lavish lifestyle at the time as he was looked upon as a hard-line U.D.A man taking the war to the I.R.A. My contact said if the money was not consistently coming in people would be beaten and kneecapped at Adair's orders. Johnny Adair also loved the publicity he gained over the years. He would never miss a chance at posing for photographs for the media. He was also known as a 'big head' who loved the limelight. He even boasted after the Shankill bombing that the I.R.A were after him – and him alone. Where as Grugg wasn't one to go posing for photographs for the news papers, Adair loved the attention and it's obvious he had a huge ego that consistently needing satisfying. To look back now I am embarrassed how I was taken in by all the Adair hype; I'd placed him on such a high pedestal. Even after his expulsion from the U.D.A he still wanted to be in the limelight, and it was reported that he received £100,000 for publishing his autobiography; I believe this figure to be true.

In addition, he later starred in a documentary made by Donald MacIntyre focused on Adair and a neo-Nazi from Germany, which made him look a right simpleton; it was truly embarrassing. By now his friends were very thin on the ground. Then in 2008, Adair appeared in an episode of Danny Dyer's deadliest men which also starred his close associate Sam McCrory. He simply could not resist the publicity and the fame. Unfortunately, his removal should have happened many years earlier. The motivation for such behaviour from Adair is sometimes difficult to piece together to people on the outside. It involved a combination of political differences over the ceasefires, feuding with the U.V.F, rivalry over control of territory, competition over the proceeds of organised crime, deep-rooted jealousy over other U.D.A members, wanting full control of the U.D.A, and not forgetting his constant craving for media attention. He has also stated that one day he will return to the Lower Shankill and reclaim his power-base. It is all talk from somebody who knows his days are over as a leading figure in Ulster loyalism.

In 2015, dissident republicans were foiled by police surveillance in a plot to 'take out' Johnny Adair and Sam McCrory – the operation was in its advanced stages. They wanted to assassinate Adair and McCrory for ordering the murders of dozens of Catholics during the troubles. Three men were eventually found guilty at the High Court in Glasgow. How would I have felt if republicans had 'taken out' Johnny Adair? In all fairness I would have been 'over the moon'. Adair may be alive for the time being, however, he must spend every second of the day looking over his shoulder knowing eventually his time will be up. But let us not forget there had also been throughout the years a number of top activists from 'C' Company, like all the other 'companies' in the U.D.A. who had more than done their bit for Ulster. The U.D.A even released a statement confirming this, and thanked the good people for their service throughout the years, which I thought was only right.

Following the removal of 'C' Company from the Shankill Road, Adair's family and supporters moved to Bolton in England, where they gained the nickname 'The Bolton Wanderers'. Before long shots were fired at Gina Adair's home (Johnny Adair's wife) and there was obviously a leak somewhere in the camp as to where they were staying. When Adair himself was finally released from prison, he headed to Bolton to link up with his small band of loyal followers. Nevertheless, the U.D.A had openly said they would seek revenge for Grugg's murder and it certainly would not be forgotten. And true to their word.......revenge was accomplished.

A loyalist named Alan McCullough who was fiercely loyal to Adair who had fled to Bolton with the Adair faction was the victim. Alan McCullough had orchestrated John Gregg's murder by orders from Adair whilst he was in jail. McCullough had been feeling home sick and wanted to return to Ulster and contacted Adair's successor for permission to return to West Belfast. His family also begged the new Brigadier in charge for consent for McCullough to return home. McCullough was told he would be safe if he returned home, however, this was a ply to get him back to Ulster. McCullough had also promised information on Johnny Adair's whereabouts in exchange for his safe return. As soon as Alan McCullough had returned home to Ulster, he was reported as missing; his body was later found in a shallow grave in Newtownabbey. The following evening a small band of people marched along the Shankill Road carrying placards and banners in protest of his killing. The U.F.F claimed the assassination, adding that it was carried out in retaliation for McCullough's involvement in the murder of John Gregg.

All this was so heartbreaking for me seeing the organisation that I loved tearing itself apart from within. It was a terrible time for me being involved in loyalism. However, if I thought this was the end of the feud – I was very wrong.

CHAPTER 25

Stan Curry who was running the West Midlands L.P.A, was staying at my house for a while before he flew out on holiday to Thailand. He had recently sold his house and as you do being one of my closest friends I offered to put him up before he flew out for his break. After all Stan had done for me over the years it was the least I could do. Karen did not mind as she liked Stan. The one morning I got up, went to work and then went out on the night to a party with Karen whilst Stan stayed in – well, so I thought he did. He had his own set of keys so it was no problem us doing our own thing. The next day it was all over the news about a bomb being placed under a car in Bolton, aimed at killing a close associate of Adair's named John Thompson. Adair and Thompson had been close friends for many years during 'C' Company's height of power. Thompson was known for being a 'hard man' who could most certainly look after himself. Nevertheless, the device placed under the car had malfunctioned and the intended victim remained unhurt. Stan and I spoke about the incident the following morning before I went to work, but he gave me absolutely no inkling of any knowledge regarding what had happened. Therefore, Stan thanked me for putting him up and flew out on his long vacation.

I had the shock of my life when Stan returned from Thailand, as he was arrested after landing back in England and held for questioning over the car bomb attack. I only found out from the teletext which I regularly scanned through to keep myself updated about events in Ulster. Stan was eventually charged with the attempt on John Thompson's life. However, like I have said, Stan never let on to me he had had any involvement, and even after knowing him for so long I had no suspicion he had been involved at any level. Being such a high-level operation it is not something he could have told me about anyway as the less people who knew the better – including friends. Moreover, Stan was all over the Birmingham newspapers.

What led to his downfall was he was spotted in the Bolton area on CCTV at the time of the attack. His CCTV picture was also in the Birmingham Mail, and if you knew Stan there was no denying it was him. There were comments in the newspaper from local residents who were saying what a nice man he was and how they were shocked that he had done such a thing. You see, Stan was a nice bloke – there was no denying that. The only difference from him and the other local residents was that he was in the U.D.A. Stan was a loyal supporter of South East Antrim Brigade U.D.A, and good friends of Grugg and Rob Carson who had been murdered by Adair's faction. This way Stan's way of trying to even out the score. But for me personally, things were about to get serious – deadly serious.

On the 3rd of February 2004, my house was raided in the early hours of the morning by Greater Manchester Police who were after more arrests for the car bombing in Bolton. Karen heard a noise out side and looked out the window and said to me: "Oh my god it's the police" I instantly knew what this was about, it didn't take much working out. They were about to baton charge my front door open, therefore, I leant out of the window and shouted that I was coming down. The police were all armed and had bulletproof vests on. It was like a scene from the film Robo-Cop. Once again, I had brought Karen trouble to the door. As the police stormed the house they instantly arrested me and I could not believe my ears when they said: "Tony Simms we are arresting you for conspiring to murder John Thompson".

You see, I only knew John Thompson by his nickname 'Fat Jackie', and this really threw me. The name John Thompson meant nothing to me at all. However, it did not take much working out my arrest was due to my connections with Stan and South East Antrim Brigade U.D.A. In addition, with Stan stopping at my house that had made the police surmise I was to some degree involved; you pay the price. I knew what I was getting involved with so I could not grumble. Don't put your hand in the fire and then moan when you get burnt. I knew I had not joined up with the Boys' Brigade and that from the word go something like this could happen. They told me to get dressed and in the panic I grabbed the nearest T-shirt – which just out of coincidence happened to be a U.D.A T-shirt. Not the wisest of choices but something I most certainly did not do on purpose. I did not even realise I had it on until I was sitting in the police car handcuffed.

As they led me away Karen was crying. They were tearing the house apart looking for evidence to link me with the car bombing. Two officers put me in the car and took me to Greater Manchester for questioning. I had loads of U.D.A regalia in the house and Karen told me they were saying to each other: "We have got our man". They found some brown tape in the house that I had been using to seal up parcels I sent to mates in Ulster – stuff like NF/BNP newspapers, badges and so on. Some brown tape had been used in the car bomb attack, to what degree I do not know, and after finding some brown tape in my house Karen said they were somewhat celebrating as this was something that they presumed put me in the frame. How many houses will have a roll of brown tape; it was ridiculous.

As I was in the car travelling to Greater Manchester, you had the old good cop, bad cop game going on. The one asked me when was the last time I had been to Bolton. I told him it was to watch the Villa, which it was. Then he started a conversation about football. I could not believe this shit was happening. The officer who was driving was very frosty towards me – it is fair to say I instantly disliked him. He's the one who pointed out the T- shirt I was wearing to his colleague. On the other hand, I was not too worried as I knew they had nothing on me. As we arrived at Greater Manchester Police station, I was told to sit in a room and wait to be booked in for questioning. The room had a little glass window in it and I could not believe what I was seeing – all the other lads from the West Midlands L.P.A were also being brought in for questioning. I could see them all coming in, however, they could not see me.

Our names, addresses and connections with South East Antrim U.D.A had been obtained from flight records and security forces intelligence. It would not have taken much working out. It was not rocket science who was frequently travelling with who and who was connected with who. I then demanded to make a phone call as that is your legal right. As a result, I phoned Karen. She answered the phone and was evidently very upset. I then asked her if they were still ripping the house apart, when the main man in charge said to me: "You can't ask that". I was raging so I told him: "Go fuck yourself", which abruptly ended the phone call as he cut me off. The police officer booking me in said: "You can't speak to him like that, he's a senior officer". I said to him: "I'll talk to him however I like". That set the tone between the arresting officers and myself.

After being put in holding cells for god knows how long, we were then all brought in for questioning one at a time. By now I had a solicitor there to represent me. We had a little briefing and he said to me that he did not care if I was guilty or not – but to go 'No comment' all the way – which I did. They were asking me questions like: "Are you a member of the U.D.A". Membership alone carries about a seven-year prison sentence. I was not a member of the U.D.A to put the record straight, I was involved with the L.P.A. That's what drives the 'Old Bill' and the security forces crazy as they are not sure who is sworn in and who is not.

They once again pointed out my T-shirt. I just grinned at them as you can purchase these from any loyalist souvenir shop, and 99% of the people who buy them are not U.D.A member's – just supporters. They then asked me: "Are you a member of the U.V.F or the L.V.F". I laughed at that question as it was blatantly obvious I had no connections whatsoever with those organisations. They then stared asking me stupid questions like: "Are you a member of the NF or BNP". What that had to do with this line of enquiry I do not know. It was common knowledge to the police I was a member of the National Front. All the other lads were also advised to go 'No comment'. The police were also asking my mates about my involvement in right-wing politics, and they told me they seemed more interested in my political leanings than the actual car bombing itself. Don't these idiots know that the NF was a perfectly legal, registered political party; it is mind-boggling. We were then put back in the holding cells and kept overnight. Despite that, worse was to come.

They then proceeded to visit all of our places of work to see if we were working on the day of the car bomb attack. Some of the lads had very highly well paid jobs working in offices and so on, and they took away all their computers to investigate further. This was totally out of order as they could have gone about this in a different way. This obviously highlighted to our employees what we were supportive of and involved in. Luckily for me, my boss was a loyalist sympathiser on the quiet so it wasn't a problem; he is very patriotic. But the question must be asked? Why not visit our places of employment first to see if we were all working on the day in question – which we were – then that would have put us out of the frame.

There was no need to raid our homes first and then visit our works. Why couldn't they of done it the other way around? I am sure to this day they just wanted to give us shit because we were loyalists and make our lives that bit more difficult. Moreover, maybe try to scare us from further involvement and to let in be known we were on their radar. That type of intimidation has never bothered me. I do not try to hide what I believe in. Unfortunately, most of the other lads had young children and it must have been terrible seeing their Dad's dragged away and their homes turned upside down. They even questioned all my mates from work asking if there was anyway I could have clocked in and then sloped off for the day. They had nothing on us apart from we knew Stan and visited Rathcoole.

We were all bailed pending further enquiries. When I finally got home I was dreading Karen's response. Fortunately, she understood the situation and was just glad to have me back. The police had torn the house apart looking for proof of my involvement and had taken away seven huge bags of so-called 'evidence'. For all that, I assured Karen that I had not been involved. She was surprisingly calm about it all – thank god. We were summonsed back to Greater Manchester on the 29th of April 2004, for an identity parade. I had no worries about this at all as I knew I was not involved. After so long we were all contacted by post that no further enquiries were needed. What a relief, even though I knew they had nothing on me from the word go. It was just the ball-ache of it all. The other lads were obviously also delighted.

When Stan Curry was finally taken to trial for the car bombing, he was found guilty and handed down a twenty-year prison sentence. I was distraught. Moreover, I owed him a lot after all he had done for me over the years. He would need my support now more than ever. After Stan had served around two years in various English jails, having to mix with all the filth you could imagine, he was eventually transferred to HMP Maghaberry, Lisburn, County Antrim, where he would serve his sentence on the same wing as Steve Irwin, Michael Stone and other prominent loyalists. I had now lost two of my closest mates – and how bizarre they were not only in the same jail together – but also on the same wing.

One last point I must make about this episode in my life is regarding the Greater Manchester Police who had arrested me at my home. The main man in charge had said to me: "We know you were involved, and if you are not charged and sentenced I'll personally write you a letter apologising for your arrest". However, all these years down the line....... I am still waiting for that letter to arrive.

CHAPTER 26

I had now left the National Front and sent of my membership for the new modernised BNP who had been winning seats at local elections. The BNP was formed out of a splinter group from the National Front in 1982 under John Tyndall, which had by now far outgrown the NF in every way imaginable. The chairman now was Nick Griffin, and it is fair to say his modernising of the party and the way he was going about things was my reason for joining the BNP. At the time I was very pro-Griffin, and refused to listen to all the rumours about him. If you listened to all the different rumours you hear about everybody you would never end up trusting a single person, therefore, I was throwing my weight behind Nick Griffin's BNP. All you were hearing about on the news was the BNP – it was an exciting time being a British nationalist. In spite of that, my passage into the BNP wasn't going to be as smooth as I was hoping for.

I was invited to my first meeting in the West Midlands region, where of all people Nick Griffin would be speaking; magnificent. I do not mean to be disrespectful to the NF – but you could see straight away that the BNP was better organised and a lot more professional. In addition, the attendance was many times bigger than that of an NF meeting. There must have been a good 100 people there. I was no longer a big fish in a little pond – I was now a little fish in a big pond. I had made the right choice. We even had the pleasure of two newly elected West Midland councillors being paraded at the meeting; that was a great experience. This is what we had been striving towards for all these years – a breakthrough for a British nationalist party. Many years of hard labour, left-wing harassment and police intimidation had gone into winning those seats. The two councillors gave a speech on how finally the British people would have someone to really turn to and a party fighting for their interests.

Some people may call me a glory hunter and say I only joined the BNP when it started winning seats, which is true. Despite that, we were involved in the serious business of saving our country – and I had to put my support into a party I really thought could make that change in British politics. Sentiment for many a year had stopped me joining the BNP due to my loyalty to the NF and my close bond with Norman Tomkinson and John Lord. All the same, I had to look at the bigger picture and what party stood the better chance of winning seats and gaining political power. After a brief chat with Simon Darby (the deputy chairman of the BNP at the time) he introduced me to the lad running Birmingham BNP who instantly did not seem too pleased to see Alan and I who had also followed me out of the NF. I do not know at the time if he felt his position might be under threat by us joining, or that he was concerned we had come over from the NF who were looked upon as hard-line. Nevertheless, the reception we got from him was very frosty to say the least.

I listened to Nick Griffin speak and as always he gave a great account of himself. When the meeting was brought to a close Alan and I then sat down with the Birmingham organiser for a chat and to see how things stood in the branch. I was not looking forward to the discussion as like I said, he had been giving off bad vibes. As we started talking it felt more like a police interview than a welcome into the BNP and it certainly was not what I was hoping for. Having said that, we exchanged numbers and I left the meeting and went home. After digesting the whole day, even though I was impressed with the set up of the BNP, I was not happy about how things had gone with the Birmingham organiser. Therefore, I contacted him the following week for a one to one meeting to see what the problem had been; he agreed to meet up. I knew there was an underlying issue that had not been mentioned. I just knew it – and I was right.

We met up in a pub in Yardley, Birmingham, where my concerns were proved correct. We sat down with a pint and then it surfaced he knew about my deep involvement in the loyalist cause and the L.P.A. Someone had wired him off about me which came as no big surprise; people love to gossip. You see, the new BNP had modernised and 'watered down' many of their policies – including Northern Ireland. However, with me being completely new to the party I was not exactly sure to what level every policy had changed. The organiser explained to me that even though the BNP still supported Ulster remaining part of the Union, it did not want to be seen to be supporting the loyalist paramilitaries for electoral reasons. They wanted to drop the sectarian tag that had been associated with the right-wing for many years. The party was cleaning up its image and openly supporting the loyalist paramilitaries was no longer on the agenda.

The Birmingham organiser was also there with his right hand man who explained that the Ulster conflict simply was not a vote winner on the mainland. I was a bit taken aback by this, however, I sat and listened as they explained that the English people were hard pushed to vote for policies at home – let alone across the water. As much as it kills me to admit this they were actually right as the majority of English people do not understand or care about what happens in loyal Ulster. Even after all the I.R.A bombings on the mainland, the English people were simply not aware of the plight of the loyalist people – the penny was now dropping. They both explained that to gain the support of the electorate we had to be totally squeaky clean if we ever wanted to make that push for power.

Little did I know at the time a lot of second and third generation Irish Catholics had joined the BNP and were helping to fight elections as they found the BNP the only party that actually spoke up for their concerns on the mainland. Birmingham has a large Irish Catholic community – the biggest outside of London – and a lot of them were now voting BNP due to being let down by the so-called big three over the years. After listening to what they had to say and digesting everything, I could see where they were coming from. The Ulster conflict had sadly never been a vote winner on the mainland; they were right about that. It was not as though the BNP were abandoning the Ulster people – not at all. It was more a case of keeping the Ulster policy in the background so to speak. The BNP were shoving forward policies that really mattered to the English electorate. Policies like asylum seekers, housing, Europe, the NHS, better schooling for our children, sending our troops to fight American wars, opposing more Mosques, the large scale use of Halal meat in our schools and prisons – and many more common sense policies that would strike a chord with the English electorate.

During my years in the NF we'd had guest speakers from the L.P.A, and I had sold U.D.A magazines at the meetings. Having said that, this was something for electoral reasons that the BNP would most undoubtedly steer clear of. There was a large Irish vote out there in Birmingham and the BNP were after it. They wanted to look and act like proper politicians and drop the old image. Some may agree with this and some may not. Certain British nationalists accused the BNP of going 'Pro-Irish' but that was nonsense. It was tactical politics. The BNP still undoubtedly opposed Sinn Fein and what it stood for. If anything the party deserved credit for attempting to make itself more voter friendly and less a party of confrontation.

I was asked if I could fall into line with the new image the party was striving for. After the initial shock and listening to what they had to say, I agreed that it was the right way forward. I did not have to change my views on Ulster (which will never change) or my support for the U.D.A. Although, it was something I could not promote from within the BNP. My membership of the BNP would not stop me visiting Ulster or attending L.P.A and B.U.A fundraisers. Nonetheless, it would be something I would do separate from the BNP and not champion in any way whilst on BNP duty. I would be serving two masters. The BNP did want me on board as I had a good record as an activist and I knew how to fight elections due to Norman Tomkinson, learning me the ropes over the years. However, I had to comply with the modernisation side of the party.

They somehow knew about my connections with Stan Curry and Steve Irwin, and were concerned about this getting out. I proceeded to tell them my wife was a Roman Catholic, as was my mother – even though neither of them followed the faith. In addition, they were both English Catholics not Irish Catholics. My wife Karen actually supported the loyalists, and even though she was brought up a Catholic she is not a religious person by any stretch of the imagination. She supported the loyalists because she was born British and that is what the loyalists were fighting to remain. I know a huge number of English born Catholics who also supported Ulster, so this is not something you never hear about. Many of my close mates were English Catholics that supported the Ulster cause. The situation in England is very, very different to the situation in Northern Ireland. Therefore, it was agreed that if ever my U.D.A connections leaked out we could fall back on that my Wife and my Mother were Roman Catholics to try to defuse the situation.

I was also asked how I felt about the watering down of the immigration policy – which I was all for. It needed readjusting as just like the Ulster policy it wasn't a vote winner come Election Day. Having an extreme line immigration policy was simply not working. We were in the market of selling our policies and I believed by now the more appealing you make them, the more they will sell. The tried and tested old ways of British nationalism had failed and something new was needed if ever we were to be taken seriously as a professional political party – whose aim was to gain political power. Moreover, as representatives of the party we must conduct ourselves in a professional sensible manner. We were asking the people to trust us with public spending, therefore, I was under no illusion that a revamp of the movement was long overdue. By now, I felt a prisoner in my own country and I was adamant to give the government a run for their money and to take our country back.

As I headed home after the meeting with the Birmingham organiser, I was now more upbeat as the slate had been wiped clean and we had agreed to work together. Now let us get on with the work of getting the BNP even more seats. I really felt like we had the chance to change the face of British politics with our breakthrough at council level. I could not wait to get started in the BNP under the leadership of Nick Griffin, with the aim of one day forming a BNP government. Let me state that after my initial dislike of the Birmingham organiser, once we thrashed things out we finished up having a very good working relationship, and I was impressed by his dedication and optimism. Building for the next wave of elections was now our target. Moreover, we were planning to stand a record number of candidates for the Birmingham council elections. I was approached and asked to be a Security Officer at Birmingham BNP meetings, which I accepted. If for example Nick Griffin was guest speaker, we could pull in over 150 members. Not to mention, the BNP were never shy of condemning the White community for their conduct when their behaviour warranted criticism.

We were out mostly twice a week leafleting and speaking to the public on their doorsteps. With our large number of activists we would split up into two teams and hit different areas. We were all asked to dress as smart as possible as we were the face of the party whilst out campaigning. The support we were getting from people was amazing as we had finally won seats on local councils – which had bumped up the image of the party and showed it was no longer a waste vote. Tens of thousands of sensible modern BNP leaflets were hitting people's doormats. Leaflets that were focusing on local issues at the heart of the area, and the people were taken in by our new approach. We did not have any need to keep mentioning immigration as everyone knew where we stood on that issue. Let us show the public that we had a wide range of policies that could solve all of Britain's problems.

The 2004 elections were a massive push for the BNP, with not only standing a record 312 candidates at council level, but also fighting the European Elections, London Mayor Elections and the London assembly elections. It was all systems go and a very hectic time as lots of campaigning needed to be done. Birmingham BNP fielded a very impressive 24 candidates at local level, up from five candidates at the last round of elections. This showed how fast the party was moving forward. The Birmingham Mail newspaper went overboard about the increase in Birmingham BNP's candidates; so much for the newspaper claiming to be non-bias towards political parties. As Election Day loomed, no person in the country couldn't of been aware the BNP where out there fighting for their rights. We had grabbed all the headlines by standing a record number of candidates all over the UK.

At local level the BNP won a further more fourteen seats to bring our total to 21 councillors. The breakthroughs were in Epping, Sandwell, Bradford, Caldermore and Kirkless. We never won any seats on Birmingham council, nonetheless, we still pulled in some fantastic results. Our Kingstanding candidate was only 300 votes short of taking a seat on Birmingham council – with a bit more campaigning in that ward we could have won that seat. The total votes at council level were an amazing 190,000 nationwide. The London assembly candidate polled a very healthy 90,000 votes – way up on the last time we fought the seat. In addition, Julian Leppert polled 57,331 votes – fighting the seat for London Mayor.

Additionally, the highlight of the night was the increase in the votes at the European Elections. Every single region totally smashed their previous record with the West Midlands vote going up from 14,344, to 107,784. That was an upsurge from 1.7% to 7.5%, and nearly polled enough votes to win the seat; we fell just short. The jewel in the crown was Yorkshire where the previous vote of 8,911 was escalated to a whopping 126,538 – an increase from 1.2% to 8.0 %. Once again just missing out on the seat. The overall vote for the European Elections was 808,200, up from 102,647 in 1999. What a night it was. We really rocked the establishment with our increased votes all over the UK. Therefore, to anybody who disagreed with our new image and changing to 'voter friendly' politics they were proved wrong by our fantastic results.

If I thought now was the time for a rest how wrong was I, as the BNP had huge plans for the general election in 2005. At the same time, the British Ulster Alliance had a schedule to mark the 30th anniversary of the Birmingham pub bombings. Republican terrorists had bombed Birmingham back in 1974, and Frank from the B.U.A wanted to mark the occasion with a remembrance meeting and a social on the night. We would never have guessed though in our wildest dreams how much media publicity this would generate. Let me make this perfectly clear though – we were not after publicity. We just wanted to mark the event in our own way, but when somehow the left-wing media caught onto our plans all hell broke loose. The Midlands, Marxist, left-wing rag called the Sunday Mercury, printed a double page story about the B.U.A's supposed links to the loyalist paramilitaries. The B.U.A was not at paramilitary organisation – it never claimed to be one. It was simply a loyalist umbrella group for all British patriots who supported Ulster. It comes as no surprise that the media do not go into overdrive when a republican event takes place in Birmingham. The anti-British lobby who run our country would like us to forget about the Birmingham pub bombings. In spite of that, we do not have short memories and we prefer to remember our people who have died at the hands of the I.R.A.

A Birmingham Irish newspaper printed a story about their concerns for the occasion and how the Irish community somehow felt threatened. What a load of nonsense – we wasn't after trouble. We just wanted to show our respects then go home, as simple as that. A political representative from the B.U.A named John Porter even went onto a West Midlands radio station to confirm to the Irish people of Birmingham that they had nothing to fear from the B.U.A. It's what makes me laugh about Irish republicans. They are so hypocritical. They hold their republican events all year round and not a word is said, then scream blue murder when the boots on the other foot. Ashamed of nothing – offended by everything.

Frank asked me if I knew of any halls we could use for the meeting. As a result, I started to look around for a suitable venue. After visiting a number of places, I found a function room in Sutton Coldfield in the West Midlands – just on the outskirts of Birmingham. Just to stay on the side of caution, I told them it was for a football team get together. I do not like lying, but as British patriots these were the hurdles placed in our way just to hold a patriotic meeting. And I didn't want to use any of the places we used for BNP meetings as I had promised to keep my BNP and loyalist activities separate. Frank visited Sutton Coldfield to have a look at the lay out of the area and to arrange some re-direction points for supporters who were coming. There was a nice little pub up the road where we could all meet up before we took the B.U.A supporters to the secret location. It was kept as tight lipped as possible to stop the venue leaking out. The last thing we wanted was a late cancellation if the person hiring us the room found out who we were. Frank also applied for a rally in Birmingham city centre which the police turned down – no surprise there. It's strange isn't it how only pro-British rallies ever get the knock back.

On the morning of the meeting, Karen and I had arrived there early to set up the function room. Suddenly, about half an hour before the meeting was about to take place endless police riot vans turned up out of the blue – apparently to make sure the occasion passed off peacefully. It was so over the top it was shocking. They surrounded the hall in a ring of steel – I have seen less police for a Villa-Birmingham match. What a waste of taxpayers money and what a waste of police resources. How the police had found out about the venue I do not know, anyhow, just by monitoring a few phone calls it would not really have taken that much homework to find out where we were congregating. As the meeting started to a packed room, there were even guests over from Ulster. B.U.A supporters gave speeches from all different regions of the UK as well as guest speakers from Northern Ireland.

As the meeting came to a close, all the names of the victims of the Birmingham bombings were read out followed by a minutes silence. The meeting was very well attended and passed off perfectly. We had achieved our goal – to remember the Birmingham people. As we left the function room, I still could not believe the amount of police officers that were parked up in their riot vans. I remember thinking next time I will book it as an I.R.A meeting as then well be left alone. In what other country in the world can't a patriotic organisation hold a meeting without police harassment? This just further confirmed to me that you cannot be proud to be British in Britain. It is looked upon as a crime.

For the social on the night we were sorted for a room as my mate Graham ran a nice big pub with a separate function room upstairs which he allowed us to have free of charge. We laid on a normal disco to start the night off, followed by a raffle, speeches from various leading people in the B.U.A, accompanied by a loyalist disco. Everyone present had a good drink and we all had a loyalist singsong. There was also a collection for the B.U.A, aimed at raising money to go towards helping the people over in Ulster and to set up more projects. The good thing also about the night was the assortment of people there from all patriotic groups and different football clubs, without one bit of the usual crap you sometimes get when large crowds gather. The B.U.A put a stop to all this bickering, which was a good thing to come out of the organisation. No one person was more important than the next man, regardless of what political organisation or football team you supported. The victims of the pub bombings and their families would of been proud of the day we held in remembrance for them. Having said that, if anybody had not previously heard of the B.U.A – thanks to the left-wing rag the Sunday Mercury, they certainly had now.

Moving on from here, the Villa Hardcore would be in involved in three more major football related incidents which would signal the end of the firm as we knew it. Now I am not condoning or promoting football violence in anyway, but I think it is only right to end this chapter regarding the lads I used to travel with to the football. Villa were playing away at Charlton Athletic in London, and a huge firm of the lads had travelled down south because on the Monday they were in all in court for the 'Battle of Rocky Lane' against the Zulu Warriors. All the lads were expecting to be sent down and whilst they were down in London they came across a mob of Chelsea's lads. Chelsea have always had a top hooligan firm stretching back many years. Police rushed to the Kings Cross area of London as the Villa Hardcore clashed with the Chelsea fans, in what officers described as a 'pre-planned event'. It took the police over thirty minutes to bring the trouble under control. Five Villa Hardcore lads were jailed for this incident at London's Snaresbrook court. The leader of the Villa Hardcore, Steven Fowler, also received a prison sentence for the 'Battle of Rocky Lane' along with a number of other lads that I knew.

But worse was to come against our local rivals West Bromwich Albion away in August 2004. Now I do not want to sound like 'my old self' but let me take this chance to state the Villa do not rate West Brom at all – never have done, never will. In all the years West Brom have only ever brought a firm to Villa Park twice to my knowledge, once smashing up the Little Crown pub when it was totally empty. If they want to claim that as a result then that shows them for what they are. They would never dream of coming to the Adventurers. For many seasons going to West Brom was like a day out at the seaside. Dating back to the late 1970's - early 1980's, the C-Crew used to regularly go in the home end and face little if no resistance. We would just land there and go on the piss because they had no organised firm; they mean nothing to us. Despite that, West Brom hate the Villa as much as they hate their Black Country rivals the Wolves.

The two sets of hooligans clashed at the Uplands pub in Handsworth, which borders West Bromwich – in what was the worst ever football related trouble between the two clubs. Eight supporters were injured and twelve fans were arrested on the day as between 80-100 people were involved in running battles in which one eye witness described it as 'pure savagery'. The West Brom firm were armed to the teeth, ranging from baseball bats to iron bars – and a number of the Villa lads received injuries that required hospital treatment. After a series of dawn raids on both sets of fans, 60 men were jailed for the disturbance with the judge handing down sentences totalling over 80 years – as well as further banning orders. Notorious Hardcore lad Steven Fowler was jailed for a further twenty months for his part in the disturbance at the Uplands pub.

From being around myself many years ago and seeing the making of the firm during its early years, it had developed into one of the England's most notorious and organised outfits. Every club in England had now heard of the Villa Hardcore. A West Midlands Police representative said after the events at the Uplands: "This was a lengthy investigation that resulted in 58 people being banned from football matches for a considerable period of time. If you go to football matches intent on causing trouble you will be arrested, put before the courts, and banned from watching the game. It should be made clear that while these people may claim to be football fans, they are in fact criminals".

Nevertheless, something needs pointing out. I knew most of these lads personally, and even though it is right they were criminals who had broken the law, they were still 100% Villa fans. Some of the lads in the Villa Hardcore had followed the Villa home and away for 20-30 years, therefore, to say they were not Villa fans was wrong. The only difference was they liked a meet up with other like-minded lads and to have a punch up on match day.

People may say I am wrong, but these lads were Aston Villa through and through and loved their club as much as the next man – if not more. The final straw for the Villa Hardcore as an active firm came on the 9th March 2005, when we played Birmingham City away. A mob of Zulus had travelled to Aston looking for the Villa Hardcore who were drinking in the Vine pub on Lichfield Road. Fair play to the Blues for having the balls to travel to Villa territory. What followed was dozens of hooligans from both sides clashing in the street armed with bottles, glasses and pool balls. Eyewitnesses said that at one point up to 200 hooligans from both sides were involved in the confrontation. Sixteen people were arrested as the fighting spilled out across the road. A number of the Villa lads had only recently been released from prison for football charges, and were still on banning orders. The clashes occurred about five hours after the game had ended, therefore, it was most certainly pre-planned again using mobile phones.

The following few days afterwards detectives were shifting through CCTV footage from cameras on Lichfield Road to identify the rest of the fans involved in the trouble who were not arrested on the night. A detective from Queens Road C.I.D said further arrests would follow – which they did. This was one battle too far for the Villa Hardcore and a large number of the lads dropped out after this. A number of the lads had already done prison sentences for the 'Battle of Rocky Lane' and the 'Battle of the Uplands' and they decided it wasn't worth the risks no more. Many lads had dropped out years ago, nevertheless, the main faces had carried it on and took it to another level. However, they now realised enough was enough. Moreover, that any further sentences handed down would be for a very long stretch indeed.

The firm had most certainly left its mark on the Villa Park terraces as well as the England national scene. The new up and coming lads at the Villa now call themselves the Hardcore Youth – but as for the older lads the journey was now over. They had accomplished what they set out to achieve. It was time to hang up their boots up.

CHAPTER 27

After the BNP's gains at the last round of local elections and the superb votes in the European Elections, hopes were high for some good results at the 2005 general election. Not for one second did we think we would actually win a seat in parliament; it was not time yet. Nevertheless, it was still looked upon as another stepping-stone to building up the parties election-fighting machine. The BNP was undoubtedly moving forward from standing in 33 seats at the last general election, to fighting 119 seats at the 2005 general election. We had been campaigning pretty heavy in our Birmingham target wards and managed to stand in a record four parliamentary seats. Come the day of the election Birmingham BNP managed to save two deposits, which was a great result and showed we were moving in the right direction. Rob Purcell stood in Yardley ward, 1,523 votes – 5.2%, and saving his deposit. Dennis Adams stood in Hodge Hill ward, 1,445 votes – 5.1%, also saving his deposit. Dennis would sadly pass away a few years later on. He was a real decent bloke who I had a hell of a lot of time for. It was not only a major loss for the BNP, but for me personally as we had built up a very good friendship. Sharon Ebanks stood in Erdington ward and nearly saved her deposit with 1,512 votes – 4.8%.

Additionally, Mark Cattell stood in Northfield ward, 1,278 votes – 4.1%. We were delighted with the results (especially saving two deposits). All the same, we had put the work in.

Bradford was looked upon as a strong region for the BNP, with all three candidates saving their deposits. L. Cromie – Bradford North, 2,061 votes – 6.0%. Paul Cromie – Bradford West, 2,525 votes – 6.9%. And the best of the night was J. Lewthwaite – Bradford South, 2,862 votes – 7.8%. Another North West target ward was in Burnley, where Len Starr gained 4,003 votes – a very impressive 10.3%. These were amazing results as only a few years ago we could only have dreamed about obtaining such high percentages. Our party chairman Nick Griffin stood in Keighley ward, and pulled in a fantastic 4,240 votes – 9.2%. In Dagenham, Lawrence Rustem obtained 2,870 votes – 9.3%. Simon Darby stood in Dudley North, 4,022 votes – 9.7%. Another strong region for the BNP was in Stoke where we also pulled in some breathtaking results. S. Cartlidge – Stoke North, 2,132 votes – 6.9%. Mike Coleman – Stoke Central, 2,178 votes – 7.8%. In addition, the best result of the night from Stoke was M. Leat – Stoke South, 3,305 votes – 8.7%.

Another strong area for us was West Bromwich, in the West Midlands. C. Butler, 2,329 votes – 6.6%, and J. Lloyd gained a very impressive 3,456 votes – 9.9%. However, the two outstanding results of the night were David Exley – Dewsbury, 5,066 votes – 13.1%. And the 'jewel in the crown' Richard Barnbrook – Barking, 4,916 votes – 17%. What a result. We also pulled in some very decent votes in Ashton under Lyne, Batley and Spen, Blackburn, Halifax, Hyndburn, Morley, Pontefract, Rother Valley, Sheffield, Thurrock and Walsall. In spite of that, we also had a few disappointing results in areas we expected to do well. The votes in Leeds and Oldham were very poor, with us even failing to save our deposit in Oldham East. Having said that, overall it was a very good election with some remarkable votes coming our way. We polled in total across the seats fought 192,746 votes – our best ever for a general election. We also fielded 41 candidates at local level, obtaining 21,775 votes, however, most councils were not up for re-election this year. Over at the National Front, they had increased their number of candidates for the general election from five in 2001, to thirteen seats in 2005 – but once again failed to save any deposits.

What had made our votes even more impressive to me was that due to my promotion at work I had been travelling around the country visiting customers to bring in more work for the company and to deal with any issues that may have needed addressing. Whilst doing so, I visited most regions in the UK and spent a day or two in these areas. I could not believe how even in little towns and villages the immigrant population was growing in such large numbers. What we were now facing was a non-British population explosion, which also included all the recently arrived Eastern Europeans. In places like Bradford and Luton, you could go an hour without seeing a White face and then when you did they were from Eastern Europe. Large parts of London were to say the least now like outposts of Pakistan, Bangladesh, India and the West Indies. They like to call it a multi-racial/cultural society but where were the White British people? I dread to think of the amount of illegal immigrants in London. If we allow illegal immigration, then there is obviously no point to legal immigration. London had previously overcame the plague, survived the great fire, and withstood the blitz...but now it had been destroyed by mass immigration.

I am not for one second saying all these immigrants were bad people – not at all. Nevertheless, our culture and way of life were not compatible. Of course, I understand that some immigrants and their off-springs do work hard and pay their taxes like the rest of us do. In addition, that large numbers of them are well-educated, skilled and intelligent people who contribute to our nation. On the other hand, these skilled people do not compensate for the many that either do not work – or work in non-skilled jobs and need welfare assistance to survive. Moreover, how is it right that these skilled, educated, and intelligent immigrants are working in Britain when their Third World countries desperately need such people themselves?

Do you think it is right that the British government have imported all the best doctors and nurses from countries that are far more in need of them than we are? Repatriation – what greater gift could we give? Mass immigration is a short term fix for a long term problem. The answer is to train up the indigenous population to suit the labour requirements of the UK. Every imported immigrant needs and uses our public services, creating more strain on the already overstretched system. For example the National Health Service – or should I call it the International Health Service – is at breaking point due to uncontrolled mass immigration. Our masters then turn around and say we need more immigration to fill these roles – it's a con trick and a complete swizz.

This was the first time it struck me regarding the BNP that we were now on a race against time; time was no longer our friend. With our ever-shrinking numbers would we actually have the people left to vote us in? Tony Blair had made a promise he wanted to make Britain truly 'multi-cultural'. Whilst driving around the country he had most certainly achieved his goal. We all know Tony Blair is a warmongering, lying, duplicitous piece of scum – who has the blood of British soldiers and thousands of innocent Middle-East civilians on his scrawny hands. What's less well known is that Blair is employed by the power hungry Israeli spy agency – Mossad – and is willing to do their bidding at any cost. Furthermore, in 19996, the Times exposed Blair's Jewish donors. "Tony Blair has been receiving hundreds of thousands of pounds in undisclosed donations through a private account, despite the Labour parties commitment to openness about its funding. A Sunday Times investigation had discovered some of Britain's richest tycoons have given huge donations under an arrangement made by Blair's fraudulent office to disguise their identities. And let us not forget these donations come at a price. Moreover, the Conservatives and Lib Dems are no different.

But one thing is for certain The present leadership of all the mainstream parties are on the verge of rendering themselves as wholly unelectable, as the British public are waking up to their betrayal and consistent bombardment of lies and misinformation. White people; the only race you can legally discriminate against. I could not believe the government had allowed the same mistake to happen twice. Firstly, the invasion from Asia and the West Indies during the 1950's and the 1960's, and now the door flung wide open to low paid workers from Eastern Europe. This was not a question of race, it was a question of space – Britain was full. How can you have an open door immigration policy when there aren't enough jobs to go around for the British people as it is? The answer is simple. To bring the job market down to its knees and have everybody eventually on the minimum wage; it's called control. They talked about the 'minimum wage', however, the fact of the matter is in most jobs it is now also the 'maximum wage'. That's if your not unfortunate to be on a 'zero hour contract'. The young White British worker has been described as being lazy and not wanting work – but how can you expect young lads to get motivated for so little in return. A good job for most people now was impossible to find.

I had done all right for myself after many years of struggling. I'd had a promotion at work and a company car. I had a nice house in a nice area, and could have quite easily said: "Well I'm alright, that suits me". However, I wanted something better for my people. I wanted to drag my country out of this mess and give my nation a little glimmer of hope. All the same, I admit after travelling the country due to my work commitments, it was the first time I had concluded that it was now maybe too late to save the United Kingdom. And in the 'well to do' areas that were still White (not that there was many left) they could not foresee the oncoming problems and were still engaged in voting for the mainstream parties – mainly the Conservatives.

It was at this stage that I was not only convinced that the new BNP image being shoved forward was right – it should have been done twenty years ago when the numbers were still greatly in our favour. Had we left it too late? Only time will tell. After travelling the country it gave me that sinking feeling that a right demolition job had been done on our people. Yes, we were winning seats at council level. Yes, we were standing record number of candidates at the general election, nonetheless, we were now in a race against time; that was for sure. And at the end of the day, the true British people were getting what I considered a 'raw deal'.

Then the one morning I had a phone call that my Karen had been mugged on the way to work. Fortunately, she was not hurt. She'd had her handbag snatched of her from behind by a person of 'Eastern European' appearance. Karen never put up a fight or tried to retrieve the bag, which was the correct move as for a start there was nothing in there of any real value. But let me make this perfectly clear. If I would have been there, or witnessed it taking place, I would now be serving a very lengthy prison sentence that's for sure; I make no bones about that. I would not have contacted the police. I would have sorted that out myself there and then and worried about the repercussions at a later date. This is my wife I am talking about and I am meant to protect her. My blood was boiling. The government let these people in then they attack our women. My Karen is the most decent person you could wish to meet and she certainly did not deserve this whilst on her way to work to earn some money to keep our house afloat. The first thing I did was book her a crash course of driving lessons to rush through her driving licence, and then when she passed I brought her a car so she would be safe on her way to work. The cost of immigration hey?

With Steve and Stan both in Maghaberry Jail, I did not only have one prisoner to support now I had two. It was crazy how things had turned full circle. Stan was the one who had put me in contact with Steve, now Stan was serving his sentence on the same wing as Steve. You could not have made it up. With both of them being in jail I used to take it in turns to visit them whilst over in Ulster. On the one visit to see Steve, I was given a lift by two of Steve's mates from North Belfast – Big Davy, and Little Davy. I had met them before, but only briefly. For all that, we were about to become real close mates – just like with the lads I had befriended from

Rathcoole. Up until then, I only really had what you could consider close mates from Rathcoole. I also used to regularly visit East Belfast and drink in the Avenue one Bar and the Bunch of Grapes, which were both U.D.A. bars. I'm not sure why, but I never made any solid contacts over in the east even though I met two cracking lads called Tubby and Jimmy from Tullycarnet.

Nevertheless, all this was about to change with the lads from North Belfast. We instantly hit it off together. Big Davy and Little Davy were a lot younger than me, but two brilliant lads who were very much on my wavelength. As you do, we liked a play up and a piss take. As the months and years progressed the two Davy's would also become very important people in my life – just like the friendship I had built up with Stan, Steve and Sammy from Rathcoole. The one weekend whilst over in Ulster, the two Davy's invited me over to their area in North Belfast to meet some of their lads and have a drink in their local pub called McKenna's Bar, which was on the Crumlin Road. Like the Alpha, it was a U.D.A bar and the U.F.F used to hold their meetings there.

The Bar was situated in an area called Ballysillan, which was a well-known loyalist stronghold. Ballysillan is a huge estate with smaller estates within like Benview, Silverstream, Glenbryn and Alliance. Even so, like all loyalist areas it had an ever-sneaking republican population increase. It had seen its fair share of 'the troubles' over the years, as it fell only 300 meters from the I.R.A stronghold of the Ardoyne. It's amazing how one second you're in a loyalist area, then within virtually seconds you can be on the border of a republican area; this was the situation with Ballysillan. Two leading figures in North Belfast U.D.A at the time were the Shoukri brothers who were of Egyptian descent. All the lads spoke very highly of them and said you could always turn to them for a favour or two.

There was also an estate called the Tyndale in Ballysillan, that also fell under the control of North Belfast U.D.A. Sammy from Rathcoole warned me that years ago the Tyndale was the murder capital of Belfast – that was his words not mine. He used to worry himself sick when I went over there as it was a very dangerous place to say the least. On the Tyndale estate they would throw some great street parties to celebrate events in the loyalist calendar. They were always a great occasion. Ballysillan had other strong connecting loyalist areas like Shore Road, Tigers Bay, York Road, Shore Crescent, Mount Vernan, Wheatfield, White City and the West Land. Additionally, there were also a number of republican strongholds like Ligoneil, Cavehill, Antrim Road, Old Park, Cliftonville and the Ardoyne. Make no mistake; the republican areas were as dangerous as the loyalist areas – no two ways about that.

The lads in McKenna's bar were as welcoming as the lads from Rathcoole, and made me feel very welcome to say the least. Just like with the lads from Rathcoole, I would have been equally as proud to have served in North Belfast U.D.A with Big and Little Davy. Most of the lads who drank in there were a lot younger than me and I nicknamed them 'The Barmy Brigade', as they were all stark raving bonkers. There was certainly something in the water over in Ballysillan. They most certainly knew how to have a laugh I can tell you that. My obvious loyalties lay with South East Antrim Brigade who were the first to take me in. Nonetheless, at the end of the day, I was an English loyalist who also liked to visit other areas to show my support.

When I visited Ballysillan, I would not have to put my hand in my pocket as the lads kept on piling me with drink. It was their way of welcoming me into their company. You don't forget gestures like that. McKenna's bar also had a function room upstairs where they would hold events like Remembrance Sunday; the place would be rocking. The one weekend when I was over with a load of English lads they even supplied us with a free bar, which I was led to believe was laid on by the Egyptian. Still to this day, they always treat me like a special guest when I am over. It's one of those places you know they are always on the look out for your safety whilst you are in their company. The one lad I met at McKenna's bar was called Gerald, and he is up there with craziest type of person you could ever wish to meet. The lad's nuts – totally lost the plot. He is hilarious, and he has you falling of your seat with laughter. He always made a beeline for me when I was over and I could not wait for him to sit down next to me with his pint and start to entertain me. The guy is a bloody legend in my eyes – and if you wanted an afternoons entertainment just simply take a seat next to Gerald.

On a more serious note, I was standing one day outside McKenna's bar having a pint and a fag, and I got talking to some women whose husband had been shot dead by the I.R.A many years ago. She explained the story to me, and even took me to the spot where he was murdered. It was virtually yards from McKenna's bar and it made me realise that even after all the laughs and play up's I had over in Ulster, this is serious shit that were involved in. Her husband was not a U.D.A man or anything, he was just a normal civilian who was murdered because he happened to be a Protestant. I did not know what to say to her and it was a very moving conversation with a very nice lady who had suffered the loss of a loving husband at the hands of the I.R.A. It made me take stock of what the people in Ulster had been through throughout the years. Behind all the laughs and jokes also bears a lot of tears and bloodshed, which you sometimes tend to forget when you're over there having a good drink and a play up. The Ulster loyalists, like the English people, have most certainly been dragged through the mud by the British government.

In 2006, South East Antrim U.D.A who I was affiliated with, withdrew from the rest of the U.D.A/U.F.F after personal differences. I was informed it was due to certain people being allowed back into the U.D.A who should have been frozen out. They then reconstructed themselves as a separate movement still using the U.D.A/U.F.F name. South East Antrim Brigade is no longer considered part of the wider U.D.A. To this day, they still operate as a separate Brigade where my support for them continues. We will probably never know the real reasons behind the split, but the Mainstream U.D.A said South East Antrim Brigade were not following suit and accused them of doing their own thing. Nonetheless, a friend from Rathcoole told me on good authority that South East Antrim Brigade tuned into the Mainstreams agenda – did not like what was going on – and had the balls to stand up and say: "No thanks, we will look after ourselves". But a friend from North Belfast U.D.A gave me his honest opinion on the U.D.A as a whole: "The war is over – the U.D.A are finished. It's just a load of wannabe gangsters running about now. I wouldn't even consider them loyalists. They are all just selfish power hungry – money grabbing cunts".

Be as it may be, I must give my own account on South East Antrim Brigade. Since the untimely death of John

Gregg, Rathcoole has never been the same. I am certainly not criticising the people who took over from Grugg, but the area just feels so different and I know that many others have the same opinion. It's like the heart and soul has been ripped out the area, and it is all down to that scum bag Johnny Adair. Don't get me wrong, I'm still made as welcome and I could turn up there any time unannounced and there would be dozens of people willing to put me up; no question about that. But I'm being perfectly honest in saying I don't enjoy my trips across the water as much as I used to. For all that, no one can take away the memories I have of Rathcoole – under John Gregg's leadership. Over and above, in 2005, the old Eastway Social Club was knocked down and a new club was built in its place. Even though it is a very modern building and no one can deny its very eye catching, I preferred the old club as it had more character. I had so many fantastic nights in the old club I suppose whatever was built in its place would never live up to my expectations. I admit to being a sentimental old fool, and I think losing Grugg and the club being knocked down in a short space of time was a lot to take on board.

In 2009, South East Antrim Brigade claimed to have decommissioned a substantial amount of guns and explosives in the presence of the chairman of the Independent International Commission on decommissioning. The brigade representatives refused to give any details about how many weapons or how much explosives were destroyed during the day long exercise. On 8th February 2010, British Prime Minister Gordon Brown announced that the brigade had completed decommissioning. The process was confirmed as complete by the Independent International Commission on decommissioning and came in the last 24 hours of the commissions existence. The decommissioning was completed at the same time as that of the republican Irish National Liberation Army (I.N.L.A) and the Official Irish Republican Army (O.I.R.A). Accusations have surfaced that the brigade have remained active; that they stringently deny. And further on down the line the Independent Monitoring Commission confirmed that the spilt between the Mainstream U.D.A and South East Antrim Brigade had not ended.

Back home I had some serious political work to do for the BNP, as we were planning to stand a record number of council candidates for the 2006 local elections. Nick Griffin knew we were on a roll support wise and wanted as many seats fought as possible; he was not disappointed. We finished up with a very impressive 363 seats nationwide and polled in total over all the wards 229,389 votes – averaging a superb 18%. Despite that, the story of the night was in Barking and Dagenham down south, which had seen a huge rise in the immigrant population into the area – mostly from Africa. The area was changing by the week. The BNP fielded thirteen candidates and won an amazing eleven of the seats it contested. This made the BNP the opposition party on the council, which had also happened before in Burnley in the North West. This was a major victory as only a few years ago BNP candidates would be lucky to get 5% of the vote. Even after all the barrage of hostile anti-BNP stories in the newspapers and endless politicians slagging us off on TV, we somehow still managed to pull of this amazing result. It put me on such a high.

For days on end the media focused on nothing else – and you would have thought we had formed a government by their reaction. But little did people know this wasn't just a slice of good fortune. For many years the BNP had been putting in a very intense and professional campaign in Barking and

Dagenham, with the view to one day taking full control of the council. Their hard work was finally paying off. We also won many more seats in wards where we already had BNP representatives – three seats in Epping Forest, three seats in Stoke on Trent, three in Sandwell, two in Burnley and two in Kirkless. Additionally, seats were also obtained in Bradford, Havering, Solihull, Redditch, Pendle and Leeds – what a night. On the night, 33 new BNP councillors were elected taking our total to 49 seats – what a move forward. Unfortunately, we also lost a few seats that we were defending. This happens in politics. As well as your ups you are going to have your downs. A Conservative councillor from Lincolnshire also defected to the BNP, which was a smack in the face for the Tories. We also gained our first Parish councillor in Wales, named Mike Howard in a place called Flintshire. What also achieved us great publicity was that we fielded a full slate of candidates in Sunderland, Kirklees, Leeds and Birmingham. Birmingham was a story within itself as I will explain now.

Birmingham BNP put forward a full slate of candidates which was 40 seats. Never been done before, never been done since and will most certainly never be done again. We did it really as a 'one off'. It took some hard work getting all the signatures for the wards (you need ten signatures per ward). Moreover, in the non-White areas of which there are now many in Birmingham, this really took its time and held us back a lot from doing other work in the party that needed doing. Nonetheless, after a lot of running around and driving around for days on end all over Birmingham, we finally achieved our goal. Everybody was exhausted. Large parts of Birmingham were now lost to the immigration invasion, nevertheless, we wanted to show the country that Birmingham BNP were growing in force – and what better way than to stand a full slate of candidates. We knew in the non-White areas that the vote would be low, but we wanted everybody to have the chance to vote BNP no matter where you lived. Furthermore, credit must be given to everyone involved as this was a very difficult task indeed.

We had two target wards in sight – Shard End and Kingstanding. Large-scale campaigning had been going on in these wards and we were being tipped to take both the seats. The support on the doorsteps in these wards was as I have never witnessed before, or since. Whole roads were saying they were voting for us; it was incredible. The Kingstanding ward was looked upon as the better of the two wards, therefore, we used our heads a put forward a female candidate. This was a clever move as female candidates seem to get less mud thrown at them by the media, and it also helped to give the party a 'softer' image as well as moving away from the 'male only' representation the party had gained over the years. We got our tactics spot on. We also used our heads and never even campaigned on the immigration issue as everyone already knew where we stood on that. We campaigned on more local issues like housing, fighting crime, better schooling, more police on the beet and buying British produce from British owned shops; local issues at the heart of the area.

Come the night of the election I was working away as I had been visiting a new customer in Southampton. But I had more than done my bit after many months of heavy campaigning. Due to my job promotion and the BNP, I'd hardly had five minutes with Karen over the last four months. I asked the candidates at the count in Shard End and Kingstanding to keep me informed of the results as they came in. I had the first late night phone call to tell me that we had pushed Labour close in Shard End – but fell just short of taking the seat. People were that sure of us taking the seat that the Conservatives did not even put in a campaign. We were hoping for this ward and fully well expected to win it by a fair margin; I was very disappointed. I then had a phone call from a member at the Kingstanding count who said to me in an excited voice: "Were in Tony, we have won the seat". I was ecstatic. I could hear all the celebrations in the background and after three recounts we had won the seat in Kingstanding ward – to say I was thrilled would be an understatement. As I have said, there were three recounts as the result was that close. Despite that, every time the BNP candidate came out on top. Make no mistake – this was won fair and square and the result was solid.

The following morning though things were about to take a huge U-turn regarding the result. After the newly elected BNP councillor left the hall with her supporters, it was announced that some of the BNP votes had apparently been counted twice and the validity of the result was now in question – what a load of bollocks. The problem here was the winning BNP candidate and her supporters left the count straight after the victory was announced to go and celebrate in a nearby pub – and why not? After three recounts there was no questioning the result. I firmly believe that this gave the establishment parties the chance to prevent the BNP from taking the seat by claiming some of the votes had been counted twice. If this was the case then why wasn't it spotted after three recounts?

My opinion is once the BNP team had left the count the other parties took part in a combined effort to prevent the BNP victory. As one member Mick said to me afterwards: "We should have stopped behind with the boxes of votes and sat on them until everyone had left the hall". And he was right. With no one left behind from the BNP, I stand by this till this day that the votes were tampered with – and why? It is quite simple. They did not want a BNP councillor on Birmingham council. Birmingham council is one of the most left-wing councils in the UK, and the embarrassment of a BNP councillor was too much for them to stomach. Therefore, they snatched the victory away from us. So much for democracy hey?

I was spitting feathers as I knew all the hard work that had gone into the area. It was eventually taken to court by the Labour Party where surprise, surprise, the result was overturned. Still to this day, I get so angry and upset how we had won the seat honest and aboveboard only to have it stolen from us by the traitors of the Labour Party. And since the BNP 'victory' in the ward of Kingstanding, the area has been totally flooded with a huge influx of immigrants. Every single council house that has come on the market, immigrants have been moved in. And this is still going on to this day – and why? To prevent the BNP vote ever being achieved again. You have never seen an area change so fast in such a short space of time. Moreover, as you can maybe guess the BNP vote in Kingstanding has now fallen away rapidly.

Moving on from here, my Dad had been complaining to me for months about having problems with his breathing and his chest not feeling right. He had previously had a nasty fall which really shook him up. I remember him saying to me: "Something isn't right son, I know it ain't". Therefore, I made him go the Doctor's. He went to see his Doctor and they sent him away with an asthma spray. After a while still no improvement, so he went back again. The same as before, they told him it was asthma and gave him a back up inhaler – this was to go with his other spray. This was now going on for months and I could tell by now it was certainly not asthma as he still had the breathing problems and other issues with his chest.

I was not happy with the Doctor he was seeing so we made him go and see another Doctor at the same surgery. You see, my Dad was very much old school and would only see the one Doctor who he had been seeing for years. As soon as he saw another Doctor he was sent straight up the hospital that second for a scan – exactly as he should have been at the beginning. My Dad and I headed up the hospital for his scan, and on the way home he received a phone call from the hospital before we had even reached the front door; they needed him back up there as soon as possible. I knew then as he did, that he was in trouble.

When we went back up the hospital they told him they thought they may have found a shadow on his lung and further tests were needed. After a few weeks that seemed like months, he went back for his results and was told the news there was nothing they could do for him. I was waiting in the house when he returned home with my sisters as I had been working away, and when he said to me: "There is nothing they can do son" - my world totally fell apart. We were all speechless. My Mom was at home, nonetheless, she was suffering from Alzheimer's which is the most common form of dementia (a general term for memory loss and other intellectual abilities serious enough to interfere with daily life) where she could not remember anything or anybody. She had no idea of the situation that was going on. The strange thing was she could remember things that happened 30-50 years ago but not things that had happened today or yesterday; that's how the illness is.

They had given my Dad between 6-24 months to live, in spite of that, I was convinced he was going to beat it. I got myself into a positive mindset for my Dad's sake and I really believed we could get through this and beat it together – I had to have hope for us both. But things only got worse. Whilst my Dad was in hospital after having his chemotherapy to fight the cancer and to try and give him more time, my Mom was taken really ill at home with a water infection and also sent to the same hospital. They even ended up on the same ward. They were seconds away from each other, yet neither one knew the other one was there. My Mom with her Alzheimer's would not have understood anyway, and my Dad was too ill to need any more bad news; he still thought that my two sisters and I were at home looking after Mom.

It was heartbreaking to have them both on the same ward together and we used to take it in turns to jump from one side of the ward to the other to go and see them. We used to make out to my Dad we were going for a coffee or a cigarette and go and visit my Mom – it was truly horrific. Whilst my Mom was in hospital she caught a bug on the ward which totally knocked her side ways and I could tell she would not be coming back from this one. She was so motionless and was fading away fast; she had stopped eating and drinking by now. My Dad knew by know he was dying and said he wanted to go home to die. It seemed to us that the chemotherapy had only made him worse – but that's my own personal opinion. As a result, the hospital let him return home.

I will never forget the drive home and how terrible he looked – the cancer had really gripped him by now. It made me so ill, however, I tried to hide my emotions for him. My hopes of him making a miraculous recovery were gone. He knew by now Mom was in hospital, but in all fairness he was too ill to give any support or to go and visit her. After a week of us all looking after him at home he started to really fall away, moreover, his breathing was terrible. Word's cannot explain what it did to me seeing him like this. We were all visiting Mom every day, however, she was rapidly slipping away and doing nothing but sleeping all the time – she did not even know we were there. Our hearts were all broken in two. The one day my Dad's breathing was that bad we called out the nurse and the Doctor and we were told the news he would be lucky to see out the night. It hit me like a sledgehammer; I was numb. He died early the following morning. My sisters were there with Karen and I – and we held his hand to the end. I loved that man like I have never loved anybody and my life would never be the same again. We'd had our differences through the years but by god what a good father he had been – always there for us. I can still remember now sitting there feeling numb and trying to take it all in. It knocked me for six and put me on another real bad bout of depression as I have suffered from before.

The strange thing was on the day of the funeral I was not that upset. It was as if I was blocking it out and was at someone else's funeral – strange but true; it did not feel real. My head and my emotions were all messed up and on the day I did not even cry. I wish I had the answer why? I was unaware how it would hit me though after wards. Two days after my Dad's funeral we had a phone call from the hospital saying to get up there quick regarding my Mother's condition. My sisters and I jumped in a cab, but before we reached the hospital my Mother had passed away. We knew this was coming – she had given up. We all stood around the bed sobbing our hearts out. How could this be happening so close to Dad's death? They had been together for over 50 years. My Dad was 72 years old and my Mother 76 years old. The strange thing was at my Mom's funeral it was as if my emotions had shut down again – just like at my Dad's funeral. I can't explain how or why this happened again? It's crazy how the human brain works.

Something I must touch on though is the support I received from Ulster. I received that many cards I had to have a separate shelf in the house to accommodate the cards sent from my friends across the water. It was lovely to know so many people had thought about me at this hard time. My contacts in Rathcoole, Ballysillan, The Woodvale and Rathfern did me proud. The Orange Lodge, of which I was a member, sent me a beautiful card signed by all the members of the Lodge. Steve and Stan were consistently on the phone to see how I was. It made me realise that when I had became involved in Ulster loyalism that I had also joined a family of friends and brothers who stick by you in times of need. All types of offers of support were there and I will always be grateful for that. I had numerous offers from all my close contacts in Belfast to get myself over for a week if I needed to get away and get my head cleared, and I know fully well I wouldn't have had to put my hand in my pocket. These were genuine offers from genuine people. I also received endless text messages and voice mails from people in the BNP – including some leading party officials (Nick Griffin was one of them) sending their condolences. As you can see, the support stretched far and wide.

However, something I touched on earlier was my fight with depression. I had been battling with depression and anxiety on and off for many years. To people who did not know me well, I seemed like a fun chap – always laughing, joking and playing up. I was known as a wind up merchant and a joker who to the outside world looked like someone at peace with himself. But I had learnt very well to hide my emotions whilst being around people. Deep down inside I had these demons I was fighting on a daily basis. I had everything really – a good job, a nice house, a caring wife, a nice car, loads of good loyal friends – yet still the depression and anxiety was always lurking there in the background. I had led a busy and active life with the football, politics and my trips across the water to Ulster. Yet still, I was suffering from this life crippling illness. In addition, it does affect your quality of life without a doubt. Looking back now I do not know how I kept up with such a busy schedule for so long feeling the way I felt. I must have been on autopilot. I tried all types of medication and therapy but nothing seemed to work. The only thing that worked for me was Valium but I got addicted to that and trying to come off it was pure hell. It took me four months to get of the Valium as it is a very addictive drug where you just want more and more of it – then eventually it stops working.

With my Mom and Dad dying so close together this put me on a deeper than ever before depression and I went into a shell and shut away. I did not want to know anything or anybody. I did not want to go out or meet people. I did not want to answer phone calls or be involved in politics. It made me into a kind of a recluse. Like I have said, on the days of the funerals I was OK, but it was afterwards when it all hit me. I was also carrying around with me a burning rage with my Dad's Doctor for telling him he had asthma for all those months, when maybe if his cancer had been caught earlier something could have been done about it? I had visions about going to my Dad's surgery and having it out with the Doctor who had been responsible. Although I honestly do not think at the time I could have controlled my anger and my Dad would not have wanted that; he was not that type of person. I was in a dark, dark place, and it took me three long years to accept and get over the loss of my Mom and Dad. You never actually get over it – you learn to live with it I suppose. Moreover, nothing in this world prepares you for it. I am still battling with my depression and anxiety to this day.

At the local elections of 2007, the BNP put forward a breathtaking 754 candidates – more than double the amount at the last round of elections. Nevertheless, I only played a very small part in this election as I was still in that 'dark hole' following the death of my Mother and Father. Even after standing so many candidates the party only made a net gain of one councillor. We still won ten seats on the night – Windsor and Maidenhead, Hugglescote and Whitwick in Leicestershire, but also lost seats three seats in Burnley for example. Losing the Burnley seats did not surprise me though because of the ever-growing Muslim population in the area. The number also fell due to party resignations and expulsions; several of them associated with a failed leadership challenge in the summer of that year. I was unaware that the party was beginning to tear itself apart from within. Just when you think everything is going great the same old situation pops up again – party infighting. I had hoped all that was behind us. We always seem to do more damage to each other than our enemies ever could. A lot of it is about over inflated egos. I had seen this before with the NF now the same was happening in the BNP.

I also had my suspicions that there may have been state involvement to some level who send in people to stir things up when things are going smoothly. I do not believe for one second that infiltrators would not have been active in the BNP, when we'd had this happen to us twice to my knowledge in the NF – remember state money is never short. It's happened before and it will surely happen again. We now had 50 councillors nationwide. It may have only been a tiny number in proportion – but from having non-in 2000-2001 to having 50 in 2007, no one would have grumbled about that. When faced with an ever-growing immigrant population and a hostile media, it was a miracle in itself.

In the 2008 London Assembly elections, the BNP pulled off a minor miracle and won a seat on the London Assembly. This was a shocking result as after previously visiting London I honestly did not think there were enough Londoners left to vote us in. In certain parts of London the non-White communities range at about 80% of the population but are still somehow called ethnic- minorities. Richard Barnbrook gained 5.3% of the vote, which was enough to take the seat – another breakthrough for the BNP. The party fielded 612 candidates at local level which was down on the year before. But that was due to all the campaigning and financial input going into the London Assembly seat. The BNP polled 14% across all the local council wards contested, with 240,968 votes. The party also gained another fifteen seats, bringing its total to 55 councillors after a few losses here and there; overall another great night. A lot more council seats were expected to be won though if I am honest. Nevertheless, we had achieved the prize we were after with the London Assembly seat. A greater even bigger victory shortly lay ahead for the party at the European Elections – a night that years ago we could only have dreamed about.

What transpired next at the party was another attempt to shut us down for good and to change the face of the BNP forever. The Equality and Human Rights Commission, sent the BNP a letter in 2009, ahead of legal action setting out concerns about the BNP's constitution and membership criteria. It alleged that the parties constitution restricting membership to 'White people only' was unlawful under the race relations act. The BNP choose to fight this in the high court. The commission issued court proceedings against party leader Nick Griffin and other leading party officials (one who I knew very well). The conclusion of the case saw costs awarded against the BNP. Nick Griffin had told members to prepare to concede the case because it would be too expensive to fight and would 'strip the party of the ability to fight any further elections'. Nick Griffin announced he would ask BNP members to accept the courts decision and allow non-White members to join the party. This move would 'outflank' the Equality and Human Rights Commission. The BNP anticipated that its members would accept the change on financial grounds.

The BNP agreed to suspend further membership applications until after a general meeting confirming changes to the constitution. When the new constitution was altered, the courts declared it still breached equality laws and was still indirectly discriminatory. Judge Paul Collins ordered the BNP to pay costs and said its membership applications must remain closed until it complied with the race relations laws. The BNP claimed it had a waiting list of non-White members and actually appealed for more to apply – to what level this was true I do not know. The BNP was accused of lying over the matter by the E.H.R.C, who claimed that the offending passage had not been removed but merely altered. After many more court hearings, the E.H.R.C finally released a statement stating: "Eighteen months and seven court hearings later,

Mr Griffin has finally amended the constitution to bring it in line with what the commission had originally requested". Nick Griffin replied with: "This is a great day because the BNP has won a spectacular David and Goliath victory".

Now I can guess people are asking what was my opinion on this matter. What did I think about allowing non-White members to join the party? Well, I was neither for nor against it. I was happy to go with what was best for the party. If it meant us staying legal and not being shut down, then that was the decision I was happy to go along with. The same had happened in Belgian with the Vlaams Blok in 2004, when the party was blocked from entering any level of government as it had breached anti-racism laws – and shortly afterwards reorganised itself as the Vlaams Belang. Make no mistake – this was an underhanded ploy to shut the party down, therefore, adjustments to our constitution had to be made. After winning council seats and a seat on the London Assembly, the government and other sources wanted the BNP shut down before the European Elections. The funny thing was the National Front who had a far more hard line stance on immigration than the BNP, and additionally a ban on non-White members joining the party – were left alone as they were not looked upon as a threat. The establishment knew how popular we were with the electorate and their plan was to bankrupt us and get us out the way; it did not work.

At the European Elections of 2009, the BNP would send shock waves through the whole British political system winning two seats in the European parliament – and pulling in near on 1 million votes. This made all other victories tiny in comparison. This really put us in the big league at the time and finally confirmed us as a mainstream party.

Andrew Brons was elected in the Yorkshire and Humber constituency with a superb 9.8% of the vote. In addition, Nick Griffin was elected in the North West region, with 8% of the vote – the media went hysterical. I was watching it all unfold on Sky News and it was on for hours and hours on end; it was brilliant. U.k.i.p, who had fared much better than the BNP, never even got a mention. Moreover, it was a kick in the teeth for the BNP's enemies who had tried to shut us down.

Nick Griffin said live on TV: "It was a great victory, we go on from here". Meanwhile, the organisations who had worked so hard to keep the BNP out, all referred to it as a 'sad moment in politics'. They forget it was their betrayal that had made so many people turn to the BNP in the first place. The simple fact was the BNP were able to capitalise on wide spread public fears over mass immigration – and rightly so. The British people were looking for an alternative to the parties who had let them down so badly and the BNP was in the right place at the right time – with the right image and sensible everyday policies. The people had turned to the party who were not afraid to talk about immigration. We were now known through every City and Town. The British National Party – three striking words of great renown; an inspiration to bring about salvation to free our land from the chains of immigration. Standing for honour and truth – opposing communist lies – standing at the forefront to open our peoples eyes. Marching on with valour – with our Union Flags and pride.

The people in the North West had experienced first hand the wage compression, high youth unemployment, long housing waiting lists, struggle for school places and a pressure on the health services that were available. In addition, a loss of community cohesion ushered in by Labour's open door immigration policy; that's not for one second to say that the Tories were not additionally to blame. Almost all nations in the world act in the interests of their own people first. In this way, the BNP made no secret of the fact that it aimed to put the true British people first and this included ensuring that the majority population remained ethnically British. This was not a policy to hide – on the contrary – it was one to discuss openly as it distinguished the BNP from all the other parties who seek the exact opposite. Since 1982, the BNP had been warning the British people about the dangers of immigration. They were not like the other political parties who skimmed around the issue – unless that is they could sniff an extra vote or two. People knew where they stood with us; we were the voice of the silent majority.

Nick Griffin claimed that the modernisation side of the party had removed the 'extremist elements'. Griffin had denounced the parties former views on race arguing that: "The BNP is no longer a genuine White racial nationalist party". He also claimed the parties new ideology – ethno-nationalism – was based on 'concern for the well being of the English, Scottish, Welsh and Irish ethnic nations that compose the United Kingdom'. In addition, that unlike racial nationalist purists, we would be opposed to the arrival at Dover of several million German or Swedish immigrants. Nevertheless, the party was still accused of racism as it only regarded people of White British ethnicity to be British. Furthermore, the BNP added: "BNP activists should never refer to 'Black Britons', for the simple reason that such persons do not exist. These people are 'Black residents' of the UK and are no more British than an Englishman living in Hong Kong is Chinese. The BNP recognises pro-British members of assimilated minorities as British in a civic sense, but we absolutely reject the poisonous, politically correct, anti-indigenous fiction that they are English, Scottish, Welsh or Irish. They may well be very decent people, but if any of us went to Nigeria or Afghanistan, no one would dream of pretending that we were Nigerians or Afghans". The BNP still stood by the claim that they were 'prisoners in their own country' and 'strangers in their own land'.

The British government announced in 2009, that the BNP's two European representatives would be denied some of the access and information afforded to other MEP's. The BNP would be subject to the 'same general principles official impartiality' and they would receive 'standard written briefings as appropriate from time to time'. At the same time, diplomats would not be 'proactive' in dealing with the BNP representatives and that any requests for policy briefings from them would be treated differently and on a discretionary basis. However, it did not stop there. MP's imposed an effective ban on BNP members of the European parliament entering Westminster. Leader of the house Harriet Harman, who had previously had links to groups like the Paedophile Information Exchange, tabled a motion withdrawing automatic access available to all MEP's. Leader Nick Griffin had been due to attend a Commons function. Labour MP John McDonnell led the campaign and said: "I'm pleased the government has listened and decided to exclude the far-right racist BNP from Westminster – symbol of our national democracy". You couldn't make it up – they have the nerve to use that word 'democracy'.

This is the first time it struck me that fighting elections was perhaps a waste of time and money. Many people I knew had said to me that 'civil war' was the only solution as elections are 'rigged' and your playing the systems game.

But I wanted to avoid civil war by democratically electing a BNP government and putting into practice the policy of humane phased repatriation. John Mann MP, Chairman of the All Party Group Against Anti-Semitism, added: "This stops the BNP parading around here as if they are legitimate politicians". Nonetheless, this ban did not apply to I.R.A terrorists Martin McGuinness and Gerry Adams.

On the other hand, we won our first three county council seats in Lancashire, Leicestershire and Hertfordshire – as well as a by-election victory in the Seven Oaks district of Kent. Unfortunately, a small number of BNP councillors had resigned their posts which left us with 54 councillors. I admit I was very pro-Griffin at the time because of how he had moved the party forward in such a short space of time. When he used to speak at local branch meetings, he never once told the audience to take their frustrations out on the immigrant communities. He would always make a point in saying it was the government that we were fighting against and it's the government we should direct our anger towards – not the immigrants themselves; they were just taking advantage of a good situation. No one could ever say he was stirring up racial hatred at meetings because he wasn't. He used to say the best way to show your anger was to put it into political work. If anything – at the time – Griffin deserved credit for changing the face of the party and bringing it up to date. In my eyes, he could do no wrong.

Our sole aim was to challenge the policies the government had put into place to destroy us – and to convert by political persuasion people to vote for the BNP. Nick Griffin was a very clever man – statesmanlike, who could have quite easily found him self a nice comfortable place in the Tory party. However, he choose the long hard road of bringing the BNP into the mainstream. After winning the seats in the European parliament there must not have been a person in the country who did not know the name Nick Griffin, or the British National Party. He had taken us from a fringe party to a party taking on the big three – and beating them. We were now looked upon as a credible option come polling day. The parties next aim was to gain our first MP's.

At the general election of 2010, the BNP were being tipped to take it's first seats in Westminster – alternatively, as British nationalists refer to it as the 'House of Treason'. The BNP were also being tipped to take overall control of Barking and Dagenham council, so as you can maybe gather it was a very exciting time for the party. But simmering away in the background was a leadership challenge to Nick Griffin – this would near enough split the party in two. It was to be a bitter contest to say the least.

CHAPTER 28

Come the general election of 2010, everybody in the country knew we were now out there. We put forward a fantastic 338 candidates – over half of the seats up for grabs – and an all time record for a British nationalist party. Even surpassing the National Front's push for political power when they stood 303 candidates at the 1979 General Election. Moreover, three times the amount of candidates we had stood at the 2005 general election. We were being tipped by the media to take two seats – Nick Griffin in Barking and Simon Darby in Stoke on-Trent. Little did I know at the time we were being bumped up by the media of having election targets that we could never reach, so it could be reported as a failure and a defeat – which in turn would deflate our members expectations. A very shrewd trick by the establishment and one I was not personally aware of at the time. A leading party official explained it to me after the election. If I had done my homework, I would have realised that Nick Griffin somehow had to overturn Labour's 8,000 majority.

I was now finally back out campaigning after my break and I was buzzing at the prospect of gaining our first members of parliament. Loads of hard work went in up and down the country with a superb election broadcast to back it up. The party was on a high again. Nick Griffin was being tipped to take the Barking seat due to our support there in an earlier round of council elections in 2006, where the BNP won eleven of the thirteen seats contested on a four-year term. It was supposedly a straight fight between Nick Griffin of the BNP and the far-left Labour candidate Margaret Hodge, who I despised nearly as much as the anti-White bigot Diane Abbott. In 1988, Abbott claimed at a Black studies conference in Philadelphia that 'the British invented racism'. Without a doubt Diane Abbott is an out and out 'anti – white racist'.

The media had latched onto the 'Battle for Barking' and it seemed at times it was the only seat up for grabs. Reporters and so-called political experts were on TV saying how terrible it would be if the BNP got in. It was all so bias – but nothing we had not come to expect. We certainly had them rattled. I remember thinking at the time how far this party had come forward. Expectations were obviously high. Nevertheless, come the night of the election the results in our two-target wards did not come in. The membership – including myself – felt so deflated. It really put me on a downer.

After intensive campaigning from both sides, everyone had their eyes on this battleground. The BNP had the 'Truth Truck' in the area to promote Nick Griffin's campaign. All the same, the Labour lie machine kicked in which would dent the BNP's hopes. Margaret Hodge visited all the local Mosques in Barking and told them if the BNP won the seat they would: "Drop them all from an aeroplane into the sea" – typical left-wing lies. A 'lefty' is a White person who lives and breathes for the opportunity to call another White person a racist. Let us not forget the establishment have all the power of the media, a bottomless pot of money to play with and have ways to sway voters away from the BNP. To a large degree, people are told what to think and who to vote for. They may not realise it but they are. There is no democracy, just the illusion of change. The BNP had put in a brilliant campaign, however, come election night the dreams of gaining our first ever member members of parliament were crushed. Nick Griffin obtained 6,620 votes – 14.6%, which was nowhere near enough to take the seat. Griffin finished 3rd behind Labour and the Conservatives. Even though it was still a fantastic vote, deep down it did not surprise me that Nick Griffin had not pulled it off – even though I admit I had been taken in by all the media hype.

After travelling the country due to my work commitments, I had noticed in a very short space of time a huge non-British population boom and Barking was no different. It had been completely flooded by Black African's. Tony Blair's open door immigration policy whilst in power had changed the complete make up of Britain. By 2010, the number of British voters left in Barking simply was not enough. Labour had got their wish – another part of the UK lost due to immigration. For all that, let us take stock of the result anyway. To even be considered to win the seat showed how far the BNP had moved forward since the 'bad old days'. Never before had a British nationalist party been tipped to get our first MP's, therefore, was it such a bad result after all? Especially considering the large block immigrant vote we had going against us. To achieve 14.6% of the vote in a now heavily non- White/non-British ward was still a cracking result. The only disappointment was that after being tipped to take the seat anything else apart from a victory seemed like a kick in the stomach – when in the cold light of day it was still a huge vote that years ago we could only have dreamed about. Unfortunately, time was not on our side. You only had to look around to see our country was slipping away at a fast pace – and right under our noses.

Simon Darby, who I knew personally, stood in Stoke on-Trent central – he was also also being tipped to take the seat. We had won a large amount of council seats on Stoke council, hence, the area was considered a BNP 'stronghold'. Proof of this was the leaflets the Labour party were putting out under the heading: "It's either us or the BNP". Hopes were high. In spite of this, like in Barking for the same reasons I have already explained, Simon Darby finished up with 2,502 votes – 7.7%. Still a very decent result – but once again the large-scale immigrant block vote had swayed the result. This only confirmed my fears I had months ago that it could now be too late to save our country. Certain areas had changed so much in just a short space of time it was shocking. The Labour government had really done their best to wipe out the British identity of our once great land. On election night we managed to save 73 deposits which was a superb achievement. We also had some great results in Ashton under Lyne, Barnsley, Batley and Spen, Bradford, Burnley, Hemsworth, Heywood and Middleton, Jarrow, Leeds, Normanton, Pontefract, Castleford, Oldham, Rotherham, Sheffield, Thurrock and West Bromwich. Another breathtaking result was in Dagenham with M. Barnbrook pulling in 4,952 votes – 11.2%.

My old party the National Front stood in seventeen seats (A vast improvement on the previous general election), however, yet again failed to save a single deposit. Even though they did come close with Chris Jackson standing in Rochdale getting 4.9% - just short of the 5% that's needed to save your deposit. Over at Birmingham BNP we fought six parliamentary seats – saving four deposits. Trevor Lloyd stood in Edgbaston – 2.9%. Kevin McHugh stood in Erdington ward – 5.1%. Richard Lumby stood in Hodge Hill – 5.5%. Les Orton stood in Northfield – 5.5%. Lyn Orton stood in Selly Park – 3.9%. And Tanya Lumby stood in Yardley – 5.3%. The total votes calculated over the record 338 parliamentary seats was 563,743. Well over half a million people still turned to us even after all the lies spread about our party. Imagine if we had been given a fair crack of the whip, and our media coverage would not have been full of lies and misinformation over where our party truly stands.

Whilst out campaigning in Erdington and Northfield ward, two dangerous incidents developed. A team of us were delivering leaflets door to door in Erdington, when suddenly a gang of lads appeared and confronted us. They were a mixed race gang – some White, and some Black. They were saying all kind of things and threatening us and then two of them approached our team of activists. Being the biggest lad in our group – which also included women – I stepped forward to try to reason with them. Suddenly out of nowhere, I was punched twice in the face which split my lip and made my nose bleed. It could of really got out of hand, therefore, I walked away to defuse the situation. I advised all the other members to follow me. The women in our group were petrified and I did not want to play the big hero by putting them in any sort of danger. The gang was shouting stuff like: "Come back round here again and well kill you all".

Where as years ago you was safe leafleting anywhere, Birmingham had now become a city where the streets were no longer safe – mob rule – the thugs rule the streets. I am still good mates with a few lads from the NF in Birmingham and they told me that they stopped leafleting years ago in Brum as it is not safe to anymore. The NF lad's said to me that it is not fair on their members to send them out into such rough areas, knowing what the consequences may be. I suppose that after years of campaigning the odds were I would eventually come into some form of conflict. Despite that, it wasn't very nice when it happened.

When I arrived home Karen was so upset – she cried at the state of my face – which then put me on a guilt trip. She said they could have stabbed you or anything, which was true. Most of these young lads in today's society like to prove a point to their friends – they do not think about the consequences; they act first. She then reminded me about when she was mugged on her way to work by an Eastern European and how that made me feel – and she was right. It's horrific to know your partner has been involved in any sort of violence. She sat me down and explained that after this event she did not want me involved again in leafleting. She said that she could not settle every time I was out campaigning; I understood her concerns. We have most certainly lost the war against violence and crime on the streets. She said that I had given nearly twenty years to the British nationalist movement and now was the time to put her first; being attacked was the last straw for her.

I could have quite easily turned around and said no, but it would have caused severe marital problems. Therefore, I promised her no more door to door campaigning. Maybe it was time to take a step back – become less active – and start to put her first. There were new people coming into the party all the time; let someone else now do their bit for the country. I would remain a BNP member, however, just attend low-key events like meetings and helping to get signatures for the elections. Getting the signatures for the elections was never a problem for me, because I knew all the people in the areas I was assigned with. It also did no good for my depression and anxiety bringing my problems home to Karen; it creates unrest at home.

A similar situation happened to our members in Northfield ward. Whilst out campaigning door to door, a very angry West Indian male chased a number of our members up the road with a machete after putting a leaflet through his door. These were the risks you were taking whilst out campaigning for the party. You were putting your lives at danger every time you walked up someone's path to deliver a leaflet. My decision – with the help of Karen – had been made. I would be taking a backwards step in politics but not leaving the movement. British nationalism and the BNP was in my blood – and in my heart.

The bad news of the night would be at the local elections, when 26 BNP councillors lost their seats – including all of the eleven seats held in Barking and Dagenham that we had held for the last four years. Everyone was totally devastated as we had expected to take full control of the council. The tidal wave of African immigration into the ward had sealed our fate. It was a right kick in the teeth. Multiculturalism – the left-wing doctrine that encourages immigrants to keep their own culture rather than to integrate into British ways and traditions.

If the initial wave of immigrants had been sent back straight back to where they had come from, then the teeming millions of immigrants who have invaded Britain – as well as the hordes still waiting to enter – would not be thinking that it's worth their while to make the journey to the UK. I can remember sitting on the sofa watching the election news and feeling totally empty. I said to myself: "That's it. Its over. We have finally lost our country". Nick Griffin said himself that after campaigning in Barking, he could not believe how the make up of the area had changed in such a short space of time – and that was it. It was not as though the BNP had lost support in the area. The ever-growing immigrant block vote, which Labour had put into place, had come into full force and destroyed our dreams. The same went for the other wards we had lost. This left us now with 28 seats overall.

In the aftermath of the elections, the BNP further suffered from severe and bitter infighting due to concerns over the finances of the party brought about by Nick Griffin. I still at the time refused to listen to any bad rumours about Griffin. A day prior to the 2010 general election, the official BNP website was closed down after Simon Bennett – the parties website manager – slammed the leadership of the party. One of the problems that had been going on for years in the BNP was that any constructive criticism of the leadership got you sacked. You did not criticise the leadership and stay in the party. You were out of the door at the speed of light. Any criticism of Griffin was seen as disloyalty to the cause – when in reality it was nothing of the sort; Griffin didn't like having the finger pointed at him. Rumours circulated that membership dropped dramatically after the general election, but to what level I am not exactly sure. Soon afterwards three senior BNP members subsequently challenged Nick Griffin for the leadership of the party. Nonetheless, they failed to secure enough support to trigger a leadership ballot. Therefore, for now, Nick Griffin's position as leader was safe. All the same, there was no denying the party was being ripped apart by infighting.

Next up was the 2011 local elections, but the party was still divided from all the infighting going on. The BNP fielded 268 candidates and defended thirteen council seats. Unfortunately, we lost eleven of the seats we were defending including losing all of our councillors in Stoke on-Trent; I was distraught. I knew how hard the people in Stoke had worked over the years to secure those seats. They were really good people form Stoke, who deserved to hold onto their seats. Two councillors were re-elected in Queensbury and West Yorkshire and another one in Leicestershire. Overall, it was not a very good night to say the least; moral was at an all time low. The infighting had torn the party apart; we do more damage to each other than our enemies ever could. The saddest thing about betrayal and infighting is that it always comes from within the movement – never from your opponents. I have had this happen to myself on a number of occasions, and it is something that will always happen within the right-wing movement – as it does between the rival loyalist paramilitaries.

Following the disappointing 2011 election results, another leadership challenge was taking place from Andrew Brons – Nick Griffin's fellow European parliament member. From the highs of winning the Euro seats to this. This contest once again got very nasty, very personal and it reached a new all time low. All types of rumours were flying around about Nick Griffin; I am now led to believe a lot of them were true. Hindsight is a wonderful thing. A letter was sent out to all BNP members from Andrew Brons camp slating Nick Griffin. Even though this came from Andrew Brons camp, Andrew himself did not directly sanction it. Andrew Brons instantly denied any involvement in the letter and I affirm this to be true. As before – I firmly believe that there was to a certain extent, state involvement in this latest tear up to split the party in two. They are masters at turning people against each other. I do not believe that for one-second agent provocateurs would not have been active in the BNP, especially after winning the seats in the European parliament.

In 2003, it emerged that a number of leading people running the National Democratic Party of Germany, were in fact undercover agents and informants of the German secret services. Therefore, if anybody believes that this does not happen in British politics they are living in cloud cuckoo land. After a postal ballot of all members, Nick Griffin secured a very narrow victory. But the damage had been done – the two factions could never work together again. After all the struggles of breaking through at local level, winning a seat on the London Assembly, to winning seats in the European parliament – we had now torn the party apart from within. Well who did I vote for and why? I voted for Nick Griffin and I will now explain my reasons for doing so at the time.

When Nick Griffin took over the leadership of the BNP, it was a tiny party on the fringe of British politics. He then transformed us in a few short years into a party with representatives at all levels of government – apart from Westminster. Moreover, this was not any fluke by the way. His clever changing of the parties image and the re-adjusting of policies played a major part in our success. When he flopped on Question time many members were disappointed with his performance – myself included. But it was not a fair debate – anyone could see that – and as much as some members liked to think so, Nick Griffin does not walk on water and he cannot turn water into wine. He threw himself into the lions den called Question Time and did the best he could have done under extreme circumstances, in what can only be described as 'verbal domination'. That was my stance anyway. He was not prepared for the questions that were being thrown at him as it was meant to be a political debate on a number of key policies – not a kangaroo court on some comments made by Nick Griffin many years ago.

The whole format of Question time was changed to attack Nick Griffin. Unfortunately he looked way out of his depth and the perfect chance to show the country we were a professional party was smashed to smithereens. Nine times out of ten Griffin chews up any panel and spits them out. All the same, Question Time caught him on a bad night. Having said that, you only have to watch his other interviews on TV and see how well he always conducted himself. No one could match Griffin for handling hostile journalists and broadcasters. I was sure he would pull it off; such was my loyalty towards him at the time.

With all the black propaganda being aimed at Nick Griffin and so many important people being expelled from the party, I did for a second think about maybe – just maybe – voting for Andrew Brons. I examined the election results before Nick Griffin took over the leadership and then examined the results after he took over the helm. There was no denying that when Griffin took over and modernised the party, the votes nationwide just kept going up and up before the inevitable collapse. The membership had sharply increased with Griffin as leader, before the bitter infighting took place and membership plummeted due to Nick Griffin falling out with many leading party officials. We all know that at the last two rounds of elections the votes were to some extent poor, losing seats here and there. But was this solely Griffin's fault? I do not think so for two reasons. Whoever at the time would have been BNP chairman, the votes would have still dropped dramatically. You see in the wards where we were winning seats, as the years were going by the immigrant population boom was growing in such large numbers that it was only a matter of time before they finally gained enough numbers to 'vote us out'. As I have said, time is not on our side anymore. The non-White/non-British block vote across the whole country was the reason behind us having two poor elections. In addition, let us not forget the apathy of the British voters.

Another thing was after the Tory/Lib Dem coalition coming together, voters were looking to punish them big time. Unfortunately, the public turned to Labour at the expense of all parties – including the BNP. I remember thinking at the time: "People have short memories how far Nick Griffin has brought us forward in such a short space of time, and why are they so quick to jump on his back after some poor results". That's politics for you. Unknowingly, not being in the inner circle I did not realise Griffin was tearing the party apart from within – due to his personal vendettas against anybody who dared to speak out against him.

I remember thinking everyone is your best friend and worship you when it is going well, then you have a set back and it is all doom and gloom and their looking for a scapegoat. Griffin was also not a leader to sit back and do nothing apart from be a face of the party. He was always up and down the country attending events all over the UK, and was always out on the streets helping to fight elections nationwide. I know this to be true as saw it with my own eyes. That's why at the time I would not have a bad word said about him. I had been warned years ago he was a 'bad apple' who ruins every organisation he gets involved in, however, I just would not listen. Personally, I did not think at the time that Andrew Brons was the man to lead the party. For a start, I thought he was too old – even though without a doubt Andrew is a great speaker and a fine British nationalist. I thought if ever we were to replace Griffin it will have to be to a young up and coming leader with similar qualities to Nick Griffin. At this particular leadership ballot I though Nick Griffin deserved another crack at putting things right. How wrong was I? If I knew then what I know now and I could turn the clock back, I most certainly would have voted for Andrew Brons.

At the 2012 council elections, the BNP faced more loses at the at the hands of a Labour party being used to 'protest' against the Tories and Lib Dems – this happens all the time. The British people vote Labour in – get sick of them – vote the Tories back in – then once the Tories fail to keep their promises again use Labour to boot them out. It's a vicious circle the British public play. A consistent game of musical chairs. Are the British public really that dumb? Well, yes. Do the British public somehow think the parties of failure and betrayal have actually changed? It's shocking.

The BNP lost all six of the seats it was defending in the local elections. They lost two councillors in Amber Valley, one in Burnley and one in each of the wards of Epping Forest, Rotherham and Pendle. In the London Mayor elections after putting in a very intense, professional and expensive campaign, our candidate Carlos Cortiglia finished in 7th place gaining 28,751 first preference votes. In addition, in the London Assembly elections the BNP lost the seat it had held for four years by finishing 6th with 47,024 votes. London is now so multi racial/cultural that it was only a matter of time before we would lose this seat – you did not need to be a maths teacher to work this one out. It is now official that true Londoners are the minority in London; we have lost our capital.

All in all a very poor night to say the least – with no new gains – although we were up against a British public who wanted to hammer the Tories – with Labour as their choice. Nick Griffin released a statement after the election: "Hammered by Labour, same as everyone. No surprise, no disgrace. How can Labour take seats of us when Ed Millband is so un-popular? Is there something wrong with the British National Party or the public? The answer is Labour will be seen to have taken seats off everyone. And yet again, the plain truth is this includes the BNP. And why? Because voters wanted to punish the Lib Dems and teach the Tories a lesson, and because since British nationalism's voter base is overwhelmingly working class, nationalist parties always do far better in elections when Labour is in power. When Labour is in opposition people unfortunately forget their misdeeds when in power". Even after two very poor elections, Nick Griffin said the BNP 'was not going away' and would carry on fighting for British freedom and contesting elections.

As we all predicted at the 2013 county council and local elections, the pumped up United Kingdom Independence Party (Ukip) pulled in all the anti-immigration votes which we had worked so hard for over the years. They had the full backing of the mainstream media and endless invites to all political debates on TV – debates that the BNP were banned from; they are nothing more than 'controlled opposition'. To ban freedom of speech or freedom of expression of any kind just because somebody may get offended – is the sign of a society in deep trouble. We have to stand up against such 'left-wing fascism' whenever and wherever it rears its ugly head.

Nigel Farage went from being someone you could have walked past in the street, to being the most identifiable face in British politics. He was suddenly being hailed as the new saviour of the British people. It was heartbreaking seeing our votes being stolen by Ukip. But the fact of the matter is the British public are easily fooled as I have stated many times before. With the help of the establishment at our expense – and a very clever promotion as an 'anti-immigration party' – Ukip obtained some breathtaking results winning a huge number of seats. The majority of people do not realise Ukip are only a splinter group from the Conservatives and would jump straight back into bed with the Tories if only the Tories would withdraw from Europe.

Ukip have been propelled forward to give an 'illusion of choice' protest and dissent against the parties of failure, when in reality it is nothing more than a sideshow. Its main purpose is to siphon away potential voters away from the BNP since our European Election victory. The traitors in power are afraid that the British people may wake up before their Marxist plan of globalisation and the destruction of the British nation is complete. Many BNP members are very optimistic about Ukip gaining huge votes as it will not last forever. Thanks to the promotion of Ukip, the very issues that we have been highlighting for years have become common debate – so much so that even the Liberals and the Labour party have been forced to try and fool the public that they will do something about the policies ruining our country. Moreover, as Ukip get 'found out' and become more politically correct, that will eventually lead to the door being open for us again.

Proof that Ukip are part of the 'establishment' and most certainly 'politically correct' surfaced when they suspended their West Lancashire General Election candidate Jack Sen for apparently making 'anti-Semitic' tweets. He had described himself as 'unapologetically incorrect pro-British'. He was a rising star in Ukip, but it wasn't enough to save him from the chop. A Ukip spokesman said: "Mr Sen, has expressed views that in no way reflect the views of the party and any other of our hard working dedicated candidates".

Regardless of what people like to believe, Ukip are not an anti-immigration nationalist party. In fact, Ukip bans any contact with the BNP and any other 'nationalist party'. When you join Ukip you have to state for the record that you have never been a member of the BNP. You are then grilled about your past political involvement. Although Ukip claims that this is due to the stigma attached to the BNP, I am not convinced. Ukip do not care about ethnic interests and it is quite apparent that Ukip's agenda starts and ends with big business. Jack Sen is now a member of the BNP and he added that there is a Jewish plot to take over Ukip: "I'm afraid at this point it has been taken over. All signs point to the fact – the donation from the Daily Express, Desmond is Jewish – he is a Zionist. There are so many friends of Israel supporters within Ukip".

The biggest problem has always been getting the British public to have the guts to voice their disapproval at the policies that have been staring them in the face since the end of World War Two. Since the end of the Second World War our people have gone to sleep. However, Ukip's 'False Flag' immigration policies have smashed that dam wide open. As for Nigel Farage, let us take a look at the man. Is he the man to save the British people? I think not. He is the leader of a splinter group from the Tories, who is a known supporter and admirer of Margaret Thatcher. The same Margaret Thatcher who helped to destroy this country, crippled the unions, privatised everything she could get her hands on, and who also like Nigel Farage claimed to be 'anti-immigration'. Furthermore, killed off the old National Front in the 1979

General Election by promising to do something about immigration. Are you getting the picture here?

This is actually nothing new. This has happened many times before. Politicians come along swearing blind they will do something about immigration, then once their in office they turn into jellyfish. Nigel Farage is too comfortable in his 'politically correct' Tory splinter group to ever get his hands dirty. He does not have the steel to face all the political harassment that the BNP has suffered over the years. Ukip is nothing more than a 'safety valve' party for the establishment to pump up – as and when needed. The ruling elite fear the British National Party more than they fear any other party. Great effort has been made to divert attention away from the BNP and onto Ukip.

Ukip have been in the European parliament since 1999. They never even mentioned immigration until growing support for the BNP broke the taboo on discussing it freely. Another problem with Ukip is that it isn't bonded together by any firm 'ideology' unlike the BNP. Recently, Nigel Farage has stated that Ukip's policy is to 'limit immigration' to a net increase of 50,000 a year'. Sounds reasonable? I think not, because the devil is in the detail with that word 'net'. To Ukip it is only a question of numbers, therefore, for every Brit who emigrates they are happy to let in an African or Asian immigrant. Their leader Nigel Farage said in the European parliament: "We welcome immigration – we want immigration". It may appear that Ukip is facing 'EU totalitarianism'. Ukip is opposed to the EU not because they want to preserve British culture, heritage, tradition and identity. Ukip is opposed to the EU because the EU interferes with the ability of Ukip's wealthy backers from making even more money. What they fear is a European wide financial transactions tax. THEY DO NOT OFFER SOLUTIONS TO IMMIGRATION!!!!!!

Ukip are the confidence trick of 'phoney patriotism'. Ukip's membership base is mostly made up of what are described as 'civic nationalists'. They believe that anybody can be British as long as they embrace our culture and way of life. Civic nationalists do not care about race – they only care about culture. Yet, they fail to understand that once the race who created the culture disappears, then the culture disappears with it. All that matters to Ukip is whoever is living in Britain respects our flag and integrates into our society. This stance by Ukip is severely damaging to our future as a racial group in Britain. It would not – and could not – sort out our immigration problems. We deceive ourselves if we imagine that Ukip could save our country.

Even if Ukip formed a government, we would still be facing an immigration problem that is wholly unacceptable. This is a huge obstacle that the BNP have to try and over turn. We are working on it now; it will not be easy. Up and down the country over the years the BNP have been banned from many meeting halls, both private and public – a majority of the time due to left-wing intimidation. As I have stated, this has forced us into booking halls under false names. We have been denied the right of assembly and the right to hold perfectly legal political meetings. In addition, bans on meeting halls have only been the tip of the iceberg.

We have had the whole of the mass media against us, which has included a consistent barrage of lies and misinformation about where our party truly stands – followed by when it suits a silence that pretends we no longer exist. It is difficult to convince the ordinary person in the street that these situations really occur in what is supposed to be a 'democracy'. Most people are led to believe that we have free speech in Great Britain. It is even harder to explain to the British public that hidden corporations control the press and broadcasting services. Ukip have never once pointed out this fact, therefore, they are as much to blame as the people in power. That the BNP has been able to survive all this is nothing short of a miracle. It was the BNP that investigated tax theft by our MP's, warned the British people about the grooming scandal and uncovered the expenses scandal. In addition, it was the BNP who scuppered David Cameron's plan to bomb the Syrian people after three BNP delegates travelled to Syria and opened up diplomatic negotiations with the Syrian government – why weren't the British people informed about this? The wall of silence from the media was deafening.

Another obstacle we have faced is organised violence against our members by the far-left. The Red, rent a mob's are sent to cause mayhem at our activities and then the media turn it around and blame us for the trouble and violence that arises. Due to this, we are penalised by further banning orders on holding meetings and demonstrations. Ukip do not have any of these hurdles placed in their way, and if they did I truly believe that their membership would not have the courage to withstand it like the BNP have. This campaign of violence is backed up by everyone on the left of the establishment and accepted by everyone on the supposed right of the establishment – including David Cameron. If our opponents think they can silence us by physical force and intimidation, we will as we have done before – prove them wrong. As things stand though the Red, rent a mob's have a licence to do almost whatever they like – with little or no oppression from a 'politically paralysed' police force.

When we cry out for politicians to stand up and take control of the situation we have received nothing back in return; Nigel Farage is no different. Every step of the way has been a bitter struggle for the BNP. When you add up everything that is stacked against us, it is a miracle in itself that we have even ever won a seat on a local council. From being the world's greatest power we are now living on borrowed money from foreigners and invaded by foreigners. We believe that the whole nature of British society must be changed. We believe that the whole political institutions must be changed. We are the only true 'revolutionary' party in British politics. Make no mistake about that. We will face them head on.

As expected at the European parliament elections of 2014, Ukip came out on top gaining 24 seats – compared to Labour gaining 20 seats and the Tories 19 seats. This came as no surprise to anybody with half a brain. The funny thing was Labour's promotion of Ukip was solely aimed at taking votes of the Tories. However, it backfired as Ukip also took a huge slice of the Labour vote. Labour were hoping this would have led to them having a clean sweep at the European elections; it didn't work. It was the first time a political party other than the Labour Party or Conservative Party had won the popular vote in a national election since the 1910 general election. No election can be taken on its own. The important thing is how they fit into the overall pattern of events over a longer time-scale. Ukip's sweeping victory has shown that the British people are willing to stand up and oppose immigration and that our core issue is a legitimate one in the minds of the electorate and one they will vote for on a national level.

In promoting Nigel Farage first as a block to the BNP and then a tool to split the Conservative vote, the BBC has let the genie of open dissent out of the bottle. Which means that when the inevitable happens and the Ukip hype begins to subside, people will turn to the party they know they can really trust on immigration – our time will come. It's up to us to build an organisation that can seize the moment of opportunity when it comes. Even after all Ukip's publicity – at the 2015 General Election it only gained one MP – due to the first past the post system, even after gaining four million votes. They had been hoping to win between 10-20 seats. The Conservatives swept to power after promising a referendum on Europe; a referendum that will certainly be rigged. The Tories, like Labour and the Lib Dems want us to remain in Europe, and they will use all the tricks up their sleeve to convince the British public it is in our best interests to remain in Europe and be controlled from Brussels.

The BNP lost the two European seats it had held since 2009, but by now Nick Griffin had frozen Andrew Brons out of the BNP. The BNP took just 1.8% of the vote in the North West, compared with 8% when Nick Griffin was elected. The result was a victory for the 'Nick Griffin Must Go' campaign – set up by Unite Against Fascism with the support of the trade unions and countless activists. Griffin's defeat would lead to being the final nail in his BNP leadership. In the middle of July 2014, after leading the BNP for fifteen years, Nick Griffin stepped aside as party chairman after a meeting of the Executive Council. He had been given a vote of 'no confidence'.

Adam Walker was appointed as acting leader, pending the routine leadership election under the party constitution in which he won. Nick Griffin stated at the time that he would be staying with the party and would take up his role as President of the BNP. Moreover, he would be there to offer Adam Walker support and advice as he slots into his new role as acting leader. Just as I thought all was well and good, I received a phone call that Nick Griffin had been expelled from the party; I was god-smacked. A conduct committee established by new Party Chairman Adam Walker took the step in a letter to Mr Griffin. The conduct committee stated: "We believe that since being given the title of honorary president, you have put all your efforts into trying to cause disunity by deliberately fabricating a state of crisis. The aim of this was to again embroil the BNP in factionalism designed to destabilise our party".

A statement from the committee read: "This has been a difficult decision to make and not one taken lightly. Although we all appreciate that Nick has achieved a lot for our party in the past, we must also remember that the party is bigger than any individual. Nick did not adjust well to being given the title of honorary president, and it soon became obvious that he was unable to work as an equal member of the team – and alarmingly his behaviour became more erratic and disruptive". I felt so let down by Nick Griffin after all the support I had given him over the years. I had defended him all the way and even fell out with people over my support for Griffin. I suppose I had a blind loyalty towards him, and even though I knew deep down he was tearing the party apart I still stood by him. I had been truly hoodwinked by Griffin; more fool me. Anderson and Griffin were both cut from the same cloth. Everyone who had warned me about Griffin years ago were saying to me: "Told you so".

What had torn the BNP apart was Griffin ignored problems that should have been faced with and dealt with at the right time – when they could have been solved. Nick Griffin would not and could not face up to the fact that the BNP had many issues that needed sorting out. Anybody who raised the problems or pointed out the fact that the party was in enormous debt, were sacked, expelled or frozen out of the party. This happened to many long-standing and hard-working party members who had given many years service to the BNP. Griffin would not tolerate questions being asked about his leadership capabilities. He has to take full responsibility for the collapse of the party. I am not saying for one second that Griffin was a state sponsored plant – but if it wasn't deliberate, then it was grossly incompetent. Everyone I spoke to said how they now wish they had voted for John Tyndall, when Nick Griffin democratically took over the leadership of the party in 1999. And furthermore, voted for Andrew Brons at the 2011, leadership election; both times we had certainly 'backed the wrong horse'.

It now all fitted in with a pattern. His history with the NF was the same – falling out with everyone. Then the same with the I.T.P and now the BNP. And as per usual, he blames everybody apart from himself. If I had to describe Nick Griffin, I would put him down as a 'confidence trickster'. The rot started when he was elected to the European parliament. He should have stepped down as leader – but with his over inflated ego he wanted to be 'leader for life'. Things now will only get better now Nick Griffin is out the way. Although undoubtedly, no one can deny he has many talents.

As one long-standing member put it who had been expelled by Griffin for speaking out about his leadership: "I am personally not in the least bit sorry to see Nick Griffin finally leave the party. Since he won an MEP seat the party has gone nowhere, bitterly disappointing many members who I have spoken to. He had too much 'baggage' surrounding him which attracted huge public dislike. Especially since modern politics is all about image. Let's all hope the party can move forward in a positive and professional manner, and ex-members like myself will renew their membership with a renewed faith in the leadership. It's time to shine again. Griffin had a silver tongue who fooled a lot of people, but not anymore". Nick Griffin is now in the 'political wilderness' with no where to turn to. He has many qualities – but I don't think even the National Front would touch him now. Is this the last we have seen of Nick Griffin? Only time will tell...........

CHAPTER 29

As my story ends I would like to explain a few things. Firstly my involvement with the football. Yes, I know that for many years I travelled the country with a load of football hooligans even though I was not directly one myself. I was only a face in the crowd – nothing more – nothing less. I have no regrets about this because at the time I was a young lad looking for an identity and a family of like-minded friends I could relate to – with the same interest in Aston Villa Football Club. It was also a bloody good social outing. I must say a big thank you to the older lads who took me under their wing and accepted me as one of their own even though I was a lot younger than they was. For that, I will be forever grateful; what a great bunch of lads who looked out for one another.

With me being the 'baby' of the crowd, from about 1987 onwards when I was low on money at the away games, they used to have 'whip-rounds' for me – mostly orchestrated by Andy O'Keefe and Mark Webb (aka The Bear). These were the initial Villa lads who were around years before The Hardcore. That's what they were like – good decent people. By knowing these lads, suddenly I knew everyone down the Villa and it just snowballed from there. I was never a 'hard man'; I must get that point across as I have done so many times. However, still I was embraced as one of the firm. It was just a big piss up whilst also taking in a football match at the same time.

Now I am older and wiser I realise that football hooliganism is wrong. I have seen too many people jailed, injured, and lose their jobs to say any different. Even so, I was a young lad at the time looking for some thrills at the weekend. No one can deny that travelling away for weekend with your mates was a brilliant buzz and it made me feel part of something. Some of the happiest days of my life were spent following the Villa all over the country. The only 'buzz' that has ever matched it were my weekends away in Ulster. The friends you make are friends for life, even if you drift away from the football yourself. If you do not see someone for years then bump into them – that old camaraderie is still there.

One of our lads from Kings Norton, moved to Australia years ago and we all had a meet up in the Aston Hotel to see him off. It was brilliant to see all the old lads again and talk about some of the old days and the play ups we used to have. Some of the things we used to get up to I would not dream of mentioning, as our idea of having a laugh knew no boundaries. I am sure most football lads can relate to this. Times had moved on and most of the lads were now not active, but the spirit and friendship was still there between us. Some of the best people I met at the Villa were hooligans, nonetheless, they were still in my eyes cracking people who would stand by you all day long. It's just how it is. Moreover, even though times had changed and the lads have moved on, I do not regret it for one second. That is apart from the hassle it brought my wife Karen after my arrest and court case after the incident with Man United at the Adventurers pub.

The government had totally abandoned my people and to a lot of us it gave us a purpose in life to attend the football after a long boring week at work. We were all Aston Villa barmy. Being a Villa fan is in our blood. We can't simply switch it on and off – we care about the club. There will be times we question an appointment of a certain manager or the signing of a player – but we will never stop supporting Aston Villa. It's not just a stadium – it's our home. It's not just a kit – it's our skin. Were not only eleven – were many thousands. Were not just a crowd – were a family. It's not just 90 minutes – it's a lifetime. It's not just a passion – it's an emotion. It's not just a game..........it's our life.

Was the Hardcore a racist firm? Well no, it was a patriotic firm who followed England all over the globe. As a result, that was enough to call us a 'racist firm' in certain people's eyes. As I have said before, I do not need to name them – they know who they are. Admittedly, there were some people in the firm with right-wing views, but as for paid up members of right-wing groups you could have counted them on one hand; myself being one of them. Additionally, no more than our hated rivals from across the city at that hovel Saint Andrews. Unfortunately, Fowler copped a lot of the flak when he had nothing to do with politics. The 'racist tag' gave our enemies a stick to beat us with. The same people with communist, Marxist and republican leanings. What is the problem with a load of patriotic lads following their country abroad? Nonetheless, some people did not like that, whilst at the same time being proud of their culture and history – hypocrisy springs to mind.

I have had phone calls before from Birmingham lads saying Fowler has been spotted drinking with Black lads and what's all that about ? I just laugh at them. Fowler has also been accused of attending NF and E.D.L marches by the Blue noses, and I know this to be true as I have heard it for myself. I just listen to them ramble on and quietly laugh to myself as I know this to be complete bullshit. Another time I couldn't help but laugh was when some Blue Noses spotted Fowler at Birmingham Airport during the 12th of July celebrations, and surmised he was going over for the Orange marches. He was actually there to head to Spain for someone's birthday bash. However , the rumour spread like wild fire that Fowler was on his was to Northern Ireland; it's ridiculous.

Fowler had Black lads in his firm. There was even a lad years ago known as 'Paki Mark', who travelled with us – he gave himself that nickname. It was never a problem. People want to believe the lies they hear about Fowler and his lads. The old saying comes to mind – throw enough mud and it sticks. In all my years at the football, I have never known a lad get as many false accusations thrown at him as Fowler – a lot of the time by ex-Villa hooligans who did not like Fowler stealing the limelight from them. My own personal opinion is they were jealous of the recognition he had gained, therefore, they took it upon themselves to smear him with the racist tag. I have also read in other hooligan books people having a pop at Fowler; they haven't got anyone who can match him. The lads having a pop at Fowler have either copped a slap of him in the past, or have never seen him in action.

Was the Hardcore a pro-loyalist firm? Large elements of the firm certainly were pro-loyalist without a doubt. When I was a nipper, Gary Reid used to teach me the loyalist songs. You only have to look at the flags we took away to the Villa away games to answer that. On match day in the Adventurers pub we would always sing 'No surrender to the I.R.A' and the 'Sash My Father Wore'. So much so, that one game we had a visit from the Anti-Nazi League who did not take too kindly to our patriotic songs, however, it didn't stop us. Could somebody please tell these people we are in Great Britain! Make no mistake though, the Villa Hardcore was not anti-Irish – we were pro-loyalist; it's a big difference. We had Irish lads travel with us and it was never a problem at all. Many of my mates were from Irish Catholic backgrounds but considered themselves English and supported the Ulster loyalists. Fowler himself was half-Irish and he was leading the Hardcore, therefore, the anti-Irish tag some people choose to give the firm was way out of line. Moreover, as I explained earlier, what is the problem with English football lads supporting another pro-British cause? Should it be looked upon as a crime? I do not think so.

Now to my involvement in right-wing politics. Do I regret it? Do I hell. Absolutely no regrets at all. Look at the damage done in only sixty-plus years of endless mass immigration. No one knows me better than Karen and even though she would say I may have 'mellowed' over the years my opinion has still not changed at all – mass immigration is the greatest threat to our precious and unique British identity. Let's get down to the recent 'refugee crisis' according to figures from the U.N.H.C.R.; The UN Refugee Agency. The breakdown of refugees are 13% women – 12% children – and 75% men aged between 19 – 45 years old. This is not the profile of an humanitarian disaster, but the demographics of an alien invasion.

I joined the NF at a young age because my country was going to the dogs and I foreseen the problems mass immigration was bringing. Can anyone honestly say the multi-racial/multi-cultural experiment has worked? I think not. Even some MP's from the three main parties have been forced to admit this – including Trevor Phillips from the race relations board who has done a complete U-turn and confessed that the multi-cultural experiment has failed. Obviously, Trevor Phillips isn't someone I will suddenly have on my Christmas card list, however, I do admire him for coming out and saying the truth. There are many decent folk from all walks of life. In addition, there are also many bad White people around; I fully well admit that without a doubt. For all that, having cultures worlds apart living together simply does not work. Just look over the water in loyal Ulster to see the problems it causes. You only have to look today at the numerous pro-Black, pro-Asian and pro-Irish republican groups that operate in mainland Britain to see that I was doing no different for my people than other people were doing for their people. You may not be aware that there are over 12,000 non-White, non-British organisations operating in Great Britain alone.

All of these organisations have been established to represent the views, aspirations and culture of the non-White and non-indigenous population of Great Britain. Another example is how the Muslim community vote on issues affecting back home, rather than issues affecting the UK. The fear of losing the Muslim vote actually effects what policies the mainstream parties put forward. Do they really have any loyalty to Britain or actually look upon themselves as being British? Even though at the same time I have met some decent Muslim people through the years, most have absolutely no loyalty to this country. Their religion and what they consider their homeland comes first. I have heard this straight from the horse's mouth. Muslim integration simply has not worked.

People from the Caribbean are no different. At the 2012, London Olympic Games, the majority of British born Black people were supporting Jamaica and not Great Britain. Even after many years of England being their home, they do not or ever will consider themselves truly British. This is not to say for one second that I have not had good friends from the Black community over the years – I have. My Mother's female Jamaican friends were the nicest people you could have wished to have known – they were church going Black Christians. In spite of this, none of them are proud of Britain – its history – or its culture. They class themselves as Caribbean, West Indian and African etc – that is a fact. I should know as I was close to a number of Black people. It's the same at the cricket. When England play Pakistan, India or the West Indies who do the immigrant population turn out in their droves to support. Do I need to answer that? The proof is in the pudding.

Look at the London riots that manifested in the summer of 2011. What started as a peaceful demonstration over the shooting of a Black man Mark Duggan in Tottenham, ended up with copy cot rioting all over the country. Before his death, he was considered one of Britain's most violent gangsters who was linked to ten shootings and two murders. Scotland Yard had also put him under surveillance because he had 'come to prominence' as an active member of the notorious Tottenham ManDem gang. The Tottenham riots took me back to the Handsworth riots in Birmingham, in the 1980's. The demonstration was hijacked by a mob hell bent on trouble; let us make no bones about that. It spiralled into the worst civil unrest in this country since the early 1980's. Every news channel showed 'hoodies' Black, Asian and

White in pitched battles with the police – including large scale looting, setting fire to cars and businesses.

How can torching Black owned businesses have anything to do with protesting against a White Police officer? This had absolutely nothing to do with the shooting of Mark Duggan – it was just the excuse the low-level scum needed to go on the rampage. It will eventually reach a stage where a White police officer will be frightened to shoot a Black gangster in case he is accused of 'racism' or it triggers more rioting. Don't people realise that police officers also murder White people – but these incidents never make the headlines. Could it be for instance in London that so many young Black lads are involved in gangs – thus the police have Operation Trident which works to prevent Black gun culture. Not to mention my home city of Birmingham, which has saw the worst in-fighting between rival Black gangs (most of it drug related) ever seen according to a senior local police chief.

It is the same as the Rodney King incident years ago in Los Angeles. Yes, what happened to Rodney King was completely unacceptable, however, you can bet your bottom dollar that this also happened to a large number of White people. The only difference is Rodney King's assault made the headlines, which triggered the events in which 53 people were killed and over 2,000 were injured. This sets a pattern of 'White police guilt' and 'Black innocence'. As a result, it triggers instant mob violence demanding revenge on the 'perpetrator' who was White, while the 'victim' is looked upon as innocent because he is Black. The analysis of the rioting is becoming one of a generalised protest against the alleged oppression of Blacks by White society. Moreover, it only ended when the military were sent in.

The same goes for the Michael Brown shooting in Ferguson, Missouri. Other Blacks kill 93% of Black people killed in America. The police in America spend a majority of their time in Black areas because that is where the bulk of the crimes are committed. In hundreds of episodes in more than 50 cities since 2010, Black gangs are roaming the streets of America – assaulting, intimidating, stalking, threatening, vandalising, stealing, shooting, stabbing – even raping and killing. But local media and public officials are silent. Crime is colour blind says a Milwaukee police chief. Race isn't important a Chicago newspaper editor assures his readers. Anybody offended by facts should take a good hard look at themselves.

The Tottenham riots signified to me a complete break down in society, which the government were to blame for due to their weak and feeble policies that they have inflicted upon us over the years. Buildings and property were set ablaze with evidently little thought given to who was inside. Images were shown around the world of lawless London and a broken Britain. All this from a country that was once respected and admired. How did that make our country look in the eyes of the world? Additionally, look at how the police treat White male football fans. It does not matter if you are a hooligan or not, you're the scum they love to hate. I have seen it with my own eyes. Normal fans baton charged just for attending a football game – with the police knowing they can get away with it. People of all racial and religious backgrounds suffer from police brutality, but only one is ever highlighted.

When the rioting stopped in Tottenham, there had been over 3,000 arrests. The government and the police tried to play it down and say that the riots were not 'racially motivated' when anybody with half a brain knows the truth. Moreover, when a group of young White lads took to the streets to defend their area from the rioters, they were ripped apart by all sections of the media as the ones provoking the trouble; you could not make it up. There were also sadly a number of deaths due to the rioting. Is multi-culturalism really worth dying for? And take my word for it these riots will happen frequently and steadily get worse, until it reaches a stage where the police will no longer be able to bring them under control. I dread to think of the out come. In addition, what was the response by the Conservatives after these riots? They axed the old style 'Bobby on the Beat' as over 10,000 police officers were ditched and replaced with 'plastic police' known as police community support officers – who do not have the same powers of arrest under Section 24 of the police and criminal evidence act. They do not even have the power to search you unless it is in the presence of a police officer. They are nothing but a waste of time and public money. The future of policing in Britain is nothing short of a joke – whilst third-word aid just keeps going up and up.

Wouldn't it have made more sense to plough millions of pounds into the police force and tackle crime head on, instead of giving the racist anti-White and British hater Robert Mugabe of Zimbabwe over £100 million per year, the Argentinians £9 million per year and oil rich Nigeria £450 million per year. The big question though has to be asked – how will the police cope as Britain faces a surge in immigrant crime, people trafficking, drug cartels and Islamic grooming gangs?

The death of Lee Rigby in Woolwich, South East London, who was hacked to death by Muslim extremists, is another example of a failed multi-racial/multi-cultural society. These Muslim converts were radicalised from within a London Mosque and trained to carry out Jihad. All this is happening right under our noses. Lee Rigby was brutally murdered by two men who were not of his race – two men who were motivated by an evil form of Islam. Lee Rigby was British by birth, British by heritage, tradition, culture – and more importantly, British by blood. The animals who killed Lee Rigby, were the sons of West African immigrants; they were British by bits of paper. British because a document issued by a faceless bureaucrat said that they were British. The men who killed Fusilier Lee Rigby, were a product of multi-culturalism – of a multi-racial society that allowed them to live in Britain and preach their hateful alien beliefs. They were both known by the British security forces. Misguided tolerance of 'diversity' created the conditions in Britain that allowed the poison that directed the killing of an unarmed British soldier on a British street. And take it from me, Lee Rigby will not be the last.

Worse still, Greenwich Council initially refused to have a memorial in Lee Rigby's name in case it cost them votes from the Muslim community. If you need any proof that our puppet politicians and their left-wing followers are still adhering to their PC, anti-British agenda, then look no further than this. You might also bring up the fact that Stephen Lawrence, more than twenty years after his death, is still getting more media coverage than Lee Rigby. Greenwich Council should hang their heads in shame for bowing down to their Muslim voters.

Having said that, let me make this perfectly clear. It is not the Muslims who are doing this – it's our own race of people on Greenwich Council. Always remember who we should direct our anger towards. The multi-cultural dream lies tattered and crumbled in the gutter. In years to come people will look back and say: "Did we really let them conduct this evil experiment?". These same deluded politicians still refuse to see the truth. It's as if they are frozen in the headlights of the mess that they have created, and to admit the truth is just too dreadful to think about. We now face decades of racial and religious tension because of some clowns utopian delusion of everybody living in harmony. But authorities worldwide are terrified of those who have seen through their lies – and the number is growing by the hour.

The government refuse to address these issues for two reasons. Firstly, we are controlled from Brussels and secondly the government would not dare to upset their Zionist paymasters who control the purse strings in not only Great Britain, but also America and beyond. At the end of the day the true British people get the sharp end of the stick. The immigrants who have settled in the UK have no problem seeing large parts of our towns and cities turned into outposts of Asia and the West Indies. Are we just supposed to roll over and take it? I am sure if the situation was reversed that they would not stand for it in their homelands. Therefore, why should we be any different? Look at how every event in the ethnic calender gets celebrated UK wide, but then on St George's day it gets swept under the carpet and labelled racist if anyone dares to fly the cross of Saint George. This is a fact that no one can deny.

The alarming thing is we have now lost most of our major towns and cities to the third world invasion. Looking at things from a realistic point of view maybe it is now too late to save Great Britain. I am not really in a position to be the one to say if it is, or if it is not. Nevertheless, we must carry on fighting back regardless. We must give our people some party to vote for and some one they can really turn to. We must give them that choice come Election Day. We owe it to our fallen heroes who sacrificed everything so that we may be free. It's better to be ostracised by certain people for holding a political ideology that you truly believe in, than to be accepted for what you don't believe in.

Now I am with the BNP this will be my last home, as all the other right-wing parties are just not worth bothering with. They are either too small or too radical (or both) for the British people to ever turn to them in their droves. If ever I was to leave the BNP it would be to retire from politics. Who knows what the future holds? By the time you read this I may be sitting on a balcony in Spain – sipping cocktails and covered in sun tan lotion. The NF was once a huge party, however, this is no longer the case. They are simply wasting their time – but there will always be a handful of people willing to carry on with its name – even though it should have ceased to exist years ago. I do not know any of the people who are now running the NF, therefore, it would be unfair of me to comment on the present leadership. I am sure like when I was a member, that there are a healthy number of good British nationalists in the party. Despite that, even though they are standing more candidates than when I was involved, it is still a very tiny party with very limited resources. And like the BNP, it is still racked with infighting.

In all its years as a political party it has never even won a seat at council level and present votes do not look like that trend is ever going to change. Furthermore, the fact of the matter is its name is not 'voter friendly'. Even though the NF name is known in most houscholds, it is simply not an electable party. It is true the NF have stayed solid on their policies and not watered any of them down unlike the BNP – and they are the only true racial nationalist political party in Britain. However, in my opinion this has simply held them further back by not attempting to improve their image.

You also have a number of tiny groups like the British Freedom Party, British Movement, English Democrats, Britain First, Liberty GB, Pegida UK, National Action, British Democratic Party, British Unity and far too many more I could mention. There are little off-shoots of groups springing up all the time all doomed to failure; it's a joke. They are too tiny to make any impact at all – a total waste of time. That's not to say you will not find decent patriots in all these organisations. Although, they spend most of their time slagging off the BNP instead of focussing on their own shortcomings. I have been on the opposite side of the fence myself, therefore, I know this to be true.

And as for the E.D.L (English Defence League) they are looked upon by the public as no more than a street gang and will never get the British public on side with how they go about things. They only oppose Islam, when we all know even if Britain was 'Islam free' there would still be major problems in our multi-racial/multi-cultural society. To only oppose Islam it shows that their ideology is way of the mark and not fit for purpose. Many of their members turn up at events in Saint George 'hooligan masks' which brings shame upon our cause. Then after a booze-fuelled afternoon end up in running battles with the police – bombarding them with bottles and pint glasses. These idiots give the left-wing media the ammunition to use against us. Whilst at the same time, scare of sensible decent people from getting involved in our struggle; they are helping the enemy. They do more damage to our movement than the media ever could.

Whilst the E.D.L has continued to stage rallies, it no longer has any meaningful existence as an organisation. The problem with the E.D.L is it draws most of its support from football gangs and angry young males who enjoy E.D.L marches and rallies, but at the same time are unwilling to engage in serious political activity. For example, having staged a march against a mosque – what do you do next? The E.D.L has never had any real long-term solutions, so was always likely to have a short political shelf life. To me it is like a modern day NF grabbing all the wrong headlines for all the wrong reasons. That's not to say I do not respect how they have awoken many thousands of angry, young, White people into political action as I do. But it is the wrong kind of political action. Moreover, the E.D.L are a Zionist financed front group from beginning to end – do some research and you will see there is nothing English about it; the E.D.L are now on the road to oblivion.

The BNP are our only chance of doing anything. Some people will not like to hear that – especially people who have left our party or are in a so-called 'rival' party. However, this is the reality of the situation and the fact needs pointing out that the BNP are our only hope. Even after the past infighting and huge reduction in membership, the BNP is still the only game in town regarding British nationalism. The BNP are now on a rebuilding programme and the sad fact of the matter is if the BNP fail, Britain is finished. Yes, it's that bleak – I refuse to try to sugar-coat the situation at all. Beyond us, there is nothing but obliteration. Our destiny hangs by a thread. The establishment have many clever ways to put people off from turning to the BNP – and they will use them. We are the only party with the real policies to change Britain. Despite that, the 'face-less' people that control our government have a bottomless pit of money to play with. This country will not be ruined by those who betray us, but by those who know what's going on and do nothing.

As things stand now the indigenous British population of Birmingham are doomed. Current government estimates put the ethnic minority, soon to be majority, at around 30% in Birmingham. Demographic experts predict that the indigenous population of Birmingham will become a minority in a blink of an eye. In about twenty years time from now, Birmingham will be an unrecognisable patchwork of conflicting ethnic groups – with the remaining British population packed into ever shrinking ghettos. Immigration without integration is a recipe for the balkanisation of society. Most of the people in places like Birmingham, Burnley, Rotherham, Bradford and East London for example, who can afford to will have fled. Those that remain will eventually be assimilated into whichever dominant culture that surrounds them like Pakistani, Bengali, Polish, West Indian, Somalian or Indian etc. The proof is out there for all to see. You only have to have a drive around Birmingham and open your eyes.

We have had more immigration into the UK in the last ten years, than in the previous 50 years. You will here politicians saying they made a huge mistake and 'got the sums wrong' but this is yet another lie. This could only have happened through a deliberate open door immigration policy, which has been promoted and financed by people hell bent on destroying our British race and identity. We have been replaced by the foreign invasion; it's genocide. The strain this has put on the NHS, Housing, Schools and communities in general, is a result of the government failing to act yet again. You need to ask yourself these questions. The masses have sat by quietly for too long watching their soap operas and voting on reality TV shows as our country gets destroyed from within.

I must without question give a mention regarding my friends and contacts in loyal Ulster. Even after all the heartache of the loyalist feuds and losing our leader John 'Grugg' Gregg in such horrific circumstances, I do not for one second regret getting involved in the L.PA/U.D.A. I have made many true friends over the years. People like Stan, Steve, Sammy, Monkey, Julie, Stevie and John McCartney, Stuart Gregg, Lynn Carson, Big and little Davy from Ballysillan, Davy Elwood and Gerald from Ballysillan, Jackie from Rathfern, my fellow members in the Orange Lodge and many more I could mention. These are now friends for life who all stood by me when my parents passed away. You don't forget that – people who were there for you when you needed them.

I am not talking now on behalf of the NF or the BNP as a whole, but I never considered the loyalist paramilitaries as terrorists. I looked upon them as soldiers fighting a war against Sinn Fein and the I.R.A. To me they were freedom fighters defending Ulster in times of needs. I was only doing what other people do worldwide. Standing by my kin-folk and supporting fellow British patriots. Let us never forget that Ulster is the most loyal part of Great Britain – and they deserved my support. It's something I will never regret. Northern Ireland is the last part of the United Kingdom that is truly British in culture, heritage and patriotism – we must fight with all our heart to keep it that away.

Now I will touch on two taboo subjects regarding the loyalists of Ulster. First and foremost, about the collusion with the British security forces. Yes, it is well known that certain sections of the security forces passed on information to the loyalist paramilitaries regarding the whereabouts of Irish republicans, which resulted in the targeting and killing of high-ranking I.R.A men. How did I feel about this? Well in all honesty, I didn't care. We were at war against the I.R.A and any help that came our way I saw no problem with that. You really expect me to show any remorse to a bunch of child killers. I think not. Nevertheless, something that is never mentioned is the same happened regarding the Irish Garda and the I.R.A, in the setting up of Protestant/Unionist people, but not many people know about this. My opinion was simply tit for tat. It most certainly happened on both sides. Even though it has always been the loyalists who are considered the 'bad guys'.

Another thing that the loyalist paramilitaries have been accused of is drug dealing and protection rackets. In all fairness, this did go on and still goes on to this day. But in all honesty, no one I had had any dealings with was involved in any of this extortion. All the people I was in contact with had jobs and were loyalists for all the right reasons; not financial gain. All my friends lived in standard housing and like most people had to watch every penny that they spent. The people I have associated with over the years were proper decent loyalist people and always made me feel like a special guest whenever in their company. Nonetheless, certain loyalists used their positions of power for the wrong reasons. I am sure the same must go on inside the republican movement.

A huge problem we face in Mainland Britain is the support for the I.R.A, even from 'certain' second and third generation people from Irish backgrounds. Moreover, like all Britain's enemies they do not even try to hide it then scream blue murder when the boots on the other foot. Actually, the 'in your face' support for the I.R.A had a lot to do with me getting involved in Ulster loyalism. I do not mind confessing that as the years progressed I loathed everything and anything Irish nationalist or republican. I would never wear any clothes that were green, or drink a pint of Guinness. To say any different I would be a liar. After all, I think my hatred was justifiable after what the I.R.A had done to my country and my people. If people want to call me a 'sectarian bigot' then so be it – I can live with that. I did not hate everybody Irish, that would have been plain stupid. I had a huge number of decent Irish Catholic friends but not any with republican leanings. That just would not have happened.

Some people will call me a 'racist' for my anti-immigration views, however, I can stand a bit of silly name-calling. Was I a racist? No, not in my eyes – I was a British nationalist. I had Black and Asian friends. The people I opposed were the people doing damage to my country – the likes of Anjem Choudary. I suppose some people could even say I am a bit of a hypocrite, but I don't look at it that way. I love Chinese and Indian food. I still to this day listen to the old-style Jamaican Ska and the 2-Tone music that hit our charts between 1979-83. In the past, I have had best mates at school who were Black. Be as it may be, people who don't know me still like to throw the racist tag my way.

I have had Black and Asian people walk up to me in the past and say: "We didn't know you were in the BNP as you don't fit the bill. We would never have guessed you was involved in right-wing politics". Talk about 'stereotyping'. What did they expect from me? To be walking around in a Nazi armband with a tattoo of Adolf Hitler on my forehead? However, the Black and Asian people I have as friends know I am a decent lad, therefore, I am happy with that. In my eyes, the people who accuse me of being 'racist' are the real racists themselves for denying another person a political opinion. It's about time the word 'racist' was ripped up and put back in the closet; it has worn itself out.

I would like to finish now on my support for Stan Curry and Steve Irwin. Yes, both of these lads broke the law of the land and were sent down for lengthy prison sentences. For all that, I stood by them and still support them to this day. They are still two of my closest friends and always will be. Stan was the man who brought me into the L.P.A/U.D.A and for that I will be forever grateful. He took me under his wing and introduced me to some of the best people I have ever met. South East Antrim Brigade U.D.A/U.F.F took me in like one of their own and gave me some of the happiest times of my life. As I have already mentioned a number of times, Stan also financially looked after me in the early years when I was struggling for money and had hit hard times. He paid for endless trips to loyal Ulster and you don't forget things like that. The only thing about it all that gutted me was that Stan was imprisoned due to a loyalist feud from within the U.D.A – I found that hard to take.

I had no reservations about getting in contact with the loyalist paramilitaries. I went into it with my eyes wide open and it was no one else's choice bar my own. Nevertheless, this is not something that everyone does on the right-wing circuit. This is just my own personal story. Some British nationalists refused to go near the paramilitaries for a number of reasons. I have had people say to me: "Why get involved in someone else's conflict ?". But I would like to put this point across very firmly. The struggle to keep Ulster British does not start and end at Belfast docks. It is every British patriots duty to support loyal Ulster as they fight to remain part of

Great Britain. I felt a duty to get involved, if only to a level of supporting prisoners and attending loyalist parades. As far as I was concerned, it was as much my duty to fight for Ulster as it was for the Ulster loyalists themselves. I consider myself an Ulster loyalist even though I'm an English man – and I am proud to say that aloud. Some mates said to me: "Why don't you 'beef' up your story by saying you did this or did that for the U.D.A". That thought never entered my mind. I wanted this to be an honest account of my involvement in loyalism, and even though I never lifted a gun for the U.D.A or served a jail sentence, I am perfectly happy with the contribution that I made.

Now on to my friendship with Steve Irwin. Steve was sent down for the Greysteel shootings and given eight life sentences in what was described as one of the worst atrocities during 'The Troubles'. As a result, he played a major part in forcing the I.R.A into calling a cease-fire. For that alone he deserved my support. He had been one of the many Ulster soldiers who'd had the republican war machine on the back foot during the height of the conflict. I obviously at the start did not know the lad – but our friendship, just like my friendship with Stan – just grew and grew. In any other country apart from Northern Ireland, Steve would have led a normal life and landed himself a decent job as he's a very switched on lad, despite that, situations in Ulster made him defend his country. Like he once said to me: "I didn't just wake up one morning and decide to shoot up a bar, situations in my country forced me into defending my people. The I.R.A were nothing but evil". He admitted to me that Greysteel was a 'dirty job' brought on by the I.R.A bombing the Shankill Road a week previous, and that the U.D.A had no alternative but to 'strike back'.

I had no second thoughts about supporting Steve. People of Irish republican leanings have supported I.R.A prisoners before, so what was I doing that was any different. Another thing about Steve, he understood my depression as he'd had dark episodes himself and he was always there to try to advise me and talk me trough my darkest days. He was the one in jail, yet I was giving him my problems to sort out – not the other way around. He really tried his best to help me out on numerous occasions when my depression struck. Let us not forget he had enough on his plate already being stuck in jail. Now and again after speaking to Steve on the phone, I would realise I never even asked how he was doing as he was listening to all my problems due to my anxiety and depression; it was always followed up with a letter from him which included more advice and support. Steve has said to me a number of times: "I could never repay you back for all the support you have given me over the years". However, this is not true. As he has been there for me as much as I have been there for him. Steve has never asked me for anything. He was just grateful for the books I sent him in once a month. Little things like that mean a lot to a prisoner; believe me. If it helps them get through a night or two, you have done your job as a prisoners supporter.

In addition, by knowing Steve, I met the lads from Ballysillan who would also become dear friends of mine. A great bunch of lads who really knew how to have a good play up. As with the lads from Rathcoole, I instantly felt one of them from the word go. Like I have already said – I know that deep down Stan and Steve think they owe me one for all the support I have given them. However, they owe me nothing at all – you do it because you want to do it. They were two comrades and friends in need of support and I was there for them. It's as simple as that. No one owes anyone anything at the end of the day. After all, I know if the situation had been reversed that they would have been as equally supportive towards me. If there is one thing you don't do in life it's turn you're back on your friends and fellow compatriots when they are in need. For me a meaningful life was never about being rich, highly educated, or being perfect. It was about standing up for my people and being able to touch the lives of others. Like many others before me, I put my country and it's people before anything; including family. Steve Irwin was eventually released from Maghaberry jail on August 2013, after serving a further nine years in jail.

As my story ends, I would like to make one final statement regarding our governments, past and present. This story is not a complete history of British nationalism, nor does it speak for everybody involved in our movement. It was never meant to be like that from the beginning. Rather it is a cautionary tale of how even a nation as strong as Great Britain, who once had an empire and vibrant communities, can be destroyed with never a backward glance from our own government who have sold us out. And let's never forget our troops serving abroad in conflicts that have nothing to do with the United Kingdom; especially the ones who return home in body bags and the endless families torn apart with bereavement. The unwanted being underpaid who will go unappreciated, doing the unthinkable for the ungrateful.

No one will ever convince me that the people of mainland Britain and the loyalist people of Ulster have not been betrayed beyond our worst wildest dreams. Your government thinks you're weak and feeble – it's about time the British people rose up, and kicked these traitors into the dustbin of history. In our minds we must ensure what our heroes have died for – not forgetting that Ulster is free.

"They shall grow not old, as we that are left grow old:

Age shall not weary them, nor the years condemn.

At the going down of the sun and in the morning

We will remember them"

Quis Separabit'

CPSIA information can be obtained at www.ICGtesting.com
Printed in the USA
LVOW07s1833201016

9 781532 718182